Global Perspectives on Changing Secondhand Economies

Providing interdisciplinary and global perspectives, this book examines historical and contemporary changes in secondhand economies, including the emergence and specialization of secondhand venues, the materials involved, as well as the cultural significance of secondhand things and the professions associated with them.

The objects in focus range from used clothing, scrap and waste materials, to antiquities and used cars, thrift stores and circular economies. Growing concerns with sustainability in the West have helped bring about the 'rediscovery' of practices of clothing re-use, re-purposing and re-cycling at the same time as major high-street retailers are establishing programs to return used clothing to their stores for re-sale or recycling. As the contributions to this edited volume demonstrate, recent concerns with the fast pace and adverse effects of global commodity flows have increased the scholarly attention to secondhand economies, both in terms of their history and their significance for livelihoods and sustainability.

The chapters in this book were originally published as a special issue of the journal, *Business History*.

Karen Tranberg Hansen is Professor Emerita of Anthropology at Northwestern University. Her publications include *Distant Companions: Servants and Employers in Zambia*, 1900–1985 (1989), *African Encounters with Domesticity* (1992), *Keeping House in Lusaka* (1997), and *Salaula: The World of Secondhand Clothing and Zambia* (2000).

Jennifer Le Zotte is Assistant Professor of History at the University of North Carolina Wilmington, specializing in gender, race, capitalism, and material culture, especially dress. Her publications include *From Goodwill to Grunge: A History of Secondhand Styles and Alternative Economies (2017)*.

Global Perspectives on Changing Secondhand Economies

Edited by
Karen Tranberg Hansen and Jennifer Le Zotte

Routledge
Taylor & Francis Group

LONDON AND NEW YORK

First published 2022
by Routledge
2 Park Square, Milton Park, Abingdon, Oxon OX14 4RN

and by Routledge
605 Third Avenue, New York, NY 10158

Routledge is an imprint of the Taylor & Francis Group, an informa business

British Library Cataloguing in Publication Data
A catalogue record for this book is available from the British Library

ISBN: 978-1-032-19237-6 (hbk)
ISBN: 978-1-032-19238-3 (pbk)
ISBN: 978-1-003-25828-5 (ebk)

DOI: 10.4324/9781003258285

Typeset in Myriad Pro
by Newgen Publishing UK

Publisher's Note
The publisher accepts responsibility for any inconsistencies that may have arisen during the conversion of this book from journal articles to book chapters, namely the inclusion of journal terminology.

Disclaimer
Every effort has been made to contact copyright holders for their permission to reprint material in this book. The publishers would be grateful to hear from any copyright holder who is not here acknowledged and will undertake to rectify any errors or omissions in future editions of this book.

Contents

Citation Information

The chapters in this book were originally published in the journal, *Business History*, volume 61, issue 1 (2019). When citing this material, please use the original page numbering for each article, as follows:

Introduction
Changing Secondhand Economies
Karen Tranberg Hansen and Jennifer Le Zotte
Business History, volume 61, issue 1 (2019), pp. 1–16

Chapter 1
Domestic textiles and country house sales in Georgian England
Jon Stobart
Business History, volume 61, issue 1 (2019), pp. 17–37

Chapter 2
'Fence-ing lessons': child junkers and the commodification of scrap in the long nineteenth century
Wendy A. Woloson
Business History, volume 61, issue 1 (2019), pp. 38–72

Chapter 3
Jews, second-hand trade and upward economic mobility: Introducing the ready-to-wear business in industrializing Helsinki, 1880–1930
Laura Katarina Ekholm
Business History, volume 61, issue 1 (2019), pp. 73–92

Chapter 4
Shylocks to superheroes: Jewish scrap dealers in Anglo-American popular culture
Jonathan Z. S. Pollack
Business History, volume 61, issue 1 (2019), pp. 93–105

Chapter 5
The mass consumption of refashioned clothes: Re-dyed kimono in post war Japan
Miki Sugiura
Business History, volume 61, issue 1 (2019), pp. 106–121

Chapter 6

The work of shopping: Resellers and the informal economy at the goodwill bins
Jennifer Ayres
Business History, volume 61, issue 1 (2019), pp. 122–154

Chapter 7

Valuation in action: Ethnography of an American thrift store
Frederik Larsen
Business History, volume 61, issue 1 (2019), pp. 155–171

Chapter 8

History as business: Changing dynamics of retailing in Gothenburg's second-hand market
Staffan Appelgren
Business History, volume 61, issue 1 (2019), pp. 172–186

Chapter 9

Second-hand vehicle markets in West Africa: A source of regional disintegration, trade informality and welfare losses
Abel Ezeoha, Chinwe Okoyeuzu, Emmanuel Onah and Chibuike Uche
Business History, volume 61, issue 1 (2019), pp. 187–204

Chapter 10

Urban prototypes: Growing local circular cloth economies
Lucy Norris
Business History, volume 61, issue 1 (2019), pp. 205–224

For any permission-related enquiries please visit:
www.tandfonline.com/page/help/permissions

Notes on Contributors

Staffan Appelgren, School of Global Studies, University of Gothenburg, Gothenburg, Sweden.

Jennifer Ayres, The Department of Social and Cultural Analysis, New York University, New York, NY, USA.

Laura Katarina Ekholm, Department of political and Economic Studies, University of Helsinki, Helsinki, Finland.

Abel Ezeoha, Department of Accountancy and Banking & Finance, Ebonyi State University, Abakaliki, Nigeria.

Karen Tranberg Hansen, Department of Anthropology, Northwestern University, Evanston, IL, USA.

Frederik Larsen, Department of Education and Research, Design School Kolding, Kolding, Denmark.

Jennifer Le Zotte, Department of History, University of North Carolina Wilmington, NC, USA.

Lucy Norris, Design Research & Material Culture, Kunsthochschule Weißensee, Berlin, Germany.

Chinwe Okoyeuzu, Department of Banking and Finance, University of Nigeria, Enugu, Nigeria.

Emmanuel Onah, Department of Banking and Finance, University of Nigeria, Enugu, Nigeria.

Jonathan Z. S. Pollack, Department of History, Madison Area Technical College, and Center for Jewish Studies, University of Wisconsin, Madison, United States of America.

Jon Stobart, Department of History, Politics and Philosophy, Manchester Metropolitan University, Manchester, UK.

Miki Sugiura, Faculty of Economics, Hosei University, Machida, Japan.

Chibuike Uche, African Studies Centre, Leiden, The Netherlands.

Wendy A. Woloson, Department of History, Rutgers University, Camden, Camden, USA.

Changing Secondhand Economies

Karen Tranberg Hansen and Jennifer Le Zotte

ABSTRACT

Research interest in secondhand economies has expanded in recent years among scholars of diverse disciplines, especially anthropology, history, geography, and sociology. The introduction to this Special Issue discusses a number of interdisciplinary and regional perspectives on the topic. After an overview of scholarship relating to secondhand economies, historical and contemporary, we introduce a number of themes that have attracted particular attention, including the growth and expansion of secondhand exchange, the emergence and specialization of diverse secondhand venues, the material objects involved, influences on these modes of exchanges, and the cultural significance of second-hand things and the professions connected with them. Finally, we turn to the articles included in this Special Issue, identifying some of the major issues to which they speak.

As contemporary consumers, we are encouraged to re-use, recycle and resell, and to approach waste as a renewable resource. The re-use and resell aspects, in particular, invite us to approach secondhand goods as a potential source of recreation. Social media sites such as Facebook are peppered with ads for ThredUp, 'The Largest Online Thrift Store and Consignment Shop,' and 'upcycled' wares flood independent dealer sites such as Etsy. In America, National Public Radio regularly encourages listeners to donate their old cars, and Goodwill and Salvation Army storefronts grace nearly every town. In Paris, the *Marchè aux Puces*, the original so-named flea market including 17 separate markets and thousands of dealers, counts more than 180,000 visitors daily, many of them with a penchant for unusual material goods and seeking a unique consumer experience. Elsewhere in Europe, Flohmärkte and car boot sales continue to flourish after decades of popularity, reflecting and supporting rich local and global histories. These unfolding histories include diverse engagements across the Global South, where the surplus of the North's hyperconsumption of a variety of goods, from secondhand clothing through used cars to electronic waste, is given a new life.

Concerns with sustainability and circular economies feature prominently in popular media and scholarship across many disciplines as the future of our livelihoods and the consumption practices that underpin them are challenged on many fronts: by environmental changes, demographic shifts, global wealth disparities, and economic growth-oriented models that are both wasteful and polluting. A circular economy minimises waste through reusing, repairing, refurbishing, and recycling existing materials and products. While the rise of schol-arly attention to secondhand consumption and commodity recycling may be recent, the circulation and exchange of a wide range of secondhand goods and materials are anything but new. Long before the worldwide net and today's global connections in secondhand goods exchange, itinerant 'old clothes men,' rag pickers and waste collectors, often immi-grants, many of them of Jewish background, linked villages, towns, and cities in occupations that sourced and exchanged clothing and used goods across vast distances in Europe and North America. Decades before Kate Moss, Miley Cyrus, and Beyoncé graced magazines and the red carpet in 'vintage' Chanel, artists and musicians in Europe and the United States helped craft subcultural styles reliant on used materials, sometimes while pushing against long-propagated xenophobic, anti-Semitic, and classist stigmas against the professions and people associated with secondhand trades.

Rather than being historically marginal, secondhand economies paralleled and over-lapped general economic exchanges, and all these processes have changed markedly with the rise of global capitalism. Similarly, styles visibly reliant on secondhand consumption have long reflected and affected firsthand fashion, and now advance alongside the accel-eration of firsthand 'fast fashion,' fueled both by a superfluity of goods and a desire to counter top-down cookie-cutter trends. Popular media reflect the voluntary use of pre-owned cloth-ing, from Fanny Brice's 1923 hit song 'Second-Hand Rose' to the 2013 hit single 'Thrift Shop' by duo Macklemore and Ryan Lewis, the latter of which portrays secondhand economies as a way of consuming creatively and smartly, of curating personally associated objects by buying off the beaten path, especially in the global North. What is most new about contem-porary recycling and reuse practices, of which the secondhand trade is considered a part, is 'the sheer scale of global trades in used materials.'[1] Today at the click of a mouse, buyers and sellers of secondhand goods meet on websites, continuing one of the world's oldest trades but with an unparalleled global scope.

Focusing on secondhand markets and economies involving a variety of commodities, this Special Issue presents interdisciplinary scholarship on historical and contemporary processes that examines the flow of secondhand objects and materials, their transformations and reval-uations, and the persons, policies, and markets involved with them. Central to many of these examinations are the social and cultural responses, outcomes, and intentions of such exchanges and valuations. Our introduction begins with an overview of scholarship on secondhand econ-omies, historical and contemporary, to provide a general backdrop for the articles. We then discuss themes, contexts, and approaches to the topic, including objects themselves, the growth and expansion of the global secondhand trade, conceptual and practical influences on the various modes of exchanges, and the cultural significance of secondhand objects and professions, all within a variety of regional and temporal settings. Subsequently, we turn to the articles included in this Special Issue, identifying some of the issues to which they speak or about which they invite future inquiry. While the introduction emphasizes the recent surge of wide-ranging scholarly interest in the topic of secondhand economies, the breadth of con-tent in the articles that appear within this double issue best attest to that fact.

Research background

As a research focus, scholarship on secondhand goods draws from a broad array of disci-plines, including anthropology, history, economics, sociology, geography, and cultural theory. Considering secondhand economies broadly provides rich opportunities for inter-disciplinary inquiry, and for bridging gaps in understanding global economies, the circulation of goods, and the ways people value and revalue objects. Whereas too often the cultural and social meanings of objects are analyzed separately from their economic purpose and monetary value, evaluations of secondhand commodities invite simultaneous inclusion of both factors, something many authors within this special issue manage successfully. Examinations of clothing and textiles, well represented in these pages, are prominent in this respect, as their historical and contemporary relationship to both profitability and cultural expression are well-noted and inextricable from each other. Where much previous scholar-ship on secondhand economies focuses on preowned clothing rather than on other sec-ondhand objects, this double issue offers a rare inclusive approach to secondhand trades and consumption.[2] The variety in types of objects examined here, ranging from automobiles to personal accessories, provides an unprecedented glimpse into the multitude of economic and social functions secondhand trade serves, and the issues scholars have addressed when studying them.

Research on secondhand goods often relies on seminal scholars such as Marcel Mauss, Mary Douglas, and Arjun Appadurai, whose pivotal understandings of the relationships between humans and objects are at least implicit in nearly all scholarly assessments of used goods exchange.[3] These early approaches to the topic underpin much of the work presented in this issue. Mauss, a sociologist, described in his 1925 work *The Gift* the central ideas of a 'gift economy' helping spur a large field of anthropological study of reciprocity and exchange. The notions that object value often relies on the context of exchange and can be variably and contingently interpreted continue to influence scholarship today.

As with gifts, secondhand exchange of goods creates value, both economically and socially, in addition to facilitating re-use. In social terms, the recasting of secondhand objects is often rooted in local cultural notions that may help redefine the relationship between waste and value in new contexts. Analyzing such transformations, two particular explanatory approaches from anthropology have stimulated scholarship across disciplines. They are both inspired to some degree by the work of Mary Douglas on the way in which societies establish boundaries between purity and dirt to handle 'matter out of place.'[4] Michael Thompson, Douglas' student, argued in *Rubbish Theory* (1979) that although many goods become rub-bish as they wear out and lose value, wear and tear actually add value to some. In effect, rubbish is a condition that emerges and then sometimes recedes, rather than an-end point.[5]

This approach resonates with the 'social life of things' perspective associated with Arjun Appadurai. In the course of their flow, objects may pass through several regimes, during which their value may be ambiguous, or they are reassessed and either disposed of or given new use and exchange value. Or, as in networks of global recycling, they connect different regimes of value, involving several smaller operators and agents rather than large transna-tional corporations.[6] Also, secondhand objects do not always cross value regimes, but may be in limbo, awaiting the removal of their previous lives or be recommodified for new exchanges.

While scholars may draw from one or more of these and other theoretical or disciplinary approaches, studies of secondhand goods and materials do tend toward some loose cate-gorization, either by the type of product, consumer perception and valuation, or the methods of redistribution. Below we discuss a few of those categories and some of the important scholarship produced on them.

Clothing and textiles

Used clothing in particular is an ambiguous category in flux between value regimes, appearing intermittently as 'gifts/donations', organized or formal 'charity/philanthropy', or 'markets'. The cultural value of secondhand clothing is as liminal and fluctuating as its economic value. Dress appears to the broader world as a link between private and public, and as visually expressive of its wearer's values and assumptions, yet all clothing has been and remains subject, as a category of style, to both misinterpretation and appropriation. Sociologist and fashion scholar Elizabeth Wilson notes the variable ways in which the wearing of decades-old items are pursued, and the recurrent cycles of fashionability, tradition, and rebellion which secondhand clothing often suggests or even establishes. Even more complexly, such cycles may be concurrent among different populations, where the same garment might represent irony, nostalgia, practicality, or rebellion to different wearers.[7]

Of all secondhand objects, clothing and textiles claim the single largest share of work, especially by historians, and more recently by scholars from several other disciplines. This is not surprising. Textiles set proto-industrialization into motion and were the main driver of the industrial revolution. Today, the garment and apparel industry is one of the largest industries globally. With yearly growing volumes of clothing production and consumption in the global North, there are lots of clothes to go around, in first-hand as well as secondhand cycles. In effect, widespread concerns with the global scale of clothing production and the complicated value chains on which it depends have helped to attract fresh attention to secondhand economies both in terms of their history and their contemporary significance for livelihoods and sustainability.

The secondhand clothing trade across national borders and between continents has a long history explored mainly in fragments, connecting European countries with the North American colonies and nations, and Europe with Africa, Asia and Australia.[8] Scholarship on the growing scope and value of the international secondhand clothing trade in the neoliberal era has begun to explore the role of charitable organizations in the global North in the export of donated used clothing.[9] Throughout the twentieth century, commercial textile recyclers operated alongside the charitable organizations and, like them, grew into economic prominence after the post-World War II years.[10] Processing the vast surplus of used clothing the charitable organizations are unable to resell in their stores, the textile recyclers sort still-wearable garments, shipping them for export, and reprocess fibers for industrial use and remanufacturing across the world. Agents, brokers, importers, wholesalers, retailers, and remanufactures play parts in this global commerce that is fuelled by the unwanted clothes of affluent consumers. While the textile recycling industry today includes some transnational corporations, charitable organizations like the Salvation Army and Goodwill Industries continue to be the largest single source of used clothes for export.

In Great Britain, secondhand clothing consumption has prompted both historical and contemporary works.[11] The cultural preoccupations of young German consumers with 1960s 'retro' styles have been detailed as well.[12] The Jewish transnational involvement with clothing, textiles, and trade has received recent attention, extending across the Atlantic to the US. In the US, historians have explored the ways in which cultural and societal perceptions, including anti-Semitism, influenced the public acceptance of secondhand economies.[13]

The sourcing, handling, buying, and selling of secondhand objects and materials rather than their subsequent use have drawn the most central attention by scholars. Most works, historical as well as contemporary, stop their analysis at the point of purchase, such as Beverley Lemire's seminal examinations of preindustrial British secondhand trade and Wendy Woloson's monograph on American pawn shops.[14] Clothing is probably the chief exception to this observation because of its intimate relationship with the body and the importance of embodied dress performance to identity formation both individually and socially.[15] As an object of material culture, dress becomes an agentive vehicle of social relationships. Some research has focused on dress practice of individuals and changing generations in specific situations, examining the social relations that emerge in the process and the ways desire helps consumers imagine new social worlds and cultural meanings.[16] Le Zotte's recent study of changing secondhand styles throughout the twentieth century highlights the complicated intersections of identity formations and consumer desires. Her vivid account of changing secondhand exchanges and styles compellingly demonstrates the significance of the material culture of dress in social, economic, and cultural history.[17]

Although the international secondhand clothing trade has a long history, scholars have been slow to examine the significance and meanings arising from local appropriations of the global North's used clothing. Tracing the commodity flow from the global North to Zambia, Karen Tranberg Hansen explored sourcing, handling, buying, selling, and use, showcasing creative recommodification of imported secondhand clothing and widespread style experimentation inspired by local norms rather than faded imitations of 'Western' dress.[18] The cultural and economic results of incorporating used garments into the national stream of commodities are complex. In some countries, especially in Africa, secondhand clothing imports are banned as their effects on domestic textile/clothing industries are questioned.[19] India, for example, prohibits the import of secondhand clothing for commercial resale purposes yet allows the entry of 'mutilated' secondhand clothing for use in the recycling and reprocessing of fiber.[20] Much of the machinery used for reprocessing clothing is imported from Prato in Italy, once the site of Europe's major wool reprocessing center. By the turn of the last millennium, the local and global forces influencing the circulation of imported secondhand clothing and the economic and cultural consequences of its availability were being examined in numerous locations from the border between Mexico and the United States, to several countries in eastern Europe, and to the Philippines and elsewhere.[21]

Trash and treasure

In addition to clothing, in and across the global North and South, scrap, waste, and trash are receiving considerable scholarly attention as discarded goods are brought into circulation and given new use and exchange value, often along with adverse transformations of livelihoods and environments.[22] Since the early modern era in northwestern Europe and North America, and today across the globe, secondhand exchanges have been practiced in changing economic and political contexts in accommodation, or in conflict, with prevailing regulatory frameworks and shifting socio-cultural norms and practices. Xenophobia and shifting expectations of hygiene often color public perceptions of such professions and their societal value, while also helping to determine the location and structure of exchange venues.

Related trade in durable goods, including automobiles and large household appliances such as washing machines or ovens, remains an underresearched topic with the potential to reveal much. As one article in this issue indicates, since higher legal barriers to such trade are often at issue, research on secondhand durable trade can reveal instructive details about conflicting interregional economic goals and priorities. Further explorations of secondhand automobiles might expand inquiries to encompass discussions of the history of secondhand car sales, the cultural meanings of vintage car culture, and the environmental costs and benefits of the trade.[23]

For the most part, studies of secondhand goods focus on objects and materials whose value is ambiguous, shifting, and subjective, even when addressing primarily practical commodities such as automobiles. The valuation of established categories of antiques and collectibles is comparatively stable, and unlike other secondhand often included sales recorded and cohesive practices of professional assessment. Even so, some methods of historical and contemporary analysis for antiques and collectibles mirror or overlap with those of second-hand exchange in general; there are very many conceptual similarities between antiques and collectibles and vintage clothing, for example, as trade categories that imply a worth elevation beyond the expansive classification of 'used.' Marketing, in other words, and its historical development in connection with reuse and redistribution, link certain aspects of antiques and collectible to other second-hand trades.

Scholars have examined the growth of antiquing as a professional and recreational field across the globe, but especially in Europe and the United States. Though literature on antiques is ample, much of it is in the form of instructional guides. Informative analyses on the topic come from an array of disciplines; for example, philosopher Leon Rosenstein follows in the vein of the above-mentioned anthropological explorations, such as those of Douglas or Thompson, by unpacking the development of non-use-oriented material valuation.[24] Historians have explored the origins and growth of antiques and collectibles from regional perspectives, describing modes and methods of secondhand distribution also relevant to less-valued items.[25]

Resale venues

A focus on the specific goods and materials recirculated is one common approach used in studies of secondhand exchange. Another approach examines the means of recirculation. US colonial and early Republic historians have emphasized the role of auctions in building a consumer citizenry and in solidifying national identities.[26] Wendy Woloson, who contributes an article here based on new research, focused her second book's attention on a premier secondhand venue of early to industrializing America, pawn shops.[27] The anti-Semitic biases associated with these persisted, as Jennifer Le Zotte shows in her recent work on the business and culture of twentieth century secondhand trade and consumption in the United States. Le Zotte identifies three major innovations in twentieth-century used goods trade—thrift stores, flea markets and garage sales—and explores the cultural process of overcoming various biases against secondhand goods.[28]

Predating these historians' focus on secondhand venues, anthropologists Gretchen Herrman and Ruth Landman conducted some of the earliest studies of secondhand exchange sites with their explorations of the social roles of American garage or yard sales, and John F. Sherry has similarly looked at the sociocultural dimensions of consumption at flea markets. Explorations of non-US sites include variations on these venues, including car boot sales in Britain and open-air markets in Africa.[29]

At the outset of the twenty-first century several scholars in Europe and North America are examining the proliferation of exchange venues and new sales practices of secondhand clothing including Internet-based sites.[30] Some explore the complicated relationship between first-hand and secondhand clothing consumption to 'fast fashion' production practices and the overconsumption of clothing in the global North that results in outright incineration and the destruction of huge volumes of discarded clothing in landfills.[31] Meanwhile, growing concerns with sustainability in the global North are spurring still others to "rediscover" practices of clothing re-use, re-purposing and re-cycling at the same time as major high-street retailers (e.g. Eileen Fisher, Hennes & Mauritz (H & M)) are establishing programs to return used clothing to their stores for re-sale or recycling.[32]

Increasingly, ecological as well as fair-labor issues have attracted international interest and scope. It is around global recycling, in particular, that recent social science scholarship on secondhand economies has begun to address environmental concerns.[33] At stake are the disassembly and destruction of discarded goods from the global North in the global South in order to recover resources for new phases of commodity production with questionable labor practices that often produce hazardous and toxic effects. Global recycling networks may create wealth for some at the same time as they entail liabilities to others.[34] Examples include the destruction of end-of-life vessels for scrap; nuclear operators sending away spent uranium for re-enrichment; hospitals shipping discarded medical supplies to poor countries; and electrical and electronic equipment used in refurbishment, as well as small firms involved in buying and re-selling e-waste. Scrap, according to the editors of a recent book presenting many of the examples we just listed, comprised the largest export from the United States, the world's largest economy, to China, the next biggest economy, in the first decade of the twenty-first century.[35]

Methodological interventions

Because secondhand circulation and exchange have no central archives due to legal categorization and the small size of many of the enterprises on which the secondhand economy depends for its operations, and because the very categorization of secondhand items is shifting and often ambiguous (for example, from trash to used, pre-owned, or gently-worn, to retro or vintage), research in this area invites methodologically creative approaches. Historians have, for instance, set about establishing their own archives of primary sources, gleaning historical details from traditional resources such as public records, historical associations, and institutional archives as well as cultural artifacts such as music, movies, literature, advertisements, and the objects and materials themselves. In recent years, by examining the sites, practices, materials, and professions of secondhand exchange within various historical contexts, historians have joined scholars from other disciplines to include informal economies in their studies of capitalism and business.[36]

Complementary to the source-finding, quantitative methods of economists and historians, anthropologists often rely on insights based on direct observation and interviews as well as an arsenal of supportive methodologies involving use of materials from statistics to historical records. In doing so, anthropologists have raised new questions about the long taken-for-granted international commerce in secondhand clothing and begun to examine the value creation of waste on a global scale. Meanwhile, geographers, museum curators, and design scholars focus on the various spaces, places, and physical materials that comprise such trades.[37] These material-based analyses are often primarily interested in the aesthetic and cultural meaning of the objects investigated, and the physical structures of the venues of exchange. All draw on interdisciplinary secondary sources to inspire analysis and explanation.

Articles in this special issue

When issuing our call for papers for a Special Issue of Business History on Changing Secondhand Economies, we hoped to solicit examples of new research that demonstrates how secondhand circulation and exchange matter in a variety of different contexts, addressing concerns about changing livelihoods, economy and society, both past and present. We deliberately cast our net wide, inviting interdisciplinary contributions on historical and contemporary topics ranging from scrap picking, used clothing, pre-owned cars, antiques, and electronic waste to the break-up of merchant ships. By and large the topics in the proposals we received fell into two broad categories, one focusing on secondhand objects and things, including clothing, and the other delving into the means and venues of redistribution. In light of our overview of scholarship earlier in this introduction, it is perhaps not surprising that we received fewer historical than contemporary proposals. This pattern, we suggest, reflects the current state of scholarship and, above all, the ambiguity at the heart of all secondhand objects, their instability as categories, and their transformations, disappearance, and reappearance, only to be revalorized or discarded, which makes them especially elusive historical research targets. There are no massive, curated archives of sources on secondhand trade and many exchange systems were intentionally unrecorded and essentially untaxed, leaving few verifiable records for historians to use. This very scarcity, however, also makes the topic a vital and fascinating one for historians. Moreover, to a keen and creative historical eye, evidence of the use and meaning of secondhand materials appears in almost every type of major scholarly source, making their research both possible and imperative. The structures and meanings of secondhand economies and materials reveal much about societies to which consumerism is central.

The issue's title, 'Changing Secondhand Economies,' addresses both the historical and present-day dynamism of the used goods trade as well as the topic's shifting role within various scholarly disciplines. Since the functions of secondhand exchange have changed markedly with the rise of global capitalism, the temporal scope of the articles is limited to the period from the mid-eighteenth century to the present. Geographically, the articles nearly span the globe, with most attention given to Western Europe and the United States but extending to Japan and West Africa. The articles are organized roughly chronologically, an arrangement which places more contemporary (sociological, anthropological) assessments in the second half of this double issue.

Jon Stobart starts the first section of the special issue with a consideration of the role of Georgian England house auctions in early modern ideas of gentility and class. Like many of this issue's contributions, Stobart focuses on a particular venue of secondhand goods sales, but he also hones in a category of object within that venue. In looking at one of the oldest and most universal methods of secondhand sales, he specifically uses eighteenth and early nineteenth century textile recirculation to frame an argument about how the acquisition of secondhand materials offered opportunities for gains in personal respectability at a time before the second industrial revolution vastly expanded the accessibility of such or similar goods to Great Britain and its colonies.

Next, Wendy Woloson shifts gears away from the upwardly mobile in '"Fence-ing Lessons": Child Junkers and the Commodification of Scrap in the Long Nineteenth Century," which offers a rather Dickensian tale about young, nineteenth-century American urbanites. Woloson examines scrap reprocessing through the incipient professions' youngest members, using the sort of innovative source-finding that has become the hallmark of historians of second-hand exchange. By energetically scouring American streets and using assumptions of inno-cence to their advantage, Woloson finds, children helped to shape an expanding junk industry, one intimately connected, through a series of sometimes illicit links, to first-hand manufacturing.

Laura Ekholm likewise utilizes a wide range of source materials in order to underscore the role of Jewish-run secondhand businesses in the development of newly produced, ready-to-wear clothing industry in industrializing Helsinki, Finland. 'Jews, Second-hand Trade and Upward Economic Mobility: Introducing the Ready-to-Wear Business in Industrializing Helsinki, 1880-1930', demonstrates that members of the European Jewish diaspora forged vital connections between numerous new and used goods industries, from scrap metal to clothing, in an underresearched locale. Ekholm contributes a valuable perspective to liter-ature assigning Jewish entrepreneurs a key role in creating and sustaining many secondhand economies. Though without civil rights until 1917, Jews in Finland were able to leverage obscure, widespread transnational connections to expand personal business opportunity and influence mainstream consumer choices.

In a similar vein, Jonathan Pollack's 'Shylocks to Superheroes: Jewish Scrap Dealers in Anglo-American Popular Culture', follows the Jewish diaspora through much of the twenti-eth-century United States. Pollack traces the cultural evolution of the depiction of Jewish scrap dealers from sinister cheats to strong heroes, quite literally in his example of the DC Comic superhero and mystic vigilante Rag Man. While delving deeply into the practical relationship between scrap metal businesses and Jewish entrepreneurs in industrializing America, Pollack also takes the reader on a romp through prominent cultural representations of the same, from the pages of Shakespeare, to Vaudeville stages, and into late twentieth-cen-tury comic books.

Miki Suguira rounds out the historicized contributions with an exploration of highly unusual large-scale commercial re-use of textiles in Japan in the mid-twentieth century. 'The Mass Consumption of Refashioned Clothes: Re-Dyed Kimonos in Post-War Japan' recounts an instance of post-consumer textile waste management, arguing that the re-dyeing of kimonos helped Kyoto retain its prominence in the dyed kimono industry. Coordinators, the intermediaries who arranged the cleaning, mending, quality assessment, redesign, and re-dyeing, established long-term relationships with customers in a nationwide made-to-order network. Their work claimed a large market for refashioning that became an integrated segment of the clothing industry and acted as an engine of broader economic growth. Despite this article's specific context, it holds potential instructive value for manufacturers looking to incorporate strategies of re-use.

The remaining articles in this double issue treat contemporary or ongoing circumstances of secondhand goods exchanges, all of which indicate the importance of the historical variety of trade in pre-owned items. Though tracking vastly different modes and meanings of sec-ondhand trades, these five authors all focus on ways in which recirculation today, locally

and globally, requires both economic and cultural flexibility, and continues to attract participation through social as well as fiscal reward. Jennifer Ayres and Frederik Larsen both use
case studies involving California thrift stores. In 'The Work of Shopping: Resellers and the
Informal Economy in the Goodwill Bins,' Ayres provides a case study of consumer/producer
participation at a Northern California Goodwill Outlet in 2010 that examines the fluid boundaries between work and leisure associated with much secondhand trade. Larsen's 'Valuation
in Action: Ethnography of an American Thrift Store' focuses attention on the relationship
between objects and people, and the subjective practices of assigning value. Using Mary
Douglas as an explanatory framework, Larsen closely examines colloquial practices of cat-
egorizing and assessing value with the motive of mitigating impressions of disorder.

Staffan Appelgren traces recent developments in secondhand commerce in Gothenberg,
Sweden, concluding that motion and adaptability are the most important attributes of successful used-goods businesses. 'History as Business: Changing Dynamics of Retailing in
Gothenburg's Second-hand Market' shows that even amidst accelerating consumer interest
in the goods, purveyors are required to show a willingness to incorporate or shift to digital
means to advertise and sell various sorts of secondhand items, from books to clothing. Abel
Ezeoha and his colleagues take the discussion of contemporary secondhand trade to the
sparsely examined category of durables, specifically automobiles in West Africa. In
'Secondhand Vehicle Markets in West Africa: A Source of Regional Disintegration, Trade
Informality and Welfare Losses,' the authors reveal how the trade across national borders
between Togo, Benin, Niger, and Nigeria has failed to thrive optimally in part due to differing
import regulations that result in conflicting motivations for market participation. Used vehicles imported legally into ports in Togo and Benin are re-exported via Niger to Nigeria.
Effective regional integration of the trade remains elusive as long as the benefits to one
nation result in losses for another.

In the issue's final contribution, Lucy Norris returns attention to secondhand clothing
economies and the ongoing relevance of textiles to issues of sustainability by focusing on
developing global modes of redistribution. Norris analyzes technical innovations in textile
recycling, specifically the driving force of Circular Economy (CE) models.[38] She pays particular
attention to how these models provide alternative forms of sociality and property relations
among small-sale designers and producers in urban areas. In effect, Norris assigns cloth
economies broad agency, arguing for their potential to remake social worlds and challenge
existing patterns of valuation.

Conclusion

Secondhand objects flit in and out of view, submerging as trash and then reappearing as
pre-owned, used, vintage, collectible, or some other transitorily valued category. As the
articles in this Special Issue demonstrate, secondhand objects were never peripheral, but
overlapped with and contributed to overall economic developments, reflecting and affecting
changes in them. All this, they still do. Because of this mutual interaction, the consumption
of secondhand objects and materials is not always or necessarily linked to social and environmental agendas or efforts to reduce consumption, but may even enable more, not less,
first-hand consumption.[39] This has implications for the way in which we understand the role
of secondhand consumption in the fraught relationship between production and consumption as the twenty-first century unfolds.

Yet many consumers and scholars have long assumed that secondhand exchange is exempt from the social, environmental, and economic critiques of primary production—or, that the scope of secondhand trade is too insignificant to warrant serious attention. Even though many consumers of secondhand goods are concerned with sustainability, the manufacturing industry is preeoccupied with growing markets and profitability. Often intending to subvert, but sometime unintentionally supporting, the ongoing commercial project of increased novelty and obsolescence, secondhand trade's success arguably compromises stated environmental and social aims by undermining more extreme notions of thrift and minimalism that involve severely minimizing consumerism—not just altering the form of consumerism practised. Understanding the practical and personal outcomes of secondhand economies may help to better inform activist entrepreneurs and ethical consumers, while maintaining or increasing the market value of used materials.

Beyond their direct and practical contributions to the field of business and consumer histories and contemporary economic inquiries, the articles in this Special Issue present the innovative theories and methodologies needed to thoroughly consider the fluid positioning of used-goods exchange, thus adding to the arsenal of academic tools in a variety of areas. Taken together, scholarship in this emerging field offers rich inspiration for future research ranging from historical perspectives on the flow of a single commodity across time to multi-site approaches by research teams of geographers or anthropologists exploring the extensive biographies of things through space and time. Research on secondhand materials clearly adds to scholarly inquiries expanding out from informal economic studies and the new histories of capitalism as well. The broad-based content in this issue also showcases ways in which cultural and economic insight benefit from each other, and how historical and contemporary treatments of a theme can similarly complement each other. The subject itself encapsulates exciting and relevant global matters, and the methods used introduce innovative resources for interdisciplinary researchers from an array of backgrounds.

Notes

1. Alexander, Catherine and Joshua Reno, "Introduction," in Alexander and Reno, eds. *Economies of Recycling: The Global Transformation of Materials, Values and Social Relations* (London: Zed Books, 2012), p. 3.
2. A couple of notable exceptions to this include Staffan Appelgren and Anna Bohlin, "Circulating Stuff Through Second-hand, Vintage and Retro Markets," *Journal of Current Cultural Research* (Thematic Section, Vol 7, 2015); Jon Stobart and Ilja Van Damme eds., *Modernity and the second-hand trade: European Consumption Cultures and Practices, 1700–1900* (Basingstoke: Palgrave, 2010) offers an exception to this by including various venues and types of second-hand exchange in a broad-spanning examination of 200 years of European used goods trade.
3. Marcel Mauss, *The Gift: Forms and Functions of Exchange in Archaic Societies* (London: Routledge, 1990, orig. published 1922); Mary Douglas, *Purity and Danger: An Analysis of the Concepts of Pollution and Taboo* (London: Routledge & Kegan Paul, 1966); and Arjun Appadurai, ed. *The Social Life of Things: Commodities in Cultural Perspective* (Cambridge UK: Cambridge University Press, 1986).
4. Douglas, *Purity and Danger*.
5. Michael Thompson, *Rubbish Theory: The Creation and Destruction of Value* (Oxford: Oxford University Press, 1979), p. 15.
6. Mike Crang, Alex Hughes, Nicky Gregson, Lucy Norris, and Farid Ahamad, "Rethinking Governance and Value in Commodity Chains through Global Recycling Networks," *Transactions of the Institute of British Geographers*, vol. 39 (2013): 12–24.

7.   Elizabeth Wilson, *Adorned in Dreams: Fashion and Modernity* (Berkeley and Los Angeles, CA: University of California Press, 2005), 5.
8.   Laurence Fontaine, ed., *Alternative Exchanges: Secondhand Circulations from the Sixteenth Century to the Present* (New York: Berghahn Books, 2008); Lemire, "Consumerism in Preindustrial and Early Industrial England"; Adam Mendelsohn, *The Rag Race: How Jews Sewed Their Way to Success in American and the British Empire* (New York: New York University Press, 2015).
9.   Hansen, *Salaula*, 99–126.
10.   In years past, recycling tended to apply to consumer waste disposed of through centers recycling products by material for industrial re-use. However, textile industries, as well as recent scholarship, also apply the term to the re-use, re-distriction, and re-production of cloth products.
11.   See for premodern context, Lemire, "Consumerism in Preindustrial and Early Industrial England"; Lemire, *Dress, Culture, and Commerce*; For more contemporary analyses, see Angela McRobbie, "Second-Hand Dresses and the Ragmarket," in *Zoot Suits and Second-Hand Dresses: An Anthology of Fashion and Music*, ed. Angela McRobbie (Boston: Unwin Hyman, 1988); Gregson and Crewe, *Second-Hand Cultures*.
12.   Heike Jenss, *Fashioning Memory: Vintage Style and Youth Culture* (New York: Bloomsbury Academic, 2015).
13.   Le Zotte, *Goodwill to Grunge*; Mendelsohn *The Rag Race*; Woloson *In Hock*.
14.   Lemire, "Consumerism in Preindustrial and Early Industrial England"; Woloson, *In Hock*.
15.   Terence Turner, "The Social Skin," in C. B. Burroughs and J. Ehrenreich, eds. , *Reading the Social Body* (Iowa City: University of Iowa Press), pp. 15–39.
16.   Hansen, *Salaula*.
17.   Le Zotte, *From Goodwill to Grunge*.
18.   Hansen, *Salaula*.
19.   Andrew Brooks and David Simon, "Unravelling the Relationship Between Used-Clothing Imports and the Decline of African Clothing Industries," *Development and Change*, vol. 43, no. 6 (2012): 1265-1290; Hansen, *Salaula*.
20.   Norris, *Recycling Indian Clothing*.
21.   See for example, Melissa Gauthier, "Mexican "ant traders" in the El Paso/Cuidad Juarez border region" in *Globalization from Below: The World's Other Economy*, eds. Gordon Matthews, Gustavo Lins Ribeiro, and Carlos Alba Vega (New York: Routledge, (2012), 138–153; Lynne B. Millgram, "Activating frontier livelihoods: Women and the transnational secondhand clothing trade between Hong Kong and the Philippines," *Urban Anthropology and Studies of Cultural Systems and World Economic Development*, Vol. 37, Issue 1(2008): 5-47; and Niko Besnier, "Consumption and Cosmopolitanism: Practicing modernity at the second-hand marketplace in Nuku'alofa, Tonga. *Anthropological Quarterly*,"Vol 77 (2004): 7–45.
22.   See Eriksen and Schober, "Waste and the Superfluous"; Minh T. N. Nguyen, "Trading Broken Things: Gendered Performance and Spatial Practices in a Northern Vietnam Rural-Urban Waste Economy," Joshua Reno, "Waste and Waste Management," *Annual Review of Anthropology*, Vol 44 (2015), 557–572; Melanie Samson, "accumulation By Dispossession and the Informal Economy—Struggles Over Knowledge, Being and Work at a Soweto Garbage Dump," *Environment and Planning D; Society and* Space, Vol 22, no. 5 (2015), 813–830; Raymond Stokes, Roman Köster and Stephen C. Sambrook, eds., *The Business of Waste: Great Britain and Germany, 1945 to the Present* (New York: Cambridge University Press, 2013); and Carl Zimring, *Cash for Your Trash: Scrap Recycling in America* (New Brunswick, NJ: Rutgers University Press, 2000 and "Dirty Work: How Hygiene and Xenophobia Marginalized the American Waste Trades, 1870–1930," *Environmental History*, Vol. 9, no.1 (2004), 80–101;
23.   See for examples of literature on secondhand automotive trade, J. Joost Beuving, "Cotonou's Klondike: African Traders and Second-hand Car Markets in Bénin," *The Jounral of Modern African Studies* (Vol. 42, Issue 4, Dec. 2004), 511–537; Yali Yand, Hao Chen, and ruoping Zhang, "Development of Used Car Market in China," *Modern Economy* (Vol. 4, Issue 6, 2013), 453–460. Carl Zimring broadens his interest in scrap recycling with his pertinent article "The Complex Environmental Legacy of the Automobile Shredder," *Technology and Culture* (July, 2011, Vol. 52), pp. 523–547.

24. Leon Rosenstein, *Antiques: The History of an Idea*, (Ithaca and London: Cornell University Press, 2009).

25. Briann Greenfield's history of antiquing in the United States is a good example. Greenfield, *Out of the Attic: Inventing Antiques in the Twentieth-Century New England* (Amherst: University of Massachusetts Press, 2009); Alison Isenberg's forthcoming book uses antiques in tandem with less valuable secondhand trade as a lens to understanding the relationship between racial re-configuring of nineteenth and twentieth-century United States cities, and the politics and economy of preserving and redistributing objects of American heritage. Alison Isenberg, "Second-Hand Cities: Unsettling Racialized Hierarchies," (paper presented at the 2013 American Historical Association Conference, New Orleans).

26. Joanna Cohen, "'The Right to Purchase Is as Free as the Right to Sell': Defining Consumers as Citizens in the Auction-House Conflicts of the Early Republic," *Journal of the Early Republic*, (20, no. 1, 2010), 25-62; T.H. Breen, *The Marketplace of Revolution: How Consumer Politics Shaped American Independence*, (New York: Oxford University Press, 2004).

27. Wendy Woloson, *In Hock: Pawning in America from Independence Through the Great Depression* (Chicago: University of Chicago Press, 2009).

28. Jennifer Le Zotte, *From Goodwill to Grunge: A History of Secondhand Styles and Alternative Economies* (Chapel Hill: University of North Carolina Press, 2017).

29. Gretchen Herrmann has written extensively on garage sales, beginning with Stephen M. Soiffer and Gretchen Herrman, "For Fun and Profit: An Analysis of the American Garage Sale," *Urban Life*, Vol. 12 (1984): 397–421; Herrmann's later garage sale work focused on gender and the role of gift-giving and haggling in the exchanges. For example, Herrmann, "Gift or Commodity: What Changes Hands in the U.S. Garage Sale", *American Ethologist*, Vol 24, No 4 (1997): 910–930; and Herrmann, Hannling Spoken Here: Gender, Class, and Style in U.S. Garage-Sale Bargaining," *Journal of Popular Culture*, Vol 38, no 2 (2004): 55-81. See also Ruth L. Landman, "Washington's Yard Sales: Women's Work, But Not for the Money," *City and Society*, Vol. 1, no 2 (1996): 703–728. For more on flea markets, see John F. Sherry, "A Sociocultural Analysis of a Midwestern American Flea Market," *Journal of Consumer Research*, Vol. 17, no. 1 (1990): 13–30; Nicky Gregson and Louise Crewe, "The Bargain, the Knowledge and the Spectacle: Making Sense of Consumption in the Space of the Car Boot Sale: *Environment and Planning D: Society and Space* (Vol. 15 (1997): 87–112; Kathryn Watt and Bernhard Dubbeld, "Enchanting the Worn-Out: The Craft of Selling Second-Hand Things at Milnerton Market, Cape Town," *Social Dynamics*, vol. 42 (2016): 143–160.

30. Staffan Appelgren and Anna Bohlin, eds., "Circulating Stuff Through Secondhand, Vintage and Retro Markets," theme issue. *Culture Unbound: Journal of Current Cultural Research*, Vol. 56, no. 1 (2015).

31. Andrew Brooks, *Clothing Poverty: The Hidden World of Fast Fashion and Second-hand Clothes* (London: Zed Books, 2015); Elizabeth Cline, *Overdressed: The Shockingly High Cost of Cheap Fashion* (New York: Penguin, 2013).

32. Kate Fletcher, *Sustainable Fashion and Textiles: Design Journeys* (London: Routledge, 2014).

33. Nicky Gregson and Mike Crang, "From Waste to Resource: The Trade in Wastes and Global Recycling Economies," *Annual Review of Environment and Resources*, Vol 40 (2015), 151–176.

34. Crang, Hughes, et al, "Rethinking Governance and Value in Commodity Chains Through Global Recycling Networks."

35. Alexander and Reno, "Introduction," 3–4.

36. See for example, Beverly Lemire, "Consumerism in preindustrial and early industrial England: The trade in secondhand clothes," *Journal of British Studies*, vol. 27, no 1 (1988), p. 1–24; Lemire, *Dress, Culture, and Commerce: The English Clothing Trade Before the Factory, 1600-1800*, (New York: St. Martin's Press, 1997). Lemire, "Shifting currency: The culture and economy of the sec-ond hand trade in England, c. 1600–1850," in A. Palmer and H. Clark (Eds.), *Old Clothes, New looks: Second Hand Fashion*, (New York: Berg, 2005), pp. 49–82; Wendy Woloson, *In Hock: Pawning in America from Independence through the Great Depression* (Chicago: University of Chicago Press, 2009); Jennifer Le Zotte, *From Goodwill to Grunge: A History of Secondhand Styles and Alternative economies*, (Chapel Hill, NC: University of North Carolina Press, 2017).

37. Important anthropological contributions include Karen Tranberg Hansen's *Salaula: The world of secondhand clothing and Zambia* (Chicago: University of Chicago Press, 2000); Lucy Norris's

Recycling Indian Clothing: Global Contexts of Reuse and Value (Bloomington: Indiana University Press, 2010); Alexander and Reno, 2012; Thomas H. Eriksen and Elisabeth Schober, "Waste and the Superfluous: An Introduction," *Social Anthropology*, Vol. 25, No. 3 (2017), pp 282–288. Social geographers Nicky Gregson and Louise Crewe offer an excellent space-based study of second-hand exchange with focus on car boot sales and charity shops in Britain in *Second-hand Cultures* (Oxford: Berg, 2003), and Alexandra Palmer and Hazel Clark edited a collection of studies of the interactions between secondhand clothing and fashion industries in *Old Clothes, New Looks,* 2005.

38. For more on circular economy (CE) models, see for example, Fenna Blomsma and Geraldine Brennan, (2017) "The Emergence of Circular Economy: A New Framing Around Prolonging Resource Productivity," *Journal of Industrial Ecology* 21(3): 603-614; Desrochers, Pierre (2000)., "Market Processes and the Closing of 'Industrial Loops,'—A Historical Reappraisal," *Journal of Industrial Ecology* 4(1): 29–43.

39. Nicky Gregson, Mike Crang, Jennifer Laws, Tamlynn Fleetwood, and Helen Holmes, "Moving up the waste hierarchy: Car boot sales, reuse exchange and the challenges to consumer culture and waste prevention," *Resources, Conservation and Recycling*, Vol. 77 (2013): 97–107.

Literature cited

Alexander, Catherine and Joshua Reno (2012a). Introduction. In C. Alexander and J. Reno (Eds.). *Economies of recycling: The global transformation of materials, values and social relations* (pp. 1–32). London: Zed Books.

Alexander, Catherine and Joshua Reno (Eds.). (2012b). *Economies of recycling: The global transformation of materials, values and social relations*. London: Zed Books.

Appadurai, Arjun (Ed.). (1986). *The social life of things: commodities in cultural perspective*. Cambridge UK: Cambridge University Press.

Appelgren, Staffan and Anna Bohlin (eds.). Circulating stuff through second-hand, vintage and retro markets. Theme issue. *Culture Unbound: Journal of Current Cultural Research*, Vol. 57, Issue 1, (2015).

Besnier, Niko (2004). "Consumption and Cosmopolitanism: Practicing modernity at the second-hand marketplace in Nuku'alofa, Tonga," *Anthropological Quarterly*, 77: 7–45.

Beuving, Joost (2015). American cars in Cotonou: Culture in African entrepreneurship and the making of a globalizing trade. *Journal of Modern African Studies*, 53(3): 317–338.

Blomsma, Fenna and Geraldine Brennan (2017). "The Emergence of Circular Economy: A New Framing Around Prolonging Resource Productivity," *Journal of Industrial Ecology* 21 (3): 603–614.

Blonde, Bruno, Cocquery, Natacha, Stobart, Jon, and Ilja Van Damme (Eds.). (2009). Fashioning old and new: Changing consumer patterns in Europe (seventeenth-nineteenth centuries). *Studies in European Urban History (1100–1800)*, 18. Turnhout: Brepols.

Breen, T.H., *The marketplace of revolution: How consumer politics shaped American independence*, (New York: Oxford University Press, 2004).

Brooks, Andrew (2015). *Clothing poverty: The hidden world of fast fashion and second-hand clothes*. London: Zed Books.

Brooks, Andrew and David Simon (2012). Unravelling the relationship between used-clothing imports and the decline of African clothing industries. *Development and Change*, 43(6): 1265–1290.

Crang, Mike, Alex Hughes, Nicky Gregson, Lucy Norris and Farid Ahamad (2013). Rethinking governance and value in commodity chains through global recycling networks. *Transactions of the Institute of British Geographers*, 38: 12–24.

Crawford, Margaret. "The Garage Sale as Informal Economy and Transformative Urbanism," in *The Informed American City: Beyond Taco Trucks and Day Labor*, ed. Vinit Mukhija and Anastasia Loukaitou-Sideris (Cambridge, MA: MIT Press, 2014), 21–38.

Cline, Elizabeth L. (2013). *Overdressed: The shockingly high cost of cheap fashion*. New York NY: Penguin.

Cohen, Joanna, "'The Right to Purchase Is as Free as the Right to Sell': Defining Consumers as Citizens in the Auction-House Conflicts of the Early Republic," *Journal of the Early Republic*, (20, no. 1, 2010), 25–62.

Desrochers, Pierre (2000). "Market Processes and the Closing of 'Industrial Loops,'—A Historical Reappraisal," *Journal of Industrial Ecology* 4(1): 29–43.

Douglas, Mary (1966). *Purity and danger: An Analysis of the concepts of pollution and taboo.* London: Routledge & Kegan Paul.

Eriksen, Thomas H. and Elisabeth Schober (2017). Waste and the superfluous: An introduction. *Social Anthropology*, 25(3): 288–287.

Fletcher, Kate (2014). *Sustainable fashion and textiles: design journeys.* London: Routledge.

Fontaine, Laurence (Ed.). (2008). *Alternative exchanges: Secondhand circulations from the sixteenth century to the present.* New York: Berghahn Books.

Gauthier, Melissa (2012). Mexican" ant traders" in the El Paso/Cuidad Juarez border region. In *Globalization from Below: The World's Other Economy*, eds. Gordon Matthews, Gustavo Lins Ribeiro, and Carlos Alba Vega (New York: Routledge), 138–153.

Gregson, Nicky and Louise Crewe (2003). *Second-hand cultures.* Oxford: Berg.

Gregson, Nicky and Louise Crewe "The Bargain, the Knowledge and the Spectacle: Making Sense of Consumption in the Space of the Car Boot Salem: *Environment and Planning D: Society and Space* (Vol. 15 (1997): 87–112.

Gregson, Nicky and Mike Crang (2015): From waste to resource: The trade in wastes and global recycling economies. *Annual Review of Environment and Resources*, 40: 151–176.

Hansen, Karen Tranberg (2000). *Salaula: The world of secondhand clothing and Zambia.* Chicago: University of Chicago Press.

Hansen, Karen Tranberg (2004). Helping or hindering? Controversies around the international second-hand clothing trade. *Anthropology Today*, 20(4): 3–9.

Jenss, Heike (2015). *Fashioning memory: Vintage style and youth culture.* New York: Bloomsbury Academic.

Lemire, Beverly (1988). Consumerism in preindustrial and early industrial England: The trade in secondhand clothes. *Journal of British Studies*, 27(1): 1–24.

Lemire, Beverly (1997). *Dress, culture, and commerce: The English clothing trade before the factory, 1600–1800.* New York: St. Martin's Press.

Lemire, Beverly (2005). Shifting currency: The culture and economy of the second hand trade in England, c. 1600–1850. In A. Palmer and H. Clark (Eds.), *Old clothes, new looks: second hand fashion* (pp. 49–82). New York: Berg.

Le Zotte, Jennifer (2013). 'Not charity, but a chance': Philanthropic capitalism and the rise of American thrift stores. *New England Quarterly*, 86 (1): 169–195.

Le Zotte, Jennifer (2017). *From goodwill to grunge: A history of secondhand styles and alternative economies.* Chapel Hill, NC: University of North Carolina Press.

McRobbie, Angela (1988). Second-hand dresses and the role of the ragmarket, in *Zoot suits and second-hand dresses: An anthology of fashion and music*, ed. Angela McRobbie (pp. 23–49). Boston: Unwin Hyman.

Mendelsohn, Adam D. (2015). *The rag race: How Jews sewed their way to success in America and the British empire.* New York: New York University Press.

Millgram, B. Lynne (2008). "Activating frontier livelihoods: Women and the transnational secondhand clothing trade between Hong Kong and the Philippines," *Urban Anthropology and Studies of Cultural Systems and World Economic Development*, 37(1): 5–47.

Nguyen, Minh T. N. (2016). Trading broken things: gendered performance and spatial practices in a northern Vietnam rural-urban waste economy. *American Ethnologist*, 43(1): 116–129.

Norris, Lucy (2010). *Recycling Indian clothing: Global contexts of reuse and value.* Bloomington: Indiana University Press.

Palmer, Alexandra and Hazel Clark (Eds.). (2005). *Old clothes, new looks: second hand fashion.* Oxford: Berg.

Reno, Joshua (2015). Waste and waste management. *Annual Review of Anthropology*, 44: 557–572.

Samson, Melanie (2015). Accumulation by dispossession and the informal economy–Struggles over knowledge, being and work at a Soweto garbage dump. *Environment and Planning D: Society and Space*, 33(5): 813–830.

Samuel, Raphael, *Theaters of memory: Past and present in contemporary culture* (London: Verso, 2012).
Stobart, Jon and Ilja Van Damme, (Eds). *Modernity and the second-hand trade*. Basingstoke: Palgrave, 2010.
Stokes, Raymond; Roman Köster; and Stephen C. Sambrook, eds., *The Business of Waste: Great Britain and Germany, 1945 to the Present* (New York: Cambridge University Press, 2013).
Strasser, Susan (1999). *Waste and want: A social history of trash*. New York: Henry Holt and Company.
Thompson, Michael (1979). *Rubbish theory: The creation and destruction of value*. Oxford: Oxford University Press.
Turner, Terence ([1980] 1993). The social skin. In C. B. Burroughs and J. Ehrenreich (Eds.). *Reading the Social Body*, pp. 15–39. Iowa City: University of Iowa Press.
Kathryn Watt and Bernhard Dubbeld, "Enchanting the Worn-Out: The Craft of Selling Second-Hand Things at Milnerton Market, Cape Town," *Social Dynamics*, vol. 42 (2016): 143–160.
Wilson, Elizabeth (2005). *Adorned in dreams: Fashion and modernity*. Berkeley and Los Angeles, CA: University of California Press.
Woloson, Wendy (2009). *In hock: Pawning in America from independence through the great depression*. Chicago: University of Chicago Press.
Zimring, Carl. *Cash for your trash: Scrap recycling in America* (New Brunswick, NJ: Rutgers University Press, 2000.
Zimring, Carl "Dirty work: How hygiene and xenophobia marginalized the American waster trades, 1870–1930," *Environmental History* 9, no 1 (2004): 80–101.

Domestic textiles and country house sales in Georgian England

Jon Stobart (ID)

ABSTRACT

Textiles are central to our understanding of the second-hand trade in Georgian England, but the focus is generally on clothing; much less attention has been given to domestic textiles in the form of linen, beds and drapery. This article draws on auction catalogues from Northamptonshire, 1761–1836, to identify the changing quantity and nature of textiles being sold, the ways in which they were promoted and valorised, and what this might tell us about consumers' motivations. It highlights how the continued appeal of second-hand textiles was framed in a rhetoric of gentility and respectability, and reveals the country house auction as a key institution in the recirculation of second-hand goods.

A CATALOGUE of the Entire Genuine Household Furniture of Thomas Medlycott, Esq; deceased. Consisting of Variety of Beds, with silks, Damask, Tabby, Harrateen, and other Furniture; Cabinet Work in Mahogany and Walnut Tree ... Marble Tables, Chimney, Pier, and Sconce Glasses; Pictures, Plate, Linen, useful and ornamental China; Kitchen Furniture and Brewing Utensils; a Post Chaise and Harness; a large quantity of Port and other Wines; Likewise an elegant Collection of Books ... which will be sold by AUCTION (By Order of the Executors) At his late Dwelling-House in Cottingham, in the County of Northampton.[1]

Thus ran the front cover of a catalogue for an auction taking place at a small country house in 1761. It speaks of the material richness of the English gentry – a wealth of goods that had grown and spread through most social groups during seventeenth- and especially eighteenth-century Europe. This involved the growing supply of goods, especially semi-luxuries, which made homes increasingly comfortable and certainly much fuller.[2] Whilst much attention has focused on the role of imported goods and the imitations that they spawned,[3] the second-hand trade played an important part in supplying household goods to all sections of society through the eighteenth century and beyond.

The consumption of second-hand goods has received growing interest in recent years, yet remains surprisingly marginal to broader narratives of consumer change that still focus on luxury, novelty and fashion as the key drivers of change.[4] Indeed, these are also seen as key drivers in the provision and consumption of use goods.[5] Focusing especially on clothing, Lemire has recently posited a three-stage model of the changing character of the second-hand trade.[6] In the first stage – the transition from scarcity – all sections of society were engaged, goods being used as non-monetary exchange by rich and poor alike, in part due to the lack of small coinage and the moral imperative of thrift, but also because of the absolute scarcity of goods.[7] By the later seventeenth century, there was a growing abundance of goods on the market and in the home, which marked stage two of Lemire's model. This encouraged a growth in second-hand exchange as used goods were released onto the market, but also a bifurcation of that market: the poor continued to draw heavily on second-hand goods, especially clothing, whilst the wealthy largely withdrew as buyers, other than of collectibles such as books or art.[8] However, they still pumped unwanted items onto the market: unfashionable clothing and furniture, for example, which were acquired by labourers and artisans in a trickle-down of goods and tastes.[9] This division was heightened further in the third stage, industrial plenty, although by the second quarter of the nineteenth century certain categories of second-hand goods were increasingly attractive as curios and antiques, old things being valued by elites and others for their scarcity and their seeming authenticity.[10]

This very brief sketch of the changing second-hand trade opens up two key points. One is the meaning that second-hand goods held for their new owners; the other is the ways in which these objects were promoted and marketed to potential buyers. Goods carry many different meanings, but these have often been conceived as a binary of economic and cultural value, with the latter becoming increasingly important through the transformation of consumption in the long eighteenth century.[11] Whilst conceptually distinct, these different meanings or values overlapped in particular objects. As Riello notes, a bed might be redolent with social and cultural associations, yet it remained an economic asset with a monetary value that could be realised.[12] This dual meaning is apparent from the care with which testators itemised specific belongings as bequests: they were desirable for their economic value and their emotional resonance.[13] It is all the more surprising, therefore, that engagement with second-hand consumption is persistently linked most directly to financial necessity, be it the purchase of old clothes by the urban poor described by Lemire or the bartering of unwanted furniture by cash-strapped French aristocrats detailed by Coquery and Charpy.[14] Yet, as all these authors make clear, used goods could be valued for their cultural meanings: the second-hand beau and the use of old furniture as a means to express difference or invent/ augment pedigree. This links to the insights offered by studies of contemporary second-hand consumption. Gregson and Crewe acknowledge the importance of financial necessity to some of those buying second-hand goods, but argue that consumers might also be driven by other motivations.[15] One possibility is that they might be engaged in attempts to capture value or get a bargain, acquiring higher value or better quality goods for less money. Buying second-hand thus becomes 'clever' consumption. Another motivation is the desire to 'capture difference'. Here, consumption links closely with social identity, and the role of goods in marking the taste, judgement and individuality of the consumer becomes critical. For Gregson and Crewe, this involved developments such as retro-shops; for those studying the eighteenth century, it has been recognised in what Stewart terms 'the search for the authentic object' or the desire to 'share in another's "genuine" world', as Wall puts it.[16]

If second-hand goods were sought after for varied reasons, it follows that they would be actively marketed in ways that addressed these different motivations, especially as the supply of goods grew from the later seventeenth century; indeed, knowledge of goods – their availability, quality, etc. – was important in structuring demand. Some knowledge was tacit and experiential, as Lemire makes clear in the context of textiles, but much was learned from visiting shops and auctions or by perusing advertisements in the printed media, including newspapers and pattern books.[17] Auctions were especially important in this regard because the goods were available for inspection; the catalogues described real objects rather than designs. The ways in which goods were described is therefore particularly useful in linking objects to different systems of meaning: value, taste, gentility and utility. They could affect the attractiveness of goods (and ultimately their price) by communicating messages about quality of raw materials, product design and so on.[18]

In this article, I want to explore some of the ways in which meaning, motivation and marketing came together in the catalogues of 21 country house auctions that took place in Northamptonshire between 1761 and 1736 – a period in which new and used goods were increasingly plentiful and immediately before the emergence of a strong and specialist antiques trade. Northamptonshire was an essentially rural county with many gentry families, including Thomas Medlycott, and a few larger magnates such as the Earl of Halifax, whose possessions were auctioned a decade after the sale at Cottingham. The sample thus contains a cross-section of the landowning elite of Georgian England. Auctions were well established as a mechanism for clearing the possessions of the deceased or bankrupt, or for cash-strapped landowners to realise assets.[19] They were institutions which bound together buyers and sellers, and embedded transactions in a familiar and structured set of practices which encouraged trust.[20] Rather than focus on the auctions as events – something which Nenadic and Pennell have both done in the past[21] – I am interested in what was available and how it was presented in catalogues, which offer both a comprehensive listing of the goods being sold and (sometimes very full) descriptions of many items, allowing assessments to be made of their quality as well as type. I focus on domestic (that is household) textiles for three key reasons: first, they have been somewhat neglected as a category of second-hand goods (as opposed to clothing, which has received considerable attention); second, they were a varied group, comprising goods that were everyday and practical (sheets and blankets) as well as those that were more status oriented (bed hangings) or associated with enhanced physical comfort (carpets); third, they included goods that might be thought increasingly problematic when second-hand for reasons of hygiene (bedding) or changing fashion (curtains).

The discussion is organised under different categories of textiles – household linen, beds and bedding, and drapery and carpets – but running through the article are three key questions: what household textiles were offered for sale and how did this change in terms of type and quality over the study period; how were different types of textiles described and valorised in the auction catalogues; and what can this tell us about the market for second-hand goods and the possible motivations of consumers who chose to buy used goods, recognising that the catalogues themselves do not ascribe motivation or tell us anything about who bought the goods being promoted?

Country house sales: Promoting and selling lots

Country house sales were promoted via notices placed in the local and sometimes the national press.[22] The wording of these advertisements was often reproduced, sometimes verbatim, on the covers of auction catalogues which themselves formed a mechanism for promoting the sales. These were made available at the auctioneer's offices and via local booksellers, inns and the like, allowing potential buyers to assess the nature of the goods on offer ahead of the sale itself. They could then be examined over several days of viewing immediately before the auction, during which those with catalogues were allowed to access the house and wander through its rooms, seeing the various lots *in situ* and often en suite. The auction itself almost invariably took place in the house, the lots often being knocked down room by room – just as they appeared in the catalogue.

Auction catalogues thus offer a useful insight into the promotion and organisation of the sale, as well as itemising the goods available. Reading the front covers, it is clear that the identity and fate of the previous owner was important in legitimising the sale and the goods on offer.[23] The name of the owner is noted in all but one case and the goods frequently lauded as genuine, elegant, genteel, valuable, useful and even modern – a language which echoes that noted by Coquery in the advertisements of Parisian furniture dealers.[24] This gives us some immediate clues about the motivations to which the auctioneers hoped to appeal. They were keen to assure buyers that the goods really were the effects of the house owner, had belonged in that property and were, in that sense, genuine and authentic. More broadly, they were bound into the cultural norms of gentility and thus portrayed as appropriate goods for genteel households or those with aspirations to such status. Assurances of modernity reflected an attempt to present them as retaining cultural currency, even if they were not at the height of fashion; playing on ideas of value and utility appealed to a sense of thriftiness that lay at the centre of the well-managed household, both genteel and middling.[25] Potential buyers could thus see themselves as canny and careful, able to identify culturally appropriate goods and secure them at a good price. William Beckford's goods undoubtedly carried 'noble' kudos, as might those of the Earl of Halifax, and the belongings of men like R.J. Tibbits, esq. (Geddington House) or Henry Green, esq. (Rolleston Hall) might have carried meanings and associations amongst local buyers, but it is less clear whether people thought of themselves as acquiring part of another's genuine world, as Wall and Charpy argue.[26]

What is also apparent from the covers of the catalogues is that textiles were rarely the main attraction: only half of the sample included any mention of textiles and seven of these were before 1805. Just once were textiles the first set of goods to be mentioned, in the catalogue for the 1761 sale at Cottingham quoted at the start of this article.[27] More often, they were featured lower down the listings, in the mix with furniture, books, tableware and wine. The Cottingham catalogue was also unusual in naming a range of textiles on the cover; most only mentioned household linen. This fits with Pennell's argument that, whilst second-hand textiles had been an important part of the strategies of even quite wealthy consumers when it came to furnishing their homes – and especially their beds – this importance slipped during the course of the eighteenth century.[28] However, it would be a mistake to assume from their absence from the covers of auction catalogues that domestic textiles were also missing from the sales themselves. If we open up the catalogues and read through the lots on offer, it quickly becomes apparent that a large quantity and range of textiles were available, especially in the later decades of the eighteenth century. This pushes any decline in the importance of the country house sale as a source of textiles into the opening years of the nineteenth century at the earliest.

In all, there were 5518 items and 149 different types of textiles offered for sale (Tables 1 and 2), ranging from napkins and knife cloths to beds and Brussels carpets. Unsurprisingly, linens were most numerous, despite the fact that they appeared in only 10 of the sales, averaging 271 items per sale; blankets and quilts were the next most common, followed by

Table 1. Second-hand textiles sold at Northamptonshire country house sales, 1761–1836: number of items.

Year	Location	Hangings	Beds	Blankets	Quilts	Curtains	Carpets	Table cloths	Napkins	Sheets	Pillow cases	Towels	Total items
1761	Cottingham	10	12	47	11	17	5	0	0	0	0	0	105
1772	Horton	41	48	122	50	50	5	72	161	102	12	102	766
1779	Bramton	8	8	22	7	14	13	0	0	0	0	0	75
1784	Barton	13	13	37	11	13	13	0	0	0	0	0	100
1788	Stanwick	6	7	10	6	5	7	56	46	58	19	102	323
1792	Stanford	13	23	57	18	21	7	50	131	74	36	70	501
1797	Brixworth	16	17	45	17	24	15	0	0	0	36	0	134
1801	Rolleston	11	12	24	8	15	18	50	86	52	36	24	336
1801	Laxton	20	19	58	19	27	25	0	0	0	0	0	173
1802	Hazlebeach	10	12	27	11	7	16	54	50	28	14	133	362
1805	Wollaston	24	20	58	20	36	19	74	154	96	36	147	685
Total 1761–1805		*172*	*191*	*507*	*178*	*224*	*145*	*351*	*610*	*410*	*153*	*578*	*3534*
1815	Thorp Malsor	14	13	46	12	11	18	0	0	0	0	0	114
1816	Pychley	17	12	37	11	10	23	36	190	0	0	26	363
1823	Geddington	9	13	38	18	20	24	36	94	76	24	0	355
1823	Stamford Baron	6	6	19	13	9	17	56	142	60	42	76	446
1826	Rushton	7	6	15	6	6	16	0	0	0	0	0	56
1828	Geddington	9	11	39	11	8	22	13	100	38	26	20	297
1829	Geddington	3	7	23	7	6	21	0	0	0	0	0	67
1830	Welton	17	18	54	54	12	23	21	52	50	46	48	396
1836	Hollowell	4	3	10	1	6	14	1	0	0	0	0	39
1836	Sudborough	7	5	16	4	8	10	0	0	0	0	0	50
Total 1815–1836		*93*	*94*	*297*	*137*	*96*	*188*	*137*	*578*	*224*	*138*	*170*	*2157*
													218.3
Total		*265*	*285*	*804*	*315*	*320*	*333*	*315*	*1188*	*634*	*291*	*748*	*5518*

Source: Auction catalogues held at Northamptonshire Central Library.

Table 2. Second-hand textiles sold at Northamptonshire country house sales, 1761–1836: number of types.

Year	Location	Hangings	Beds	Blankets	Quilts	Curtains	Carpets	Table cloths	Napkins	Sheets	Pillow cases	Towels	Total
1761	Cottingham	8	1	2	3	5	3	0	0	0	0	0	25
1772	Horton	9	2	2	5	7	4	6	4	3	2	3	48
1779	Bramton	3	1	2	3	3	3	0	0	0	0	0	18
1784	Barton	7	3	3	3	5	5	0	0	0	0	0	26
1788	Stanwick	4	2	1	3	3	4	4	2	4	1	7	36
1792	Stanford	9	3	3	6	5	5	5	5	3	2	5	52
1797	Brixworth	8	2	2	3	6	4	0	0	0	0	0	25
1801	Rolleston	7	2	4	6	8	7	5	5	4	2	3	53
1801	Laxton	7	3	2	3	4	6	0	0	0	0	0	30
1802	Hazlebeach	8	3	3	5	4	6	6	4	3	1	7	50
1805	Wollaston	11	2	4	4	9	8	9	5	4	3	8	68
Total 1761–1805		*20*	*5*	*7*	*12*	*14*	*14*	*12*	*8*	*10*	*6*	*14*	*137*
1815	Thorp Malsor	8	4	4	4	6	11	0	0	0	0	0	37
1816	Pychley	3	2	2	2	2	5	3	3	0	0	3	26
1823	Geddington	3	4	4	4	6	5	3	3	3	1	0	39
1823	Stamford Baron	3	1	2	4	3	6	5	4	3	1	3	35
1826	Rushton	4	2	2	1	3	5	0	0	0	0	0	17
1828	Geddington	4	1	1	1	4	8	2	2	2	1	3	29
1829	Geddington	2	2	2	4	3	9	0	0	0	0	0	22
1830	Welton	7	2	2	2	4	7	2	4	2	2	1	36
1836	Hollowell	3	2	3	1	4	5	1	0	0	0	0	19
1836	Sudborough	4	3	1	3	3	7	0	0	0	2	8	21
Total 1815–1836		*12*	*6*	*7*	*7*	*10*	*15*	*7*	*8*	*7*	*2*	*8*	*94*
Total		*20*	*6*	*7*	*12*	*14*	*15*	*13*	*10*	*11*	*6*	*14*	*149*

Source: Auction catalogues held at Northamptonshire Central Library.

carpets and curtains, but even beds were widely available, with an average of over 13 per sale. Quantities decreased over time, from an average of 324 items per sale before 1805 to just 218 after 1815, with carpets being the only category of textile goods that were more numerous in the second part of the study period. However, the range remained steady at 8–9 categories of textiles per sale, suggesting that country houses remained an important source of a wide variety of domestic textiles well into the nineteenth century. Moreover, like their metropolitan counterparts, these sales afforded the opportunity to acquire both every-day goods and a considerable variety of high quality items.[29] Writing ahead of the sale at William Beckford's Fonthill estate in 1801, *The Times* assumed that the items on offer would be 'old-fashioned and worn-out articles'; but the correspondent at the auction itself was struck by the quality of goods being sold: 'there never was … a collection of finer or more superb furniture, in proportion to its quantity'.[30] Whilst the Northamptonshire sales were not in the same league, there were still some remarkable pieces, including: 'two sets of beautiful striped and flowered chintz pattern cotton festoon window curtains, 13 feet long, 3 breadths each, lined with calico and fringed, to correspond with the bed' at Stamford Hall (1792) and a 6-foot carved mahogany bedstead, 'with beautiful modern needlework furni-ture, lined throughout, silk fringe and full drapery, with black and gilt cornice poles' at Welton Place (1830).[31] Such goods might attract high status buyers. Back at Fonthill, *The Times* had been scathing, writing that: 'the principal competition is expected among the Farmers', whereas the sale accounts list amongst the buyers numerous gentlemen and aristocrats, including the Earl of Ilchester and the Duke of Somerset.[32] Country house auctions thus appealed to a wide range of buyers and second-hand goods did not necessarily descend down the social ladder.

Household linen: Practicality and respectability

Household linen falls into two broad categories – for the table and for beds. Both were important to a well-furnished home, serving practical functions linked to comfort, sociability and hygiene, and signalling status through displays of plentiful and clean linen.[33] In quan-titative terms, only the availability of napkins and pillowcases held up over time: tablecloths, sheets and especially towels were found in much smaller numbers after 1815 than had been the case earlier (Table 1). Even so, the quantities available at certain auctions remained impressive. The 1823 sale of Henry Fryer's belongings from Stamford Baron included 56 tablecloths, 142 napkins, 60 sheets, 42 pillowcases, and 76 towels and kitchen cloths; selling them all took up much of the fourth day of the auction.[34] Choose the right sale, then, and the late Georgian householder could still acquire an impressive array of linen second-hand. This suggests a continuation of the practices noted by Nenadic in her analysis of auctions in late eighteenth-century Glasgow where the up-and-coming merchant class happily acquired a variety of goods, including household linen. The attraction of these goods was their usefulness in facilitating rituals of hospitality centred on the table – a key part of mid-dling and genteel sociability at this time.[35] They were 'capturing value' by acquiring good quality and useful goods at a lower price than they would pay for new items, but they were also drawing on and reinforcing the cultural value of table linen for the middle ranks. The upshot for individual householders was that they might end up owning a variety of linen acquired from many different places and perhaps carrying the marks of many different earlier owners. Indeed, Nenadic notes just this in the case of William Crawford, a wealthy Glasgow merchant, whose large store of linen was all carefully marked with initials, but none with his own or those of his wife.[36]

Part of what made country house sales so attractive to such people was the range of linen available. Across the 11 auctions where it was being sold, there were 13 different types and qualities of tablecloth, many with napkins en suite; 10 sorts of sheets and 6 of pillowcases, and 14 varieties of towels, cloths and dusters (Table 2). To flesh this out a little, the catalogue for the auction of Sir Thomas Cave's goods from Stanford Hall in 1792 lists tablecloths in fine damask and diaper, plus damask breakfast cloths and servants' tablecloths. There were also napkins in fine damask, damask and diaper, and a variety of doylies.[37] A similar range of table linen was listed amongst the property of the Earl of Halifax, auctioned in 1772; but here a note against some of the damask tablecloths that they were 'almost new' heightened the attraction of these items by hinting at their currency and lack of wear.[38] Buyers could thus acquire table linen for a wide variety of purposes, from the everyday to impressive cloths brought out when entertaining guests – as Elizabeth Shackleton did with her 'handsome new damask tablecloth which looks most beautiful'.[39] Having a range of table cloths and napkins was important in making the right statement through qualitative distinctions, but it also helped to ensure that clean linen was always available – a very material consideration when dirty linen was a signal of a poorly managed household and a slur on the moral standing of the housewife.[40] The availability of such variety and choice via country house sales meant that some of this demand could be readily met via second-hand goods.

Much the same could be argued for sheets and pillowcases, which were also available in a range of different qualities, from diaper through Irish and huckabuck to Russian and even homespun. A plentiful supply, perhaps augmented by second-hand purchases and often carefully marked to indicate the room for which they were intended, again signalled good household management, as Vickery's analysis of Lancashire families makes clear.[41] The position with towels and cloths was made more complex because of the wide variety of uses ascribed to them. At the Wollaston Hall sale in 1805, for instance, there were huckabuck, common, round and hand towels, but also knife, kitchen and glass cloths.[42] The former would have been used by family members and guests as part of the process of cleaning the body, perhaps during dining, but increasingly in dressing rooms as part of the toilette. The latter were for servants to dry or clean tableware, again ensuring the presentation of clean tableware as a symbol of a respectable and orderly household.[43]

Buying table and bed linen at country house auctions was thus linked to motives other than financial necessity. Respectable householders were no doubt attracted by the prospect of securing a bargain, but also by the variety and choice available. In addition, they may have been interested in marking distinction through the purchase of particularly fine linen that might act as a status symbol. Qualitative descriptions added to the listings of table and bed linen were comparatively brief and generally centred on distinguishing some pieces as particularly fine. Quality and size came together in some descriptions, as at Wollaston Hall where we see a 'very fine large damask table cloth, 4¼ yards long & 3 yards wide, and a layover', followed by another the same and a further 12 that were slightly smaller.[44] These were impressive pieces – objects of desire that would add distinction to the table of the new owner, rather than everyday items snapped up because they were a bargain. They were exceptional both in their quality and in the way that they would stand out in all but the wealthiest homes. They were the equivalent of Elizabeth Shackleton's handsome damask tablecloth: objects of pride but also affection and sentiment. After using her cloth for the first time, Elizabeth noted in her diary: 'Good luck to it, hope it will do well'.[45]

Most household linen could be slotted in alongside existing pieces, even if there were slight differences in size or fabric. The process of integration was assisted by the relative ease with which linen could be cleaned, removing any physical traces of previous use and previous ownership – always a concern with second-hand goods.[46] Laundering was an important consideration in selecting textiles, as Lemire has demonstrated in the context of the growing demand for Indian textiles,[47] and second-hand goods were far less problematic if they could be washed. What of those that were less amenable to such processes of purification?

Beds and bedding: A problematic purchase?

In many ways, beds and bedding were also readily integrated into existing assemblages of goods as the constituent parts of a well-made bed in a prosperous house were fairly stand-ardised across the study period: a mattress, bed, pillows and bolster, plus blankets and a quilt or counterpane.[48] That they might be acquired second-hand is understandable given the considerable cost of the assemblage of bed, bedstead and hangings.[49] However, there was a growing distrust of used beds and bedding, most frequently expressed in terms of cleanliness and anxieties about infestations of insects. Pennell argues that this was already apparent in the second quarter of the eighteenth century, being heightened by the publi-cation of John Southall's *Treatise on Bugs* in 1730.[50] As they could not readily be washed, beds, bedding and bedsteads were particularly suspect as potential carriers of vermin, a concern that prompted the emergence of a range of patent and homemade concoctions to kill the offending insects. Yet Pennell also notes that demand for used bedding and beds remained buoyant well beyond this date, good quality and well-maintained articles retaining their value in the second-hand market. Something of this tension is captured by Elizabeth Dryden, a widowed landowner living at Canons Ashby in Northamptonshire, when she was contemplating a move to London in 1816. She wrote to her sister-in-law that 'I have much fear of the bugs … [and] must be at the expense I fear of a new bed as all old furniture in London is dangerous'.[51] It is telling that second-hand was something that she would con-template, if then reject, and that the attraction was the relative cost of new and used.

The auction catalogues indicate that the supply of, and by implication the market for, used beds and bedding fell notably from the late eighteenth century. A total of 191 sets of beds, pillows and bolsters were offered at the 11 sales before 1805; just 94 were listed in the 10 sales after 1815. For blankets, the figures were 507 and 297 respectively. It appears, then, that others may have shared the concerns expressed by Elizabeth Dryden, eroding the demand for second-hand bedding. That said, the earlier figures are inflated by the huge quantities of beds and bedding being sold from the estate of the Earl of Halifax (some 449 items in all – see Table 1) and there were still significant amounts available at the Welton Place sale in 1830.[52] Clearly, demand did not dry up completely, maybe because beds from known and local sources, and accessed through an auctioneer with a reputation to maintain and perhaps therefore seen as trustworthy, might have been less worrying than those from London.[53]

Turning from quantity to quality, there is evidence of qualitative distinctions within a fairly constant assemblage of goods. Aside from the bedstead (not considered here), the fundamental element was the bed itself. With the exception of a handful of straw-filled beds sold from Pychley Hall in 1816,[54] feathers were the standard in attics and servants' rooms as well as the family and guest bedchambers – a standard of provision seen by Crowley as an indication of growing comfort in English homes.[55] It would be a mistake, however, to view all feather beds as uniform in their socio-cultural or economic value. The best rooms were often differentiated by the provision of goose feather beds or by those described as 'fine' or 'seasoned', semantic and material distinctions which marked the status of the rooms and their occupants. Moreover, comfort, status and cost were often determined by the weight of the bed, a point made explicit in the catalogue for the sale at Hazlebeach, wherein a note against each bed informed buyers that they were to be sold 'per lb'.[56] The significance of this is twofold. First, it helps to explain the difference in estimated price (and economic value) marked by the auctioneer against each bed in the 1761 Cottingham sale catalogue.[57] Those in the garrets were expected to fetch between £1 and £1 2s 6d, whereas those in the main chambers had estimates ranging from £1 14s to £2 10s. Second, selling by weight hints at the likely fate of many beds once they were purchased and taken home; rather than being used in their current form, they would be cut open and the feathers used to stuff existing or new beds. This was common practice within households, Mary Leigh being charged £1 15s by the upholsterers Bradshaw and Smith for 'ripping the porters bed & bolster & taking out all the feather, well waxing the tick, driving & dressing the old feathers & putting 12 lb best season'd feathers in addition, sewing up the tick'.[58] Cleaning the feathers in this way may have helped to alleviate some of the concerns about infestation and cleanliness.

Bedding was less amenable to this kind of repurposing, but was readily incorporated into the purchaser's home, either as individual items or in the sets in which it was invariably sold: three blankets, plus a quilt, coverlet or counterpane. Most blankets were described in simple terms, with little to distinguish one from another and relatively few superlatives. Some were 'large' or described in terms of the number of quarters (12 being most common); rather more than 10% were lauded as 'fine'. More occasionally, the catalogues refer specifically to Witney blankets – a rare example of a 'proto-brand' which communicated material qualities through a place name.[59] They had a reputation for being particularly soft and had an excellent white-ness, and would presumably have been particularly attractive to buyers at these auctions; the distinctive blue or red stripes signifying their dimensions also served as a kind of brand-ing.[60] Like sheets, blankets were utilitarian items: a necessary part of any comfortable night's sleep. To judge from the Cottingham catalogue, their price varied comparatively little in relation to their location in the house and, at just 2–3s, it was very modest. Direct comparisons are difficult, but only five years later Edward Leigh was charged £1 apiece for fine large blankets and 8s for more workaday under-blankets for his refurbished bedchambers at Stoneleigh Abbey. Even with a difference in size and quality, it is clear that buying blankets second-hand made them much cheaper – a cost saving which must have underpinned many purchases as an effective way of capturing value.[61]

With quilts, coverlets and counterpanes, qualitative differences were more important in determining price and perhaps also in rendering them attractive to potential buyers. There were, of course, physical differences between these items: quilts had a filling (increasingly of cotton) between two outer layers, whereas counterpanes and coverlets were often woven in squares and sometimes embroidered.[62] As the uppermost covering on the bed, they were visible in a way that sheets and blankets were not, making their physical appearance far more important. This is reflected in the auction catalogues, which noted the material com-position of around one-third of bedcovers, thus highlighting to potential buyers their cultural value alongside their utility as another layer of insulation on the bed. There were bedcovers made from silk, damask, dimity, camblet, chintz, printed and plain cotton, checks and stripes; some were adorned with needlework. Material differences helped to distinguish these items as markers of taste and status, a function which was underpinned by their price. Vickery notes that cotton counterpanes were found in even cheap furnished lodgings by the 1790s,[63] but different materials and finishes made for very different prices and cultural meanings. At Cottingham, the auctioneer suggested that a plain white quilt might fetch 8–10s – an impressive amount compared with a blanket and even an ordinary feather bed, but easily overshadowed by the £2 and £2 2s put against a silk and a needlework counterpane.[64] Like the crimson silk and crimson damask counterpanes sold off from the Earl of Halifax's estate a decade later, these were not simply useful items; they were desirable objects that would add a layer of luxury to the purchaser's bed. Unsurprisingly, then, these items were valorised through the deployment of adjectives that emphasised their aesthetics qualities and linked them to familiar tropes of taste and status, much as Coquery notes of Parisian upholsterers.[65] For instance, we see a 'neat' needlework counterpane at Stanford Hall (1792), a 'beautiful' Marseilles quilt at Rolleston Hall (1801) and a 'handsome' 12-quarter white cotton counterpane at Geddington Hall (1823). These were words redolent with meaning for eighteenth-century householders. As Vickery argues, they 'embodied the social distinctions of provincial gentility', communicating ideas of good taste rather than ostentatious grandeur, but lifting both the goods and their prospective owners above mere respectability.[66] Consciously or not, then, auctioneers were tapping into broader cultural norms to make these used goods more appealing. These auction catalogues, of course, were more than simple listings of goods to be sold; they promulgated the cultural values that imbued goods with meaning as well as promoting the cultural value of the goods themselves. In praising a needlework counterpane as 'neat', for instance, the auctioneer no doubt sought to make it more desirable to buyers, but also encouraged those buyers to value neatness in such products. These same ideas came out more strongly in the final category of textiles I wish to consider: bed hangings, curtains and carpets.

Curtains and carpets: Home comforts or status symbols?

All household textiles served a variety of functions, both practical and symbolic. One key benefit that they brought was to help make the country house more comfortable – an aspiration that grew in importance through the eighteenth century and into the nineteenth. Whilst we might contest the timing and emphasis which Crowley outlines, there is no doubt that people took increasing trouble to make their homes physically comfortable and sociable places – an important part of the growing material richness of the home.[67] Alongside technological developments like stoves and lamps, furnishing textiles were deployed in a variety of ways that enhanced comfort: upholstered seats were more accommodating; carpets offered some measure of insulation on a cold floor (especially important in bedchambers); and curtains reduced drafts and offered some privacy – an extension to the room of earlier imperatives for the bed with its hangings. At the same time, of course, these textiles also expressed the taste and wealth of their owner. The state bed had long been a key focus for expressing aristocratic wealth and power through the opulence of fine and luxurious fabrics; window curtains and carpets offered further opportunities for such display.[68] The appearance of these items in the sale catalogues thus raises a number of important questions about how they were conceived as practical objects or symbols of taste, and what this tell us about the possible motivations for acquiring such things second-hand.

In total, there were 265 sets of bed hangings, 320 pairs of window curtains and 333 carpets and rugs offered for sale across the 21 auctions (Table 1). The amount of drapery being offered for sale declined sharply in the nineteenth century, roughly halving for both bed hangings and curtains. This mirrors the decline in beds and may, as Riello argues, have been prompted by similar concerns for hygiene, particularly as beds, hangings and window curtains were often conceived and supplied as a set for bedchambers.[69] The catalogues reflect this process, grouping on the page the assemblage of bed, bedding, curtains and furniture that comprised a comfortable bedchamber. However, as the ensemble was usually split into different lots and sold separately, it is by no means certain that the same motivations or reservations were in the minds of buyers when it came to purchasing beds, blankets, hangings and curtains. In the absence of sale accounts, we do not know whether buyers acquired individual lots or the whole set.[70]

As with other kinds of textiles, country house sales offered an impressive variety of drapery, especially in the eighteenth century: bed hangings appear in a total of 20 different types of cloth and window curtains in 14, each with dozens of variants in terms of colour and pattern. Even in a single auction, the choice available could be impressive. At Brixworth Hall, for example, the catalogue for the 1797 sale lists bed hangings in green check, green morine, needlework, Manchester, white calico, green damask, crimson check, crimson morine, white morine, corded dimity, calico, and red and white cotton; there were curtains in green morine, calico, green damask, striped cotton, white morine, corded dimity and chintz – several of which appear both as hanging and festoon.[71] Variety declined over time, in part reflecting the overall decline in the quantity of drapery appearing in the auctions, although this was more manifest in terms of fabric type than colour and pattern. Morine, sometimes referred to as stuff,[72] became increasingly common, displacing other woollen cloths such as cheney, harrateen and serge. More striking, though, was the increasing use of chintz, which became widespread in both bedchambers and living rooms at the expense of damask and woollens (Table 3). Here, the drapery available from auctions undoubtedly followed the prevailing taste both for patterns and for textiles that could be kept clean and free from vermin.[73] They fitted with Vickery's assessment of provincial genteel taste for

Table 3. Changing textile types used in bed hangings and curtains: three sample house sales.

		Cottingham (1761)	Stamford (1792)	Welton Place (1830)
Woollens	Morine/stuff	4	6	6
	Harrateen	1	2	0
	Cheney	1	0	0
	Total	6	8	6
Silk/damask	Silk/tabby	2	1	0
	Damask	4	7	0
	Total	6	8	0
Needlework	Needlework	1	2	3
Linen/Cotton	Stripe/check	1	0	4
	Dimity	3	0	1
	Cotton	0	2	2
	Printed	2	0	2
	Chintz	0	6	12
	Total	6	8	21

Source: Auction catalogues held at Northamptonshire Central Library.

wallpapers that were 'neat and not too showy',[74] allowing such objects to slot into non-elite domestic arrangements in a way that might have been more problematic with an earlier generation of silks and damasks.

Curtains would have added to the comfort as well as the aesthetics of the home, but it is with carpets that this imperative becomes more apparent. Hearth-rugs and bedside carpets, rarely listed in catalogues before 1800, became commonplace thereafter – part of the general rise in number of carpets listed in the auctions catalogues (Table 1). Bedside carpets were often sold in pairs, set either side of the bed, whilst hearth-rugs would have protected larger carpets against sparks from the fire. Both were integral to making rooms more comfortable, but it is the growing number of carpets in passageways and stairs that did most to add to the overall comfort of domestic life by taking some of the chill from what were often described as cold and draughty spaces.[75] As with curtains, their availability at auctions signals both their presence within the homes of the gentry and their availability to others. Read in this way, a carpet for the stairs or the bedside might be seen as a utilitarian item, purchased at auction because it offered good value for money; but carpets were also hugely important in shaping the aesthetics of the room. The catalogues make no mention of colours or patterns, but the style and character was communicated through place names: Turkey, Wilton, Scotch, Kidderminster and Brussels. It is telling, then, that Scotch and Wilton carpets dominated before 1815, but disappeared thereafter, whereas the opposite was true of Kidderminster and Brussels carpets. With Scotch and Kidderminster, this was a shift in name rather than type, both being thinner ingrain carpets which were less expensive; the move from Wilton to Brussels was more significant because the former had a thicker velvet pile whilst the latter had a smooth looped pile.[76] Velvet cut-pile carpets were considered more luxurious, but those with a close pile had a better defined pattern, more in keeping with fashionable taste in the later eighteenth and early nineteenth century.

The appeal to genteel taste in both carpets and curtains is apparent in the language used to describe these goods. They were elegant, neat, genteel, beautiful and above all handsome – an adjective deployed in nearly one-third of the catalogues to describe these goods. As with quilts and counterpanes, then, auctioneers were active in blending the goods they were selling into the cultural norms of gentility. As one auctioneer put it in an advertisement placed in the local press, these were not the 'Scraps or Scrapings of Time' but pieces in which 'Beauty and Art are so happily blended … that, it is hoped, Criticism will lose her Sting on the Day of Viewing and give an assenting Nod on the Day of Sale'.[77] Linked to this, we also see attempts to portray particular pieces of drapery as genuine and modern: chintz curtains sold from the drawing room at Thorp Malsor (1815) were described as being of a 'real Indian pattern', whilst a set at Welton Place (1830) were in 'beautiful modern needlework'.[78] Conversely, there is nothing to suggest that the auctioneers sought to portray these textiles as useful or valuable – other adjectives deployed in newspaper advertisements from the time. Both utility and economic value are apparently taken as read, something which is underscored by the price difference between new and used, which appears to have been greater here than was the case with bedding. Whereas Edward Leigh was charged £5 10s 11d for a pair of green morine window curtains and £17 1s 9d for a four-post wainscot bedstead with green morine furniture, the auctioneer organising the Cottingham sale estimated that four large morine curtains would fetch £2 2s and a four-post bedstead with green damask furniture £2 15s.[79] Of course, we do not know about the relative quality of the textiles or the condition of the drapery at Cottingham, but, with prices well under half and perhaps as little one-sixth, second-hand again emerges as offering the careful householder real bargains.

We should be wary, though, of assuming that buyers were simply weighing considerations of cost against those of taste and wear-and-tear. The lengthy and persuasive descriptions of window curtains which some auctioneers included in their catalogues suggests that they were trying to promote these as desirable objects which would add lustre to the purchaser's home. James Denew, who organised the 1823 sale at Geddington House, waxed lyrical, describing 'a suite of elegant lofty French curtains for two windows, lined with yellow, full drapery valens, trimmed with silk fringes and lace' and 'a very elegant suite of Parlour Curtains for 2 lofty French windows, made of fine dove coloured morine, bordered with brown silk velvet, full drapery valens, trimmed with a rich deep fringe, displayed on black and gold cornices'.[80] Even if we strip away the rhetoric, these were undoubtedly impressive objects, and of course the rhetoric is important: Denew clearly sought to portray these and many other things in the sale as positional goods with the power to bolster or enhance social status. As Coquery argues for Parisian upholsterers, the material qualities of the objects are linked adjectivally to aesthetics and broader cultural values.[81]

Two things are important here for our understanding of second-hand consumption. The first is that these were not goods that would fit into just any house. Although the state bed was acquired for the Theatre Royal in Bath, most items at Fonthill were bought according to the status of the buyer and their desire either to augment their houses with choice items or to pick up handsome but useful furniture. Mr Bracher, who owned land in the neighbouring parish, bought an oval mahogany dining table, whereas the Earl of Ilchester and the Duke of Somerset both acquired four-post carved mahogany bedsteads with japanned cornices and chintz furniture at a cost of £27 6s and £32 11s respectively.[82] Quite apart from their grandiose appearance, the curtains at Geddington House were simply too large to make them practical for smaller rooms – curtains with a 12 or 14 feet drop, carpets measuring over 40 square yards and beds standing 12 feet tall required big rooms. Of course, all might be cut into small pieces or modified to fit other spaces, but even so they needed to fit into the existing décor if they were to be integrated properly into the new domestic setting.[83] This links to the second point, that these items were powerful social statements – even second-hand they could communicate wealth and status. This is apparent from the list of titled and genteel buyers at the Fonthill sale, but also from the intrinsic character of the drapery and carpets, as well as the books, pier glasses and furniture available in the Northamptonshire auctions. None of these things would have been bought second-hand from financial necessity or for their economic value alone – they were luxuries and were written into the catalogues as such. In the absence of information about purchasers, it is impossible to be certain, but it seems most likely that what motivated them was a desire to acquire items that were commensurate with or enhanced their homes. That the identity of the previous owner made them more attractive in this sense is possible, but less certain: difference was marked by status symbols rather than allusions to another's world.

Conclusion

Country house sales offered a wide range of goods through the late eighteenth and early nineteenth century. Whilst they rarely formed comprehensive clearances of the entire moveable estate, these auctions offered much more than the 'scraps and scrapings of time' – things that might be bought from financial necessity. All the sales included in this analysis released into circulation things that were worth owning and which could augment the existing material culture of respectable and genteel homes – things like damask tablecloths, Brussels carpets and chintz counterpanes. In part, this reflected the slower cycle of change in household goods in comparison with clothing: they could retain both cultural currency and economic value much longer. Old furniture was sometimes bought because it offered authenticity to the bourgeois home or formed part of collectible types[84]; but domestic textiles did not readily align with such priorities, in part because of their semi-durable nature – they wore out rather than obtaining an attractive patina. This goes some way to explaining the declining quantity of textiles sold at the Northamptonshire sales, as does the growing concern about cleanliness and infestation. That said, we should not overstate this decline: a variety of domestic textiles remained significant in all the Northamptonshire sales in the 1810s–1830s and the language used to describe these goods consistently emphasised their alignment with the norms of gentility. In identifying bed hangings, counterpanes and carpets as neat, handsome or elegant, the auctioneers highlighted their aesthetic qualities in a way that chimed with the sensibilities of those who were or aspired to be genteel. More detailed descriptions of the workmanship involved (for example, curtains being lined and fringed), or assertions that sheets or tablecloths were fine, served to underline the material qualities and durability of these objects. This links to Pennell's argument that clean and well-maintained textiles retained a value for middling sort householders exercising thrift and looking to secure a bargain.[85] Both the language and the goods themselves blended a concern with economic and cultural value; these were things worth buying because of their relative price, their symbolism and, indeed, their utility – a combination perhaps seen most clearly in household linen. Purchased second-hand, I would argue that domestic textiles were less about authenticity and distinction (as Charpy argues for old furniture and Gregson and Crewe assert for present-day buyers of retro clothing), and more about belonging. They helped to mark membership of a broadly defined set of genteel and respectable households, in terms of both the quantity and variety of domestic textiles that it should contain and their material and aesthetic qualities.

Country house auctions played a particular and important role in this process. As commercial institutions they were a key mechanism through which a wide range of household goods – from the magnificent to the mundane – were brought back into circulation, feeding consumer demand amongst a middling sort that, in contrast with the trade in used clothing, remained firmly engaged with the second-hand market.[86] Auction catalogues were a key source of consumer knowledge. They smoothed information asymmetries by advertising the range of goods available and fostered trust through the identity and standing of the previous owner, the reputation of the auctioneer and the location of the sale.[87] This allowed auction lots to escape from some of the anxieties that surrounded used goods, especially in terms of their authenticity. In asserting the owner's name and holding the sale in the house, the risk of buying shoddy newly made goods dressed as old was minimised. In their use of language, auction catalogues also spread knowledge about the value systems which framed the demand for these goods. The Times might have struck a moralising tone in its reflections on the 1801 Fonthill sale, arguing that luxury and fashion were 'false taste and superfluous gaiety' spread through society through events such as public auctions.[88] However, the Northamptonshire auctions brought taste and material objects firmly into the realm of respectable gentility: second-hand domestic textiles were solid and virtuous, just like the people who had and would own them.

Glossary

(based on Edward, *Encyclopedia of Furnishing Textiles*)

(1) Calico – rather coarse and lightweight cotton, sometimes printed; often used as a generic term for all Indian cottons, although later manufactured in Europe

(2) Camblet – plain-weave woollen, traditionally with a watered pattern

(3) Cheney – worsted, often with bold colours and embossed, watered or striped pattern; similar to harrateen and morine

(4) Chintz – painted or stained cotton, originally from India but increasingly manufactured in Europe

(5) Damask – woollen or woollen–silk mix, woven with an elaborate figured design, sometimes in contrasting colours

(6) Diaper – linen, woven on the damask principle

(7) Dimity – plain-weave cotton and linen mix with a distinctive rib effect

(8) Doily – small ornamental linen mat used at dessert

(9) Harrateen – worsted, finished by watering and stamping, often in imitation of damask; similar to harrateen and morine

(10) Huckabuck – stout linen with rough or bumpy surface

(11) Morine – strong woollen with stamped or watered pattern in imitation of camblet

(12) Russian – heavyweight, coarse linen

(13) Serge – worsted and woollen mix with distinctive diagonal rib

(14) Stuff – generic term of worsted cloth with a nap or pile (including camblets, harrateens and morines)

(15) Tabby – silk with watered or plain finish

Notes

1. Northamptonshire Central Library (NCL), M0005644NL/2 Cottingham, 1761, 1.
2. See Weatherill, *Consumer Behaviour*; Ago, *Gusto for Things*; Crowley, *Invention of Comfort*; DeJean, *Age of Comfort*.
3. Berg, *Luxury and Pleasure*, 46–110.
4. Recent collections on second-hand include Fontaine, *Alternative Exchanges*; Stobart and Van Damme, *Modernity and the Second-Hand Trade*; Fennetaux, Junqua, and Vasset, *Afterlife of Used Things*. In contrast, second-hand is absent from Berg, *Luxury and Pleasure*, and marginal in de Vries, *Industrious Revolution*, and Trentmann, *Empire of Things*.
5. for example, Coquery, "Fashion, Business, Diffusion."
6. Lemire, "Secondhand Clothing Trade."
7. On thrift, see Vickery, *Gentleman's Daughter*, esp. 174–7; Berg, "New Commodities"; Rasmussen, "'Recycling a Fashionable Wardrobe." On goods as currency, see Fontaine, "Exchange of Secondhand Goods"; Coquery, "Fashion, Business, Diffusion"; Ago, *Gusto for Things*, 18–26.
8. Lemire, "Secondhand Clothing Trade," 153.
9. On furniture, see Coquery, "Fashion, Business, Diffusion"; Charpy, "Auction House."
10. Van Damme, "Second-hand Dealing"; Charpy, "Auction House"; Westgarth, *Emergence of the Antique*.
11. Ago, *Gusto for Things*, 15–39; Weatherill, *Consumer Behaviour*, 8–13.

12. Riello, "Fabricating the Domestic," 49–51.
13. Ago, *Gusto for Things*, 26–30, 58–9; Berg, "Women's Property."
14. Lemire, "Second-hand Beaux"; Lemire, "Secondhand Clothing Trade"; Coquery, "Fashion, Business, Diffusion"; Charpy, "Auction House."
15. Gregson and Crewe, *Second Hand Cultures*, 11–12.
16. Stewart, *On Longing*, 133; Wall, "English Auction," 14–15.
17. Lemire, "Secondhand Clothing Trade," 148; Coquery, "Language of Success," 73–7; Wall, "English Auction."
18. See Jeggle, "Labelling with Numbers," 36.
19. Ohashi, "Auction Duty Act"; MacArthur and Stobart, "Going for a Song?"; Gemmett, "Tinsel of Fashion."
20. See de Munck and Lyna, "Locating and Dislocating Value," 4.
21. Nenadic, "Middle-rank Consumers"; Pennell, "All but the Kitchen Sink."
22. Gemmett, "Tinsel of Fashion," 381–8; MacArthur and Stobart, "Going for a Song?"
23. MacArthur and Stobart, "Going for a Song?," 180–82.
24. Coquery, "Language of Success," 86.
25. Whittle and Griffiths, *Gender and Consumption*, 26–48; Vickery, *Gentleman's Daughter*, 127–60; Harvey, *Little Republic*, esp. 64–98.
26. Wall, "English Auction," 14–15; Charpy, "Auction House," 219.
27. M0005644NL/2 Cottingham, 1761, 1.
28. Pennell, "Making the Bed." Domestic textiles are not mentioned amongst the goods traded second-hand by Parisian upholsterers – see Coquery, "Fashion, Business, Diffusion," 73–4.
29. Charpy, "Auction House"; Wall, "English Auction."
30. Quoted in Gemmett, "Tinsel of Fashion," 383.
31. NCL, M0005646NL/11, Stanford Hall, 1792, 5; M0005644NL/13, Welton Place, 1830, 37.
32. Gemmett, "Tinsel of Fashion," 383–4.
33. On the importance of clean linen, see Vigarello, *Concepts of Cleanliness*; Lemire, "Education in Comfort," 18–20.
34. NCL, M0005644NL/9, Stamford Baron, 1823, 57–62.
35. Nenadic, "Middle-rank Consumers"; Collins, "Matters Material and Luxurious," 114.
36. Nenadic, "Middle-rank Consumers," 131.
37. NCL, M0005646NL/11, Stanford Hall, 1792, 6–7.
38. NCL, M0005647NL/6, Earl of Halifax, 1772, 35.
39. Quoted in Vickery, "Women and the World of Goods," 285.
40. Vickery, *Gentleman's Daughter*, 148. See also Smith, *Consumption and the Making of Respectability*, 189–222.
41. Vickery, *Gentleman's Daughter*, 150–51. See also Nenadic, "Middle-rank Consumers."
42. NCL, MM0005644NL/5, Wollaston Hall, 1805.
43. Smith, *Consumption and the Making of Respectability*, 130–38; Vickery, *Gentleman's Daughter*, 149.
44. NCL, M0005644NL/5, Wollaston Hall, 24. Emphasis in the original.
45. Quoted in Vickery, "Women and the World of Goods." 285.
46. See Jones, "Souvenirs of People."
47. Lemire, "Education in Comfort."
48. Pennell, "Making the Bed," 31–3.
49. Riello, "Fabricating the Domestic," 49–50.
50. Pennell, "Making the Bed," 39–40. See also Vigarello, *Concepts of Cleanliness*, 41–5.
51. Northamptonshire Record Office, D(CA)/361, Letter, August 18, 1816.
52. NCL, M0005647NL/6, Earl of Halifax, 1772, 33–7; M0005644NL/13, Welton Place, 1830, 32–4.
53. See de Munck and Lyna, "Locating and Dislocating Value," 4.
54. NCL, M000564NL/15, Pychley Hall, 1816, *passim*.
55. Crowley, *Invention of Comfort*, 7.
56. NCL, M0005647NL/7, Hazlebeach, 1802, 5.

57. NCL, M0005644NL/2, Cottingham, 1761, *passim*. These prices are printed in the catalogue. Pennell notes that, at a 1753 house sale in London, the prices realised for beds and bedding were 10–50% higher than these estimated prices – see Pennell, "Making the Bed," 39. Whilst not uncommon practice, this is the only catalogue in the sample which marks prices in this way.
58. Shakespeare Central Library and Archives, DR18/5/6023a.
59. See Richardson, "Brand Names."
60. Kerridge, *Textile Manufactures*, 35.
61. SCLA, DR18/3/47/52/15 bill from Thomas Burnett, 1765. Similar cost savings were apparent with beds: Leigh paid a minimum of £6 14s for a feather bed, bolster and two pillows – four times the cost of the most expensive bed in the Cottingham sale.
62. Edwards, *Encyclopedia of Furnishing Textiles*, 60–61, 173–4.
63. Vickery, *Behind Closed Doors*, 214.
64. NCL, M0005644NL/2, Cottingham, 1761, 6.
65. Coquery, "Language of Success," 86; Coquery, "Fashion, Business, Diffusion," 73.
66. Vickery, *Gentleman's Daughter*, 161. See also Vickery, *Behind Closed Doors*, 180–82.
67. Crowley, *Invention of Comfort*, esp. 142–9. See also DeJean, *Age of Comfort*, 102–30, 156–8; Vickery, *Behind Closed Doors*, 207–30.
68. DeJean, *Age of Comfort*, 165–77; Riello, "Fabricating the Domestic."
69. Riello, "Fabricating the Domestic," 63; Stobart and Rothery, *Consumption and the Country House*, 218–23.
70. For examples of purchasing behaviour, see Gemmett, "Tinsel of Fashion"; Bristol, "A Tale of Two Sales," 9–24.
71. NCL, M0005646NL/15, Brixworth Hall, 1797, *passim*.
72. Edwards, *Encyclopedia of Furnishing Textiles*, 203.
73. Lemire, "Education in Comfort," 18–20; Edwards, *Encyclopedia of Furnishing Textiles*; Riello, "Fabricating the Domestic," 63.
74. Vickery, *Behind Closed Doors*, 166–83.
75. Fowler and Cornforth, *English Decoration*, 225–6.
76. Edwards, *Encyclopedia of Furnishing Textiles*, 34–5, 117–18, 188, 240.
77. *Northampton Mercury*, January 3, 1780.
78. NCL, M000564NL/14, Thorp Malsor, 1815, 19; M0005644NL/13, Welton Place, 1830, 37.
79. SCLA, DR18/3/47/52/15.
80. NCL, M0005644NL/8, Geddington 1823, 14.
81. Coquery, "Language of Success," 86. See also Jeggle, "Labelling with Numbers," 33.
82. Gemmett, "Tinsel of Fashion," 383–4.
83. See McCracken, *Culture and Consumption*, 118–29.
84. Charpey, "Auction House"; Westgarth, *Emergence of the Antique*.
85. Pennell, "Making the Bed."
86. See Lemire, "Secondhand Clothing Trade," 153–4.
87. De Munck and Lyna, "Locating and Dislocating Value," 4; MacArthur and Stobart, "Going for a Song?," 177–82.
88. Gemmett, "Tinsel of Fashion," 388.

Acknowledgment

This research was undertaken as part of the AHRC project AH/H008365/1.

Disclosure statement

No potential conflict of interest was reported by the author.

ORCID

Jon Stobart ⓘ http://orcid.org/0000-0002-9771-4741

Bibliography

Ago, Renata. *Gusto for Things. A History of Objects in Seventeenth-Century Rome.* Chicago, IL: University of Chicago Press, 2013.

Berg, Maxine. "Women's Property and the Industrial Revolution." *Journal of Interdisciplinary History* 24 (1993): 233–250.

Berg, Maxine. *Luxury and Pleasure in Eighteenth-Century England.* Oxford: Oxford University Press, 2005.

Berg, Maxine. "New Commodities, Luxuries and their Consumers in Eighteenth-Century England." In *Consumers and Luxury: Consumer Culture in Europe, 1650–1850,* edited by Maxine Berg and Helen Clifford, 63–85. Manchester, NH: Manchester University Press, 1999.

Bristol, Kerry. "A Tale of Two Sales: Sir Rowland Winn and no. 11 St James's Square, London, 1766–1787." *History of Retailing and Consumption* 2, no. 1 (2016): 9–24.

Charpy, Manuel. "The Auction House and its Surroundings: The Trade of Antiques and Second-Hand Items in Paris During the Nineteenth Century." In *Fashioning Old and New: Changing Consumer patterns in Western Europe (1650–1900),* edited by Bruno Blonde, Natacha Coquery, Jon Stobart and Ilja Van Damme, 217–233. Turnhout: Brepols, 2008.

Collins, Brenda. "Matters Material and Luxurious – Eighteenth and Early Nineteenth-Century Irish Linen Consumption." In *Luxury and Austerity: Papers Read before the 23rd Irish Conference of Historians,* edited by Jacqueline Hill and Colm Lennon, 106–120. Dublin: University College Dublin Press, 1999.

Coquery, Natacha. "The Language of Success: Marketing and Distributing Semi-Luxury Goods in Eighteenth-Century Paris." *Journal of Design History* 17 (2004): 71–89.

Coquery, Natacha. "Fashion, Business, Diffusion: An Upholsterer's Shop in Eighteenth-Century Paris." In *Furnishing the Eighteenth Century: What Furniture Can Tell Us about the European and American Past,* edited by Dena Goodman and Kathryn Norberg, 63–77. London: Routledge, 2007.

Crowley, John. *The Invention of Comfort: Sensibilities and Design in Early Modern Britain and Early America.* Baltimore, MD: John Hopkins University Press, 2000.

De Munck, Bert and Lyna, Dries, "Locating and Dislocating Value: A Pragmatic Approach to Early Modern and Nineteenth-century Economic Practices." In *Concepts of Value in European Material Culture, 1500–1900,* edited by Bert de Munck Lyna and Dries, 1–30. Aldershot, UK: Ashgate, 2015.

De Vries, Jan. *The Industrious Revolution. Consumer Behaviour and the Household Economy, 1650 to the Present,* Cambridge: Cambridge University Press, 2008

DeJean, Joan. *The Age of Comfort. When Paris Discovered Casual and the Modern Home Began.* New York, NY: Bloomsbury, 2009.

Edwards, Clive. *Encyclopedia of Furnishing Textiles, Floor Coverings and Home Furnishing Practices, 1200–1950.* Aldershot: Lund Humphries, 2007.

Fennetaux, Ariane, Amelie Junqua, and Sophie Vasset, eds. *The Afterlife of Used Things.* Recycling in the Long Eighteenth Century, London: Routledge, 2015.

Fontaine, Laurence, ed. *Alternative Exchanges: Second-Hand Circulations from the Sixteenth Century to the Present.* New York, NY: Berghahn, 2008

Fowler, John, and Cornforth, John, *English Decoration in the Eighteenth Century.* London: Barrie and Jenkins, 1974.

Fontaine, Laurence. "The Exchange of Second-Hand Goods: Between Survival Strategies and Business in Eighteenth-Century Paris." In *Alternative Exchanges: Second-Hand Circulations from the Sixteenth Century to the Present*, edited by Laurence Fontaine, 97–114. New York, NY: Berghahn, 2008.

Gemmett, R. J. "'The Tinsel of Fashion and the Gewgaws of Luxury': The Fonthill Sale of 1801." *The Burlington Magazine*, CL (2008), 381–388

Gregson, Nicky, and Louise Crewe. *Second Hand Cultures*. London: Berg, 2003.

Harvey, Karen. *The Little Republic: Masculinity and Domestic Authority in Eighteenth-Century Britain*. Oxford: Oxford University Press, 2012.

Jeggle, Christof. "Labelling with Numbers? Weavers, Merchants and the Valuation of Linen in Seventeenth-Century Munster." In *Concepts of Value in European Material Culture, 1500–1900*, edited by Bert de Munck Lyna and Dries, 33–56. Aldershot, UK: Ashgate, 2015.

Jones, Robin. "Souvenirs of People Who Have Come and Gone: Second-Hand Furnishings and the Anglo-India Domestic Interior, 1840–1920." In *Modernity and the Second-Hand Trade*, edited by Jon Stobart and Ilja Van Damme, 111–135. Basingstoke: Palgrave, 2010.

Kerridge, Eric. *Textile Manufactures in Early Modern England*. Manchester, NH: Manchester University Press, 1988.

Lemire, Beverly. "'Second-Hand Beaux and Red-Armed Belles': Conflict and the Creation of Fashion in England, c.1660–1800." *Continuity and Change* 15 (2000): 391–417.

Lemire, Beverly. "The Secondhand Clothing Trade in Europe and Beyond: Stages of Development and Enterprise in a Changing Material World, C.1600-1850." *Textile: The Journal of Cloth and Culture* 10 (2012): 144–163.

Lemire, Beverly. "An Education in Comfort: India Textiles and the Remaking of English Homes Over the Long Eighteenth Century." In *Selling Textiles in the Long Eighteenth Century*, edited by Jon Stobart and Bruno Blonde, 13–29. Basingstoke: Palgrave, 2015.

MacArthur, Rosie and Stobart, Jon. "Going for a Song? Country House Sales in Georgian England." In *Modernity and the Second-Hand Trade. European Consumption Cultures and Practices, 1700–1900*, edited by Jon Stobart and Ilja Van Damme, 175–195. Basingstoke: Palgrave, 2010.

McCracken, Grant. *Culture and Consumption*. Bloomington and Indianapolis: Indiana University Press, 1988.

Nenadic, Stana. "Middle-Rank Consumers and Domestic Culture in Edinburgh and Glasgow 1720–1840." *Past and Present* 145 (1994): 122–156.

Ohashi, Satomi. "The Auction Duty Act of 1777: The Beginnings of Institutionalisation of Auctions in Britain." In *Auctions, Agents and Dealers: the Mechanisms of the Art Market, 1660–1830*, edited by Jeremy Warren and Adriana Turpin, 21–31. Oxford: Wallace Collection, 2007.

Pennell, Sara. "All but the Kitchen Sink: Household Sales and the Circulation of Second-Hand Goods in Early Modern England." In *Modernity and the Second-Hand Trade*, edited by Jon Stobart and Ilja Van Damme, 37–56. Basingstoke: Palgrave, 2010.

Pennell, Sara. "Making the bed in later Stuart and Georgian England." In *Selling Textiles in the Long Eighteenth Century: Comparative Perspectives from Western Europe*, edited by Jon Stobart and Bruno Blonde, 35–41. Basingstoke: Palgrave, 2014.

Rasmussen, Pernilla. "Recycling a Fashionable Wardrobe in the Long Eighteenth Century in Sweden." *History of Retailing and Consumption* 2, no. 3 (2016): 193–222.

Richardson, Gary. "Brand Names before the Industrial Revolution." *NBER Working Papers*, 13930 (2008).

Riello, Giorgio. "Fabricating the Domestic: The Material Culture of Textiles and the Social Life of the Home in Early Modern Europe." In *The Force of Fashion in Politics and Society: Global Perspective from Early Modern to Contemporary Times*, edited by Beverly Lemire, 41–65. Aldershot: Ashgate, 2010.

Smith, Woodruff. *Consumption and the Making of Respectability, 1600–1800*. London: Routledge, 2002.

Stewart, Susan, and On Longing. *Narratives of the Miniature, the Gigantic, the Souvenir, the Collection*. Baltimore, MD: John Hopkins University Press, 1984.

Stobart, Jon, and Mark Rothery. *Consumption and the Country House*. Oxford: Oxford University Press, 2016.

Stobart, Jon and Van Damme, Ilja, eds. *Modernity and the Second-Hand Trade*. Basingstoke: Palgrave. 2010.

Trentmann, Frank. *Empire of Things. How We Became a World of Consumers, from the Fifteenth Century to the Twenty-First*, London: Allen Lane, 2016

Van Damme, Ilja. "Second-Hand Dealing in Bruges and the Rise of an "Antiquarian Culture", C.1750–1870." In *Modernity and the Second-Hand Trade. European Consumption Cultures and Practices, 1700–1900*, edited by Jon Stobart and Ilja Van Damme, 73–92. Basingstoke: Palgrave. 2010.

Vickery, Amanda. *The Gentleman's Daughter: Women's Lives in Georgian England*. New Haven, CT: Yale University Press, 1998.

Vickery, Amanda. *Behind Closed Doors: At Home in Georgian England*. New Haven, CT: Yale University Press, 2006.

Vickery, Amanda. "Women and the World of Goods: A Lancashire Consumer and Her Possessions, 1751–81." In *Consumption and the World of Goods*, edited by John Brewer and Roy Porter, 274–301. London: Routledge, 1993.

Vigarello, Georges. *Concepts of Cleanliness: Changing Attitudes in France since the Middle Ages*. Cambridge: Cambridge University Press, 1988.

Wall, Cynthia. "The English Auction: Narratives of Dismantlings." *Eighteenth-Century Studies* 31 (1997): 1–25.

Weatherill, Lorna. *Consumer Behaviour and Material Culture in Britain, 1660–1760*. London: Routledge, 1988.

Westgarth, Mark. *The Emergence of the Antique and Curiosity Dealer, 1815–1850*. Aldershot: Ashgate, 2011.

Whittle, Jane, and Elizabeth Griffiths. *Gender and Consumption in the Early Seventeenth-Century Household*. Oxford: Oxford University Press, 2013.

'Fence-ing lessons': child junkers and the commodification of scrap in the long nineteenth century

Wendy A. Woloson

ABSTRACT
This article considers the circulation of junk in nineteenth-century American markets, concentrating on its various stages of commodification – and the people responsible for that commodification – as scrap was transformed from worthless garbage found on the streets into lucrative materials suitable for industrial use. The study adds to historians' understanding of the emergence of capitalism, whose formation happened as much from the bottom up as the top down. The often-overlooked populations who engaged in petty and often illegal entrepreneurship, including the children discussed here, had a very real impact on the emerging economy. Looking at scrap more clearly elucidates the processes of commodification and the logic of capitalism at work – the transformation of miscellaneous, valueless goods into aggregated abstractions with significant economic worth.

On a May morning in 1857 New York City police rousted a number of little boys from their beds and arrested them on charges of robbing empty houses 'of all the brass, lead and iron they could find in them'. Having been at it for some time, the boys knew what they were doing: like modern day drug dealers, they stashed their choice goods in heaps of rubbish, bringing out items one at a time for buyers. And they used lookouts who signalled crews to scatter when the police approached.[1] Like the 30 boys arrested just a few months earlier for committing similar robberies – all between the ages of 14 and 19 – they were 'ragged and filthy, and sometimes barefooted.'[2]

Far from being anomalies, gangs of marauding young thieves had in fact become commonplace in nineteenth-century urban America, many of them nourished by their cities' daily diet of poverty, abuse, and neglect. Although working and living on the very margins, the boys were key participants in an emerging market for scavenged raw materials. To secure these things, they were highly organised, abided by a code of ethics, understood the value of their stock, and knew how best to resell it given variable market conditions. Well known to authorities, thieving youth comprised a thriving culture of often illicit activity that was the initial – and crucial – link in the economy of junk that would take scrap from city streets through channels of dealers and brokers and at last to American manufacturers. And then back again.

This article considers the circulation of junk in nineteenth-century American markets, concentrating on its various stages of commodification – and the people responsible for that commodification – as scrap was transformed from worthless garbage found on the streets into lucrative materials suitable for industrial use. Taking a closer look at the movement of junk adds to what historians are understanding about the development of capitalism, whose formation happened as much from the bottom up as the top down. The often-overlooked populations who engaged in petty and often illegal entrepreneurship, had a very real impact on the emerging economy. In fact, for economic, social, and cultural reasons children – and poor boys in particular – were uniquely suited to do this kind of work. Beyond those who have studied the evolution of the scrap trades and recycling, however, few scholars have seriously considered the crucial role that child junkers played in the emergence of American industry from the mid-nineteenth to the early-twentieth centuries and the mutual dependence of the two.[3]

This article more directly connects the activities of child junkers to the rise of American industry, arguing that they played an essential role in the emergence of industrial capitalism. Although their activities were stigmatised at the time and mostly lost to history today, these children were nevertheless important participants in far-flung commercial networks and themselves agents of capitalism, who were by turns exploited and opportunistic. Their contributions in this regard – although seemingly marginal, often illicit, and impossible to quantify – were as essential to the growth of industry as were its labour and machinery.

What is more, the very process of commodification effectively obscured this form of child labour within the market, rendering it invisible to all but a few keen observers, such as social welfare advocates and reform-minded journalists. Through circulation and recirculation, contextualisation and recontextualisation, discarded items were transformed from individual miscellanies into larger, aggregated abstractions which made them valuable and viable commodities within the logic of capitalism. This process, however, erased the involvement of the young agents who introduced these things back into the supply chain. By the end of the nineteenth century, the commodification of scrap was amplified in the increasing organisation and consolidation of junk-dealing itself. What was once a fringe economic sector reliant on supplies of largely ill-gotten goods and channeled by the most disenfranchised had by the early-twentieth century grown into a viable and lucrative industry in its own right. By then, its reliance on child labour, which had become intractable, could no longer be ignored.

Eighteenth-century Americans were by necessity scroungers and recyclers. Families often supplemented their income by trading and selling ash, fat, and other by-products of daily life. [4] In an era predating sophisticated, large-scale industrial processes and extensive trade networks, local soap makers, iron workers, paper makers, and even jewellers relied on these bits of raw material for their livelihoods and constantly sought them out. Requests for scrap clotted the advertising columns of newspapers. In 1776 Philadelphia, for example, pewterer William Will and coppersmith Benjamin Town both promised 'ready money' for 'any quantity' of old copper and brass. In 1797, residents of Albany could purchase 'a large quantity of the first rate sleigh shoes, made of West-Point Ore and Scrap Iron.' Desperate to make paper to print on, stationer William Trickett offered threepence a pound for clean linen rags and 'the best price' for old sails. James Gallagher offered money for money: hard cash for 'ragged Newcastle and Maryland money' (i.e. paper currency) that he would turn into paper.[5]

Smaller and more remote manufactories also faced chronic shortages of raw materials, and enterprises such as nail manufacturer Chamberlin & Alden, situated inland, in Pittsfield, Massachusetts, included in advertisements for their finished products pleas to buy scrap metal as well.[6] In contrast, cities on the coast were lousy with scrap. In 1816, New London, Connecticut blacksmith John Manierre, for example, was selling 1.5 tons of scrap iron and 2 tons of 'old' iron. In 1821 Boston merchant Edward Peters had on hand some 50 tons of pig and scrap iron.[7]

Early in the nineteenth century America's ships supplied and used up surprising amounts of junk, be it shards of iron, brass, and copper, inches of cordage, or bits of linen and cotton. 'Junk', in fact, originally referred to old cable and rope that was cut up and used for making fenders on ships, and 'junk shop' was synonymous with marine store.[8] The 'Sundry Articles' Joseph Ripley was selling from a decommissioned ship on Lewis wharf in Boston were representative:

> About 50,000 [feet] of pine and spruce Plank and refuse Boards – about 3,000 feet of Joist – 1 small Cable, good – 1 middling size d[itt]o. good – 1 very large do. for junk – a quantity of different qualities of Junk, some of it excellent for ship use – copper Pots and Boilers – Blocks, of various kinds among them a set of excellent purchase blocks – large Anchor, about 4,000 wt … a quantity of old Iron … and a great quantity of articles worthy the attention of those who keep junk shops.[9]

Ships were both terrific consumers of and sources for scrap, laden as they were with valuable materials. Even before being decommissioned their various parts and pieces made their way into secondhand markets. Occasionally sailors were arrested for selling stolen junk from their own ships, but more often thieves conducted organized raids that included off-loading cargo onto small boats at night.[10]

Scrap material was also generated by industry. By the second decade of the nineteenth century, the Springfield Armory, for instance, was employing some 250 workers making about 45 muskets a day. Manufacturing processes generated so much waste that 'large quantities' of scrap were being auctioned in 1816, including 'Scrap Iron for Smiths', 'Scrap Iron for Forgemen', 'Refuse Gun Barrels', 'Refuse Gun Stocks', and 'Refuse Grindstones'.[11] It was easy to envision how such ready supplies of relatively cheap materials would be a boon to local tradesmen like blacksmiths, as this ad suggests.

Cities, too, produced their own scrap materials. As urban areas filled with more people making, using, and throwing away more stuff, waste became ubiquitous – a persistent nuisance to local residents. At the same time, scrap materials were becoming increasingly necessary to help supplement the raw materials required for the country's nascent domestic manufactures. The papermaking sector, for one, was constantly short of the rags it needed; advertisements to purchase clean rags for cash appeared throughout the century in local newspapers, city directories, and even published books.[12] In the early decades of the nineteenth century New England paper mills looked to nearby markets for their cotton and linen rags – 'the paper maker's most important raw material and his single greatest expense.'[13] As local populations increased, so, too, did their consumption of clothing. Even so, papermakers faced constant rag shortages, thus their numerous printed appeals to the public.

By the 1830s, paper mills had to explore ever more distant markets to supply the rags they needed, first turning to coastal cities like New York, and soon to Europe, which ended up supplying some 75% of the rags for paper mills at that time; in 1850, 90 million pounds of rags were imported, a figure that increased to 123 million pounds by 1875.[14] The Panic of

1857 forced rag prices skyward, coinciding with a global rag shortage as well. From the 1830s to the 1850s, the cost for many kinds of rags doubled, an expense which was difficult for papermakers to pass on to their customers, especially those purchasing cheap newspaper and wrapping paper.[15]

One way for papermakers to economise on rags was by streamlining the sorting, grading, and cleaning processes. Papermakers benefitted from being able to purchase the kinds of rags best suited to making their specific types of paper, and all papermakers preferred to work with the cleanest, most uniform kinds of rags possible, and of the grades best suited to the kinds of paper they made. Even so, rags still required a great deal of processing up front. Hence, the growing importance of dealers to help mill owners keep their costs as low as possible:

> Rag dealers lowered fine paper makers' raw material costs primarily by guaranteeing them a market for refuse rags, threads, lint, and trimmer shavings. ... Alternatively, rag dealers offered fine paper makers the option of eliminating sorting costs entirely by purchasing new white rags, scraps that dealers bought from shirt makers.[16]

So while these raw materials were quite humble and worthless *in situ*, they were highly sought-after by manufacturers, who obtained them through much expense and effort.

The iron and steel industries likewise became increasingly reliant on scrap at this time, and were in constant need of raw materials from which to forge finished products. In order to create mill cranks, spindles, and other kinds of iron machinery, the Franklin Iron Foundry, established in New Hampshire in 1829, sought out 'Scrap Iron, wrought or cast', for which proprietors would offer 'a fair price'.[17] The Massachusetts firm of Pierce & Lee, makers of ploughs, shovels, and assorted housewares, was ready to buy 'Old Cast Iron, Brass, Copper[,] Pewter and Lead' in 1835.[18] It was much more affordable for mills to use scrap iron, if they could, than mining virgin ore themselves. The Bessemer steel process used some amounts of scrap iron but not a lot. But open-hearth furnaces, operating at higher temperatures, were able to burn off the impurities in scrap metal, enabling them to make 'purified steel from a greater range of materials than was previously possible'. Metals from the open-hearth process could be made with up to 90% scrap materials, but more common were 50–50 ratios.[19] The open-hearth process could be used for other metals, too, like strengthening copper, which was especially prized due to its scarcity and used to make everything from metal buttons and wire to the lining of ships' hulls.

The expansion of the steel industry by the end of the nineteenth century spurred an even greater demand for scrap metal. More and more structures were being constructed of steel, including industrial machinery, railroad engines and rails, automobile parts, and the skeletons of skyscrapers. Men of capital responded in kind by seizing new opportunities – Andrew Carnegie's monopoly on the high-quality iron ore in Minnesota forced competitors to seek out other modes of production, including a large-scale embrace of open-hearth processes. By then, the use of scrap materials was not a choice but a necessity for steel producers, thus exerting pressure further down the supply chain, much as the rag trade had experienced in previous decades.[20]

While industrial pressures for raw materials became acute in the closing decades of the nineteenth century, they certainly were not new. Already by the 1840s and 1850s suppliers and producers were being forced to source rags, scrap metal, glass, rubber, and other materials outside of regional markets, necessarily turning to cities to meet their increasingly voracious demands. Early port cities tended not to generate much of their own industrial waste, but as home to any number of ships, were sites of opportunity for scavengers. As *Harper's* would remark later in the century, 'our wharves receive the multiform commodities that make up the commerce of New York, and the very vastness of our exports and imports tends to exalt the consequence of all the parasites that prey upon them.'[21]

Additionally, rising urban populations themselves produced scrap in greater quantities, and the number of dispossessed, impoverished, and marginalised among them were available to perform labour in service of the scrap supply chain. Scavengers – typically young, unskilled, illiterate, foreign-born, and/or otherwise disenfranchised economically and socially – were as cast off as the things they collected. Scavenging was low status, dangerous 'dirty work' that attracted few native-born people.[22] But because it required little start-up money, scavenging was a venture open to enterprising people, especially those in vulnerable economic and social circumstances. Among their few available livelihoods, scavenging kept many from the poorhouse. What was more, scavenging and related occupations became quite specialised according to the particular commodity, often mapping onto race or ethnicity. For example, legions of rag and bone pickers, mostly German immigrants (men, women, and children), trod their way through city dumps with hooks and pokers, picking at rubbish heaps in search of cast-off clothes (Figure 1).[23] They often established and worked their own territories, taking rotting produce home to feed their animals and carting rags and other salvageable items to the junk shop.[24]

In a similar fashion, Jews dominated the used clothing and rag (and, related, pawnbroking) trades by the middle decades of the nineteenth century, while many Irish ran the junkshops.[25]

DUMPING GROUND AT THE FOOT OF BEACH STREET, NEW YORK CITY.—[SKETCHED BY STANLEY FOX.]

Figure 1. The trickle-down economy at work. 'Dumping Ground at the Foot of Beach Street,' *Harper's Weekly*, September 29, 1866. Library Company of Philadelphia.

Not surprisingly, those occupying the lowest rungs of the recycling trades did the dirtiest work. James Francis, a resourceful African American, was for a time Philadelphia's 'Dog-Killer-In Chief.' In the early 1860s Francis was earning about $1000 each summer catching stray dogs who were subsequently killed and boiled down into wheel grease. He also could be enlisted to catch feral pigs, and he oversaw a team of chimney sweeps in the winter.[26] Over time, these ethnic groups tended to graduate occupationally as they saw economic success: German scavengers headed west to become farmers. Jewish peddlers became shop owners, trading their carts for stationary storefronts, and pawnbrokers became bankers. Irish junk dealers moved into pawnbroking. And African Americans came to find junk dealing more amenable than dog catching.

While not the only ones, impoverished boys were especially well-situated and -suited to do scavenging work. They were particularly good at 'junking' – retrieving (often illicitly) scrap metal, rope, and glass to sell to the junk dealer. Among the most disempowered of urban dwellers, they were largely untethered from the clannish boundaries that defined ethnic and familial groups. With knowledge of and access to the streets and possessing a desire for excitement and freedom, these boys were among the most enterprising and opportunistic scavengers. More commonly known as vagrants, loafers, cotton-pickers, mud-larks, trunk smashers, bone-sellers, gutter-snipes, and street-rats, they became some of the most reliable suppliers of raw materials for the junk trade, especially when they organized into groups that stole things like the ones who so terrorised New Yorkers at mid-century.[27]

It was in fact their very status as marginal, neglected, and often victimised figures in the urban landscape, that enabled them to be such effective junkers. Many thieving youths came from broken homes, resulting in lax or utterly absent parental oversight. The same could be said for children for whom both parents were still alive and perhaps together, but who were overburdened with work. Social and economic conditions alike contributed to many impoverished children's virtually unlimited access to the streets and freedom of movement. Parents struggled, often unsuccessfully, to enforce their children's duties to go to work or attend school, if they were present in the household at all. This was particularly true of boys, who lived under much lighter surveillance than did girls. 'When the parents are both employed, or are working long hours' surmised one later account, 'their influence on the children is very slight, and they are left to range at will in the tenement and street. This freedom can hardly be good for them.'[28]

The economic stresses of urban life and increasing industrialisation also impinged more directly on children's lives, since parents were often forced to send them out explicitly to supplement the household's income; young ones had to earn money any way they could. New York City Police Magistrate J.W. Wyman wrote in 1830 of the perils faced by members of households run by single mothers whose 'inadequate compensation' was not enough to live on. He noted that the women often had no choice but to demand that their children go out to beg or in search of 'petty plunder' which 'finds a ready market at some old junk shop, and the avails are in part carried home as the earnings of honest labor.'[29] Their very exploitability enabled them to be effective revenue generators.

Countless nineteenth-century police officers, reformers, and cultural critics duly remarked on the close relationship between thieving gangs and tenement life. What they did not acknowledge, however, was the equally undeniable yet crucial contribution that the marginalised of all sorts, and thieving children in particular, made to the nineteenth-century commodities trade and the development of the industrial economy – the very one that kept them so disenfranchised. As a group, junkers and scavengers helped amass scrap from a variety of sources, bringing it to junk dealers for eventual consolidation and channeling back into industrial use. As individuals, these children learned through their first-hand experiences in the streets about the economic value of the things they scrounged and what outlets to seek in order to unload them.

Already by the mid-century child junkers had become an indelible part of American urban life, but public opinion of them was decidedly mixed. Some appreciated their street smarts and commercial acumen. One police officer in 1850 described scavengers as 'cunning and adroit', able each day to pilfer 'immense quantities' of 'plunder', using 'sly and artistical' approaches in their 'petty depredations'. In addition to taking off-loaded cargo from the wharves, 'they wrench the knobs from doors, steal building hardware from unfinished dwellings, lead and copper pipe, and even tin roofing!'[30] Others, however, excoriated them for embodying a darker side of the market. In his 1849 work *The Mysteries of City Life,* writer, James Rees called young junkers 'miserable creatures' who skulked around Philadelphia's wharves 'stealing old iron, hoops, copper sheathing, lead, empty barrels, boxes, &c., while in the more popular streets, they carry off door-rugs, [and] brass work from the doors.'[31] When police arrested the young James M'Manus, he had $6 on him, earned by selling stolen gas fixtures to a junk dealer ('one of those pests of Boston'). A reporter asked rhetorically, 'Is it a common thing for a laborer's children to have a dollar or two about them at a time?'[32] Well, yes. If they were good scavengers and could recognise the potential capital that was for the taking throughout the urban landscape. A group of 'youths of Irish parentage' no older than 16 tried to pawn a stolen clock worth $500, but Simpson the pawnbroker would not take it, surely knowing it to be stolen. Frustrated at their lost revenue, because they knew a working clock should command a lot of money, 'they ruthlessly broke it into pieces and sold the works for old metal at the junk shop.'[33] Another observer also recognised the sophistication of young thieves, characterising their operations as 'enterprises' that were made 'thoroughly efficient by ample capital and competent, systematic direction, both as to the "acquisition of property," and the proper market and means for its disposal.'[34] A later study pointed out the same thing, noting that a good number of children knew what they were doing, and stole 'to get a desired result', like the boy who 'steals iron or brass from the cars standing on the railroad tracks and sells his booty to the junk dealer in order to get money for some amusement.'[35]

Not only could they be smart, but young junkers were opportunistic – organised and seemingly all over the place. This makes sense, for bands of roving young boys from the tenements were uniquely situated to serve the key roles they did. Having such free access to and intimate knowledge of the city's streets, they forged the first and most necessary link in a long commodity supply chain. Hundreds of newspaper accounts appeared throughout the nineteenth century addressing the seeming intractable problem of child thieves. Articles with such headlines as 'Young Burglars and Their Abettors', 'Nurseries of Crime', and somewhat contradictorily, 'Encouraging Youthful Enterprise' merely confirmed that child junkers were not anomalies but actually quite common, their activities driven, ultimately, by hidden yet urgent industrial imperatives. Between 1850 and 1856 alone, New York City police arrested nearly 800 'dock thieves', who represented a mere fraction of all of the thefts that must have occurred at the time. Between the ages of 16 and 20, these boys organised themselves into gangs called the 'North Grabbers' and 'South Grabbers'.[36] Undergirding these dramatic headlines were more concrete figures that represented the real and growing problem of juvenile delinquency in America's burgeoning cities and the various ways it was encouraged by industrialisation. Through 1868, the total commitments of the 'much crowded' New York Juvenile Asylum, for example, numbered 13,796; of these, 3191 children were in for 'pilfering', although this figure was much higher if we could also tease out the young thieves who happened to be categorised as 'vagrant', 'bad', and 'disobedient and truant'.[37] By the end of 1899, these numbers had risen almost threefold.[38]

Accompanying these figures were reformers' observations, which reiterated in a different manner the sensational accounts in newspapers' police blotters. In *Darkness and Daylight*, Helen Campbell wrote that even with so many city schools and juvenile asylums, there were still 'surplus children' with nowhere to go and nothing to do: 'No Home can reach them all', she wrote, continuing:

> … even with every power thus far brought to bear, fifteen thousand unreclaimed children rove the streets [of New York City] to-day, a few of them peddlers of matches or small notions, but the majority living by their wits. Swill-gatherers and ragpickers employ some of them, but the occupation is hardly better than roaming at large. … There are gangs of many orders – 'copper pickers', 'wood stealers', young garrotters and burglars.

She also shared the story of Jack, a member of the 'Daybreak Boys', 'a whole gang what steals from small craft below Hell Gate, an' sell their stealin's for whatever they get, which is mostly nothin'. [39]

These accounts did not merely reveal the social and economic conditions of urban America's growing numbers of impoverished. Nor were they simply testaments to the ability of urban youth to seize the few social and economic opportunities that presented themselves. They also suggested something of larger market needs to be satisfied: after all, it would not have been worthwhile to steal were there no aftermarket for these kinds of raw materials, especially procured by the cheap labour of the similarly commodified 'surplus' and 'unreclaimed' children.[40]

Beyond helping sustain poor youth materially, street enterprises such as junking and rag-picking also created important social milieus for vagrant children, often providing essential personal protection and semblances of family life when 'loafing' on the streets was safer than living in their own homes. Representative intake records from the New York House of Refuge document the perilous lives of urban children throughout the century. A few descriptive examples, just a small sample taken from a few months in 1855, are telling. One of the youngest residents was five-year-old John McCarthy, who ended up at the House of Refuge, charged along with 'several other boys', for stealing cotton on the dock.[41] Motherless Andrew Reinhard, aged 14, lived with his father, and 'frequently played truant and went about the streets with bad boys, and pilfered'. His crime was 'stealing a piece of lead valued at four dollars'.[42] His biological parents having died, 14-year-old John Kennedy lived with his stepfather, who tended a market stall near the Five Points. He 'was in the habit of stealing old iron, and selling it at the junk shops'.[43] Edward Pounder, who 'gathers wood in the streets', was arrested for stealing eight cents worth of old iron.[44] Anthony Witz, 14, was in the habit of running away from home, 'sleeping in stables, carts, and old boxes. … He was associated with a band of young thieves with whom he used to go about the streets stealing whatever came in their way, that they could turn to account'.[45] When not working as a riverboat cook, 14-year-old John McDonnelly 'roved about the streets with other idle boys like himself and commenced to steal'. He was arrested for stealing four shillings worth of copper. 'He seems a hardened case', the record noted.[46] Neither Casper Cohen nor Valentine Treehart could speak English. Both entered the House of Refuge in May of 1855, Treehart for 'stealing wood and old brass', and Cohen, who had been seen 'picking up old iron, chips &c.,' was brought in for 'stealing a quantity of old iron'.[47] As is no doubt true for similar institutions in other cities, intake records for the New York House of Refuge are rife with accounts of young boys consorting with 'loafers', 'the idle', and gangs of 'bad boys' who would 'sleep out' and frequent the theatres when they were not getting arrested for theft or vagrancy. (While boys also stole from their workplaces – taking money out of store tills and pilfering stock – girls tended to steal from the homes in which they worked as laundresses, cooks, and domestic helpers; they were not typically involved in the illicit junk trade.)

Groups of young junkers adopted codes of honor among themselves even though what brought them together was their stealing from other people. By their early teens, these children had, through their gang apprenticeships, developed a keen sense of where to find the most abundant scrap and how best to obtain it. Evincing 'systematic direction', junking gangs were organised and they practiced profit-sharing. A 'feeler' ventured from the group and brought back anything of potential value. The older boys then sold the material at nearby junk shops and meted out the spoils. If spotted while 'on the lay', all the boys scattered except the youngest feeler, who was too young to be sent off to jail. This was yet another reason why young junkers were practically the only population that could do this work: because much of it involved theft, the youngest, everyone knew, could get away with it.[48]

Tight-knit, the gangs also defended each other in fights and offered a family structure of sorts when children had no other. Thirteen-year-old African American William Jackson, for instance, knew only absentee parents – his father, a sailor, was gone for years at a time and his mother, a washerwoman, had sent him to live with another woman for whom he worked as an errand boy. When she turned him out, 'Not having anything to do, he commenced to go about the streets with bad boys and steal'.[49] Joseph Grimm, 15, son of a 'partially intemperate' 'longshore man', did not much like his job driving horse carts. So 'he became acquainted with a gang of young thieves, who induced him to accompany them to steal. On this occasion [of his arrest] they commenced to rob a house of the lead on the roof, but were caught in the act and arrested'.[50]

Two older boys taught 14-year-old Henry Turner how to steal; 'he was very quick to learn these habits, and soon became the leader of the gang'.[51] A former resident of the Newsboys' Lodging House recounted that he had no recollection of his parents, and his aunt took him in when he was eight. When she married and moved to Boston, he was left 'to shift for myself in the streets', pilfering fruit for sustenance and 'finding a resting place in some box or hogshead' for the night. 'The boys that I fell in company with would steal and swear, and of course I contracted those habits too. I have a distinct recollection,' he added, 'of stealing on to the roofs of houses to tear the lead from around the chimneys, and then taking it to some junk-shop and selling it'.[52]

An exposé published in *Harper's Monthly* described the 'nests' built by dock rats out of 'patch[ed] together odds and ends of plant and drift-wood.' Some of these nests, under piers, would also have 'contrivances' providing heat for cooking and staying warm. There, gangs would eat, sleep, plot strategy, and take account of their booty in relative safety and privacy.[53] Being a member of a junking crew offered occupational training, physical protection, a sense of belonging, and a small but steady income for the child without a stable home life (Figure 2).

NEST OF YOUNG "DOCK RATS"—INTERIOR.

Figure 2. The streets could provide physical protection as well as a livelihood for the city's most vulnerable. "Nest of Young 'Dock Rats,'" *Harper's Monthly*, October, 1872. Library Company of Philadelphia.

But protection and community could also come at a steep price for a city's wayward youth. The often harrowing, mean, and unforgiving life of urban poverty could be one of exploitation as much as opportunity. Plenty of accounts in fact suggest coercion as much as camaraderie among members of thieving gangs: Joseph Walch was arrested for stealing $5.00 worth of cigars, claiming that 'larger boys told him to do it.'[54] Since 17-year-old Hiram Patterson's family 'broke up', he 'has had no steady home … [and] became acquainted with some bad boys … and was induced to go with them and steal.'[55] Bartholomew Chaffer, just 16, was lured from a stable home and a steady job as a butcher by 'some bad boys … [who] go about the streets stealing'. They 'finally tempted' him to steal his mother's gold watch, which his 'comrades' sold for $18, dividing the spoils amongst themselves. He earned a mere $4.50, plus the ire of his mother, who had him arrested.[56] Jacob Kepler, who often picked rags 'to help his father support the family', offered to help another boy carry a load of copper for sixpence. The copper was stolen and when the police approached, the other boy ran off while Kepler 'stood still and was arrested.'[57] Two boys in Boston were convicted of 'stealing a brass kettle from the yard of a dwelling house'. After the trial, the boy who had testified against the pair 'confessed that he committed the theft himself, and that the other boys sold the article at a junk shop for him.'[58]

Voluntary or not, the robust activity of young scavengers illustrates that already by the antebellum era scavenging, pilfering, and theft of raw materials was becoming commonplace, and would become even more so in the following decades.[59] The physical and economic exigencies of urbanisation that led to street youths' disenfranchisement also created more trash. The sheer number of arrests for the theft of various things, including wood, lead, iron, and copper, illustrate quite clearly that all of this stuff was circulating in the urban environment and finding ready aftermarkets. Urban populations rose steadily throughout the nineteenth century, increasing by 64% during the 1830s and by 92% during the 1840s.[60] In addition, more cities sprung up over time with westward expansion to Pittsburgh, Cincinnati, Chicago, and beyond. What was more, urban population densities increased as

Figure 3. The very signifiers of bustling commercial activity – robust store stock and the crates, barrels, and other containers that carried them – would also in various form become scrap, trickling back up the supply chain by enterprising junkers and junk dealers. James Queen, *Newmarket Hardware, Cutlery, and Nail Store* (Philadelphia: Pinkerton, Wagner & McGuigan, LIth., [August 1846]). Library Company of Philadelphia.

well, with a city's poor often packed into ever-tighter geographical footprints where they lived in substandard conditions.[61]

At the same time, domestic production and the expansion of global trading networks opened up new consuming possibilities by offering more and cheaper goods to greater numbers of the population. Feral pigs roving about the city streets readily dispatched uneaten food scraps. Human waste ran along the streets. Worn clothing was disassembled and refashioned into new garments and eventually sold to the rag picker when beyond repair. Lard was rendered into candles and suet. But what could be done with pieces of broken iron from heating grates, kettles, and sadirons? Or the glass bottles, whole and broken, now drained of their magical elixirs and panaceas? Or the bits of rope once used for hauling and baling, and the pieces of twine unwound from packages? In nineteenth-century images, urban commerce is often enthusiastically depicted as bustling activity in the form of barrels, crates, and boxes being carted about from wharf to wholesaler to retail shop (Figure 3). But once consumables were actually consumed – the flour scooped from its barrels, fabric unsheathed from its wrapping paper – that packaging and other detritus was discarded, cast out into the street since households and small enterprises did not have the resources to transmute such materials into something other than the waste it was. The material by-products of mounting industrialisation and mass consumption gave rise to and sustained all of those thieving gangs and the junk dealers they patronised. They monetised scrap as they dispatched it; were it not for scavengers and pilferers, in fact, cities would have been drowning in the trash they created, suffocating in the detritus left from what they had consumed.

Whether they were the first to retrieve scrap from the streets or to reappropriate it from houses, ships, factories, and other materials-rich sites, junkers worked on the front lines of urban waste. But they could not be successful junkers (or junkers at all) were it not for the peddlers and dealers ready to buy the spoils they had to sell.[62] As a law enforcement manual put it a century later,

> The first role of the fence is that of <u>providing a market</u> for stolen property, and hence for theft crimes themselves. By showing a continued willingness to receive and purchase stolen property, the fence gives economic or commercial value to stolen property which it would not otherwise have. This willingness to acquire stolen property provides the incentive for its theft in the first place.[63]

No fences, no junkers. One commenter explained that youth often looked to 'some sage old hag or some Fagin of a junk dealer' who acted as 'special counsel and adviser extraordinary'[64] (Figure 4).

Activities attendant to junk – from junking itself and the theft of stolen goods to the increasing viability of junk dealing and more strident calls for their licensure – signalled the unremitting creep of capitalism in the nineteenth-century American city and its conse-quences, especially among the most marginal. It was equal evidence, too, of industrial con-cerns' increasing reliance on the dogged activities of society's most marginal, and the degree to which their success – the success of big capitalism – depended on the meanest and pettiest entrepreneurialism, including illicit activity and the exploitation of the very young. Already by the antebellum era the country's cities were beginning to see their first profes-sional junk dealers, who were responding to the growing needs of American manufactures: in 1845 there were six rag dealers and 18 iron dealers in Baltimore; in 1847 Philadelphia was supporting four dealers in tin plate, copper, and sheet iron, 18 dealers in paper and rags, and 35 iron merchants and dealers; 32 ship stores and 36 junk dealers made their homes in Boston in 1848.[65]

By the mid-century, cities were teeming with junk shops and scrap dealers. In the early 1850s New York City police officer William Bell, like many of his colleagues, went on daily rounds not only to inspect known junk shops but to identify new ones. He routinely came upon storefronts 'having signs out to buy old rope, rags, &c.' Many of these businesses popped up, and disappeared, seemingly overnight.[66] Official records in New York City alone tallied some 250 junk dealers and another 300 'keepers of junk carts and boats' operating each year during the 1850s.[67] This figure did not include the countless other folks, like the 10 unlicensed junk shop keepers arrested in one week in 1852, or the 11 unlicensed traders running junk shops and the nine with boats who were arrested in one week in 1858.[68]

Most junk dealers situated their shops near opportunity, often directly down streets lead-ing to the waterfront. Many were closer still to the wharves that witnessed bustling activity on the docks, harboured materials-rich ships, and supported any number of legitimate and illegitimate trades, from junk dealers and marine stores to thieving sailors and loafing wharf rats.[69] Stolen goods travelled easily and often, in carts and pockets, across streets and down

A FENCE-ING LESSON.

MOTHER JUNK—" *Now, then, yer lazy waggabones, is this the vay yer vurk for a livin'? Here yer been and haint stole nothin' since yisterday but yer daddy's razor and a hammer, and yer mammy's weddin-ring! Wot'll become of yer if yer keep on in this here, idle, vicked, unmoral vay? Scollyvogs!*"

Figure 4. In this cartoon, a female junk dealer rewards boys who steal good scrap and chides those who don't. "A Fence-ing Lesson," *Frank Leslie's Budget of Fun,* April 15, 1861. Library Company of Philadelphia.

alleyways. They also were transported on the water, like the $30 worth of pig iron robbed from a sloop docked off New York City in 1846. The iron was loaded at night into a small boat and rowed with dispatch across the East River to Patrick White's basement junk shop in Brooklyn.[70] A few decades later, the city appointed a special squad of harbour police just to oversee illicit activities transpiring in the water and along the waterfront.[71]

Most junk peddlers and dealers themselves lived on the margins, and were only able to stay in business because they were able to exploit the young junkers who were more disenfranchised still. Toward this end, many junk dealers set up outlets near schools. John Hetherington, Cormick O'Hare, Thomas Casper, and Thomas English, to name but a few, operated junk shops just a block or two away from a public school, a high school, and the orphan asylum in New York.[72] At the mid-century dealers were primarily Irish immigrants – and many of them women.[73] They counted their profits by the penny, and their notorious reputation for being receivers was well earned: with the exception of professional fences who traded in higher-end items like bonds and securities, jewellery, and fine clothing, junk shops were undeniably the most prolific traffickers of pilfered things[74] (Figure 5). City officials issued, revised, and reissued ordinances year after year in futile attempts to discourage the trade in stolen goods. Lowell, Massachusetts directed the City Marshal in 1857 'to prosecute all known violations of the law relating the purchase of old junk, &c.,' suggesting that it was becoming an increasing problem.[75] The *Cleveland Daily Herald* complained in 1869 that violations of the law had become 'frequent', causing 'trouble and vexation' to victims of theft.[76] And the *Inter Ocean* quixotically suggested that Chicago's junk dealers pay higher license fees and post a sizeable bond with the mayor, provide police with daily lists enumerating the previous day's transactions, hold goods for five days before reselling them, and only purchase from children if accompanied by a note from their parents.[77] Likewise, newspapers daily carried reports of some junk shop owner or another getting arrested for receiving stolen goods. Complaints to the mayor about nuisance junk shops also filled newspaper space and included postings such as 'A junk-shop in Seventh-avenue is in the habit of receiving stolen goods and encouraging crime' and 'James Matthews, junk-shop keeper, Third-avenue, was fined $5 for purchasing from children.'[78]

Figure 5. The Irish ran most of the junk shops during the nineteenth century, and purchased a variety of articles, from scrap metal and rags to old cordage and bottles. "In Hefferan's Junk Shop," *Puck*, February 5, 1896. New York Public Library.

Figure 6. People assumed, quite rightly, that junk shops were common receptacles of stolen goods. "Receiver's Office," *Yankee Notions,* November, 1865. Courtesy, American Antiquarian Society.

Critics throughout the nineteenth century condemned all low-level junk dealers as being receivers. It was a fairly accurate characterisation (Figure 6). Even though in most cities they were required to register with authorities, secure an annual license, submit to regular inspections, prove their 'good character' to the mayor, and keep ledger books documenting transactions, most of them never did.[79] A beleaguered officer Bell came upon more unlicensed than licensed dealers while making his rounds near the Five Points; and despite their dubious status, many owners had the temerity, even, to solicit the officer's business. During a typical day in 1851 Bell reported that he:

... called at James Duffys Junk Shop on 7th Avenue ... his wife told me they had no License. +
she offered to sell me an old Iron Chain for 3/- and buy old rags of[f] me for 1 ½ cts a pound.
John Manning No. 648 Greenwich St. Running a Junk Shop without License. The woman in the
shop could not tell me the price of any articles. I called on Michael Madigan in Christopher near
Greenwich St. he is Keeping a Junk Shop without License he promised to get out his License this
month. ... I called at Mrs. Mary Anne McAfee No. 68 Hamersly St. Keeping a Junk Shop without
License. Thomas Sherry a young man in her employ offered to sell me an old Chain for 2/-.[80]

Their boldness in dealing with the authorities despite the fact that they were operating
illegally suggested it happened all the time, and that operating legally was more the exception than the rule.

There is no way to quantify precisely how many junk shops operated at any one time, nor
the quantity or value of their stock, nor even how much of it was stolen. But a good percentage of it certainly was. New York City police admitted in 1847 that their 'very imperfect'
estimate of 215 'Junk Shops, Receivers of Stolen Goods' (which were considered to be the
same thing) was probably only about half of those actually operating.[81] Although authorities
tried to control junk dealers, their sheer numbers confounded even the most assiduous
officers like William Bell. The number of known junk shops – to say nothing of the underground operators – overwhelmed authorities, making compliance of no more than a passing
concern to dealers. Part of Bell's rounds during a day in 1850, for example, consisted of visiting
the junk shop of Patrick Cooney ('who was very abusive + impudent') to see about some
stolen wool. Cooney 'said he did not know who he bought it from or who he had sold it to
as he kept no books for that purpose.' 'While I was in there,' Bell continued, 'I saw him buy a
Bottle from a Boy about 6 years old for one cent.' Then Bell went to a cellar junk shop where
the officer 'saw 3 small Boys there who were recognized as Theives [sic]' by his partner. 'They
had just sold some old rope.' Bell continued to walk his beat and:

> ... on going down South St. I met a gang of small Dock Theives [sic]. One of them had a bag full of
> short peices [sic] of old rope & Iron. He told me he was in the habit of selling his stuff to Mullins.[82]

Shop proprietors had no way of knowing where junk had really come from. They didn't ask
and they didn't much care – overly inquisitive junk dealers risked alienating their suppliers,
thus putting themselves out of business. Bits of rope, shards of iron, and pieces of paper
could be literally picked up off the street and totally legitimate. Sometimes, raw materials –
copper piping, wood planks – were collected from abandoned buildings. More often, though,
things like brass doorknobs and tin roofing materials were stripped from new construction.
And sometimes junk had 'just fallen off the ship.' Definitions of property and ownership were
fluid and the difference between 'finding' and 'stealing' something of value was a matter of
interpretation.[83] Even if caught, it was extremely difficult to convict junk dealers of being
knowing receivers.

Junk shop owners' refusal to acquiesce to these attempted municipal controls was due
in part to resisting the authorities on principle. But as members of some of the most marginalised and disempowered populations themselves, they often could not afford license
fees and had no knowledge of how to keep formal books, let alone the inclination to do so.
Like the vulnerable youth who supplied them, keepers of junk shops were both victimised
by intensifying urbanisation and also able, occasionally and modestly, to capitalise on it. The
very factors that marginalised them in fact created slivers of opportunity as well. For example,
the rise of urban development that pushed the poor into ever-tighter quarters also enabled
the market in stolen goods to flourish, since the same materials needed for expansion – to

build new buildings and create new infrastructure – were also the kinds of things that had resale value in the secondary market. And so, in the process of reporting increasing amounts of theft, contemporary accounts also chronicled the fast pace of urban development as well.

Newly-built but unoccupied structures proved irresistible to petty thieves like William Kelly and Henry Lyons, who were arrested in 1853 for stealing 'a quantity of lead pipe' from a just-erected building that they tried to sell at a junk shop.[84] With more building came more tradesmen, too. And with more tradesmen came their tools. Made of materials with an aftermarket, they were in high demand among junk shop proprietors like David Cooney, who was arrested for being in possession of an adze worth $1.25. When police searched his place, 'in the company of four or five shipjoiners who had lost adzes and other tools', they also came upon 'a large number of adzes, chisels, and hammers … discovered in a desk, and in kegs, and on the floor'.[85]

What was more, the expansion of transportation networks meant that the thriving trade in junk was no longer confined mainly to coastal cities which relied considerably on marine scrap and urban waste. Nearly every part of a railway line, from the locomotives and cars to the tracks and ties (to say nothing of the valuable cargo within), had worth on the secondary market. Sites of railroad accidents – of which there were countless in the nineteenth century – were prime scavenging opportunities for scrap dealers (Figure 7). The very things 'strewn in confusion on the ground' could find ready resale as scrap.[86]

Like that of ships, the rich concentration of materials encouraged an illicit trade in railroad parts as well, since they, too, were tempting sources of easily-convertible raw materials. The arrest of the Felsenthal brothers was a case in point. The junk dealers were indicted in Chicago for possessing 'a lot of brass journals for locomotive axles, stolen from the cars of the

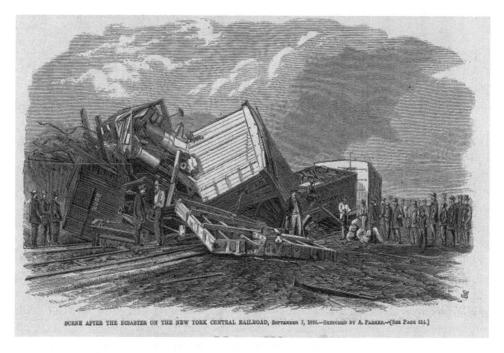

SCENE AFTER THE DISASTER ON THE NEW YORK CENTRAL RAILROAD, September 7, 1866.—Sketched by A. Parker.—[See Page 614.]

Figure 7. "Scene After the Disaster of the New York Central Railroad," *Harper's Weekly*, September 29, 1866, 609. Library Company of Philadelphia.

Northwestern Railway.' By failing to obliterate the identifying ownership marks individuating one piece of scrap from another, the men broke the cardinal rule of trafficking in stolen goods – the journals were not yet anonymous, and still carried the letters C. and N.W., G.D. (Chicago and Northwest, Galena Division).[87] 'That a significant relation exists between juvenile junking and railroads has already been indicated,' asserted one later observer, noting that:

> … twenty-eight out of the 100 boys studied were accustomed to secure junk from railroad yards or tracks … over 50 percent of them, lived less than 6 blocks from the tracks … this accessibility was thought to have an important bearing on the practice of securing material from railroad yards and cars. [88]

One railroad detective described a group of six Lithuanian 'brass thieves' who were adept at taking the brass bearings from the journal boxes of railroad cars, requiring 'considerable expertness', since the cars had to be carefully jacked up.[89] By the same token, scrap was also used to make railroad parts, such as 'good reliable locomotive car axles, cranks, connecting rods, and other forgings.'[90] Although lawful reuse was also common, it was difficult, if not impossible, to distinguish ill- from legitimately-gotten material.

Fences played a decisive role in shaping the market, influencing what things boys would steal and what they avoided according to the demands of larger market pressures exerted by wholesalers and commodities brokers who bought the materials from the junk dealers in order to resell further up the supply chain. It remained paramount that dealers continued to encourage reliable suppliers to bring them choice materials that could be quickly turned over. Particularly amenable junk dealers were well known among 'sneak thieves.' Timothy O'Leary was one such buyer who asked few questions. For weeks before his arrest in 1847 he purchased a few dollars' worth of stolen canvas at a time, $100 worth in total, from a boy named Samuel Thorp.[91] Before being apprehended for trafficking in stolen rope, sails, and tarpaulins from the wharves, a 'robber gang' had been 'doing a large business' through its 'junk agent.' And 'at several times' junk shop keeper James Maloney purchased lead from a boy who worked for a white lead manufacturer.[92] Additionally, many junk dealers were accused of being in the 'habit' of purchasing from children, and junk shops were commonly described as being 'nurseries of crime' and 'resorts of young thieves.'[93] A study from the early-twentieth century showed that the practice had continued, stating matter-of-factly that 'Junkmen sometimes actually instigate robberies on the part of the gang boy or his group.' It explained:

> A dealer lent a saw to a gang of boys on the Northwest Side [of Chicago] and instructed them to saw out the lead pipes in a vacant house and bring them to him … the junk-dealer regularly met the young fellows in a poolroom on Twelfth Street, where the robberies were planned and assignments given out. According to the police, the value of loot from Chicago robberies alone during the past sixty days amounted to over $100,000.[94]

Instances like these reveal a decades-long pattern of criminal activity feeding on and facilitating the expansion of urban areas.

Myriad critics decried junk dealers' practices on both moral and economic grounds, but reserved their outrage mostly for junk dealers rather than their passive abettors in big industry. Not only did these 'most prolific sources of crime' 'foster and encourage' larceny and delinquency among urban youth, but when buying junk, the reports frequently pointed out, dealers only gave 'a consideration equivalent to three cents on the dollar of its value.'[95] Eighteen-year-old Peter O'Brennan learned this the hard way, selling two stolen copper plates engraved with a map of Canada, reportedly worth $50, to a junk dealer for a mere $3.[96] Young Patrick Riley sold some $40 worth of stolen carpenters' tools for just $3.50.[97] And 'appropriately named' junk man John Bottle paid 4 cents for a stolen block of tin worth ten times as much.[98] Thieves though they might be, the boys were getting a raw deal. The marginal economies of junk only worked because young junkers could be maximally exploited by people who would face few, if any, consequences.

The unfortunate reality was that although junk dealers were dependent on boys to bring them scrap, the boys possessed relatively little transactional power. Often, they simply did not understand the market, especially those who were new to the game and working on their own. But just as often, by dint of their dubious if not outright illegal trading, the youth had little recourse if junk dealers did not give fair market value, since they could hardly complain to the police about their paltry returns on stolen loot. Junk dealers pressed their advantage knowing, too, that the boys were desperate and destitute. That was the cost of doing business in the black market, and crooks, however young, accepted that junk shops were the only outlets for their ill-gotten goods. Many young thieves such as those who were unable to pawn their $500 clock at Simpson's pawnshop had a reasonable idea of what they could realistically get from the junk dealer for their stuff: in this exchange sphere, 'fair market value' was a matter of context, and greatly depreciated because the materials were stolen or presumed to be.

Junk dealers' efforts at collecting, amassing, and sorting enabled these various articles to be funneled back up the supply chain; as such, they played an important yet unheralded role in the growth of the nineteenth-century economy, contributing to humble manufactures and massive infrastructure projects alike. Dealers put in motion the scrap they collected from junkers, selling sorted and graded stock in bulk to middlemen – brokers and wholesalers in metals, fibres, and glass – who then in turn sold it again at ever-greater markups to better capitalised agents or directly to papermakers, iron foundries, bottlers, and other industries. One contemporary writer remarked that junk dealers 'relieve our houses and stores, our lumber rooms and cellars of useless and bulky materials, and send them on their way to be shaped into new forms and appear in other combinations.'[99] The 1863 advertisement for William Bowman of Baltimore properly captured the 'omniverous maw' of the junk shop:

> BOWMAN, WILLIAM, dealer in WROUGHT AND CAST SCRAP IRON, Old Copper, Brass, Lead, Pewter, Zinc, &c. all kinds of Paper Stock, such as Rags, Canvas, Old Ro[p]e, Bagging, &c., which he is prepared to purchase in large or small quantities, at the highest market prices, Cash. A large assortment of Second Hand Cotton, Linen, and Gunny Bags constantly on hand, for sale low, suitable for Bark, Feed, Grain, &c., second hand Blacksmith's Goods, such as Anvils, Bellows, Vices, Hammers, &c. MACHINERY such as Pulleys, Shafting, and Leather Belting. A general assortment of the above articles always on hand. N.B. Old Iron suitable for Blacksmiths, &c., Iron Yard.[100]

With each subsequent transaction facilitated by the likes of Bowman and his fellow junk shop keepers in cities around the country, cast-off materials became even more valuable, increasing the profit margins of those who were, by degrees, distanced from scrap's original sources. An author late in the century noted:

> A piece of iron worth but five dollars in the market in its simple state, may become ... when combined with a proportion of carbon ... as steel, and wrought into balance-springs for watches, worth two hundred and fifty thousand dollars.[101]

Some 40,000 bottles *a month* passed through the hands of just one San Francisco junk dealer, destined for soda factories.[102] *The Scientific American* magazine estimated in 1871 that over

$15 million in waste cotton, woolens, iron, tin, and other metals 'is annually worked over in New England.' The mills alone each purchased an estimated $3000–$4000 of used fibre a year, and paper mills 'have standing orders with the largest dealers for thirty and forty tons of stock per week.' Regional ironworks 'consume from sixty to seventy tons of scrap' each week. And shovel companies 'stand ready to take all the old wrought iron offered in the market.'[103]

The domestic production of axes alone, 'one of our largest and most important business interests', required substantial amounts of raw material. In the early 1870s axe company Collins & Co. of Hartford, but one company of many, was making 3000 tools a day, using 1100 tons of steel and 5000 tons of iron annually. There were, additionally, the pressing needs of enterprises small and large: makers of everything from wire, ornamental ironwork, and hardware to plows, hoes, stoves, and even massive architectural structures such as bridges.[104] The addition of scrap added strength and durability to pure metal, 'hence scrap iron, lead, copper, zinc, tin, and other metals are in constant demand, and reenter speedily into the manufacture of new wares.'[105]

Because junk dealers took in scrap for pennies on the dollar, they made it possible for others further up the chain to realise their own profits and yet still deliver materials to industry efficiently and economically. For the junk dealer to see his best profits he needed to know the various properties of these materials, their potential buyers, and their particular markets. In addition, junk dealers created value by preparing commodities for trade to mills, foundries, and factories, enabling them thus to circulate in more legitimate markets. Crucially, they sorted stock, differentiating it into types and subtypes through often labour-intensive processes, and their efforts in this regard – which were much more onerous yet much less profitable – made the work of commodities traders, who could provide cheaper and necessary raw materials to manufacturers, viable.

Junk dealers' 'first business', according to one account, was to properly sort materials; doing so skillfully determined a dealer's income. Rags alone were sorted into as many as ten grades, 'each of which has a special use and an established value'[106] (Figure 8). Another contemporary source expounded on the importance of a textile mill's wool sorter:

> Each bale of wool, as well as the wool from different parts of a sheep's body, affords many different degrees of fineness, softness, strength, color, cleanliness, and weight ... the best wool in the fleece [is separated] into prime, choice, super, head, downrights, seconds, fine abb, coarse abb, and tags.[107]

Scrap iron also had to be sorted into grades, each with its own market value and specific industrial customer. For example, scrap wrought iron, which was already processed, possessed certain properties that when added to new wrought iron created a material of superior quality. Leather, too, came in several grades and could find various forms of reuse. Worn out leather hose and belting was reshaped to make the soles of boots; boots were disassembled, the leather treated, and the pieces used to make smaller shoes; smaller shoes whose leather was compromised became thin layers of shoe soles primarily constructed of other materials.[108]

Although essential to industry – to big capitalism – the trade in scrap did not enrich the junkers and dealers who were the first-line suppliers and the initial and necessary links in the chain. One account from the 1870s estimated that young junkers earned about 50 cents a day and adult scavengers about $3.00. Most dealers did little better, since, wedged between the junkers and petty brokers, they worked within especially tight margins. Representative

ASSORTING RAGS IN THE CELLAR.

Figure 8. The scrap trade relied on the hard work of individual labourers who sorted materials by type, grade, quality, and condition. "Assorting Rags in the Cellar," *Harper's Weekly,* March 21, 1874. Library Company of Philadelphia.

was the female junk dealer who told Virginia Penny in 1868 that she cleared only half a cent for each pound of fine rags she sold.[109]

Only as it was disgorged back into the American economy, to brokers and manufacturers, did scrap materials accrue any significant value. And only as the people driving its circulation became by degrees more physically removed from it, did scrap generate the kinds of profits befitting capitalists. Edwin C. Barringer's *The Story of Scrap* characterised this as 'the scrap pyramid':

> … the army of small peddlers and dealers who, in order to eke out a living, must also handle other waste materials such as rubber, rags, paper, and nonferrous metals. But as the top of the pyramid is approached specialization begins, and the larger dealers concentrate on one division of the waste trades.[110]

Over time, and especially after the Civil War, Americans were producing more scrap than ever before, a symbiotic relationship between production and consumption. Its processing required yet more organisation and greater numbers of middlemen inserting themselves into the supply chain. With each successive year city directories added more occupations to the scrap trade, all of whom were in some way handling secondhand goods. Their numbers included used clothing and furniture stores, junk dealers, rag dealers, iron scrap dealers, and any number of brokers and wholesalers who were able to leverage their superior buying power by dealing with industrial consumers on a larger scale.[111] Metal broker Nathan Caswell, for one, conducted his business on Wall Street in New York, far away from the junk dealers and scavengers who supplied the materials he traded so lucratively. His services included 'the Purchase and Sale of Railroad Iron (new and old).'[112]

Business was moving westward as well. William McGowan, of Pittsburgh, advertised his iron brokering business in the *American Railway Journal* in 1867, promising 'Prompt attention given to all business intrusted to my care.'[113] By the early 1870s, Cleveland was producing almost 700,000 tons of iron a year, using up some 125,800 tons of scrap and pig iron in order to do so.[114] By the 1890s, the west and northwest had 'thoroughly organized' its scrap rubber trade into 'channels through which 18,000 tons of scrap annually trickle from the hands of country peddlers into larger streams, until the rubber reclaiming factories receive it in carload lots.' Chicago, too, supported scrap rubber brokers, while the northeast tended not to, since 'the existence of near-by factories ... buy directly from the small dealers.'[115] Clearly, large, resource-intensive industries were dependent in part on steady supplies of scrap. And those industries at a remove from the right kinds of trash producers imported their scrap from across the country and overseas. While worn rubber boots in New England might have been shipped as waste to the northwest to be processed, iron scrap amassed in San Francisco after the 1906 earthquake – some 150,000 tons of it collected by one company alone – made its way to the Atlantic coast and to ports abroad.[116]

Without a doubt, there was value in simply gathering, sorting, and redistributing stuff. By the first decades of the twentieth century observers estimated the annual total value of salvaged junk to be about $2 billion; the industry even had its own trade organ, *The Waste Trades Journal*.[117] It had become such big business that writers in newspapers and magazines lamented the 'passing' of scavenging and peddling trades, depicting them as romantic and quaint, which was yet another way of erasing the labour of those who engaged in it.[118] But despite scrap's consolidation into full-fledged and quite lucrative industries (and, by degrees, its takeover by organised crime), scrap itself still started its cast-off life as miscellaneous by-products either from industrial production or individual consumption. In its more remote contexts and humble forms, scrap had little use and therefore negligible worth. The integration of scrap both materially and economically into the logic of big capitalism continued to require the efforts of countless anonymous and marginalised individuals to initiate the chain of reclamation, retrieving rags, iron shards, glass, cordage, rubber, and other useful materials from oblivion. And then junk dealers had to sort these disparate materials, like with like, grading them by kind and quality. In the process; they consolidated scrap into logical groups and meaningful quantities to merit the attention of brokers who enjoyed social and economic benefit in their distance from these more menial, denigrating, and much less profitable processes.

This was as true at the dawn of the twentieth century as it was in the nineteenth. Indeed, child junkers remained a vital yet deliberately invisible presence in the supply chain. Industry

saw reliable supplies of scrap as a boon (and absolutely necessary for their long-term success), yet increasingly wanted to distance themselves from its tainted connection to illicit
activity – and one that particularly harmed children. Urban municipalities additionally
labelled the rag and scrap trades as 'nuisances' since rags could catch fire and spread disease,
and scrap metal was viewed as dirty work performed by dirty (i.e. foreign) people.[119] Even
the courts preferred a hands-off approach. In nineteenth-century public nuisance suits,
judges, using 'social-cost balancing', tended to rule against injunctions on industry, believing
them to impede the progress of industrialisation. Like the physical and moral hazards of
scavenging, which were encouraged albeit indirectly by industry, pollution, also, 'was the
price one paid for the amenities of city life and economic and social progress in
general.'[120]

Reformers, however, continued to point out the problem with the source of scrap in an
attempt to make manifest what was most convenient to ignore: the inextricable relationship
between junking and juvenile delinquency. For example, in the 1894 article for *Century*
magazine, 'The Making of Thieves in New York', Jacob Riis described the conditions endemic
to urban poverty. He attributed many children's waywardness on the lack of space for them
in school, estimating that some 50,000 in New York City alone in 1891 were not served by
education. Where did they go if not to school or work? Many were out in the streets 'learning
to become thieves', stealing bottles and similar items to sell at the junk shop, he posited.[121]
In 'The Subtle Problem of Charity', an incisive and honest assessment of the disconnect
between many reformers and their objects of charity, Jane Addams recognised the blurry
lines between entrepreneurialism and exploitation:

> There are certain boys in many city neighborhoods who form themselves into little gangs. ...
> Their favorite performance is to break into an untenanted house, to knock off the faucets and
> cut the lead pipe, which they sell to the nearest junk dealer. With the money thus procured
> they buy beer, which they drink in little freebooters' groups sitting in the alley. ... In motive and
> execution it is not the least unlike the practice of country boys who go forth in squads to set
> traps for rabbits or to round up the coon. It is characterized by a pure spirit of adventure, and
> the vicious training really begins when they are arrested, or when an older boy undertakes to
> guide them into further excitements.[122]

Two decades later, however, the problem remained, prompting the Juvenile Protective
Association of Chicago to devote an entire monograph to *Junk Dealing and Juvenile
Delinquency* in 1919, which detailed 'the economic importance of the junk business as well
as its moral hazards.'[123] The two went hand in hand. Perhaps the most thorough study on
the subject, the report described the relationship between junk dealers and their young
suppliers in ways that were strikingly similar to earlier accounts, while also making apparent
the exponential increase of both the industrial need for scrap and the attendant effects of
urban poverty embodied in young junkers. One police officer reported that:

> ... the junk dealers have been doing a thriving business, buying fish plates, brass journals, etc.,
> stolen from the Railway Company's right of way. Junk dealers make a specialty of meeting boys
> at [the Grand Crossing] intersection to make deals with them.'[124]

Like the products of 'imported pauperism' whom reformers identified in the nineteenth
century, many of these boys were foreign-born, and a large number came from 'abnormal
domestic groups', i.e. broken homes.[125] What was more, the report described the enduring
and seemingly intractable interdependence of junk dealers and young junkers. The
nine-year-old son of one junk peddler offered that 'Sometimes on the North Side as many

as 25 boys come to the wagon to sell things – rags, brass and bottles. ... Every day the kids come to my house and sell things to my father.'[126] Indeed, the practice had become increasingly normalised, commonplace, and accepted. 'The attitude of parents is often one of condonement [sic] and even encouragement of boys in their stealing from railroad tracks. In some cases, the families of the boys act as receivers of stolen goods', noted one contemporary account. According to another, 'The whole neighborhood turns out to steal from the [railroad] cars at Western and Twenty-fourth [Streets].' Following futilely in the footsteps of officer Bell working over a half century earlier, 'The juvenile officers are lenient in this connection, because they know how much a part of the neighborhood mores this has become, and they do not blame the children for following the pattern of the group.'[127]

Other aspects of the business also remained relatively unchanged. Like the youth working in previous decades, boys were still readily exploited by junk dealers, who relied on their vulnerability and disempowerment for their own marginal survival. Coming from compromised bargaining positions, boys often lacked meaningful leverage during business transactions due to the familiar triad of 'inexperience, ignorance, and need.' For instance, $20.00 worth of clothes taken from a stock yard earned one boy only 20 cents. And the 30-inch, 40-lb bronze statue 'Golus', worth $800 when it was stolen from the Hebrew Institute in 1911, netted only $2.00 in the secondhand market.

But a close reading of these reports also suggests these boys possessed commercial acumen and cunning beyond their years. An eight-year-old named Martin brought a 'hunk of brass' to a junk dealer who gave him nothing in return, 'thinking no doubt that the boy had stolen it and would not dare report him.' The boy followed the dealer down an alley and stole it back. Another boy, aged 14, took his junk home for his mother to sell, knowing she would get a better price.[128] Because 'the scales of junk peddlers bore such a bad reputation' – over two-thirds of those inspected in 1918 did not meet required standards – one enterprising group carried its own set to ensure their goods would be weighed accurately.[129]

Even under the most optimal conditions, however, junkers were lucky if they earned more than a few cents a day, due to chronic exploitation and, over time, more competition. Collectively, their indispensable efforts enriched only those much higher up. While a boy might make 25 cents on a good day, the most successful junk dealers were clearing thousands of dollars annually. Perhaps exceptions, one San Francisco dealer made $30,000 a year trading largely in marine junk and a Chicago junk dealer left an estate estimated to be worth $100,000.[130] In 1920, McClure's published an article about these very inequities. 'Who,' its author asked, 'would suppose that thousands of dilapidated junk-wagons and drivers, hardly able to speak English, collect every year one and one-half billion dollars' worth of refuse?'[131] Surely, it was not these poor, unnamed souls who profited, but rather the 'kings, princes and dukes of junk ... men of affairs', who 'buy waste only in car-load quantities'. They could transmute, say, defective shell casings from the war that had been rejected by 'fussy government inspectors', into 'cocktail shakers and beverage holders, in which form they were sold in Fifth Avenue shops at the price of ten dollars each'.[132] This kind of entrepreneurship enabled some, like the men celebrated in this article, to clear thousands of dollars on even single transactions. Meanwhile, the child junkers, initially responsible, were not worth mentioning.

Tracing the circulation of scrap tells us something about the activities of a marginal but essential group of people working in a trade that has been little recognised or quantified. Due to their very disempowerment – their often immigrant status, want of parental controls,

Figure 9. By the end of the nineteenth century the problem of urban waste became even more acute, as this image of the rubbish accumulating in back alleys and privy pits shows. *The Tenement Conditions in Chicago*. (Chicago: City Homes Association, 1901). Library Company of Philadelphia.

lack of education, and limited options save for relatively free access to the streets – boy junkers were uniquely situated to do this work. Scrap's circulation and the attendant processes of commodification necessarily and efficiently obscured this work, decontaminating and adding value to scrap at each step along the way (Figures 9 and 10). As scrap moved through the market and up the supply chain, it accrued more worth through organisation, consolidation, abstraction, and recirculation. Goods flowed through increasingly well-established and respectable channels, from scavenger to junk dealer to petty commodities trader to manufacturer. In the process, these miscellanies became enriched as they were aggregated into larger quantities and ever further removed – materially, economically, geographically, and symbolically – from their origins in the suspect hands of grubby street urchins and juvenile delinquents through similarly suspect carts and stores of junk dealers, to the respectable world of commodities trading among merchant princes. Finally, scrap moved to large-scale industry, where it became the raw material to make new things – a percentage of which would surely end up being discarded once again.

It was necessary for junk to be thus sanitised (laundered, if you will), moving from the little-regarded, often illegal, and largely maligned world of petty capitalism's small-scale transactions among individual (and individuated) things associated with specific people (owners, junkers, junk dealers) to the more-worthy, value-neutral market spheres of abstract (and abstracted) commodities. In addition to usefully obscuring the work of child junkers and others who worked closer to the source, the commodification of scrap, necessary for it to be absorbed back into manufacturing, was not simply an economic or material process

NORTH END JUNK SHOP.

Figure 10. Junk shops sorted and aggregated various and miscellaneous goods, helping to funnel them up the supply chain for eventual industrial uses. "North End Junk Shop," from Louis Albert Banks, *White Slaves: Or, the Oppression of the Worthy Poor*. (Boston: Lee and Shepard, 1893). Library Company of Philadelphia.

but a mental one as well. That scrap's commodification had to occur on both concrete and symbolic levels in order for it to become useable within large-scale industry is perhaps the most fundamental 'fence-ing lesson' of all.

Notes

1. *Brooklyn Eagle,* "Juvenile Thieves," May 26, 1857.
2. *Brooklyn Eagle,* "Gang of Juvenile Burglars Arrested," November 27, 1856.
3. Carl Zimring briefly discusses the relationship between junk dealing and juvenile delinquency in the later part of the nineteenth and early-twentieth century in *Cash for Your Trash: Scrap Recycling in America*, see esp. 67–69. The issue of child labour appears throughout Martin Medina's *The World's Scavengers: Salvaging for Sustainable Consumption and Production*, which focuses on contemporary and global issues. The contributions of urban children to recycling make cameo appearances in Susan Strasser's *Waste and Want: A Social History of Trash*. Although their involvement with the junk trade is only briefly mentioned, Christine Stansell's *City of Women: Sex and Class in New York, 1789–1860* helpfully contextualises the roles of impoverished children in the emerging American city. The work of David Nasaw is likewise useful in explaining

the larger social and economic environments within which late-nineteenth-century urban children lived. He touches only briefly upon their involvement with the scrap trade, but extensively covers the newsboys, who were often involved in petty criminal activities as well. See *Children of the City: At Work and At Play*. Timothy Gilfoyle's work explores more directly nineteenth-century children's criminal activities, with a particular focus on pickpocketing. See especially "Street-Rats and Gutter-Snipes: Child Pickpockets and Street Culture in New York, 1850–1900."

4. Strasser, *Waste and Want: A Social History of Trash*. For more on the history of rubbish, see Benjamin Miller, *Fat of the Land: Garbage of New York the Last Two Hundred Years*.
5. *Pennsylvania Evening Post,* "Ready Money," January 6, 1776 and "READY Money," July 16, 1776; *Albany Centinel,* "J. & Norman Landon & Co.," December 22, 1797; *Pennsylvania Evening Post,* "Threepence per pound given," March 12, 1776 and "Ragged Newcastle and Maryland Money, Exchanged," April 13, 1776. Parts were often greater than the whole, and objects made with valuable materials became the targets of thieves who, by melting something down into its base form, could render it both more valuable to potential buyers and also unidentifiable to former owners. See, for example, *Pennsylvania Evening Post,* "Was Stolen," September 12, 1776.
6. *Pittsfield Sun,* "Iron and Nail Factory," August 15, 1821.
7. *Connecticut Gazette,* "John Manierre, Has for Sale," June 19, 1816; *Boston Commercial Gazette,* "Edward D. Peters," October 15, 1821.
8. *The Oxford English Dictionary*, volume V. See also Morison, *The Old Ropemakers of Plymouth: A History of the Plymouth Cordage Company, 1824–1949*, 10.
9. *Boston Gazette,* "By Joseph Ripley," June 12, 1815.
10. For descriptions of these enterprises, see *New York Times,* "Brooklyn News. Extensive Seizure of Stolen Property," August 8, 1864; W.O. Stoddard, *Harper's New Monthly Magazine,* "New York Harbor Police," October 1872, 672–683.
11. *Hampden (Mass.) Federalist,* "Sales by Auction," January 4, 1816; *A Description of the United States Armory at Springfield, (Mass.)* (n.p., 1818]), 3–4.
12. To cite but a few suggestive examples: Louisville grocers Tillay & Norton advertised "Cash paid for Rags, Feathers, Ginseng, &c." in *The Louisville Directory for the Year 1832*, 171; bookstore proprietor John B. Perry's ad noted, "Books bought in quantities and cash paid for Rags," *O'Brien's Philadelphia Wholesale Business Directory* for 1844, 52. The title page of the captivity narrative *God's Mercy Surmounting Man's Cruelty, Exemplified in the Captivity and Surprising Deliverance of Elizabeth Hanson*, contained an ad for rags: "The third edition … Danvers, near Salem: reprinted and sold by E. Russell, next the Bell Tavern, MDCCLXXX. At the same place may be had a number of new Books, &c., some of which are on the times. – Cash paid for Rags." Newspaper ads are even more abundant. A search in Readex's *American Historical Newspapers, 1741–1922* for the phrase "cash paid for rags" yields 1457 hits.
13. McGaw, *Most Wonderful Machine: Mechanization and Social Change in Berkshire Paper Making, 1801–1885*, 27–28. She notes that expenses for rags was about four times that of labour (195).
14. McGaw, *Most Wonderful Machine*, 67; Zimring, *Cash for Your Trash*, 19.
15. McGaw, *Most Wonderful Machine*, 191–192, 195.
16. McGaw, *Most Wonderful Machine*, 193.
17. *New Hampshire Patriot,* "Franklin Iron Foundery [sic]," March 23, 1829.
18. *Hampshire Gazette,* "Stoves!! Stoves!!," November 4, 1835.
19. Zimring, *Cash for Your Trash*, specifically 23–24, but more generally to explain steel-making processes much more adroitly.
20. Zimring, *Cash for Your Trash*, 43. See also Medina, *The World's Scavengers*, 38–40, for more extensive lists of waste items that can be recycled, and their future uses.
21. Stoddard, "New York Harbor Police," 673.
22. Zimring, *Cash for Your Trash*, 28, 30–1.
23. See [Charles Loring Brace] *New York Daily Times,* "Walks Among the New-York Poor. The Rag and Bone Pickers," January 22, 1853.
24. In Madeline Leslie's *The Rag Pickers,* two women working a field get into a skirmish over territory. See *The Rag Pickers, and Other Stories,* esp. 14–15.

25. For more on Jews in the scrap and used goods trades, see Zimring, *Cash for Your Trash,* esp. 37–38, 44–58; Mendelsohn, *The Rag Race: How Jews Sewed Their Way to Success in America and the British Empire*; and Woloson, *In Hock: Pawning in America from Independence through the Great Depression,* esp. chapter 5.

26. *Philadelphia Inquirer,* "Enforcement of the Ordinance Against Dogs," June 2, 1862. For more on the importance of marginal economies, see Luskey and Woloson, *Capitalism by Gaslight: Illuminating the Economy of Nineteenth-Century America.*

27. For more on these urchins, see Gilfoyle, "Street-rats and Gutter-snipes."

28. Hunter, *Tenement Conditions in Chicago. Report of the Investigating Committee of the City Homes Association,* 150.

29. Quoted in Carey, *An Appeal to the Wealthy of the Land,* 13.

30. *Prisoners' Friend,* "Juvenile Depravity in New York," April 1850, 339.

31. Rees, *Mysteries of City Life,* 53.

32. [Thomas Gill], *Selections from the Court Reports Originally Published in the Boston Morning Post, from 1834 to 1837,* 228–229.

33. *New York Times,* "Police Reports. Young Burglars and Their Abettors," August 16, 1860.

34. Stoddard, "New York Harbor Police," 678.

35. De Koven Bowen, *Safeguards for City Youth at Work and at Play,* 163.

36. *Daily National Intelligencer* (Washington), "With the Occasional Aid of the City Police," December 6, 1856, reprinted from the *New York Journal of Commerce.*

37. *Seventeenth Annual Report of the New York Juvenile Asylum,* 37, 40.

38. *Forty-Eighth Annual Report of the New York Juvenile Asylum,* 86. New York was representative rather than exceptional. In turn-of-the-century Detroit, crimes against property accounted for 57% of boys' arrests, a figure which certainly included the theft of scrap metal. See Wolcott, *Cops and Kids: Policing Juvenile Delinquency in Urban America, 1890–1940,* 43–44.

39. Campbell, *Darkness and Daylight; or Lights and Shadows of New York Life,* 153–154, 165.

40. *New York Times,* "Young Burglars and Their Abettors"; "Encouraging Youthful Enterprise," February 8, 1860; *Inter Ocean,* "Nurseries of Crime," May 22, 1876. In 1919 the Juvenile Protective Association of Chicago commissioned a study on the subject. See Grigg and Haynes, *Junk Dealing and Juvenile Delinquency. An Investigation Made for the Juvenile Protective Association of Chicago.* The authors estimated 'that 90% of the delinquency [among teenage boys] was traced to the junk business', 10. For more on urban youth culture see Nasaw, *Children of the City: At Work and at Play.*

41. New York House of Refuge, *Inmate Case Histories,* New York State Archives, Albany, NY. Entry for John McCarthy, April 7, 1855 (hereafter NYHR, *ICH*). For more on the history of handling disorderly children, see Shelden, *Controlling the Dangerous Classes: A Critical Introduction to the History of Criminal Justice,* esp. 196–230.

42. NYHR, *ICH,* entry for Andrew Reinhard, April 10, 1855.

43. NYHR, *ICH,* entry for John Kennedy, April 19, 1855.

44. NYHR, *ICH,* entry for Edward Pounder, April 11, 1855.

45. NYHR, *ICH,* entry for Anthony Witz, June 9, 1855.

46. NYHR, *ICH,* entry for John McDonnelly, May 16, 1855.

47. NYHR, *ICH,* entries for Valentine Treehart and Casper Cohen, May 17, 1855.

48. [Charles Loring Brace], *New York Daily Times,* "Walks Among the New-York Poor," March 4, 1853, 2.

49. NYHR, *ICH,* entry for William H. Jackson, Nov. 10, 1855.

50. NYHR, *ICH,* entry for Joseph Grimm, December 10, 1855.

51. NYHR, *ICH,* entry for Henry C. Turner, Jan. 4, 1856.

52. Letter from J.G.B. to Charles Loring Brace, transcribed in Campbell, *Darkness and Daylight,* 130.

53. Stoddard, "New York Harbor Police," 678.

54. NYHR, *ICH,* entry for Joseph Walch, April 25, 1855.

55. NYHR, *ICH,* entry for Hiram Patterson, May 5, 1855.

56. NYHR, *ICH,* entry for Bartholomew Chaffer, May 21, 1855.

57. NYHR, *ICH,* entry for Jacob Kepler, May 26, 1855.

58. *Daily Evening Transcript* (Boston), "Juvenile Depravity," June 16, 1849.

59. Girls tended to steal petty luxuries like handkerchiefs, shoes, ribbons, loose change, and occasionally clothing because they often worked as domestics and these were the most convenient kinds of things for them to take. Adults tended to steal more valuable items such as cash, pocket watches, clothing, and jewellery.
60. Hoffman and Felkner, "The Historical Origins and Causes of Urban Decentralization in the United States," (*www.jchs.harvard.edu/.../von_hoffman_w02-1.pdf*), 6.
61. Hoffman and Felkner note that in the nineteenth century 'Low-income housing developed in relatively inexpensive damp lowlands, which were most prone to flooding and unsanitary conditions', 3.
62. In *Cash for Your Trash*, Carl Zimring describes the five main tiers of the scrap trade – collectors, peddlers, dealers, processors, and brokers (52–53). These tiers were already well in place by mid-century, with dealers and processors becoming more numerous after the Civil War.
63. US Department of Justice Law Enforcement Assistance Administration, *Strategies for Combatting the Criminal Receiver of Stolen Goods*, 8, original emphasis. The report also describes 'passive' vs. 'active' fences. The former accepts everything; the latter discriminates, which in turn influences the actions of the thief, who 'will steal only those items he knows them to handle', 9.
64. Stoddard, "New York Harbor Police," 677.
65. *The Baltimore City Directory for 1845*. Copper and tin worker Charles Collier's ad noted "Old Copper, Brass, Pewter, and Lead bought or taken in exchange," 134. *McElroy's Philadelphia City Directory for 1847*; George Adams, *The Boston Directory ... 1848–9*. It is difficult, if not impossible, to disaggregate some of these numbers to determine more precisely which dealers were trading in new or used materials. Likely most dealt in both.
66. Bell, "Diary of William Bell, Inspector of Second-Hand Dealers & Junk Shops, 1850–1851." Hereafter Bell Diary.
67. *National Police Gazette*, "Receivers of Stolen Goods," July 1, 1857, 4.
68. *New York Daily Tribune*, "Arrest of Junk Shop Keepers," June 19, 1852, and *New York Times*, "Police Intelligence. Unlicensed Junk Shops," March 24, 1855. People engaged in junk dealing were hard to count because not all of them obtained licenses and were on a city's books. Many others engaged in similar occupations were not required to register with authorities, such as sellers of paper stock, iron merchants, used furniture dealers, metal workers, soap makers, secondhand clothing dealers, and others.
69. At the other end of the spectrum legally and logistically from petty theft of marine junk was the 'systematic dismantling of vessels', through ship-breaking operations such as the ones that thrived in places such as San Francisco. See Pastron and Delgado, "Archaeological Investigations of a Mid-nineteenth-Century Shipbreaking Yard, San Francisco, California," 61–77.
70. *Brooklyn Eagle*, "City Intelligence. Robbery of a Vessel," January 20, 1846.
71. Stoddard, "New York Harbor Police."
72. Based on Samuel Augustus Mitchell's *City of New York ... Entered 1850*, map and addresses taken from D.T. Valentine, *The Manual of the Corporation of the City of New-York, for the Year 1849*, 271–273.
73. City directories include many listings for female junk shop keepers. Early female junk dealers in New York included Mary Bubser, Hannah Burrows, Catharine Carroll, Elizabeth Dunican, Bridget Gallagher, Mary Holly, Jane Kirkbride, Mary McHugh, Elizabeth McManus, Mrs. M. McManus, Mary Regan, Ann Smith, and Janett Watts. See, *The New-York Business Directory for 1844 & 1845*; *Doggett's New-York City Directory, for 1845 & 1846*; *Wilson's Business Directory of New-York City*. In *Five Hundred Employments Adapted to Women*, Virginia Penny described the business enterprises of several 'junkwomen', 122.
74. Campbell, *Darkness and Daylight*, 686. She describes dealers in secondhand goods as 'the most annoying class' of receivers, 688. See also Woloson, *In Hock*, 128–129, 137.
75. *Lowell Daily Citizen and News*, "City Items," May 12, 1857.
76. *Daily Cleveland Herald*, "The Junk Ordinance," April 22, 1869.
77. "Nurseries of Crime."
78. *New York Times*, "Mayor's Black Book. Complaints," January 19, 1855 and "Mayor's Black Book; Complaints," January 23, 1855. "A junk-shop in Seventh-avenue is in the habit of receiving

stolen goods and encouraging crime" (*New York Times* January 19, 1855) and "James Matthews, junk-shop keeper, Third-avenue, was fined $5 for purchasing from children" (*New York Times* January 23, 1855).

79. See, for example, New York City Common Council, *A Law to Regulate Pawn-Brokers, and Dealers in the Purchase or Sale of Second-Hand Furniture, Metals or Clothes. Passed July 13th, 1812*, 3–4. For representative articles about receivers, see: "Capture of a Gang of Forgers, Robbers, and Receivers of Stolen Goods," *Salem Gazette* May 9, 1834; "A Gang of Thieves Broken Up," *New York Aurora* April 27, 1842; "Police Court," *Massachusetts Ploughman and New England Journal of Agriculture* December 4, 1847; and "A Junk-Shop Keeper Arrested," *New York Times* March 18, 1858.

80. Bell Diary, entry for January 23, 1851.

81. "Police Statistics," *National Police Gazette* June 12, 1847.

82. Bell diary, entry for November 25, 1850, emphasis added.

83. As Frederic Thrasher noted, 'The distinction between picking up some discarded object to sell and appropriating the unguarded property of others can hardly be very clear to the adolescent in the gangland environment' (*The Gang*, 149). I would argue, however, that most boys could tell the difference but it was likely of little concern.

84. *New York Daily Times*, "Junk Dealers," March 14, 1853.

85. *New York Daily Times*, "Court of General Sessions," December 14, 1853.

86. *Harper's Weekly*, "Scene after the Disaster on the New York Central Railroad," September 29, 1866, 614.

87. "Criminal Court. The Felsenthal Junk Dealers Sent to the Penitentiary for One Year," (Chicago) *Inter-Ocean* February 19, 1874. For more on this, see, James McCabe, *Secrets of the Great City*, esp. "The Thieves' Exchange," in which he observes that a fence's most pressing duty was to remove ownership marks, continuing, 'A melting-pot is always over the fire, to which all silver ware is consigned the instant it is received. ... Jewelry is at once removed from its settings, and the gold is either melted or the engraving burnished out, so as in either case to make identification impossible. ... Cotton, wool, rags, and old ropes, require no manipulation. When once thrown upon the heap, they defy the closest scrutiny of the owners. ... The "fence" is as well skilled as any lawyer in the nature of evidence,' 364–365. It was for this very reason that many local ordinances required junk dealers to document from whom they purchased goods and that they keep property tagged and 'in certain piles' for five days, 'without removing, melting, cutting or destroying any article thereof'. Frank Gilbert, *Bender's Supervisors', County and Town Officers' Manual*, 408. See also, *New York Times*, "Receivers of Stolen Goods," July 1, 1857.

88. Thrasher, *The Gang*, 36.

89. Thrasher, *The Gang*, 153.

90. *American Railway Times*, "Scrap Iron Forgings," January 1857, 2.

91. *National Police Gazette*, "Receiver of Stolen Goods," August 28, 1847, 403.

92. *Brooklyn Daily Eagle*, "The Robber Gang," January 10, 1850 and "Arrest," January 30, 1850.

93. *New York Daily Times*, "Minors and Junk Dealers," March 2, 1855 and "Nurseries of Crime."

94. Thrasher, *The Gang*, 153–154.

95. "Annual Report of the Boston Society for the Prevention of Pauperism," 35; *Brooklyn Eagle*, "The Courts," December 22, 1857.

96. *New York Times*, "Police Reports. Larceny and Receiving Stolen Goods," July 27, 1860.

97. *Brooklyn Eagle*, "Receiving Stolen Goods," February 8, 1860. The article gives the purchase amount as 14 shillings, each equivalent to about 25 cents. See Tim Watkins, "Some Details of Everyday Life in 1860," http://www.royalengineers.ca/lifedetail.html.

98. *Brooklyn Eagle*, "New York City News. Buying Stolen Goods," October 29, 1859. The article noted, 'He appears to be a man of good character – albeit successful in his trade ...'.

99. *Galveston (TX) Daily News*, "Junk Shops and Their Connections," June 23, 1874.

100. *E.M. Cross & Co.'s Baltimore City Directory, 1863–4*. The phrase "omniverous maw" comes from *The Great Industries of the United States*, 379. The passage continues, '[the junk shop] can digest almost every article of commerce and send it through the appropriate channels ...'.

101. *The Great Industries of the United States*, 379.

102. *Daily Evening Bulletin (San Francisco)*, "Rags, Sacks, and Bottles," July 31, 1875.

103. "Fortune in Scraps," reprinted in *The Farmer's Cabinet* 69.39 (April 13, 1871), 1.
104. *The Great Industries of the United States,* 123.
105. "The Junk Trade," *Cleveland Morning Daily Herald* May 11, 1872.
106. P.L. Simmonds, *Waste Products and Undeveloped Substances: A Synopsis of Progress,* 106.
107. The source emphasised that good sorting determined a mill's reputation 'for producing high grades of goods with uniformity'. See *The Great Industries of the United States,* 915. 'Abb' refers to low grade wool from the edge of the fleece; 'tags', to wool caked in mud or faeces.
108. *Cleveland Morning Daily Herald,* "The Junk Trade." Reprinted from the *Boston Commercial Bulletin.* See also, *Railway Times,* "Bessemer Scrap and its Uses," December 19, 1863, 401.
109. Penny, *Five Hundred Employments,* 122.
110. Barringer, *The Story of Scrap* (New York: Institute of Scrap, Iron and Steel, Inc., 1939), 6–7.
111. Barringer explains that 'Small [scrap] dealers sell either direct to consumers, or to larger dealers or brokers. Large dealers usually book orders directly from consumers, which they may fill entirely from their own accumulation or may distribute among other dealers. Brokers function without yards, frequently buying and selling without having a definite supply or an outlet, respectively.' *The Story of Scrap,* 6.
112. *American Railroad Journal,* "Nathan Caswell, Metalbroker," February 16, 1850, 108.
113. *American Railroad Journal,* "Wm. D. McGowan, Iron Broker," January 20, 1867, 79.
114. *Railway Times,* "Trade and Manufactures of Cleveland," June 10, 1871, 183. Pig and scrap tonnages were not disaggregated.
115. *Scientific American,* "Old Rubber Shoes," October 26, 1895, 267. For more on rubber and the vulcanisation process, see Zimring, *Cash for Your Trash,* esp. 25–26.
116. *Banker's Magazine,* "Twenty Thousand Tons of Old Iron in a Single Scrap Heap," December 1909, 914.
117. Grigg and Haynes, *Junk Dealing and Juvenile Delinquency,* 5.
118. *Maine Farmer,* "Passing of Trades. Features of the Old Time City Life That Are Fading Away," June 3, 1897, 6.
119. Zimring, *Cash for Your Trash,* 34–35. On immigrants, dirt, and contamination, see Bushman and Bushman, "The Early History of Cleanliness in America"; and Hoy, *Chasing Dirt: The American Pursuit of Cleanliness.*
120. Rosen, "Different Perceptions of the Value of Pollution Abatement across Time and Place: Balancing Doctrine in Pollution Nuisance Law," 319.
121. Riis, "The Making of Thieves in New York," 110, 111.
122. Addams, "The Subtle Problems of Charity," 173.
123. Grigg and Haynes, *Junk Dealing and Juvenile Delinquency,* 6.
124. Grigg and Haynes, *Junk Dealing and Juvenile Delinquency,* 7.
125. *Pennsylvania Journal of Prison Discipline,* "Annual Report of the Boston Society for the Prevention of Pauperism," 32; Grigg and Haynes, *Junk Dealing and Juvenile Delinquency,* 25.
126. Grigg and Haynes, *Junk Dealing and Juvenile Delinquency,* 30.
127. Thrasher, *The Gang,* 154, 155.
128. Grigg and Haynes, *Junk Dealing and Juvenile Delinquency,* 32–35.
129. Grigg and Haynes, *Junk Dealing and Juvenile Delinquency,* 45–47.
130. *Daily Evening Bulletin (San Francisco),* "The Junk Trade," June 30, 1870; Grigg and Haynes, *Junk Dealing and Juvenile Delinquency,* 33.
131. Kaempffert, "What Junk Has Done. Some Men Grow Rich on What Other Men Throw Away," 29.
132. Kaempffert, "What Junk Has Done," 63.

Disclosure statement

No potential conflict of interest was reported by the author.

References

Adams, George. *The Boston Directory. 1848-9*. Boston, MA: James French, 1848.

Addams, Jane. "The Subtle Problems of Charity." *The Atlantic* 83, no. 496 (Feb., 1899): 163-179.

"Annual Report of the Boston Society for the Prevention of Pauperism." *Pennsylvania Journal of Prison Discipline* 7, no. 1 (January, 1852): 30-38.

"Arrest." *Brooklyn Daily Eagle*, January 30, 1850.

"Arrest of Junk Shop Keepers." *New York Daily Tribune*, June 19, 1852.

The Baltimore City Directory for 1845. Baltimore: John Murphy, 1845.

Barringer, Edwin C. *The Story of Scrap*. New York: Institute of Scrap, Iron and Steel, 1939.

Bell, William. "Diary of William Bell, Inspector of Second-Hand Dealers & Junk Shops, 1850-1851." New-York Historical Society Manuscripts Division.

"Bessemer Scrap and Its Uses." *Railway Times* 15, no. 51 (December 19, 1863): 401.

Bowen, Loise de Koven. *Safeguards for City Youth at Work and at Play*. New York: The Macmillan, 1914.

Brace, Charles Loring. "Walks among the New-York Poor." *New York Daily Times*, January 22, 1853.

Brace, Charles Loring. "Walks among the New-York Poor." *New York Daily Times*, March 4, 1853.

"Brooklyn News. Extensive Seizure of Stolen Property." *New York Times*, August 8, 1864.

"By Joseph Ripley." *Boston Gazette*, June 12, 1815.

Campbell, Helen. *Darkness and Daylight; or, Lights and Shadows of New York Life*. Hartford, CT: A.D. Worthington, 1893.

Carey, Mathew. *An Appeal to the Wealthy of the Land*. 2nd ed. Philadelphia, PA: L. Johnson, July, 1833.

"City Intelligence. Robbery of a Vessel." *Brooklyn Eagle*, January 20, 1846.

"City Items." *Lowell Daily Citizen and News*, May 12, 1857.

"Court of General Sessions." *New York Daily Times*, December 14, 1853.

"The Courts." *Brooklyn Eagle*, December 22, 1857.

"Criminal Court." (Chicago) *Inter-Ocean*, February 19, 1874.

A Description of the United States Armory at Springfield, (Mass.). N.p.: n.p., 1818.

Doggett's New-York City Directory, For 1845 & 1846. New York: John Doggett, Jr, 1845.

"Edward D. Peters." *Boston Commercial Gazette*, October 15, 1821.

E.M. Cross & Co.'s Baltimore City Directory, 1863–4. Baltimore: E.M. Cross &, 1863.

"Encouraging Youthful Enterprise." *New York Times*, February 8, 1860.

"Enforcement of the Ordinance against Dogs." *Philadelphia Inquirer*, June 2, 1862.

"Fortune in Scraps." *The Farmer's Cabinet* 69, no. 39 (April 13, 1871): 1.

"Franklin Iron Foundery [Sic]." *New-Hampshire Patriot*, March 23, 1829.

"Gang of Juvenile Burglars Arrested." *Brooklyn Eagle*, November 27, 1856.

Gilbert, Frank. *Bender's Supervisors', County and Town Officers' Manual*. Albany: Matthew Bender, 1914.

Gilfoyle, Timothy J. "Street-Rats and Gutter-Snipes: Child Pickpockets and Street Culture in New York, 1850-1900." *Journal of Social History* 37, no. 4 (2004): 853–882.

Gill, Thomas. *Selections from the Court Reports Originally Published in the Boston Morning Post, from 1834 to 1837*. Boston, MA: Otis, Broaders, 1837.

God's Mercy Surmounting Man's Cruelty, Exemplified in the Captivity and Surprising Deliverance of Elizabeth Hanson. Danvers: Reprinted and sold by E. Russell, 1780.

The Great Industries of the United States. Hartford, CT: J.B. Burr & Hyde, 1872.

Grigg, Harry H., and George E. Haynes. *Junk Dealing and Juvenile Delinquency. An Investigation Made for the Juvenile Protective Association of Chicago*. Chicago, IL: Juvenile Protective Association, 1919.

Hoffman, Alexander, and John Felkner. "The Historical Origins and Causes of Urban Decentralization in the United States." Joint Center for Housing Studies of Harvard University, January, 2002. www.jchs.harvard.edu/.../von_hoffman_w02-1.pdf

Hunter, Robert. *Tenement Conditions in Chicago. Report of the Investigating Committee of the City Homes Association*. Chicago: City Homes Association, 1901.

"Iron and Nail Factory." *Pittsfield Sun*, August 15, 1821.

"J. & Norman Landon & Co." *Albany Centinel*, December 22, 1797.

"James Matthews, Junk-Shop Keeper." *New York Times*, January 23, 1855.

"John Manierre, Has for Sale." *Connecticut Gazette* (New London), June 19, 1816.

"Junk Dealers." *New York Daily Times*, March 14, 1853.

"The Junk Ordinance." *Daily Cleveland, Herald*, April 22, 1869.

"A Junk-Shop in Seventh-Avenue." *New York Times*, January 19, 1855.

"Junk Shops and Their Connections." Galveston (Texas) *Daily News*, June 23, 1874.

"The Junk Trade." *Daily Evening Bulletin*, (San Francisco) June 30, 1870.

"The Junk Trade." *Cleveland Morning Daily Herald*, May 11, 1872.

"Juvenile Depravity in New York." *Prisoners' Friend* 2, no.8 (April, 1850): 340-347.

"Juvenile Thieves." *Brooklyn Eagle*, May 26, 1857.

Kaempffert, Waldemar. "What Junk Has Done. Some Men Grow Rich on What Other Men Throw Away." *McClure's* 52, no. 5 (June, 1920): 29, 63-64.

Leslie, Madeline. *The Rag Pickers, and Other Stories*. Boston, MA: Henry Hoyt, 1863.

The Louisville Directory for the Year 1832. Louisville: Richard W. Otis, 1832.

Luskey, Brian P., and Wendy A. Woloson, eds. *Capitalism by Gaslight: Illuminating the Economy of Nineteenth-Century America*. Philadelphia, PA: UPenn Press, 2015.

Matsell, George W. "Juvenile Depravity." *Daily Evening Transcript (Boston)*, June 16, 1849.

"Mayor's Black Book. Complaints." *New York Times*, January 19, 1855.

"Mayor's Black Book; Complaints." *New York Times*, January 23, 1855.

McCabe, James. *Secrets of the Great City*. Philadelphia, PA: National, 1868.

McElroy's Philadelphia City Directory for 1847. Philadelphia: Edward C. and John Biddle, 1847.

McGaw, Judith. *Most Wonderful Machine: Mechanization and Social Change in Berkshire Paper Making, 1801–1885*. Princeton: Princeton UP, 1987.

Medina, Martin. *The World's Scavengers: Salvaging for Sustainable Consumption and Production*. Lanham: AltaMira Press, 2007.

"Minors and Junk Dealers." *New York Daily Times*, March 2, 1855.

Mitchell, Samuel Augustus. *[Map of the] City of New York. Entered 1850*. Philadelphia: Thomas, Cowperthwait, 1853.

Morison, Samuel Eliot. *The Old Ropemakers of Plymouth: A History of the Plymouth Cordage Company, 1824-1949*. Boston: Houghton Mifflin Company, 1950.

Nasaw, David. *Children of the City: At Work and at Play*. New York: Oxford UP, 1986.

"Nathan Caswell, Metalbroker." *American Railroad Journal* 6, no. 7 (February 16, 1850): 108.

The New-York Business Directory for 1844 & 1845. New York: John Doggett, Jr., 1844.

New York City Common Council. *A Law to Regulate Pawn-Brokers, and Dealers in the Purchase or Sale of Second-Hand Furniture, Metals or Clothes. Passed July 13th, 1812*. New York: Hardcastle & Van Pelt, 1812.

"New York City News. Buying Stolen Goods." *Brooklyn Eagle*, October 29, 1859.

New York House of Refuge. *Inmate Case Histories, 1824-1935*. Albany, NY: New York State Archives.

New York Juvenile Asylum. *Seventeenth Annual Report*. New York: Wm. S. Dore, 1869.

New York Juvenile Asylum. *Forty-Eighth Annual Report*. Albany: James B. Lyon, 1900.

"Nurseries of Crime." (Chicago) *Inter Ocean*, May 22, 1876.

O'Brien, John G. *O'Brien's Philadelphia Wholesale Business Directory* For 1844. Philadelphia: King & Baird, 1844.

"Old Rubber Shoes." *Scientific American* 73, no. 17 (October 26, 1895): 267.

"Passing of Trades. Features of the Old Time City Life That Are Fading Away." *Maine Farmer* 65, no. 31 (June 3, 1897): 6.

Pastron, Allen G., and James P. Delgado. "Archaeological Investigations of a mid-Nineteenth-Century Shipbreaking Yard, San Francisco, California." *Historical Archaeology* 25, no. 3 (1991): 61–77.

Penny, Virginia. *Five Hundred Employments Adapted to Women*. Philadelphia, PA: John E. Potter and Company, 1868.

"Police Intelligence. Unlicensed Junk Shops." *New York Times*, March 24, 1855.

"Police Reports." *New York Times*, July 27, 1860.

"Police Reports. Young Burglars and Their Abettors." *New York Times*, August 16, 1860.

"Police Statistics." *National Police Gazette*, June 12, 1847.

"Ragged Newcastle and Maryland Money Exchanged." *Pennsylvania Evening Post*, April 13, 1776.

"'Rags, Sacks, and Bottles.'" *Daily Evening Bulletin* (San Francisco), July 31, 1875.

"Ready Money." *Pennsylvania Evening Post* (Philadelphia), January 6, 1776.

"Ready Money." *Pennsylvania Evening Post* (Philadelphia), July 16, 1776.

"Receiver of Stolen Goods." *National Police Gazette*, August 28, 1847.

"Receivers of Stolen Goods." *National Police Gazette*, July 1, 1857.

"Receivers of Stolen Goods." *New York Times*, July 1, 1857.

"Receiving Stolen Goods." *Brooklyn Eagle*, February 8, 1860.

Rees, James. *Mysteries of City Life*. Philadelphia, PA: J.W. Moore, 1849.

Riis, Jacob. "The Making of Thieves in New York." *Century* 49, no.1 (Nov., 1894): 109-116.

"The Robber Gang." *Brooklyn Daily Eagle*, January 10, 1850.

Rosen, Christine. "Different Perceptions of the Value of Pollution Abatement across Time and Place: Balancing Doctrine in Pollution Nuisance Law." *Law and History Review* 11, no.2 (Autumn, 1993): 303-381.

"Sales by Auction." *Hampden (Mass.) Federalist*, January 4, 1816.

"Scene after the Disaster on the New York Central Railroad." *Harper's Weekly* 10, no.509 (September 29, 1866): 609–614.

"Scrap Iron Forgings." *American Railway Times* 9, no.1 (Jan.1, 1857): 2.

Shelden, Randall G. *Controlling the Dangerous Classes: A Critical Introduction to the History of Criminal Justice*. Boston, MA: Allyn & Bacon, 2001.

Simmonds, P. L. *Waste Products and Undeveloped Substances: A Synopsis of Progress*. London: Robert Hardwicke, 1873.

Simpson, John A. *The Oxford English Dictionary*. Vol. 5. Oxford: At the Clarendon Press, reprinted 1978.

Stoddard, W. O. "New York Harbor Police." *Harper's New Monthly Magazine* 45, no. 269 (October, 1872): 672–683.

"Stoves!! Stoves!!" *Hampshire Gazette* (Northampton, Mass.), November 4, 1835.

Strasser, Susan. *Waste and Want: A Social History of Trash*. New York: Metropolitan Books, 1999.

Thrasher, Frederic. *The Gang: A Study of 1,313 Gangs in Chicago*. 1927/2nd ed. Chicago: U of Chicago P, 1936.

"Threepence per Pound given." *Pennsylvania Evening Post*, March 12, 1776.

"Trade and Manufactures of Cleveland." *Railway Times* 23, no. 23 (June 10, 1871): 183.

"Twenty Thousand Tons of Old Iron in a Single Scrap Heap." *Bankers' Magazine* 79, no. 6 (December, 1909): 914.

U.S. Department of Justice Law Enforcement Assistance Administration. *Strategies for Combatting the Criminal Receiver of Stolen Goods*. Washington, DC: Government Printing Office, 1976.

Valentine, D. T. *The Manual of the Corporation of the City of New-York, for the Year 1849*. New York: McSpedon & Baker, 1849.

"Was Stolen." *Pennsylvania Evening Post*, September 12, 1776.

Watkins, Tim. "Some Details of Everyday Life in 1860." Royal Engineers Living History Group. http://www.royalengineers.ca/lifedetail.html

Wilson's Business Directory of New-York City for 1849. New York: John F. Trow, 1849.

"With the Occasional Aid of the City Police." *Daily National Intelligencer* (Washington), December 6, 1856.

"Wm. D. McGowan, Iron Broker." *American Railroad Journal* 23, no. 3 (January 20, 1867): 79.

Wolcott, David. *Cops and Kids: Policing Juvenile Delinquency in Urban America, 1890–1940*. Columbus, GA: Ohio State U, 2005.

Woloson, Wendy A. *In Hock: Pawning in America from Independence through the Great Depression*. Chicago, IL: U of Chicago P, 2009.

Zimring, Carl. *Cash for Your Trash: Scrap Recycling in America*. New Brunswick, NJ: Rutgers UP, 2005.

Jews, second-hand trade and upward economic mobility: Introducing the ready-to-wear business in industrializing Helsinki, 1880–1930

Laura Katarina Ekholm (iD)

ABSTRACT

This article examines the history of a 'Jewish' second-hand marketplace in Helsinki (1880–1930). This was a niche left for the Jews, who were not awarded civil rights in Finland before 1917. In utilizing a wide range of heterogeneous source material, I argue that the second-hand dealers introduced ready-made clothing to local consumer markets. The restrictions placed upon Jews provide a glimpse into the social status towards such products and trades. The article also highlights the tendency to deliberately undermine entrepreneurial success among Helsinki Jews in order to fit into the narrow social space that was historically designated to them.

Introduction

This article combines the second-hand trade and the role of the Jews by looking at ready-to-wear markets in an industrialising Helsinki from the 1880s to the 1930s. Specifically, it examines the rise of supply in ready-to-wear clothing in Helsinki with a focus on the second-hand marketplace called Narinkka.[1] It was mainly the domain of a Jewish minority which was kept on the margins of society until the independence of Finland (1917).[2]

The Jewish marketplace has been portrayed in the popular memory and the local Jewish self-narrative as a form of pariah capitalism par excellence, a peculiar form of petty-trade. Yet strikingly, over a period of 50 years, the Jews of Finland faced a proverbial from-rags-to-riches-experience. Within a couple of generations, many of the Helsinki 'cloth-Jews' came to be known as the middle-class bourgeois of Helsinki. The starting point of this study is the contradiction between the 'schmate', the rag trade as a form of forced entrepreneurship composing an ethnic niche left for the Jews, and their striking, upward economic mobility. I argue that the introduction of the mass production of clothes in series was central in this process.

Scholars have long argued for the pivotal role of commercial recycling – to use the formulation of Miles Lambert for the development of ready-to-wear markets.[3] The second-hand clothing was the first mode of buying ready-made garments at a time when clothes were either made at home or custom-made by skilled tailors and seamstresses.[4] Beverly Lemire has shown the crucial role of the second-hand trade for the European economy in different stages of industrialisation 'from scarcity to industrial plenty'. In each stage from the 17th to the mid-19th centuries, second-hand trade enabled consumption.[5]

The scholarship on cast-off trade, on the one hand, and the ready-to-wear business, on the other, focuses on the parts of Europe where industrialisation first commenced.[6] Perhaps even half of Englishmen wore ready-to-wear by the end of the 1860s.[7] It has been estimated that by the 1910s, ready-made had generally substituted custom-made clothing in the United States.[8] By contrast, in the standard works, the breakthrough of the Finnish ready-to-wear manufacturing is generally dated to the interwar period.[9] As I will show in this article, just a handful of Jewish families contributed crucially to this process.

The repairing, making and selling of clothing, both second-hand and new, has almost no barriers to entry. It was a typical start-up trade for many of the immigrants. What astonished contemporaries, and has been debated ever since, was the rapid upward economic and social mobility of Jews from Russian-dominated Eastern Europe upon emigrating to the West.[10]

In this broad dichotomy of 'east' and 'west', 19th century Finnish policy toward the Jews was decidedly eastern. Finland was an autonomous Grand Duchy of Imperial Russia. The Jewish policy of 19th century Finland was, in principle, straightforward: no Jews were supposed to permanently reside in Finland. Jews in Finland could not choose their economic activities and their temporary residential bills included restrictions in terms of their means of gaining a livelihood.

The Jewish colony in Helsinki was a by-product of the Russian military reforms of the 1860s, after which Jews who had served in the military were allowed to stay in the region where they had completed their service. Hence, most Jewish families in Helsinki had some sort of connection to garment manufacturing and trade, and all of them had roots in Russian military service. Those who wished to stay in Finland, again in principle, were forced into livelihoods in the petty-trade, repairing and selling of used clothing.[11]

The modern armies of the 19th century accelerated the demand for mass-produced men's wear. Military workshops were the first clusters of ready-to-wear factories. Ready-made uniforms were first introduced for military purposes, which were then applied and adapted to the production of civilian clothing.[12] Hence, Helsinki makes a case contributing to a set of questions on the interplay between ethnicity, the role of the military and the second-hand trade in the social and economic context of the changing demand and supply of the consumer markets in a growing urban milieu.

My research strategy is to analyse the functions and importance of Narinkka from the perspective of its different actors: the second-hand dealers, their customers, and the non-Jewish tailors and retailers. The aim of the article is to synthesise the remaining fragments of information on Narinkka to answer the following questions: What was the role of Jews in Helsinki clothing markets? How could Jews create a niche with economic advantage in such a limited scope for opportunities? What was the role of the military in this process? Why certain trades were seen as being suitable for Jews in late 19th century Finland provides a glimpse into the norms and social status towards such products and trades. This may help us to understand why the non-Jewish counterparts were so slow in doing what the Jewish second-hand dealers and their offspring did: recognise the increased consumer demand for ready-made clothing and put such products up for sale.

Methodological reflections and sources

A second-hand marketplace is often understood as the part of an informal economy operating in parallel to the world of prostitution, narcotics and stolen goods. The same applies to the case of the Jewish Narinkka in Helsinki. With regard to the context in which the marketplace is introduced in the historiography of the city, the second-hand marketplace is mentioned only in passing. It is, moreover, always mentioned in the context of urban poverty and, in most cases, as a static image of a bygone world in contrast to the fluctuating modern world. Apart from the list of rents paid for the city of Helsinki[13] and a few documents filed in the Helsinki Jewish archive, Narinkka left behind little formal documentation. The same applies to the customers of the marketplace, the growing working class and soldiers from the nearby military garrisons. Parallel to Narinkka, the scholarship of Helsinki tends to ignore the presence of the Russian military and its impact on the city. Consequently, much of the analysis is deduced from a wide range of secondary sources.

The Finnish Jews are among the very few Eastern European Orthodox Jewish communities that were not destroyed in the Holocaust. Yet their extended family and business networks perished in the Shoah. The Soviet era had a further effect on the traces left by the Jewish businesses. Thus, the sources beyond the eastern border of Finland have proven elusive. Above all, the history has had an effect on what kind of attention the local Jewish community in Helsinki has paid to their entrepreneurial history. Many of the Holocaust survivors, Zionists or Communists alike, found the traditional position of Jews as a middleman minority despicable. This ideological stand has influenced the image of the economic life of a typical Jewish shtetl.[14]

The Helsinki Jews definitely had a similar attitude towards the economic life of Eastern European Jews. Generally, the Helsinki Jewish community was known for their Zionist sympathies.[15] What is known of the Jewish second-hand trade is based primarily on a heterogeneous assortment of memoirs written by Jews as well as non-Jews. The ideological stand of the community elders has clearly affected the tone of discussion and history writing.

The methodological challenge is to set the different accounts on Narinkka that, in total, form a fragmentary body of research data into a context of rapid social change. For the men of the Jewish community who wrote about Narinkka, it uniquely symbolised oppression of times that had been left behind. Most of the Jewish authors in Helsinki had a negative stand on small-scale business. This image has been a prevalent part of the local Jewish collective memory.[16] The ideas of what a life of Jewish families should have been like has probably influenced the stories. None of the memoires' writers mentions, for example, that the local Jewish community campaigned and lobbied for decades for preserving the Narinkka marketplace when the city of Helsinki planned to close it in the 1920s.[17] Hence, what is given in the parenthesis or remains unsaid is often as important as what is actually written about Narinkka and small-scale Jewish trade and business.

Although finding information on Narinkka is laborious, defining the members of the Helsinki Jewish community is not. All Jews who stayed in Finland before 1917 were connected to the Russian military, and all had to regularly apply for a renewed permission to stay in Finland. The way to settle in Helsinki was very controlled and limited. Thus, Helsinki had detailed sources on every Jewish person legally living in the country, including information on years spent in military service, the place of birth, marriages, the number of under-aged children and occupational status. There are inconsistencies in the sources concerning the spelling of names, yet generally it is possible to follow and track the Jewish men and their families from the moment the service in the military was over until the end of their lives or, since many decided to migrate further to the West, until the date of their emigration.

For estimating the relative significance of the Narinkka marketplace, I will reconstruct the supply of clothing in late 19th century Helsinki. I use the trade directories to assemble a picture of what kinds of products were available and who sold them. Since the directories were never collected in any systematic fashion, they are by no means a reliable source for an exact number of tailors, seamstresses, retailers and wholesalers. Nevertheless, the trade directories reflect the supply of clothing in Helsinki – or as this article will show – the lack thereof.

A 'Jewish' business refers to the business of a member of the Helsinki Jewish community as defined in the registers compiled by the authorities and the Jewish congregation. Distinguishing the Jewish business-owners from the non-Jews is simple. We can find the Jewish names announced in the business directories. [18] With the information on Jewish-owned companies it is possible to further consider the share of the Jewish business owners among the Helsinki-based textile and ready-to-wear manufacturers, retailers, wholesalers, tailors and seamstresses. There were some Christian individuals with a Jewish background, yet their firms are not involved in the analysis.

The way the business directories organised the compiled data varied as to how the different firms were presented and how much information they gave. Some volumes just list names of companies in alphabetical order under broad titles such as 'textile, garments, apparel manufacturers, wholesalers and retailers', while in other volumes the firms are classified in detail, distinguishing companies with hats on sale to companies with both hats and caps. Since the main interest here is the supply of ready-to-wear clothing and the share of the Jewish-owned companies, I have sorted out the ready-to-wear manufacturers and retailers, tailors, textile wholesalers and retailers, hats, caps and furriers. The firms present under several product categories in the directories are counted only once according to the foremost activity of the firm.

Success stories are always easier to find than the failures. Those Jewish men, moreover, who had the most successful business, had their birthdays published in the local newspapers, allowing for a consideration of their career paths. Needless to say, not all the Jews of Helsinki became wealthy and successful, yet the social position of Jews shapes the narration and gives much weight on the marginal social status and underrates the achievements in business. The Jewish-owned companies were understandably stated to operate in the fields of business allotted for them in all formal contexts.[19] It is possible that some early Jewish businessmen undervalued their contribution on purpose, in order to fit the narrow social space allowed for the Jews.

Most public accounts by the Finnish Jews, such as the community periodicals, were written by men. Yet similar to the Jewish market squares of Eastern Europe,[20] and notions on the second-hand markets of early modern Western Europe,[21] also in Helsinki, the marketplace was dominated by women. In the analysis below, I apply a simple method: I employ a family document commemorating Narinkka from the inside. In her unpublished genealogy, Miriam Seligson recounts the life of her grandmother Rebecka, née Radsevitsch (ca. 1857–1921).[22] The life story of Rebecka Bensky, as recalled by her granddaughter, represents a typical life of a Jewish woman in 19th century Finland.

The author wrote the account based on extensive archival work for the succeeding generations. The chronicle includes elements that can be confirmed from other sources, revealing elements of Jewish second-hand trading practices in Helsinki. I first contrast the oral-history type of material on the Helsinki Jews with the data on the community, as derived from other sources. The life of Rebecka Bensky and her family is the starting point of the analysis.

The Jewish colony in a rapidly growing city

With her life story, Rebecka Bensky is representative of the mid-19th century Jewish life in Finland. She was born around 1857 to a Jewish soldier.[23] Since 1858, the Russian soldiers, their families and widowed wives were allowed to stay in Finland. The statute concerned did not take a stand on the ethnic background of the permitted soldiers but it was later confirmed by the Russian authorities that the right applied to the Jews.[24]

The Jewish soldiers and their wives came from the Russian controlled parts of Poland, Ukraine, Belarus and Lithuania. These areas were the homelands of the largest Jewish population in the pre-Holocaust world. They were subjects of Imperial Russia, and as Russian Jews, in principle, only allowed to reside in certain areas generally referred to as the Pale of Settlement.[25] Military service was one of a few ways of legally moving out of the Pale within the Russian empire.

No matter how much autonomy Finland had for implementing the terms of their own internal affairs, there was no way to prevent a small Jewish colony of former military personnel from settling in the country. The Finnish authorities set a decree in 1869 specifying the occupations allowed to Russian subjects staying in the country after finishing military service. The available means of gaining a livelihood included trade in tax-free products, whereas second-hand clothes and used shoes, along with other used goods and cheaper linen, scarves and hats, shoes, string, filament, needles, and other tawdry items would carry the same taxation rate as that of Finnish citizens.[26]

Finland could not stop a small number of Jews setting in the country by the permission of the Russian military, yet the policy of Finland was to make life for the Jews as unbearable as possible. The local authorities did not hide their attempts to limit the number of Jews living in Finland to an utmost minimum. The major problem for Jewish families was the status of the children. The residential permits only applied to former soldiers, their wives and widows. According to the interpretation of the law by Finnish authorities, Jews born and raised in Finland had to leave the country upon coming of age.

Military service was a filter selecting those candidates who could legally stay in Finland. For the Jewish men, the choice was either to join the military or to emigrate. The Jewish daughters avoided deportation, if they married a Jewish soldier who had finished the service in Finland and thus redeemed the residential permit. This is what Rebecka Bensky's family chose to do. At the age of 15 years she married a significantly older, retired soldier, a divorcé from Vilnius by the family name of Bensky – and thus renewed her right to stay in Finland.[27]

In striking contrast to the Scandinavian countries, where the Jews were given full civil rights between the 1850s and the 1870s the authorities did their best to avoid providing any possibilities for Jewish economic activities within the Finnish borders. This decidedly illiberal approach to the Jews collided with the general liberalisation of the Finnish economy in the 1870s. In 1876 the Senate confirmed that the above mentioned trades were the sole ones permitted to the Jews, aiming to keep them on the fringes of the formal economy. Jews could only stay in three cities with a larger military garrison: Helsinki, Turku and Viborg.[28] Without civil rights, Jews were not permitted to hold governmental offices, nor own landed property. Furthermore, any purchase of a business including peddling outside the three cities was forbidden and could lead to deportation from the country. Certainly, there were peddlers of Jewish origin trading in the Finnish countryside, but this was illegal; those who wanted to keep their permit to stay in Finland took a great risk in continuing such activities. As late as 1889, the Finnish Senate introduced a new residence license to the Jews. It gave a temporary right to stay in Finland (for six months at a time) repeating the list of means of gaining a livelihood allowed for the Jews.[29]

Retired soldiers and their families started up small businesses on these premises. The city of Helsinki especially designated Narinkka as the site for Jewish trade in the 1870s. The town of Turku also had its own version of Narinkka.[30] The Bensky made their living at Narinkka. The marketplace consisted of wooden market stalls rented out by the city of Helsinki. [31] The Jewish life of Helsinki converged around the marketplace.

A local newspaper *Hufvudstadsbladet* called the marketplace in 1894 a Jewish Ghetto, and a stain on the reputation of Finland '(…) we have towards the end of the 19th century created a miniature version of the medieval Ghetto in our country, a "Jewish quarter" of a kind that is not to be found among the nations of Western culture.'[32]

There were occasionally rumours mentioning stolen goods connected to the Jewish marketplace, yet generally Narinkka seemed to lack all the connotations to criminality often attached to second-hand markets. The Jewish community was alert to avoid drawing any

Figure 1. Photographed by Roos in 1929. The archives of the City Museum of Helsinki. 'The often-shown pictures taken of Narinkka were part of a conscious project to document the part of Helsinki that was about to vanish into history.

negative attention. An attempt to sell stolen goods by one broker could have caused trouble for the entire community.

The Jewish colony was connected to the nearby Russian military garrisons. The Governor's list for 1915 reported 54 Jews as 'narinkka vendors'.[33] The marketplace had 28 individual stalls and 30 row shops in the halls.[34] Not all vendors at the second-hand marketplace were Jews. About one-fifth of those with rented slots had Russian or Finnish names without any connections to the Jewish community.[35]

By the same token, not all Jews traded at Narinkka. There were musicians serving in the army, medical doctors, military tailors, mechanics and other skilled workers and merchants supplying the army. Nonetheless, all families had a connection to the military base, including occasionally even the rabbi because the military guaranteed religious services for the Jews.[36]

Manufacturing on the larger scale was not allowed for the Jews; but this only applied to the Finnish market. Just like the special permission to live in Finland, guaranteed by the Russian military, orders from the Imperial Army could not be forbidden by the local Finnish authorities.

Around 1900 the authorities in Finland generally accepted the small number of Jews who were born in Finland. The restrictions were never dropped until Finland's independence – the subject was discussed from the 1870s – yet strict observance of the regulations were no longer practised on the local level. The city of Helsinki donated a site for the Jewish community and the synagogue was inaugurated in 1906.[37]

The number of Jews in Finland kept rising, albeit slowly (Table 1). In other words, during the active years of Rebecka Bensky, the growth of the community was modest while the surrounding city had more than quadrupled in size. When Rebecka started her trading activities, Narinkka was located near the Russian military barracks and training field on the outskirts of Helsinki. By the time she retired its location was in practice right in the city centre.

The growth of Helsinki did not just refer to its number of inhabitants. The economy grew as well. In the decades between 1860 and 1914, the Finnish economy grew at a faster rate than the European average.[38] Finland was still extremely poor compared to Western Europe, yet the material living-standards of the workers in Helsinki were improving.[39] Consumption must have led to a constant increase in demand for suits and outfits.

Over the same period, other major social changes shaped Helsinki. As a young wife, Rebecka Bensky moved to a town with a certain linguistic and religious diversity not associated with Finland in later decades. One-fifth of the merchants in the mid-19th century Helsinki had names either of Russian or of northern German origin.[40]

Most of the new inhabitants were workers from the predominantly Finnish-speaking countryside. By the 1910s the most-spoken language in Helsinki and the ethnicity of most names in the business directories were Finnish. Consequently, the Jewish community, with

Table 1. The population of Helsinki and the Jewish community in 1880, 1915 and 1930.

	1880	1915	1930
The Helsinki Jewish community	441	894	1,132
The population of Helsinki	43,000	176,500	241,000
The share of the Jews in Helsinki, %	1.03	0.51	0.47

Sources: OSF: Recensement de la population de Helsingfors 1880, table 11, OSF: Population 1915, 15; OSF Mouvement de la population en 1930, 22; Uudenmaan läänin kuvernöörin Senaatin Siivilitoimituskunnalle laatima luettelo Uudenmaan läänissä asuvista juutalaisista [The Governors's report for the Civil Department of the Senate with a list for Jews living in Uusimaa county], He1, The National Archives of Finland.

their stores located near one another along the streets with the best public transportation lines and with Narinkka, had a more visible role in the urban milieu as suggested by the above numbers.

Urban poverty and upward economic mobility

One constant theme in the accounts written by non-Jewish authors on the Jews of Helsinki in the 19th century is the penury of the community; Helsinki Jews belonged to the sphere of urban poverty: 'the economic standards and living conditions of the poor Helsinki Jews were that of a urban proletariat'.[41] The synagogue of the 1880s was said to be as 'poor and needy' as the entire congregation.[42]

Narinkka, *der yidisher mark* in Yiddish, comes up in the texts written by Helsinki Jews as a kind of folklore.[43] Narinkka had a different meaning for the Jews, who sold their goods, as well as for their (non-Jewish) customers. The way Narinkka is portrayed corresponds well with trades which anthropologist Antony Blok calls infamous' or 'pariah occupations'.[44] These were domains open or specified for social outcasts and ethnic minorities.

Within most memoirs of the past Helsinki, Narinkka had an exotic flavour of 'orientalism' about it.[45] Jews are connected not only to the other side of a class boundary, but also as representing complete otherness and strangeness. One gentile woman recalls visits to the park in her childhood in the 1890s: [In addition to newspaper sales] 'A business of another type took place on the streets of Helsinki without any hullabaloo, yet insistent: "Ma'am has any used clothes?" (…). Most often these Jewish women were on the Esplanade, one was least safe from them on the benches there. As youths we found it so awful to be addressed like that on the street, and I was personally afraid of them and their black, glowing eyes'[46]

Another woman recalls a Narinkka merchant-woman that used to come to buy clothes from their home: She [unlike other peddlers] came through the main door and rang the doorbell:

We called her the Jew-Granny [...]. She was one of those Jews who collected used clothes, bought children's worn and used adult garments, repaired them, and sold them further for a good price. Her store was one of the stalls in the Kamppi square. This place was called 'Narinkka'. The place where the stalls were located was fenced like the souks of the Arabs. This peddler spoke some kind of *judendeutsch*, 'Yiddish-Deutsch', and walked in asking: 'Haben Sie was, gut Frau?'. If mother was unsure, she would assure: 'Na suchen Sie mahl, gut Frau': Mamma found a rag and the haggling started. To get rid of her, Mamma sold the suit for 25 pennies although she had initially asked for one markka, and was decisive that she had nothing else.[47]

Rebecka Bensky was undoubtedly one of the Jews living in the conditions of the urban proletariat. The family had seven children, two of whom died in infancy. In 1891, at the age of 33 years, Rebecka was widowed and left alone with five young children. She continued to work at the marketplace. After a second short marriage that ended in divorce, she married for a third time, this time to a Polish-Jewish soldier, who had lost his wife in 1900 and had two small children.[48] The couple had two more children together. Altogether Rebecka raised nine children while earning her living at Narinkka.

The childhood of Rebecka's eldest and youngest daughters reflected the change in the family's fortunes and the rise in living standards. The oldest daughter Anna was born in 1877.

She grew up in a rented one-bedroom and a kitchen apartment with her parents, siblings, and a maid.[49] Later on when she married – again to a Jewish soldier from Vitebsk, her husband and their new-born daughter also lived in the two-room rented apartment.[50]

In quite a different childhood, Rebecka's youngest daughter Vera, born in 1903, from Rebecka's third marriage, grew up in an apartment with three rooms and a kitchen. Rebecka now owned the apartment herself. Instead of helping at the family stall in Narinkka, Vera stayed at home and took private piano lessons.[51]

In a striking contrast to the dominant narrative of Narinkka, notable upward economic mobility, with parallels to Jewish experience in Central and Western Europe, took place among the Finnish Jews. Swedish, being the language of the middle and upper classes, soon became the predominant language of the community.[52] The family size dropped, the children were educated and, more often, women were stay-at-home mothers although many still had a primary role within the family businesses. The wealthier Jewish families in Helsinki had the life-style of the European Jewish bourgeois with visits to spas, homes in the modern new apartment buildings, piano lessons, bridge and tennis.[53]

The role of Narinkka as consumer market

How could a woman like Rebecka Bensky carry out such an upward turn in her economic mobility in turn-of-the-century Helsinki by selling cast-off clothing? The family story gives credit to Rebecka's thrift, but it also reveals the inner workings of the Narinkka trade: Rebecka managed quite well in her later years, because, as it is explained, 'she ran a small-scale banking business.'[54] Rebecka, together with other Narinkka vendors, accepted pawned goods from people in immediate need of money. While working at Narinkka as a young widow, she also developed the business into ready-made suits.[55]

Both activities are congruent with the literature on early consumer markets in other parts of Europe. Before the rise of the consumer markets of cheap clothing retailers, second-hand trade was the 'fast fashion' of clothing for workers and ordinary people.[56] The customers of second-hand markets were also people with little or no access to formal credit markets. Textiles and clothes were often the most valuable possession that people had. For the ordinary people, textile products were often the only asset that could be easily converted into cash.[57] Due to factory production, the prices of textiles fell considerably. Pernilla Jonsson and Kristina Lilja have analysed the value of clothes as a means of credit by studying the prices of second-hand clothing in the auctions in Sweden.[58] According to the analysis, prices fell during the 19th century, but clothes still held considerable value. While the income gap between Finland and Sweden grew in the 19th century, we can assume that garments in Finland formed at least as important a part of what people owned as they did in Sweden.

Nevertheless, pawning, buying, repairing and selling cast-off clothing alone cannot explain the accumulation among (some of) the Jewish merchants. None of the above is sufficient to explain Rebecka Bensky's ability to raise the living standards of the growing family.

Trade with second-hand goods has practically no barriers to entry and is one of the persistent forms of an informal economy. If trading with cast-off clothing alone could raise one's living standards, there would have been no poverty in Helsinki, let alone any other growing city.

The pawning and hawking of cast-off clothing and the informal exchange of credit and cash binds Narinkka trade to the early modern world, where clothes were inherited, sometimes stolen, repaired and resold.[59] The note in the memoire about Rebecka's other small innovation – imported clothes from St Petersburg – rather indicates a completely new form of textile and clothing business. Anecdotal evidence supporting this notion comes up in the literature on the history of Helsinki as well as the history of the Jews of Helsinki: the Narinkka traders blurred the boundaries between used clothes and new products.[60]

This bears asking: what was the supply of reasonably priced clothing in Helsinki beyond Narinkka. Where else could people buy clothing from in industrialising Helsinki?

The supply of ready-made clothing is derived from a sample of business directories from 1883, 1887, 1895 and 1898. As stated above, the directories provide a scattered evidence of the market. The directory of 1883, for example, omits all female milliners, meaning that the total numbers are not comparable between 1883 and 1887. Some of the tailors or stores were stated to have been in the markets years before appearing in the pages of the directories. Categories between tailors and merchants were fluid. For this reason, distinguishing between artisans or merchants is somewhat arbitrary.

Nevertheless, the directories reflect trends and changes in the markets even though the results must be treated with caution. In Helsinki, the manufacturing enterprises were rather small consumer goods manufactories – some aiming at the lucrative markets of St Petersburg. Large textile mills were located elsewhere in the country.[61]

Helsinki was the commercial centre and what could not be found in Helsinki, was hardly available in other towns of Finland either. Helsinki had agents for sewing machines, imported textiles, as well as those selling Finnish textile products. There was one department store, Stockmann, established in 1862, but it did not have a garment department until the 1930s.[62]

In 1884 there were no stores listed as selling ready-to-wear. Between 1887 and 1898 there seemed to be very few merchants supplying cheaper, ready-made clothes (Table 2). A few of the tailors were listed as having ready-made suits in the store.[63]

Altogether, the supply of garment-related products as represented in the trade directories did not seem to keep pace with the growth of the city. The number of tailors and furriers in the business directories was growing slowly, but hardly enough for supplying the increased demand for outfits that must have followed due to the growth rate of the city. The supply of clothing in Helsinki was based on skilled bespoke production and small-scale manufacturing. What seemed to be lacking was clothes' dealers or clothes' retailing shops selling reasonably priced clothing. Hence, Narinkka must have been an essential resource for the

Table 2. Number of textile and garment merchants and artisans in the Business directories for Helsinki in selected years and population of Helsinki (1883–1898).

Textiles, yarns	4	14	29	44
Shirts, corsets, underwear	3	6	14	13
Hats and furs	6	7	14	14
Milliners	Na	17	25	23
Tailors	24	43	70	60
Ready-made clothing	Na	3	6	9
Total	37	90	158	163
Population of Helsinki (in thousands)	43	51	75	80

Sources: Finlands Handels-kalender af Victor Forselius for 1883, 1887, 1895, and 1898.

new inhabitants, who were mostly workers from the countryside packing into the same quarters where Helsinki Jews and other urban poor were said to live.[64] In a northern town like Helsinki, finding warm winter clothes was not a matter of consumption preferences but a must. Above all, it was one of the very few places where one could walk in and look at the low-priced products without obligations to buy anything.

If we look at the supply of clothing in late-19th century Helsinki, bearing in mind the increasing number of workers, who were moving into the city, the anecdotal evidence that Jews at Narinkka started to import ready-to-wear products from St Petersburg appears in a new light. It is one thing – and not unusual in the world of second-hand trade – to mix new products with used products. It is yet another thing to be among the very first ones to introduce this innovation to growing consumer markets.

Capturing a market niche

The first Jewish tailor, Weintraub, appeared in the business directories from 1987.[65] In 1898, three ready-to-wear sellers, one hat factory owner and two tailors were Jewish.[66]

These were now registered firms, which can be traced in the Finnish Trade Register. The files of the pre-1918 companies sometimes include a paragraph made using a different kind of a pencil, adding that the purpose of the company was 'to sell used clothes and similar activities'. In these entries, 'used clothes' has been added later to be on the safe side.[67]

Since Jews were only permitted to make a living by small-scale trade with a limited range of choice, they registered their businesses as a second-hand dealer, regardless of the type of business they were engaged with in reality.

In practice, most of the second-generation Jewish families of the 1890s and 1900s were engaged with the clothing trade. Yet they no longer did this at Narinkka but, rather, in their own shops along the shopping streets, or by ready-to-wear manufacturing.

In 1909, the opening of a non-Jewish ready-to-wear store had news value in Helsinki. The article of the Business bulletin Kauppalehti (May 12, 1909) also explains why Finns, thus far, had to buy such goods from the Jews:

> It is true that they [the Jews] have inborn qualifications for fraud, and they indeed have gained their practical training in those ambiguous Narinkka stands, the customer knows that the cheap prices are a trick, yet the lack of any domestic [that is non-Jewish] options makes one visit these stores anyway. A ready-made suit is always a more economical alternative than that of a tailor-made suit – and where else could one buy [it] if not from the Jews, because the tailors only keep a limited selection on sale. Their warehouses especially lack clothes for women and children. (…)[68]

In the early 1900s, the main shopping streets of Helsinki had Jewish-owned stores opened side-by-side. Some of them were small and modest, but the most successful definitely belonged to the most notable ones, which bore importance for the development of the Finnish garment industry and trade. Considering how few Jewish families there were in Helsinki, they were well represented among the manufacturers by the beginning of the 20th century.

The business directory of 1913 announced 25 stores selling ready-to-wear products, of which 20 firms were Jewish-owned. These numbers do not include the trade on the Narinkka marketplace.

Table 3. Textiles, garments, ready-to-wear and accessories in Helsinki in the Business directory for 1913.

Product group	Number of firms in selected categories	'Jewish firms'	%
Ready-to-wear	25	20	**80.0**
Custom-made bespoke tailoring	80	1	**1.3**
Textiles, yarns	88	0	**0.0**
Hats and caps (manufacturers and retailers)	24	3	**12.5**
Furs (Manufacturers and retailers)	5	1	**20.0**
Total	222	25	**11.3**

Source: Mercators handels- och industrikalender 1913–1914, 'Branch section', 381–752.

Why were the non-Jewish counterparts so slow in doing what the Jewish second-hand dealers and their offspring did? Why did they not notice the increased consumer demand for ready-made clothing and provide for such products on sale? If explaining how an entrepreneurial innovation is born is challenging, it is nearly impossible to determine why and how business opportunities are missed.

The manufacturing census of Finland draws attention to the contemporary social position given towards the dress trades and manufacturing. How data and material is organised reflects what has been considered important and worth nothing, but the given classification also reflects the understanding between relations and hierarchies. Before the industrial mass production of clothing, ready-to-wear referred to the small scale production of ready-made stocks by an artisan.[69]

The title of the products of the ready-to-wear industry in the Finnish census from 1884 to 1908 manifests relics of the cultural position of dress-making; The census contained 13 'sections' divided further into classes and subclasses. The textile industry occupied class 7. This was a category with the large wool and cotton mills that were among the most dynamic and fastest growing industry of late-19th century Finland. The cotton mills were the second largest industrial employer after saw mills.[70] Also hosiery and stockings were considered as textile manufacturing. Tailoring, shirts, hats, caps, accessories were, in contrast, treated as completely different products. These belonged to the class category titled as 'garments and cleaning manufacturing'. Shirt factories, tailors, hat-making firms, furriers and shoemakers were considered to belong to the same class category as barbers, public baths and cleaning.[71] It was only since the reclassification of the Manufacturing census statistics in 1909 that textile and garment manufacturing were combined to successive industrial categories of textile industry (with wool and cotton mills) and garment manufactories.[72]

The skilled tailors and dressmakers, and most likely many of their customers, associated ready-made garments with the rag trade, poor quality and the lower classes. The ready-made suits, cloaks and dresses were not considered as respectable forms of clothing but, rather, as a substitute for second-hand clothing: both were products that can be bought 'off-the-rack' instead of the sell-and-make type of products of bespoke tailoring.[73] With this mindset, ready-made clothing was not considered a part of the modern industrial world but, rather, considered a by-product of cast-off goods, a little extra income for widowed women making a living in cloth selling.

There was another main stimulus of ready-to-wear clothing, which does not appear in any Finnish manufacturing census: the demand for mass-scale clothing of the Russian military outfitting. The early manufacturing censuses did not take into account the production of goods demanded by the military stationed in Finland.[74]

Table 4. Number of ready-to-wear retailers, wholesalers, textile and garment merchants and artisans in the Business directories for Helsinki in 1920 and 1929, and the share of the Jewish-owned companies.

Product group	Number of firms in selected categories (1920)	'Jewish firms'	%	Number of firms in selected categories (1929)	'Jewish firms'	%
Textiles, yarns (wholesalers and retailers)	76	3	4	176	25	14
Ready-to-wear	25	11	44	122	35	29
Custom-made bespoke tailoring	30	3	10	75	7	9
Hats and caps (manufacturers and retailers)	12	5	42	30	5	17
Furs (Manufacturers and retailers)	7	3	43	20	5	25
Total	150	25	17	423	52	12

Sources: Mercators handels- och industrikalender 1920, 361–658; Finlands Handels kalender 1929, 105–232.

Herein were the origins of the transformation from the rag trade into wealthy textile merchants and factory owners. Military workshops were the first clusters of ready-to-wear manufacturing producers. Returning once more to the story of Rebecka Bensky, at the age of 20 years, her daughter Anna married a permitted Jewish soldier, Moses Smolensky (born in Belarus, in 1875).[75] The young couple no longer worked at Narinkka. Instead, Smolensky worked at Seligson's tailoring which had developed into 'a Jewish military tailor industry'. Isak Seligson (born in 1844 in Latvia) was a military master tailor, who produced uniforms for the officers in the Russian military.[76]

Laurence Fontaine has demonstrated, in her work on peddlers and other transient communities, how economic status varied. It is often a mistake to confuse a marginal social status with a low economic status.[77] For skilled Jews in Finland, the Imperial Russian army could provide careers as suppliers, military tailors, and other skilled artisans, who served the military base.[78] The social status of such professional craftsmen and suppliers was not necessarily higher than the lower rank soldiers, but the economic prospects certainly had more potential.

In the tax unit list for the City of Helsinki in 1913, among the 75 largest companies measured by their tax unit, four were owned by Helsinki Jews: M. Skurnik, Pergament & Rung, Pergament & Linder and S.S. Strascheffkskij.[79] The owners of the businesses appeared among the highest taxed men of Finland in 1916.[80] Some of these names can further be tracked to the most prestigious addresses of art-nouveau villas, built in the most appreciated districts of the city in the early 20th century.[81]

The life paths of these Jewish military suppliers explain the astonishing change from the second-hand trade to the highest tax payers of the country. Jehuda Pergament, born as a soldier's son in Turku (Åbo) in 1863, opened a wholesale business in 1893. He supplied military and civilian uniforms for over 50 years, first for the Imperial Russian army, later for the Republic of Finland, especially for the Maritime Administration.[82]

In 1917, after Finland's independence and the end of the First World War, the Russian military garrisons were closed. Moreover, the transition to an independent Finland provided no radical change for these Jewish-owned military manufactories. During the Finnish Civil War (1918), some of the larger military suppliers continued their business with the Finnish army, supplying the side of the Whites in the civil war. Gumpler's *Finlands militär ekipering* [The military outfitter of Finland], for example, originally started up in 1902 and, in the beginning, produced uniforms in modest quantities. These orders grew, notably during the First World War. After the independence of Finland, the company continued to produce uniforms, but now for the Finnish state and civil guard.[83]

After the First World War and Finland's independence the share of the Jews decreased. In 1920, a total of 25 firms could be defined as selling ready-to-wear clothing. The number of Jewish-owned firms among these companies had dropped to 11 firms (Table 4).

By the time Narinkka was closed in 1930, there were 423 companies in the categories of 'garment wholesale and retail, furs, hats, accessories, and textiles', according to the Trade directory for 1929. Some of the Jewish firms had developed into notable textile wholesalers and bespoke fur ateliers. Of those selling ready-to-wear clothing, 35 firms can be recognised as 'Jewish'. The Jewish community was so small that the Jews could by no means 'dominate' the Helsinki clothing market, yet notably many of the stores in the 'garment districts' of the interwar Helsinki were Jewish owned. Narinkka soon transformed into a symbol of bygone times when Jews were social outcasts without civil rights in Finland.

Conclusion: introducing the ready-to-wear in Helsinki

The main argument of this article is simple: the mainly Jewish dealers of Narinkka represent the early stages of the modern garment industry in the industrialising phase of Helsinki. Since most of the new inhabitants were working-class men and women from the countryside with little or no purchasing power, there must have been a constant demand for cheap clothing. Helsinki was an expanding city with unavoidably undeveloped consumer markets. Analysing the business directories, the supply side did not seem to quite follow the growth rates of the city. Cheap ready-made suits, working clothes and outfits were not generally available in the stores of Helsinki at the turn of the 19th and the 20th centuries.

The rise of the modern garment industry with standard-sized ready-to-wear clothing is inevitably one of the markers of a modern, industrialised consumer society. The role reserved for Narinkka has, in contrast, been an antithesis of modernity: a static relic of the past, frozen in time.

The legal frame, within which the Jewish Narinkka trade originally formed, partly accounts for this interpretation. Until 1918, Finland's restrictive Jewish policy was strikingly outdated when compared to legislation in the Scandinavian countries and in Western Europe. The official policy of 19th century Finland was to limit the number of Jews living in the country. All Jews had a link to the Imperial Russian army. Beyond the army, their options for gaining a livelihood were restricted to small-scale trade such as cast-off clothes. Narinkka became a particular Jewish enclave.

Notwithstanding this, how could a little colony of former soldiers, their wives and children fill a gap between the growing demand and the limited supply of cheap clothing? Jewish tailors working for the Imperial Russian garrisons had direct access to the large demands made by the military. The owners of clothing firms and industrialists producing for the military were easily found to be among the most important ones in Finland. Despite their low social status as 'cloth-Jews', some families experienced significant, upward economic mobility. Coming from the poverty-driven working-class districts, these families achieved the middle-class status of the Helsinki bourgeois. How is one to comprehend the inconsistency between the marginal social status allocated to these Jews and the eventual outcome?

In memoires, the story is staged as an insignificant happenstance, with at most a marginal role in the local history. Quite understandably, concepts such as entrepreneurial success implied contradictions for the Jews of Helsinki. The stress has lain on the narrow social position reserved for those Jewish families, who were allowed to stay in Finland. By the 1930s when the marketplace was finally dismantled, the trade was seen as a part of a bygone world, both in terms of the trade itself as well as in terms of the Jewish policy of the Imperial Russian era. Indeed, since the number of Jews in Helsinki remained nearly insignificant, while the city around the community grew rapidly, the visible role of the Jews in the clothing business gradually decreased.

In a scholarly context, both the second-hand trade and the role of the Jews in Helsinki, appear as a part of a broader pattern. Helsinki and its Jewish marketplace appears more as a specific version of the development that has been recollected in the Western European contexts, albeit on a miniature scale and belated, as compared to the 19th century industrial nations. When looking at the history of the development of the modern garment industries, specific features can be found in Helsinki: the blurring of used and new clothes, and larges-cale orders from the military. The role of the Narinkka marketplace in modernizing the Finnish ready-to-wear trade implies another question: Why was this trade specifically left as an ethnic niche for the Jews?

I argue that the very restrictions placed upon Jews provides a glimpse into the norms and social status towards such products and trades in late 19th century Finland. The Narinkka-type of "rag" trade was generally considered with profound contempt. Jews were pushed toward the clothing trade, because it was not seen as a competitive field of economic live-lihood. This may help us to understand why the non-Jewish counterparts were so slow in recognizing the increased consumer demand for ready-made clothing and in putting such products up for sale.

Today second-hand trade is understood as a form of recycling. Before the era of mass-pro-duced clothing, textiles and garments were used as a medium of exchange for people outside the credit markets. By blurring new, ready-made clothes with the cast-off goods, they filled a commercial gap between the growing demand for and scanty supply of reasonably priced clothing in a rapidly growing urban milieu.

In this context, the Jewish widows, selling used clothes may no longer appear as the passive objects of the measures imposed upon them. Rather, one witnesses, instead, entre-preneurs with agency, introducing a new product to the markets – factory-made, stan-dard-sized clothing. The blurring of ready-to-wear with used clothes at Narinkka can thus be seen from two perspectives: on the one hand, it was about an age-old occupation within the boundaries of the formal and informal economy; yet at the same time, the women selling cheap ready-made clothing introduced a new product, the forerunner of the mass-produced fashion industry. Simultaneously, the idea of second-hand as a petty trade usually belonging to the sphere of the early-modern world is updated to 19th-century industrialising Europe.

Notes

1. In Swedish, which was then the dominant language of Helsinki, Narinken. The name is directly derived from Russian *na rynke* – meaning literally 'on the market'. For example, the 1966 Thesaurus entry for the Finnish word Narinkka describes it as a market site, either a market house or a marketplace with wooden stalls, where peddlers sell second-hand clothing and other cast-off goods. *Nykysuomen sanakirja*, 626–627.
2. The debate on Jewish civil rights in Finland started in the 1870s, but it did not result in any changes until the early 1900s. For more details, see, Ekholm, *Boundaries* , 53–59.
3. Lambert, "Cast-Off Wearing Apparell", 1.

4. Green, *Ready-to-wear, Ready-to-work*, 21.
5. Lemire, "The Secondhand Clothing", 157.
6. Lemire, "Peddling Fashion"; Fontaine, Laurence (ed.). *Alternative Exchanges;* Godley, "The Development"; Green, *Ready-to-Wear – Ready-to-Work*.
7. Chapman, "The Innovating Entrepreneurs", 22.
8. Godley, "British and American Clothing Industries", 71.
9. Ahvenainen, and Kuusterä, *"Teollisuus ja rakennustoiminta"*, 254.
10. Kuznets, "Economic Structure"; Godley, *Jewish Immigrant Entrepreneurship*; Mendelsohn, *The Rag Race*; Slezkine, *The Jewish Century*; Green, *Ready-to-wear – Ready-to-Work*.
11. On the literature concerning the Finnish-Jewish history, Ekholm, Muir, and Silvennoinen, "Linguistic, cultural and history-related Studies".
12. Green, *Ready-to-Wear and Ready-to-Work*, 29–31.
13. Helsinki City Archives, Narinkahyror 1918–1930. Rahatoimisto Gy:21.
14. Eliach, *There Once was a World*, 10–11.
15. Ekholm, and Muir, "Name Changes", 176.
16. See for example, Jacobsson, *Taistelu ihmisoikeuksista;* Weinstein, *Minneskrift*, 5.
17. Narinkka-kysymys 1929–1930, 167, The Archive of the Finnish Jews, The National Archives of Finland.
18. *Judisk årsbok för Finland;* of the Jewish family names in Helsinki, see Ekholm, and Muir, "Name Changes".
19. Ekholm, *Boundaries*, 94.
20. Eliach, *There Once Was a World*, 270–271.
21. Lemire, "The secondhand clothing trade", 152.
22. Seligson, *"Vi"*.
23. *Meliza's Genealogy*, 'Rebecka Radsevitsch'. www.amitys.com. (Accessed July 27, 2017).
24. Ekholm, *Boundaries*, 49–50.
25. The Pale refers to the areas consisting of what today are parts of Poland, Belarus, Lithuania and Ukraine in which Jews were allowed to legally reside, Klier, "Pale of Settlement". (Accessed December 21, 2017).
26. Decree 17, Helsingfors, June 30, 1869. *Storfurstendömet Finlands Författningssamling för* 1869.
27. Seligson, *"Vi"*, 56.
28. Muir, *Yiddish in Helsinki*, 19–29.
29. Ekholm, *Boundaries*, 53–59; Fenno-Judaica, ['Medborgerliga rättigheter'].
30. Wassholm, "Handel i marginalen".
31. It was first located in Nikolai Street near the city centre. Hertzberg, *Helsinki herra Hertzbergin silmin*, 152–154.
32. Translated by the author. "Narinken" (*Hufvudstadsbladet* 18 August, 1894). Finland was seeking international acknowledgement during the final years of Imperial Russia and the way the Jews were treated was troublesome for this cause.
33. Uudenmaan läänin kuvernöörin Senaatin Siivilitoimituskunnalle laatima luettelo Uudenmaan läänissä asuvista juutalaisista [The Governors's report for the Civil Department of the Senate with a list for Jews living in Uusimaa county], He1, The National Archives of Finland.
34. Narinkahyror 1918–1930, Gy:21, The Helsinki City Archives.
35. Narinkka-kysymys 1929–1930, 167, The Archive of the Finnish Jews, The National Archives of Finland.
36. Ekholm, *Boundaries*, 69–76.
37. Ekholm, *Boundaries*, 53–59.
38. Hjerppe, *The Finnish economy*, 50–51.
39. Heikkinen, "Major necessities".
40. Alongside the most important merchant houses of Russian origin were merchants from Lübeck. These families easily integrated with the Swedish-speaking bourgeoisie and were often naturalized and absorbed into the local ruling class. Wolff, "Elitinvandring och kosmopolitanism".
41. Åström, *Samhällsplanering och regionbildning*, 279.

42. Hertzberg, *Helsinki herra Hertzbergin silmin*, 152–154. Up until 1906 the synagogue was located in rented properties.
43. Muir, "Jac Weinsteinin Jiddišinkielinen revyy", 145–146.
44. Blok, *Honor and Violence, 44–66.*
45. Åström, *Stadsamhällets omdaning*, 39.
46. Translated by the author. Lüsch, "Barndomsintryck", 62.
47. Translated by the author. Ahde-Kjäldman, *Kotini vuosisadan lopun Helsingissä*, 93–94.
48. Seligson,"*Vi*", 87.
49. Seligson,"*Vi*", 70
50. Seligson,"*Vi*", 108.
51. Seligson,"*Vi*", 81–84.
52. Muir, *Yiddish in Helsinki*, 6–7.
53. Ekholm, *Boundaries*, 89, 105; Ekholm, and Muir, "Name Changes and Visions", 176.
54. Seligson,"*Vi*", 88.
55. Seligson,"*Vi*", 82; 88.
56. Charpy, "The Scope and Structure".
57. Fontaine, "The Exchange of Second-hand Goods", 99.
58. Jonsson and Lilja,"Strategier för krediter".
59. Fontaine, "The Exchange of Second-hand Goods"; Lemire, "The Secondhand Clothing Trade", 153.
60. Hertzberg, *Helsinki herra Hertzbergin silmin*, 152–154; Jacobsson, *Taistelu ihmisoikeuksista*, 104.
61. *Industri-Statistik 1884: Teollisuustilastoa: Tehtaita ja käsityölaitoksia 1884–1908.*
62. Damstén, *Stockmann genom hundra år*, 127.
63. For instance, [non-Jewish] *Stude* (est. 1880) and *Rintala* (est. 1879).
64. Åström, *Samhällsplanering och regionsbildning*, 279.
65. *Finlands Handels-kalender 1887, 39.*
66. *Finlands Handels-kalender 1898*, Pergament (est.1882), Seligson, Katsman & Leffkowitsch, Rubinstein, Skurnik.
67. Helsinki, Public trade registers by the National Board of Patents and Registers, by the name of the owner, The National Archives of Finland.
68. *Kauppalehti* was a Finnish language newspaper with an emphasis on business and economics that regularly published articles on the role of the Jews in the economic life of Europe.
69. Wottle, "Opposing Prêt-à-Porter", 25.
70. *Industri-Statistik 1884: Teollisuustilastoa: Tehtaita ja käsityölaitoksia. Jälkimmäinen osa 1884*, 10.
71. *Industri-Statistik 1884: Teollisuustilastoa: Tehtaita ja käsityölaitoksia: 1884.*
72. *Industri-Statistik 1884: Teollisuustilasto 1909.*
73. Green, *Ready-to-Wear and Ready-to-Work*, 21.
74. *Industri-Statistik 1884: Teollisuustilastoa: Tehtaita ja käsityölaitoksia 1884*, II.
75. Seligson,"*Vi*", 99; *Meliza's Genealogy.* www.amitys.com. Accessed December 7, 2017.
76. Seligson, "*Vi*", 167–168.
77. Fontaine, *History of Pedlars*, 201–204.
78. Ekholm, *Boundaries,* 50.
79. Kovero, "Helsinki liikekeskuksena", 337–342.
80. 'Skurnik', 'Rung', 'Pergament', 'Rubinstein', 'Kotschack' and 'Gumpler', Suostuntaverojen kantokirjat (1916) [Appropriation taxes], Lääninhallitus, läänien revidioitujen tilien arkisto, The National Archives of Finland. Courtesy of Petri Roikonen.
81. Nenonen & Toppari, *Herrasväen ja työläisten kaupunki*, 27 - 28; 35 - 36.
82. 'Pergament, Jehuda', biografiska avdelningen, Brages Pressarkiv.
83. 'Gumpler, Moses', biografiska avdelningen, Brages Pressarkiv.

ORCID

Laura Katarina Ekholm ⓘhttps://orcid.org/0000-0001-8282-3163

References

Ahde-Kjäldman, Aili. *Kotini vuosisadan lopun Helsingissä [My home in the turn-of-the-century Helsinki].* Helsinki: W. Söderström, 1964.

Ahvenainen, Jorma, and Kuusterä, Antti."Teollisuus ja rakennustoiminta." In *Suomen taloushistoria 2,* edited by Jorma Ahvenainen, Erkki Pihkala and Viljo Rasila, 223–261. Helsinki: Tammi, 1982.

Åström, Sven-Erik. *Samhällsplanering och regionsbildning i kejsartidens Helsingfors [Social planning and the formation of social areas in Imperial Helsingfors].* Helsingfors: Studier i stadens inre differentiering 1810–1910, 1957.

Åström, Sven-Erik. *Stadssamhällets omdaning* [Reforming the Urban Society]. *Helsingfors stads historia IV.* Helsingfors: Helsingfors, 1956.

Blok, Antony. *Honor and Violence.* Cambridge, England: Blackwell, 2001.

Chapman, Stanley. "The Innovating Entrepreneurs in the British Ready-made Clothing Industry." *Textile History* 24, no. 1 (1993): 5–25. Doi: 10.1179/004049693793712222.

Charpy, Manuel. "The Scope and Structure of the Nineteenth-century Second-hand Trade in the Parisian Clothes Market." In *Alternative Exchanges. Second-Hand Circulations from the Sixteenth Century to the Present,* edited by Laurence Fontaine, 127–151. New York: Berghahn Books, 2008.

Damstén, Birger. *Stockmann genom hundra år.* [Oy Stockmann AB]: Helsingfors, 1961.

Ekholm, Laura. *Boundaries of an Urban Minority. The Helsinki Jewish Community from the End of Imperial Russia until the 1970s.* PhD Diss. Helsinki: University of Helsinki, <https://helda.helsinki.fi/bitstream/handle/10138/41009/boundari.pdf>, 2013.

Ekholm, Laura, and Muir, Simo."Name Changes and visions of 'a new Jew' in the Helsinki Jewish community." *Jewish Studies in the Nordic Countries Today. Scripta Instituti Donneriani Aboensis* 27, (2016): 173–188. doi:10.30674/scripta.66574

Ekholm, Laura, Muir, Simo, and Silvennoinen, Oula. "Linguistic, cultural and history-related Studies on Jews in Finland: A Look into the Scholarship in the 21 Century." *Scandinavian Jewish Studies* 27, no. 1 (2016), 43–57. https://journal.fi/nj/article/view/67605. doi:10.30752/nj.67605

Eliach, Yaffa. *There Once was a World. A 900-Year Chronic of the shtetl of Eishyshok.* Boston (MA): Little Brown and Company, 1998.

Fenno-Judaica, [An online collection of the history of the Finnish Jews]. http://fennojudaica.jchelsinki.fi/se/se_about.html Judiska församlingen i Helsingfors, 2009.

Finlands Handels-kalender [Trade directory for Finland]. Åbo: Victor Forselius förlag, 1883.

Finlands Handels-kalender [Trade directory for Finland]. Åbo: Victor Forselius förlag, 1887.

Finlands Handels-kalender [Trade directory for Finland]. Åbo: Victor Forselius förlag, 1895.

Finlands Handels-kalender [Trade directory for Finland]. Åbo: Victor Forselius förlag, 1899.

Finlands Handels kalender *1929* [Business directory for Finland 1929]. Helsingfors: Suomen tukku-kauppiaiden liitto – Suomen vähittäiskauppaiden liitto. Förlags AB för Inhemskt Arbete, 1929.

Fontaine, Laurence. *History of Peddlers in Europe.* Cambridge, England: Polity, 1996.

Fontaine, Laurence, ed. *Alternative Exchanges. Second-Hand Circulations from the Sixteenth Century to the Present.* New York: Berghahn Books, 2008.

Fontaine, Laurence. "The Exchange of Second-hand Goods between Survival Strategies and 'Business' in Eighteenth-century Paris." In *Alternative Exchanges. Second-Hand Circulations from the Sixteenth Century to the Present,* edited by Laurence Fontaine, 97–114. New York: Berghahn Books, 2008.

Godley, Andrew. "Comparative Labour Productivity in the British and American Clothing Industries, 1850–1950." *Textile History* 28, no 1 (1997): 67–80. DOI: 10.1179/004049697793711111

Godley, Andrew. "The Development of the Clothing Industry: Technology and Fashion." *Textile History* 28, no. 1 (1997): 3–10. DOI: 10.1179/004049697793711067

Godley, Andrew. *Jewish immigrant entrepreneurship in London and New York, 1880–1914*: enterprise and culture. Studies in modern history. Basingstoke: Palgrave Macmillan, 2001.

Green, Nancy. *Ready-to-wear and Ready-to-work. A Century of Industry and Immigrants in Paris and New York.* Durham: Duke University Press, 1997.

Heikkinen, Sakari. Major necessities and minor luxuries: Workers as consumer in Finland at the turn of the twentieth century." *Scandinavian Economic History Review* 46, no 1 (1998): 59–70. DOI: 10.1080/03585522.1998.10414679

Hertzberg, Rafaël. *Helsinki Herra Hertzbergin silmin. Kertomus 1880-luvun Helsingin elämästä* [Helsinki in the eyes of Mr Herzberg. A story of Helsinki of the 1880s]. Edited, translated and commented by Rolf Martinson of the original work *Helsingfors för tre hundra år sedan och i våra dagar [Helsingfors 1888]*. Helsinki: Helsinki seura, 2004.

Hjerppe, Riitta. *The Finnish economy 1860–1985: Growth and structural change.* Studies on Finland's economic growth XIII, Bank of Finland. Helsinki: Government Printing Center/Bank of Finland, 1989.

Jacobsson, Santeri. *Taistelu ihmisioikeuksista* [A fight for human rights]. Porvoo: Gummerus, 1951.

Jonsson, Pernilla, and Lilja, Kristina. "Second-hand clothes and textiles as a store of value and medium of exchange in Västerås 1830–1900." *Historisk tidskrift* 135, no 3 (2015): 465–500.

Judisk årsbok för Finland 5690–1930 [Jewish yearbook for Finland 5690–1930]. Helsingfors: Surdus, 1929.

Kovero, Martti. Helsinki liikekeskuksena." [Helsinki as the center of business and trade] In *Helsingin kaupungin historia IV:1 (1875–1918)*, edited by Ragnar Rosén, Eirik Hornborg, Heikki Waris, and Eino Jutikkala, 275–347. Helsinki: Helsingin kaupunki, 1955.

Klier, John. "Pale of Settlement". *YIVO Encyclopedia of Jews in Eastern Europe.* <http://www.yivoencyclopedia.org/article.aspx/Pale_of_Settlement>. YIVO Institute for Jewish Research, 2010. Accessed December 21, 2017.

Kuznets, Simon. Economic Structure and life of the Jews." In Vol. 2 of the *The Jews: their history, culture, and religion*, edited by Louis Finkelstein, 1597–1666. 3rd ed. New York: Walter and Bros. Publisher, 1960.

Lambert, Miles. "Cast-Off Wearing Apparel': The consumption and distribution of second-hand clothing in northern England during the long eighteenth century." *Textile History*, 35, no. 1 (2004): 1–26. doi: 10.1179/004049604225015620

Lemire, Beverly. "Peddling Fashion: Salesmen, Pawnbrokers, Taylors, Thieves and the Second-hand clothes Trade in England s. 1700–1800". *Textile history* 22, no. 1 (1991): 67–82. DOI:10.1179/004049691793711342

Lemire, Beverly. "The Secondhand Clothing Trade in Europe and Beyond: Stages of Development and Enterprise in a Changing Material World, c. 1600–1850." *Textile. The Journal of Cloth and Culture* 10, no. 2 (2012): 144–163. DOI: 10.2752/175183512X13315695424392

Lüsch, Marie. "Barndomsintryck från 1880–1890-talet." [Childhood impressions from the 1880s and the 189s] In *Narinkka 1997*, edited by Minna Lavola, 57–76. Helsinki: Helsinki City Museum, 1997.

Meliza's Genealogy 'Rebecka Radsevitsch'. www.amitys.com. (Accessed July 27, 2017).

Mendelsohn, Adam. *The Rag Race: How Jews Sewed Their Way to Success in America and the British Empire.* New York: New York University Press, 2015.

Mercators, handels- och industrikalender [Mercator's trade and industry directory]. Helsingfors, Mercators tryckeri AB, 1913.

Mercators, handels- och industrikalender [Mercator's trade and industry directory]. Helsingfors, Mercators tryckeri AB, 1920.

Muir, Simo. "Jac Weinsteinin Jiddišinkielinen revyy Helsingissä." [Jac Weinstein's Yiddish language revue in Helsinki] In *Både och, sekä että*, edited by Heidi Grönstrand, and Kristina Malmio, 128–151. Helsingfors: Schildts, 2011.

Muir, Simo. *Yiddish in Helsinki. Study of a Colonial Yiddish Dialect and Culture.* Helsinki: Finnish Oriental Society, Studia Orientalia 100, 2004.

Nenonen, Kaija, and Toppari, Kirsti. *Herrasväen ja työläisten kaupunki* [A City of Gentlefolk and Workers]. Helsingin vanhoja kortteleita 2. Helsinki: Helsingin Sanomat, 1983.

Nykysuomen sanakirja [Dictionary of Modern Finnish], L-R, Porvoo: WSOY, 1966.

Seligson, Miriam."Vi" En släktkrönika ["Us". A Family Chronicle], (Unpublished manuscript) Courtesy of Laila Takolander and Leo Bensky, Helsingfors, 1981.

Slezkine, Yuri. *The Jewish Century.* Princeton University Press: Princeton, 2004.

OSF [Official Statistics of Finland]. XVIII *Industri-Statistik: Fabriker och handtverkerier 1884* [Industrial statistics: factories and manufacturers], Part II. Helsingfors: Statistical Office of Finland,1887.

OSF [Official Statistics of Finland]. XVIII Industristatistik 1909 [Industrial statistics] Helsingfors: Statistical Office of Finland, 1911.

OSF [Official Statistics of Finland]. Recensement de la population de Helsingfors 1880. [Helsinki: Statistical Office of Finland, 1882].

OSF [Official Statistics of Finland]. Väestösuhteet Suomessa 1915. Helsinki: Statistical Office of Finland, 1917.

OSF [Official Statistics of Finland]. Mouvement de la population en 1930. Helsinki: Statistical Office of Finland, 1931.

Wassholm, Johanna." Handel i marginalen. Den judiska småhandel och lokalsamhället i Åbo i slutet av 1800-talet [Trade in the margin: Jewish small trade and the local community in Turku in the late 19th century]." *Historisk tidskrift för Finland* 102, no. 4 (2017): 589–617.

Weinstein, Jac. *Minneskrift till 50 –årsdagen av Judiska församlingens i Helsingfors synagogas invdging den 30 augusti 1956, 16* [A Chronic composed to celebrate the 50th anniversary of the Helsinki synagogue, part I and II], unpublished manuscript. Archive of the Finnish Jews, The National Archives of Finland.

Wolff, Charlotta. "Elitinvandring och kosmopolitism i 1800-talets Finland." [Elite migration and Cosmopolitanism in the 19th Century Finland] In *Mångkulturalitet, migration och minoriteter i Finland under tre sekel*, edited by Charlotta Wolff and Mats Wickström, 105–127. Helsingfors: SLS, 2016.

Wottle, Martin. "Opposing Prêt-à-Porter: Mills, Guilds and Government on Ready-made Clothing in the Early Nineteenth-Century Stockholm." *Scandinavian Economic History Review* 56, no. 1 (2008): 21–40. DOI: 10.1080/03585520801948500.

Shylocks to superheroes: Jewish scrap dealers in Anglo-American popular culture

Jonathan Z. S. Pollack ⓘ

ABSTRACT

For centuries, Jewish entrepreneurs have worked in the second-hand goods economy. Closely allied with pawnbroking, dealing in second-hand goods made it possible for Jews, often forbidden from owning land or joining craft guilds and unions, to earn a living in much of Europe. As Jews left eastern and central Europe for England, the British Commonwealth, and the United States, they took their knowledge of second-hand goods with them and built on established peddlers' networks to create businesses that dealt in scrap materials like metals, paper, rags, and hides. From that foundation, Jewish scrap dealers came to deal in military surplus, used and new furniture, and auto parts. Although underappreciated and obscured in the present day, in the nineteenth and twentieth centuries, the figures of Jews who dealt in second-hand goods loomed large enough to appear in popular culture in literature, on stage, and on screen, both films and television. Even comic books – a literary genre shaped by Jewish entrepreneurs and artists – got into the scrap.

1. Introduction

In 1976, DC Comics introduced Ragman, a hero whose magical suit of rags enabled him to fly, absorb bullets, and dispatch villains with super strength. Created by Joe Kubert and Robert Kanigher, veteran comic creators who are better known for their characters Sgt. Rock, Hawkman, and Wonder Woman, Ragman is Vietnam War veteran Rory Regan, reluctantly working in his father's scrap yard, unable to find other work as he makes a slow and unsteady readjustment to civilian life. In the comic's 1991 reboot, Ragman is suddenly Jewish: the cover of the first issue boasts the legend, 'FROM THE ASHES OF THE WARSAW GHETTO TO THE BACK ALLEYS OF GOTHAM CITY … THE TATTERDEMALION OF THE OPPRESSED RISES AGAIN …'[1]

Why does Ragman's Jewishness matter? What explains this Jewish superhero's scrap-yard roots? Ragman actually was the most over-the-top conflation between Jews and rags, and other scrap materials, in American culture, a culmination of a process that had begun over a century before. Even before Jewish rag-collector characters appeared in popular fiction, theater, film, and comics, these archetypes showed up in English writers from Ben Jonson to Charles Dickens.[2]

However, the history of Jewish rag and scrap dealers in North American culture is not a static one. It follows the history of antisemitism and Jewish stereotyping across a hundred years – from Jews as otherworldly and *sinister* to otherworldly but *tough*. Where second-hand goods in other contexts can be seen as markers of subcultural or specifically genderqueer identity, Jewish scrap stereotypes follow a trajectory from disrepute to virtue, from weakness to superhuman strength. For Jewish men in the scrap business, which is a virtually 1:1 ratio – few Jewish women have worked in the scrap, surplus, and second-hand industries – pride in the Jewish presence in the scrap industry, symbolized by Jewish scrap-dealer characters, is part of a growing idea of the 'tough Jew,' in stark contrast to earlier Jewish masculine images as milquetoasts, cowards, and geeks of all stripes.[3]

In the late nineteenth century, the increasing Jewishness of the trade in scrap, surplus, and second-hand goods coincided with Populism, a theory of political economy that saw value originating in gold instead of paper money. Populists also tended to be producerist; that is, they believed that value originated in production. In a producerist economic world-view, manufactured goods – whether agricultural or industrial – were 'real' in a way that repurposed goods were not. Paper money, or 'rag' money, then, was not as 'real' as money tied to the price of gold. Concerns about the trustworthiness of Jewish rag dealers partially stemmed from producerist economic theories in this era. Jews did not fare well in an economic system that valued purity (as in gold) and production. In the 1890s, Jews were seen as a race that was not completely white, and therefore 'impure' in the eyes of people who subscribed to populist economic ideas. The 'impurity' of scrap, surplus, and second-hand goods – by definition, things that other people had deemed valueless, and given away to Jewish entrepreneurs or sold to them for rock-bottom prices – transferred to the Jews who dealt in them. The metonymic slide from 'junk' to 'Jews' recurred in North American popular culture for the next hundred years.[4]

2. Jewish dealers in second-hand goods: economic niche and analysis through the nineteenth century

Jewish involvement in the business of second-hand clothing and jewelry goes back to the early modern era, when Jews were often compelled to go into the money-lending business. When desperate creditors pawned their clothes to get money in emergencies and failed to redeem them, Jewish entrepreneurs repaired and resold them. The prevalence of Jewish merchants in the economy of pawning and second-hand goods became a stereotype that crossed the Atlantic in the early nineteenth century. As the Industrial Revolution and the expansion of the British empire continued, second-hand clothing became a critical part of the wardrobes of working people across the British empire, both free and enslaved.[5]

Pawnbrokers and second-hand dealers had unsavory reputations. Pawnbrokers were seen as exploiters of human suffering; in the 19th-century US, anyone who was so economically desperate that they would need to hock treasured family possessions were seen as figures for pity and mercy, not customers to be haggled with. In England during the same era, old clothes and rags were thought to spread tuberculosis and other chronic diseases, and the conflation of illness with immorality gave Jews who dealt in second-hand goods a bad reputation in the era's popular culture. Magazine illustrations, novels, and plays, when featuring Jewish characters, often depicted them as cruel, uncompromising dealers in scrap materials and pawnbrokers.[6]

In addition to their depictions in popular culture, early social theorists also took their shots at Jewish entrepreneurs in the second-hand economy. In the early eighteenth century, Italian physician Bernardino Ramazzini theorized that Jewish predominance in rag and paper recycling led to disease and early mortality. Following the analysis of cultural-studies scholar Jay Geller, Karl Marx, a hundred years of change later, incorporated Ramazzini's conflation of Jews, scrap materials, and disease into his 'On the Jewish Question.' Marx's collaborator Friedrich Engels wrote about the rag business, and Marx's contemporary, the English journalist Henry Mayhew, wrote about the Jewish economic niche of second-hand goods.[7]

3. American Jews and the business of scrap, surplus, and second-hand goods

Peddling was the main economic niche for Jewish men who emigrated from the German-speaking areas of central Europe to the Americas, Australia, and southern Africa in the mid-nineteenth century. Jews occasionally peddled in Europe, so the job was not unfamiliar to new immigrants, but what had changed was peddling's scope. Wholesale merchants advanced clothing, dry goods, and miscellaneous knick-knacks to peddlers, who learned English while cultivating a customer base. Peddlers who saw opportunities in a town on their regular route often partnered with their wholesalers to start general stores, and the presence of several Jewish storeowners in the same town was often the start of an organized Jewish community.

Scrap-dealing changed the peddling equation, and solved one of the main obstacles that peddlers faced. The downside of peddling was the cold-calling. Rural American families often lacked disposable income, and some were downright hostile to peddlers who showed up, unannounced. Asking a customer to buy goods that she was not planning to purchase could be stressful. Dealing in scrap and second-hand materials allowed new immigrants to travel door-to-door and offer to purchase unwanted or discarded goods at minimal prices. In many cases, farm families were eager to give their old papers, rags, and rusted-out tools to scrap peddlers, and even help them load scrap materials onto their wagons and carts.

Like peddling before it, scrap dealers built networks for the supply and distribution of their goods. Collectors with the means to do so bought land near railroads to create yards for storing their scrap materials. A successful scrap yard enabled entrepreneurs to hire more recent arrivals, often relatives and landsmen (people from the same town or region) to collect and sort the scrap materials. By the late nineteenth century, Jewish entrepreneurs who had begun their careers dealing in second-hand clothing in England had built fortunes on exporting such clothing to far-flung Australia and South Africa. In the United States at that time, Jewish peddlers were bartering for and buying used clothing, paper, rags, and disused metal objects, which they then sorted and sold to paper mills, steel mills, or back to the general public.[8]

Although many historians view the late 1800s as the beginning of American consumerism, and the time when Americans began to embrace a 'throw it out' philosophy toward the objects they bought, the market for what we would now call recycled or repurposed goods took off. The clearcutting of many old-growth American forests, coupled with the exhaustion of easy-to-reach mineral resources, meant that paper and steel mills looked for sources of fibres and metals that could be melted down and processed into new paper and steel. Jewish men who were coming to the United States from Europe often had some background in the collection and repurposing of discarded goods, and an ethnic entrepreneurial niche was born.[9]

The ubiquity of Jewish scrap dealers in large and small American cities meant that non-Jews came to associate Jews with second-hand materials. By the time that the American theater troupe known as The Larks published *The Shakespeare Water Cure*, an 1883 burlesque of Shakespeare plays that placed characters from his tragedies at a spa, American audiences would have laughed at the familiar sight of Shylock entering at the start of Act 1 by calling, 'Old clo'es, old hats, here you are, very cheap! Old hats for new ones! Old clo'es for new ones!'.[10]

The literature on Shylock as a synecdoche for Jews, especially on stage, is voluminous. Shylock is ugly, grasping, and unyielding in his pursuit of money. The character of Shylock leapt from the stage to economic life as 'Shylock' became a synonym for 'moneylender' or 'Jewish merchant' of any sort during the 19th and early 20th centuries.[11] The Larks' portrayal of Shylock as an 'old clothes man' indicates that audiences of that era would have been familiar enough with Jewish second-hand dealers to make the quick metonymic slide from Shylock to 'old clo'es!'

Other rag dealers continued to grace the American stage in the early twentieth century. As part of that era's vogue for humor grounded in ethnic stereotypes, actors Frank Bush and David Warfield portrayed Jewish characters in vaudeville, alongside Irish and Black characters. Rag dealers, pawnbrokers, peddlers, and other 'Stage Jew' types, as depicted by actors like Bush were often 'losers,' characters who earned laughs as the butt of others' jokes. At this early stage of Jewish characters in American drama, plays like Harry Lee Newton's *Second-Hand Man* (1903) used Jewish proprietors' stores full of cast-off merchandise as clues to their characters' moral corruption.[12]

The stage-Jew rag-dealer character specifically spilled over into characterizations of Jewish entrepreneurs who were beginning to enter the movie business. While some film pioneers, like Louis B. Mayer, actually worked in the scrap business before coming to Hollywood, advertisements from the Edison-led studio trust used the well-known connection between Jews and scrap to argue against their rivals. For example, in a 1911 advertisement in *The Billboard*, a leading entertainment-industry trade magazine, Edison's General Film Brokers argued, under the headline 'JEALOUS':

> Just because we had the capital and were clever enough to secure at sacrifice prices, a fine, big lot of Films That So-called Brokers Could Not Buy [,] the report is being circulated *by the junk dealer* that we handle stolen goods, just because he thinks our low prices will injure his business. He ought to know better than to circulate such scandal – it's boosting our business every day. [Emphasis in original.][13]

In this and related messages in the early 1910s, the Edison trust alternatively used and inverted the stereotype of the junk dealer. The trust stated that they beat scrap dealers at their own game – acquiring films at 'sacrifice prices' and evading claims that they were actually fencing stolen merchandise. Clearly, the grasping, unethical 'stage Jew' had bolted the stage and entered the business of film itself.

The 'stage Jews' of this type began to appear less often on stage in the 1910s, due to several factors. Along with the National Association for the Advancement of Colored People and the Ancient Order of Hibernians, an Irish mutual-aid society, Jewish organizations began to see that discrimination against Jews in employment, recreation, and society was related to derogatory images of Jews on stage and screen. The Anti-Stage Jew Vigilance Committee, organized in Chicago in 1913, brought together representatives from B'nai B'rith, the National Council of Jewish Women, and the Anti-Defamation League to protest such images. This group had some success in banning or censoring derogatory rag dealers and other stage Jews in Chicago; in the late 1910s and early 1920s, fewer 'Jew comics' graced the stage with their portrayals of Jewish scrap dealers. As more Jews began writing, producing, and distributing films, outwardly Jewish characters became less common, especially if they worked in 'dirty work' industries like scrap and second-hand dealing.[14]

Although Jewish rag dealers made fewer appearances in 1920s films, two features from 1925 stand out. The films *Old Clothes* and *The Rag Man* both starred veteran Jewish actor Max Davidson as rag dealer Max Ginsberg and Jackie Coogan as Tim, an orphan who works for Ginsberg. Although Davidson indulges in the kinds of 'stage-Jew' characterizations that offended Jewish audiences a decade earlier, the rag-dealer character is basically sympathetic, allying with other down-trodden types (in this case, an Irish-named orphan) and eventually becoming wealthy; in *The Rag Man*, the characters leave the rag business to open an antique store, a more respectable (and presumably lucrative) way of dealing in second-hand goods.[15]

4. From scrap to surplus: second-hand dealers and the by-products of World Wars

Due to the United States' late entry into World War I, American military capacity was ramping up at the exact moment that US forces helped rally the Allied forces to victory. Coupled with the traditional American impulse to muster out troops and restore the size of the military to pre-war levels, the end of the war meant that there were warehouses full of equipment, vehicles, and armaments, as well as entire military bases, which were now superfluous. As American voters elected representatives who pledged a return to pre-war 'normalcy,' what would happen to all that stuff?

Charles H. Lipsett, a pioneering publisher of scrap-industry trade magazines, worked for the Quartermaster General's office of the War Department during World War I. Applying his industry knowledge to the problem of postwar military surplus, he developed a system of advertisements and auctions that brought in millions of dollars in revenue to the War Department. A group of 'Army-Navy stores,' initially run by the Federal government, later sold to private entrepreneurs, who often had roots in other areas of the second-hand economy, brought military surplus canteens, tents, and other outdoor gear to civilian customers throughout the United States, and Army-Navy stores continued to be part of the Jewish economic niche in second-hand goods. After World War II, the pattern repeated itself, but given the relative size of that war, military surplus became an even bigger part of the American economy in the 1940s.[16]

The end of World War Two saw a new kind of Jewish scrap dealer on the stage and screen. Garson Kanin and Ruth Gordon's *Born Yesterday*, a satire of postwar American politics, featured Harry Brock, described early in the play as a 'big man. Ran a little junk yard into fifty million bucks, with no help from anyone or anything – except maybe World War II.'[17] When Brock enters a few pages later, Kanin and Gordon's stage directions describe him as 'a huge man in his late thirties. Gross is the word for him.'[18] As the play unfolds, it becomes clear that Brock is in Washington to set up a cartel that will corner the postwar market for the scrap metal left behind on European battlefields.

Clearly, Harry Brock is a new kind of scrap dealer. He is not identified as Jewish, but Kanin, who grew up in Rochester, New York, would have grown up with characters like him. Kanin claimed that Brock was inspired by Harry Cohn, the chief of Columbia Pictures. Broderick Crawford, who played Harry Brock in the 1950 film adaptation of the play, claimed that he based his character on Louis B. Mayer, the most famous scrap-dealer-turned-film-magnate. Even though Harry Brock was, for audiences in the know, a recognizably Jewish type, the fact that his Jewishness is never directly addressed in the play ensured that it did not fall victim to the censorship of earlier portrayals of Jewish scrap dealers. The play's producer, Max Gordon, opposed bringing in the Jewish comedian Judy Holliday to play Brock's girl-friend, on the grounds that 'This show is *by* Jews and *for* Jews, but it can't be *with* Jews!'.[19]

Harry Brock also stands out, as Jewish scrap dealers often talked about their trade in euphemistic ways at this time. The terms 'metals dealer' and 'metals broker' had become commonplace by this time, but in Kanin's play, Brock does not go along with this trend; he calls himself 'the top man in my racket … over twenty-five years … Junk. Not steel. *Junk*.'[20] Actual scrap dealers from this era, in letters to the editor, in trade magazines, and other contexts, were always *scrap* dealers. Brock's line indicates a kind of throwback character, who would have come across as over the top to a contemporary 1950 audience.[21]

5. Scrap Dealers as White Ethnics and Tough Jews: 1970s–1990s

The decade of the 1970s saw white people take a renewed interest in their European ethnic identities. In many cases, the so-called 'white ethnics' represented a counterpoint to the New Left and subsequent movements for social change that came with it. Celebrating one's European ancestors was a way to appeal to traditional values while opposing more radical challenges to the status quo. In an American Jewish context, examples range from the early neoconservative writings in *Commentary* and other magazines of political opinion. A kind of 'toughness' comes through in many of the *Commentary* articles, particularly in pieces like Norman Podhoretz's 'My Negro Problem … And Ours,' which asserts a tough response to African-American assertions of Black Power.[22]

In this broader context, American (and Canadian) Jewish authors reclaimed the scrap dealers of old. Part of this may have been due to the nature of the scrap industry, as postwar prosperity gave way to consolidation and corporatization. The evolution of the scrap industry in the 1960s meant that many of the small-scale Jewish scrap dealers had left the business. Sons (again, due to the masculinist nature of this field) of scrap dealers were less likely to take over their fathers' businesses as opportunities opened in the professions and academia. The tense, boom-and-bust nature of the business prompted some scrap dealers to urge their children to find other careers.[23]

The Montreal-based novelist Mordecai Richter, himself the son of a scrap dealer, included a scrap dealer in his best-known work, *The Apprenticeship of Duddy Kravitz*. Richter's novel, relatively obscure at the time of its initial publication in 1959, became better known in 1974 as a result of its successful film adaptation. In the film and novel, the title character produces an avant-garde film of a scrap-dealer's son's bar mitzvah. Cohen, the scrap-dealer figure, is the CEO of M. Cohen, Metal Merchants. He is on the executive board of the Reform temple which comes across as ridiculous in the film and in Richler's description of it. At the bar mitzvah itself, Cohen's father, described as 'an old rag peddler,' is uncomfortable with the church-like setting that his son clearly prefers. The ridiculous film culminates with the narrator intoning Shylock's 'I am a Jew; hath not a Jew eyes ...' speech from Shakespeare's *Merchant of Venice*. Cohen seems completely unaware of this reference to the classic source of anti-semitism; instead, he is entranced by seeing his family and friends on screen, thinking, 'it's worth it, every last cent or what's money for ...'[24]

Scrap dealers show up in other Richler writings. For Richler, the profession represents a middle way between the peddling and sweatshop work of his grandfather's generation and his cohort's entry into academia, big business, and the professions. Trying to get through a period of writer's block, Richler writes, 'Your father had to be out at six every morning, driving to the junk yard in the sub-zero dark, through Montreal blizzards. You work at home, never at your desk before nine, earning more for a day's remembered insults than your father ever made, hustling scrap, in a week.'[25] In 1941, when refugees were able to leave Canadian camps to settle in Montreal, Richler recalls his father eagerly awaiting their arrival:

> My father, who had never had anybody to condescend to in his life, was expecting real greeners with sidecurls. Timorous innocents out of the shtetl, who would look to him as a master of magic. Canadian magic. Instead, they patronized him. A mere junk dealer, a dolt. The refugees turned out to speak better English than we did, as well as German and French.[26]

In his semi-autobiographical *Son of a Smaller Hero*, Wolf Adler, a scrap dealer, dies when he races into his office, which is on fire. When the fire department exhumes him from the rubble, he is holding an open box, which contains some fragments of Torah scrolls. Adler is memorialized as a hero for trying to save the scrolls, but his son, the novel's protagonist, discovers that his father's brother had set the fire, and that his father also thought that the box had cash in it. Like *Born Yesterday*, the novel also plays with wartime profiteering; a scrap dealer is said to have sold scrap to Japan into 1941, after an embargo had been set.[27]

A year after *The Apprenticeship of Duddy Kravitz*, another Montreal-set film treated early twentieth-century scrap dealers nostalgically. Paul Allan's *Lies My Father Taught Me* centers on flashbacks of David, the narrator, and his relationship with his grandfather. Haggling, whether with people looking to sell their old clothes, or with second-hand-shop owners looking to buy them, is treated nostalgically. In some scenes, dealing in second-hand clothes precedes the grandfather's magical stories; in others, the grandfather's bargaining is interspersed with conversations about family. When the narrator's family moves to a better-off neighborhood, David's desire to remain near his grandfather is interspersed with the cry of 'Rags, clothes, bottles!' that the pair called out as the grandfather made the rounds of Montreal's Jewish neighborhoods.[28]

The most famous scrap dealer of the 1970s, however, was not Jewish. Fred Sanford, the lead character of the sitcom *Sanford and Son*, often comes up in the discussion of scrap dealers and popular culture. The show, based on the British series *Steptoe and Son*, featured Redd Foxx as a scrap dealer in Los Angeles. Sanford's yard, run with his son Lamont, was a return to the old-style 'junk shop' – the set features random car parts in the yard and second-hand goods in varying stages of repair inside. The nearly all-Black cast has led some observers to believe that by the 1970s, scrap dealing was a primarily Black economic niche. It was not. For its creator, Norman Lear, setting a TV show with a nearly all-Black cast in a junkyard, was a way of showing a historic Jewish connection to working-class people of all backgrounds, in line with Lear's liberal political philosophy.[29]

So, why talk about *Sanford and Son* here? By 1975, the show's fifth season, *Sanford and Son* was in a state of turmoil. Star Redd Foxx feuded with the show's (primarily Jewish) producers over characters' dialogue, casting choices, and even the design of his dressing room.

In a fascinating bit of meta-comedy, the 'Steinberg and Son' episode, which aired on 10 October, featured an alternative-universe sitcom, in which Max Steinberg (played by Borscht Belt comic Lou Jacobi) bawls out his son Murray and his rival, Aunt Ethel, enters with the same greeting employed by Molly Goldberg on her sitcom back in the 1950s.[30]

The underlying theme of the episode seems to have been 'making things right.' In response to criticism that Jewish writers could not write believable dialogue for Black characters, 'Steinberg and Son' writer Bernie Taub (whose name is an amalgam of the [Jewish] screen-writers Bernie Orenstein and Saul Turteltaub) turns out to be Black. Fred Sanford, who threat-ens to sue the network for appropriating his story, sees the show cancelled. And of course, in the alternative universe of 'Steinberg and Son,' the junk dealers are reassuringly Jewish.[31]

6. Jewish pride in comics and scrap

Talk of alternative universes prompts us to look at superhero comics in the 1970s. During this same era, thanks in part to Jewish fans of comics, collectors and fans began to discover the Jewish roots of Golden Age comics: the Jewish creators of Superman and Batman, among others; Jewish moguls in comics who ran their empires with a combination of love and exploitation, and faint traces of Jewish mysticism and folktale in the plots of comics them-selves. 1976's *Ragman*, created by Jewish artists Joe Kubert and Bob Kanigher, starred Rory Regan, the son of a junk dealer, who acquires a magical suit of rags that give him immunity to bullets, superhuman strength, and the ability to fly. To reader Leo Keil, Ragman seemed like the perfect opportunity to bring a Jewish hero, based on the Jewish-identified trade in second-hand clothing, to the DC universe.[32]

But that was not to be. In response to Keil's letter to the editor in *Ragman* #3, editor E. Nelson Bridwell replied that 'If Rory was meant to be Jewish, he would have a Jewish name,' seemingly dismissing Keil's reading of the character. The question of Regan's ethnicity was moot within a year; the original *Ragman* lasted just five issues.[33]

However, in 1991, DC decided to reboot *Ragman*. The cover of the first issue makes his new origins clear: 'From the ashes of the Warsaw Ghetto to the back alleys of Gotham City … the Tatterdemalion of the oppressed rides again …' The issue goes on to reintroduce Rory Regan, who works in his father's combination rags/junk/pawn shop. The store, called 'Rags'n'Tatters,' brings together three strands of the association between second-hand/scrap goods and Jewish merchants. In Rory's waking nightmares (in line with the first series, Regan is a Vietnam veteran coping with PTSD), he sees the Hebrew word for truth, 'emet,' which is also the word inscribed on the forehead of the mythical Golem, a homunculus made of clay who was said to have saved the Jews of Prague from attacks. The issue's back page, entitled 'The Last Neighborhood,' points up the consistent sticking-up-for-the-underdog in the orig-inal *Ragman* and in the rebooted series. Identifying Jewish scrap dealers with downtrodden social groups harks back to *Sanford and Son*, and Max Davidson's rag-dealer characters. The page reprints part of the original letter that pointed to Ragman's Jewish origins, and asserts that the new Ragman has 'powers heavily rooted in the Kabbala,' the esoteric writings of Jewish mysticism.[34]

The second issue of *Ragman* features more Jewish allusions. As Ragman prepares to throw a villain off a roof, the villain pleads for his life, saying, 'Let me go!! I didn't do anything! An' … an' if I did, then I'm sorry.' Ragman glares at him for one panel and then throws him off the roof, killing him. As the man falls, Ragman wonders to himself, 'The dying man's final words give me pause. He said that he was sorry. True repentance requires acknowledgement of sin … and he knew not what he had done. And now … never will. Is there something I could have done differently? [...] Am I sorry?' In this passage, Ragman grapples with the issues of blame and repentance in Talmudic fashion; he is troubled that he may have killed someone who was possibly, at the last minute, genuinely sorry and was not sure why he was being punished. Toward the end of the issue, Rory Regan sees the word 'emet' in the Ragman suit, and the final, full page panel introduces his spiritual master – a rabbi.[35]

Ragman #3 goes all-out on the character's backstory, leading a guided tour of four hundred years of Jewish history. We learn that the same rabbi who created the Golem of Prague created the magical suit of rags, and that the suit's power comes from the evil souls of the people killed by the wearers of the suit over time. This concept resembles the Jewish mystical idea of using the 'yetzer hara,' or humans' inclination to do evil, for good. As the unnamed rabbi continues the origin story, we learn that Rory's father, Gerry Regan, was actually Jerzy Reganiewicz in Poland, so connecting his apparently Irish name with his Jewish background. We further learn that the elder Reganiewicz led the Warsaw Ghetto uprising, after which the suit took him away from Poland, as the suit goes to where people need hope, and the fighters in the Warsaw Ghetto had lost it. Finally, we learn that the rabbi has created another Golem.[36]

In *Ragman* #4, Rory works the counter at the pawnshop, and turns down a plea to buy jewelry from his first customer. The customer, a red-haired gent who greets Rory with a 'Top o'the morning to ya, pal!' gets rejected when Rory suspects that he's trying to fence stolen goods. Rory's refusal to take the stolen goods matches the efforts that Jewish pawn shop owners made to distance themselves from fencing operations, and the customer's Irish stereotyping recalls the intertwined history of Jews and Irish in pawn and scrap businesses – Irish entrepreneurs moved into pawnshops as Jews moved out, and Irish entrepreneurs pioneered the scrap businesses that Jews began to operate at the same time, back in the late nineteenth century. Furthermore, both the Irish customer and the rabbi, who appears in the last panel to ask, 'Rory, why wouldn't you sell to that nice boy his menorah [*sic*]?' recall nineteenth century caricatures of stage Irish and stage Jews.[37]

After the copious amounts of Jewish backstory in the previous issues, the fifth and sixth issues of *Ragman* have less connection to Jewishness. We learn that DC editor Bill Kaplan worked in a scrap yard prior to breaking into the comics business, and in the strip itself we meet a present-day Golem, who is acquiring self-consciousness after 40 years of wandering, as in the Exodus story. We also see Ragman emerging as a champion of Gotham City's underclass, in contrast to the upper-class, police-connected Batman.[38]

In the back page column in issue 7, editor Bob Kahan gets into a dispute with letter-writer Mark Lucas. Lucas, reacting to the Holocaust-era setting in much of issue #3, asks, 'Must every story dealing with [Judaism] hark back to World War II?' Lucas appreciates the rabbi character but urges the DC team to present more three-dimensional Jewish characters. Kahan defends the Holocaust orientation of that issue, and maintains that Ragman is an accurate portrayal of contemporary Jewish ideas, demonstrated by Regan's/Ragman's commitment to social justice, as he defends his downtrodden neighborhood from drug dealers and the predatory real estate magnate who is trying to drive property values down in order to build an ambitious mega-development.[39]

Ragman #8 ends the mini-series. As the rabbi leaves Gotham City, flying to Tel Aviv to settle in Israel permanently, Ragman battles Batman. In the climactic final panel, the residents of Regan's neighborhood surround their tatterdemalion superhero, daring the Caped Crusader to hurt them in order to get to Ragman. As the series ends, Ragman exemplifies the connection between Jewishness and outsider status.[40]

Ragman has subsequently turned up in other DC comics, and the Jewish angle has remained strong and surprisingly coherent. In Batman #552, from 1998, Ragman kills a Nazi skinhead gang leader (a plotline suggested in the letters in Ragman #8), and the character's roots in Kabbalistic theory are explained by a Rabbi Luria, named for the foremost compiler of Kabbalistic writings. 2007's *Shadowpact 8* reprises Ragman's origin story and implausibly Irish name, and reveals that Ragman's magical suit is really something called 'The Great Collector Artifact,' which, in various forms, has existed since the time of Abraham. 2010's *Ragman: Suit of Souls* one-shot focuses on the relationship between Rory and his father, in the form of a conference between Regan and yet another rabbi, in which Rory wonders why his father was so reticent in his Jewish observance. In this issue, the magical rag suit functions as a symbol for Jewish 'chosenness' and Rory and the rabbi come to see that Gerry Regan did not feel worthy of that burden.[41]

7. Conclusion

From the earliest depictions of Jewish rag dealers on the American stage to the most recent reiterations of Ragman, Jewish scrap dealers are clearly outsiders, marked, in most cases, by their shabby clothing, their unkempt appearance, and their accent. However, from the 1920s onward, their shadiness has been replaced with a nostalgic look back at the good (or bad) old days, and a kind of toughness has emerged as these characters reclaimed and strengthened their connections to Judaism. Jewish scrap dealers in popular culture remain marginal, but essential, players in urban second-hand economies.

Notes

1. For Kubert and Kanigher's career highlights before Ragman, see Fingeroth, *Disguised as Clark Kent*, 21–22, 87, 89, 142–143; for Ragman's origins and powers, see *Ragman* 1:1 (Aug.-Sept. 1976), 3–4, 6–8, 11; for the reboot, see *Ragman* 1 (October, 1991), cover.
2. Mendelsohn, *The Rag Race*, 18–20; Stone, 'Dickens and the Jews,' 225–231.
3. Zimring, *Cash for Your Trash*, 47–48; on nebbishy, effeminate Jewish characters on stage and in film, see Erdman, *Staging the Jew*, 36–39; and Merwin, *In Their Own Image*, 41–45.
4. For the connotations of gold vs. paper money in this period, see O'Malley, *Face Value*, 114–161; for the perceived impurity of scrap materials, see Zimring, *Cash for Your Trash*, 38–41. For a thorough account of the 'metonymic slide,' see Rice, 'The New "New",' 200–212.
5. Woloson, *In Hock*, 1–53; Mendelsohn, *The Rag Race*, 112–133.
6. Mendelsohn, *The Rag Race*, 18–36; Woloson, *In Hock*, 9–19.
7. Ramazzini, *A Treatise of the Diseases of Tradesmen*, 196–200; Geller, *The Other Jewish Question*, 169–211.
8. Zimring, *Cash for Your Trash*, 45–52; Pollack, 'Success from Scrap,' 95–97; Diner, *Roads Taken*, 172–173, 177–179.
9. Pollack, 'Success from Scrap,' 97–99; Zimring, *Cash for Your Trash*, 44–66.
10. The Larks, *The Shakespeare Water Cure*, 6; see also Erdman, *Staging the Jew*, 17–18, for Shylock's villainy throughout the play. Harap, *The Image of the Jew*, 212–214, lists several similar Shylocks in Shakespeare spoofs.
11. For example, see Landa, *The Jew in Drama*, 11–14, 70–85; Friedman, *Hollywood's Image of the Jew*, 16–17; Erens, *The Jew in American Cinema*, 12; Erdman, *Staging the Jew*, 17–39.

12. Erdman, *Staging the Jew*, 75–87, 104–105.
13. For Mayer's early career as a scrap dealer, see Gabler, *An Empire of Their Own*, 82–84. General Film Brokers advertisement, *The Billboard*, 28.
14. Kibler, *Censoring Racial Ridicule*, 116–130, 147–170; for the concept of 'dirty work,' see Zimring, 'Dirty Work'.
15. *Old Clothes*; *The Rag Man*; A synopsis of *The Rag Man* can be found on the Turner Classic Movies site, http://www.tcm.com/tcmdb/title/2048/The-Rag-Man/full-synopsis.html; see also Erens, *The Jew in American Cinema*, 93–94.
16. For World War I, see Lipsett, *U.S. War Surplus*, 9–20; for World War II, Zimring, *Cash for Your Trash*, 96–101; for a less sanguine view of the military-surplus industry in both wars, see Brandes, *Warhogs*, 180–184, 260–262.
17. Kanin and Gordon, *Born Yesterday*, 8.
18. Kanin and Gordon, *Born Yesterday*, 10.
19. Kanin, *Hollywood*, 372–374; Gabler, *An Empire of Their Own*, 300; 'Broderick Crawford Dead at 74; Oscar Winner, TV Series Veteran,' *Variety*, 4, 46.
20. Kanin and Gordon, *Born Yesterday*, 24.
21. Zimring, *Cash For Your Trash*, 70–80.
22. Jacobson, *Roots Too*, 180–195.
23. Zimring, *Cash For Your Trash*, 108–123; Pollack, 'Success from Scrap,' 106–108.
24. Richler, *The Apprenticeship of Duddy Kravitz*, 145–159; *The Apprenticeship of Duddy Kravitz*.
25. Richler, 'A Sense of the Ridiculous,' 59.
26. Richler, 'My Father's Life,' 60–61.
27. Richler, *Son of a Smaller Hero*, 78–79, 149, 216, 222.
28. *Lies My Father Told Me*; in Ted Allan's stage adaptation of the same title, references to the rag-collector's cry appear on pages 7, 49, 53, and 64.
29. For more on Lear's politics, see Buhle, *From the Lower East Side*, 227–229.
30. 'Steinberg and Son'; Vider, 'Sanford versus Steinberg,' 21–29.
31. Ibid.
32. Portnoy and Buhle, 'Comic Strips/Comic Books,' 313–341; *Ragman* 1:1; Leo Keil letter in 'Junk Mail' column, in *Ragman* 1:3 [31].
33. Keil letter, op. cit.
34. Kevin Dooley, 'The Last Neighborhood,' in *Ragman* 1, 30.
35. *Ragman* 2, 18–19, 31.
36. *Ragman* 3, 1–15.
37. *Ragman* 4, 7–8; Woloson, *In Hock*, 71–73.
38. The Golem starts to express his self-consciousness in *Ragman* 5, 20–21. Kaplan's bio appears in the same issue, in 'Inside DC: What *Did* an Editor Do? Part II,' 26. Batman appears in *Ragman* 6, 24.
39. Bob Kahan letters column appears in *Ragman* 7, 25.
40. *Ragman* 8.
41. Ken Altabef letter in *Ragman* #8, 25; Batman 552; *Shadowpact 8* (DC Comics, February 2007); *Ragman: Suit of Souls* (DC Comics, December 2010).

Disclosure statement

No potential conflict of interest was reported by the author.

ORCID

Jonathan Z. S. Pollack ⓘ http://orcid.org/0000-0001-7732-5442

References

Allan, Ted. *Lies My Father Told Me*. Toronto: Playwrights Canada, 1983.

Brandes, Stuart D. *Warhogs: A History of War Profiteering in America*. Lexington, KY: University of Kentucky Press, 1997.

Batman 552. New York: DC Comics, March, 1998.

Billboard, The. April 22, 1911

Buhle, Paul. *From the Lower East Side to Hollywood: Jews in American Popular Culture*. London: Verso, 2004.

Diner, Hasia. *Roads Taken*. New Haven, CT: Yale University Press, 2015.

Edbauer Rice, Jenny. "The New 'New': Making a Case for Critical Affect Studies." *Quarterly Journal of Speech* 94, no. 2 (May, 2008): 200–212.

Erdman, Harley. *Staging the Jew: The Performance of an American Ethnicity, 1860–1920*. New Brunswick: Rutgers University Press, 1997.

Erens, Patricia. *The Jew in American Cinema*. Bloomington: Indiana University Press, 1984.

Fingeroth, Danny. *Disguised as Clark Kent: Jews, Comics, and the Creation of the Superhero*. New York: Continuum, 2007.

Friedman, Lester D. *Hollywood's Image of the Jew*. New York: Frederick Ungar, 1982.

Gabler, Neil. *An Empire of Their Own: How the Jews Invented Hollywood*. New York: Crown Publishers, 1988.

Geller, Jay. *The Other Jewish Question Identifying the Jew and Making Sense of Modernity*. New York: Fordham University Press, 2011.

Harap, Louis. *The Image of the Jew in American Literature*. Philadelphia, PA: Jewish Publication Society, 1974.

Jacobson, Matthew Frye. *Roots Too: White Ethnic Revival in Post-Civil Rights America*. Cambridge: Harvard University Press, 2006.

Lies My Father Told Me. Directed by Ján Kadár. Columbia Pictures, 1975.

Kanin, Garson. *Hollywood: Stars and Starlets, Tycoons and Flesh-Peddlers, Moviemakers and Moneymakers, Frauds and Geniuses, Hopefuls and Has-Beens, Great Lovers and Sex Symbols*. New York: Viking Press, 1974.

Kanin, Garson, and Ruth Gordon. *Born Yesterday*. New York: Viking Press, 1946.

Kibler, M. Alison. *Censoring Racial Ridicule: Irish, Jewish, and African American Struggles over Race and Representation, 1890-1930*. Chapel Hill: University of North Carolina Press, 2015.

Apprenticeship of Duddy Kravitz, the. Directed by Ted Kotcheff. Paramount, 1974.

Landa, M. J. *The Jew in Drama*. London: P. S. King and Son, 1926.

Larks, The. *The Shakespeare Water Cure*. New York: Dick and Fitzgerald, 1883.

Lipsett, C. H. U. S. *War Surplus: Its Source and Distribution, 1917–1924*. New York: Atlas Publishing Co., 1924.

Mendelsohn, Adam D. *The Rag Race: How Jews Sewed Their Way to Success in America and the British Empire*. New York: New York University Press, 2015.

Merwin, Ted. *In Their Own Image: New York Jews in Jazz Age Popular Culture*. New Brunswick: Rutgers University Press, 2006.

O'Malley, Michael. *Face Value: The Entwined Histories of Race and Money in America*. Chicago, IL: University of Chicago Press, 2012.

Old Clothes. Directed by Edward F. Cline. Metro-Goldwyn Mayer, 1925.

Pollack, Jonathan Z. S. "Success from Scrap and Secondhand Goods: Jewish Businessmen in the Midwest, 1890-1930." In *Chosen Capital: The Jewish Encounter with American Capitalism*, edited by Rebecca Kobrin. New Brunswick: Rutgers University Press, 2012, 93–112.

Portnoy, Eddy, and Paul Buhle. *"Comic Strips/Comic Books",* in Paul Buhle, *Jews and American Popular Culture*. vol. 2. Westport: Praeger, 2007.

Rag Man, the. Directed by Edward F. Cline. Metro-Goldwyn-Mayer, 1925.

Ragman. New York: DC Comics, 1976-77, 1991-92.

Ragman: Suit of Souls. New York: DC Comics, December, 2010.

Ramazzini, Bernardino. *A Treatise of the Diseases of Tradesmen, Shewing the Various Influence of Particular Trades upon the State of Health; with the Best Methods to Avoid or Correct It, and Useful Hints Proper to Be Minded in Regulating the Cure of All Diseases Incident to Tradesmen*. London: printed for Andrew Bell, Ralph Smith, Daniel Midwinter, Will. Hawes, Will. Davis, Geo. Stranghan, Bern. Lintot, Ja. Round, and Jeff. Wale, 1705.

Richler, Mordecai. *Son of a Smaller Hero*. London: Purnell and Sons, Limited, 1955.

Richler, Mordecai. *The Apprenticeship of Duddy Kravitz*. reprint ed. Toronto: McClelland and Stewart Limited, 1969.

Richler, Mordecai. *"A Sense of the Ridiculous"*, in the Great Comic Book Heroes and Other Essays. Toronto: McClelland and Stewart, 1978.

Richler, Mordecai. *"My Father's Life"*, in Home Sweet Home: My Canadian Album. New York: Alfred A. Knopf, 1984.

Shadowpact 8. DC Comics, February 2007.

"Steinberg and Son" episode, *Sanford and Son*. Directed by James Sheldon, NBC-TV, first aired October 10, 1975.

Stone, Harry. "Dickens and the Jews." *Victorian Studies* 2, no. 3 (March, 1959): 223–253.

Variety, April 30, 1986.

Vider, Stephen. "Sanford versus Steinberg." *Transition* 105, no. 105 (2011): 21–29.

Woloson, Wendy A. *In Hock: Pawning in America from Independence through the Great Depression*. Chicago, IL: University of Chicago Press, 2009.

Zimring, Carl. "Dirty Work: How Hygiene and Xenophobia Marginalized the American Waste Trades." *Environmental History* 9, no. 1 (2004): 80–101.

Zimring, Carl A. *Cash for Your Trash: Scrap Recycling in America*. New Brunswick: Rutgers University Press, 2005.

The mass consumption of refashioned clothes: Re-dyed kimono in post war Japan

Miki Sugiura

ABSTRACT

Among the strategies of post-consumer textile waste management, refashioning or the makeover of used clothes, is gaining attention as value added recycling. However, refashioning business is considered as being possible only on a small scale. This article presents a case of its mass scale operation and clarifies the factors that enabled it. From the 1920s to the 1960s, re-dyeing played an indispensable role in Kyoto maintaining its central position in dyed kimono production. This study clarifies how the coordinators of re-dyeing and makeover, the *shikkai*, established a MTO (make to order) network, forming direct and recurrent ties with customers nationwide.

Introduction

Sustainable waste management is becoming an important issue of concern for the fashion industry.[1] The management of post-consumer textile waste, such as the take-back of used clothes, is increasingly being taken up as an initiative by fashion firms. Recent literature has provided historical reconstructions of private sector's waste management in the nineteenth and twentieth centuries.[2] In contrast, the waste management of clothes initiated by the fashion industry is generally seen as a recent phenomenon, an activity that commenced after the advent of the fast-fashion culture and growing interest in environmental issues. Recycling, reusing, and refashioning are seen as three key strategies for waste management in the fashion industry. Of these, refashioning, defined as remaking used clothes into new ones, is gaining attention because it is 'a higher form of reusing which focuses on value added recovery'.[3] However, businesses using the refashioning approach, in general, form a niche market. As Dssanayake and Sinha investigated in the case of the UK, the refashioning business commonly faces difficulties in each of its operational processes, that is, in: obtaining recoverable products during the collection phase; quality assessment during the sorting and grading phases; the lack of technologies and skills during the redesign phase; and finally, self-marketing sufficient numbers of clients during the distribution and selling phases.[4]

Few historical studies show cases of overcoming these difficulties. Historical analyses highlight reuse and refashioning of clothes in the context of shortage and associates them with the pre-industrial period or with the poorer strata of society.[5] Some studies have stressed that the large scale repair and re-use of clothes under shortage had long-term influences on the later fashion industry: Oldenziel and Hard and Gerasimova and Chuikina, among others, have pointed out that the expansion of mending and makeovers during the 1930s economic recession, wartime period, or under Soviet communism had significant impacts on post-war consumerism, as well as the industry structure.[6] The authors highlight the activities' long-term links to the higher fashion of the middle and upper classes, such as do-it-yourself fabrication, and customised niche production.[7] Furthermore, the refashioning segment of the second-hand clothing (SHC) market in Africa served as a catalyst for developing tailoring skills and creating new local designs.[8] Norris provides a multi-faceted study on second-hand circulations in India as well as innovative conceptual frameworks for how the massive global supply of SHC and regional circular economy could be connected.[9]

However, there are few historical cases that show that refashioning became a major way to support mass consumption and acted as the engine of growth. The case of Japan, in turn, shows that the refashioning of clothes could be an indispensable segment integrated with the clothing industry. In order to understand how the clothing industry incorporated refashioning and made refashioned items a mass consumed product, this study examined the operations of the dyed kimono industry in Kyoto in Japan as a case study. The rapid popularization and mass consumption of kimono, which began in the 1890s, witnessed an intensive re-acceleration in postwar Japan till its peak in the early 1970s. The consumption of both woven and dyed kimonos increased, but the latter created unprecedented booms that made the dyed kimono a mass-consumed product. Kyoto, the ancient capital located in the western part of Japan, was the leading production centre of dyed kimonos, producing approximately 80% of the dyed kimonos in Japan in 1953-54.[10] Remarkably, in 1956, 46% of the 5.5 million pieces of dyed kimono produced in Kyoto were refashioned, that is, they were re-dyed makeovers.[11] The article demonstrates the extent of these refashioning operations within the industry using statistical data. It shows the reasons why Kyoto's dyed-kimono industry was proactive in integrating the reuse of clothes. Moreover, the article clarifies the occupational functions that enabled Kyoto's dye industry to have a nationwide refashioning clientele network, and discusses the influence the operation had on the industry structure.

We propose to use three approaches and set one key actor in the analysis. The first is to consider long term customer relationship that spanned an item's first purchase, maintenance, refashioning ordering, and further purchases. In our case, all these cycles were facilitated by the same coordinators, called *shikkai*, who consulted and arranged cleaning, mending, quality assessment and redesign or refashioning, as well as the coordination of re-dyeing of a kimono. The second approach posits that make-to-order (MTO) production underlay the maintenance of such long-term customer relationships.[12] Both MTO and make-to-stock (MTS) production expanded rapidly in the period extending from the 1950s to the 1970s; however, this article demonstrates that the nationwide MTO network was crucial in establishing a large market for refashioning. The third approach of this study considers how the Kyoto dye industry could provide broad choices for refashioning by making various manual and mechanised dye techniques applicable to re-dyeing. The abovementioned coordinators were again central to the coexistence of these techniques, as they could act as intermediaries to coordinate the use of any technique suitable for the item, according to customers' wishes. Finally, these coordinators, who maintained long-term relationships with customer and facilitated arrangements for re-dyeing, are the key actors of our analysis. The coordinators were collectively known by the occupational name *shikkai*, which literally means 'dealers in all-round matters'. The formation of the national network of *shikkai* between the Kyoto *shikkai* and local *shikkai* was crucial in maintaining Kyoto's centrality in kimono production.[13]

Methodology

There are few studies on the re-dyed kimono or the *shikkai*'s operations in Japan. The *shikkai*'s operations were most thoroughly investigated in a series of contemporary investigation reports and studies from the 1950s to the 1980s.[14] Iwaki and Takatera provided systematic historical overviews of *shikkais'* operational functions.[15] In addition, Yamamoto refers to the recent endeavours of the *shikkais* in Kyoto in her discussion on the highly specialised industry structure.[16] However, the extensive re-dyeing of kimonos has not so far featured prominently in the context of the 20th-century popularisation of the kimono.[17] Though these studies referred to the kimono's long-term lives as things, they have overlooked re-dyed items and the mechanisation, organisational changes, and innovations that occurred in relation to re-dyeing operations.

Methodologically, this study is based on the data and records of the abovementioned investigation reports, Kyoto's municipal records, national governmental reports, *shikkai*-related organisations' publications, and newspaper articles from the 1920s the 1970s.[18] For the earlier developments, practical surveys of the Kyoto dye techniques of that period, written by the Kyoto dye experts and the *shikkai*, were used, together with other sources.[19] For the period from the 1950s to the 1970s, the period of focus of this study, the article owes much to the abovementioned investigations, conducted in 1956, 1965, 1972, and 1980, by the Kyoto municipality and a group of scholars at Kyoto's Dōshisha University.[20] To extend their views, this article conducted additional analysis on the 1957 report on the dye-professional's discussion panel,[21] the 1966 MITI investigation report,[22] the 1967 questionnaire survey of Tokyo's *shikkai* networks,[23] and the *shikkai* guild surveys.[24] In addition, the author conducted several interviews with the Kyoto *shikkai* and kimono firms that were active from the 1950s to the 1970s.

The rest of this article is organised as follows. First, after the short overview of the Kyoto dye kimono industry, the role of re-dyeing in the popularisation phase of the kimono is clarified. Second, this study historically reconstructs how the *shikkai* established their nationwide MTO network of re-dyeing. Third, in-depth analysis is provided of the re-dyeing segment of the kimono industry in the mid-1950s and mid-1960s, followed by the reasons for the rapid decline of MTO production. Finally, the conclusion summarises the elements that made mass operation of refashioned clothes possible from the case.

Kyoto dye kimono industry

A kimono consists of a standard length and width of cloth (circa 0.36m x 13m) that is cut into eight pieces, which are then sewn together. Another straight strip of cloth is wrapped around the body as a belt. The kimono's length, width, and forms have not changed much over the years.[25] Moreover, the kimono was regularly disassembled for annual cleaning and maintenance. Sewing of the kimono could be done at home or in shops as a side business and needed no professional tailoring or fitting. These features were suitable for reuse. Moreover, because their forms and sewing patterns are unified and simple, their weave, dyes, printing, and painting patterns have diversified quickly, leading to trends that changed over short cycles.

Kyoto had maintained its leading position as a kimono production centre by providing the latest fashion patterns and refining its finishing skills, particularly in dyeing, painting, and embroidering. Kyoto is the home of the innovations in Yūzen dyed kimonos, which are hand-painted, resist-paste-dyed patterned kimonos. Successful popularisation of the dyed kimono by means of stencils, chemical dye, and mechanisation ensured Kyoto's leadership in kimono production in Japan throughout the 20th century.[26] During its popularisation phase, from the late 19th century till the 1960s, the MTS production of woven kimono fabric, including that of white kimono fabrics that were dyed, expanded rapidly,[27] In contrast, the dyed kimono expanded primarily under the MTO system. MTS production of dyed kimonos did not surpass MTO production till the late 1960s. Historically, Kyoto was the pioneer of MTS dyed kimono production, not a follower. According to one estimation, 80% of both the MTS and MTO dyed kimono production was located in Kyoto in 1953–1954.[28] In the 1960s, however, Kyoto's dyed kimono production faced both a boom for dyed kimonos and pressure from the rise of other centres, such as Tokyo, Nagoya, Fukui, Kiryu, and Tokamachi in the east.[29] In particular, Tokamachi in the Niigata prefecture started large-scale integrated production of MTS dyed kimono factories, pressuring the lower popularised segment in Kyoto.[30]

In the 1950s and 1960s, the production of Kyoto dyed kimonos doubled from 5.5–10 million kimono pieces (*tan*) per year.[31] At the same time MTS production started to increase significantly. The investigation reports of 1956 and 1965 enable us to estimate the ratios of MTS, MTO re-dyed, and MTO new dyed kimonos (Table 1). In 1956, the ratio of re-dyed kimonos far exceeded that of MTS kimonos reaching 46% of the revenue. The figure before World War II is estimated to be 60%. However, in 1966, the proportion of re-dyeds kimonos was less than half that of the MTS sort. By 1980, the re-dyeing orders had shrunk to only a small fragment of the industry.[32]

Re-dyeing and the popularization of the kimono

To understand the role re-dyeing and refashioning played in kimono consumption during the popularization phase, a quote by Shige Omura (1918–1999), who wrote books on the daily life of the period, is suggestive:

> The kimonos [that my mother owned] were divided into five types: very formal wear, formal wear, casual wear, daily wear, and work wear. Formal wear items were made of Yūzen. High-quality fabrics could be re-dyed multiple times. Therefore, first we would dye them in pale colours. After re-dyeing twice or thrice, the shade of the colour would darken, and the kimono became casual wear....The fabrics for daily wear were different. They were made of spun silk or wool. They too were made over, by cutting off the weakened sleeves, switching the front and back sides, or removing the hem.[33]

As this quote shows, the popularisation of the kimono was supported by women possessing multiple types of kimonos, according to the occasion.[34] It should be noted here that the

Table 1. Ratios of MTO re-dye, MTO new dye and MTS productions 1914–1980.

Year	1914	1938	1956	1965	1970	1980
MTS (Amounts)	10%	–	40.70%	58.40%	74.10%	93.30%
MTO Re-dye (Amounts)	54%	90%	46.25%	28.96%	25.90%	1.96%
MTO New dye (Amounts)	36%	–%	13.05%	12.64%		4.74%
Total annual production (in million *tan* pieces)	–	–	5.5	9.4	16.5	7.23

Source: For 1914 and 1938: Kyōsen oroshi shōgyōkumiai, 1974, p. 25 and p. 30. For 1965: Izushi, 1967a, pp. 19–20; Izushi,1967b, pp. 39–41. For 1970: Iwaki, 2010, p. 640; Nakamura, 1988, pp. 159–160. For 1980: Ibid., p. 342 and p. 357.
Note: Total annual production of 1956 and 1965 are estimations driven from the MTO and MTS production results. Those of 1970 and 1980 are estimations by Nakamura.

Yūzen kimonos, which were the Kyoto-originated dyed kimono with patterns, were formal wear, but they also included wear for varying degrees of formality. Moreover, much stricter dress codes were laid down for the patterns that should be worn according to the occasion, season, and age. These consumption patterns matched those for re-dyeing. It became common to re-dye the patterns of kimono every 4-5 years.[35] Moreover, Omura's quote suggests that customers were willing to a pay a higher price if the fabric could withstand re-bleaching and re-dyeing. Weavers developed techniques that involved the imprinting of complicated carving patterns on the white cloth, so that the fabric had the potential to take on shades and nuances in the process of re-dyeing.

The re-dyeing option was crucial for the popularisation of kimono owing to a supply-demand mismatch; the demand for white fabrics often surpassed production capacity until the 1960s. These white fabrics were retailed as finished products as well. Consumers kept several white kimono fabrics in stock, dyeing them under MTO (a process termed as 'MTO new dye').[36] A re-dyed kimono was able to reduce its cost, relative to that of a new kimono based on the purchase cost of new fabric, and had around one-third the cost of a new kimono (fabric + dye fee).[37] However, the re-dyeing fee was higher than the new dyeing fee mentioned above, simply because re-dyeing included the preparation costs of bleaching and removing stains. Innovations in the techniques and chemicals in the preparation process allowed the second-hand kimono to be dyed using the same process as that for new fabrics.

This meant that consumers were able to choose from various dyeing techniques in re-dyeing, as was the case for new dyeing. Figure 1 shows the rate of re-dyeing orders in 1955 by product category. Impressively, the proportion of re-dyeing orders was equally high, except in hand-painting; for the others they were in the 72–78% range; mechanised printing stood out with 96% of their orders comprising re-dyeing. At the retail level, in 1967, the desirable dye fee proposed by the Tokyo *shikkai* was 16,000 yen for hand painting, 4,900 yen for stencil painting, 2,400 yen for mechanised pattern printing, 2,000 for plain colour dye.[38] The price of white fabric at that time is assumed to be 15,000-30,000 yen. Thus, customers could choose their re-dyeing methods from the variety of options available and had flexibility in deciding the fashionable attributes that the re-dyed item should regain.

Re-dyeing was pursued almost exclusively under the MTO system. Despite the presence of active second-hand kimono markets, MTS re-dyeing production never grew as much. MTO production was adopted because re-dyeing was considered an extension of consumers'

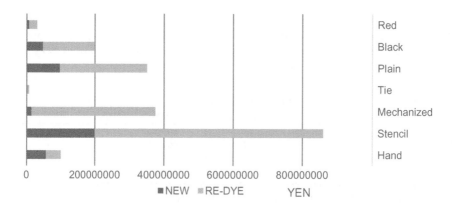

Figure 1. Re-dye ratio per dye techniques in 1956. Source: Kuroiwa and Munakata, 1959, p. 124.

regular cleaning, maintenance, and repair. Minute re-dyeing, refilling, and changing of colour nuances were done during these stages.[39] Although re-dyeing was closer to a complete makeover, it was natural to put it within this context, and utilise the broadly spread out channels (local *shikkai*) close to consumers. In this way, they could connect refashioning to the long-term and regular customer relationships. In the mid-1950s, the re-dyeing segment was evaluated as a reliable revenue source of the industry that could count on stable and constant demand.

For the MTO re-dyed refashioning business to flourish and attain the level achieved by dyed kimono, both the distribution network and production system had to meet certain conditions. First, it required a centre where the industry could cluster. Re-dyed items had to be more than simple makeovers; they had to be refashioned items, produced at the kimono production centre, which followed the latest fashion trends. Kyoto, which stood at the top of the luxurious kimono production setup, was the most appropriate for gaining redesign skills and techniques. Second, re-dyeing could not be integrated or centralised by several dye factories. MTO re-dying involved piece-by-piece operation, customisation, and coordination of the multiple steps of washing, bleaching, and dyeing of each item. Thus, the workshops became highly specialised in a particular process. Kyoto, with its highly segmented and specialised dye workshops developed over centuries, was the only option for re-dyeing MTO kimonos. The massive demand for re-dyeing, in turn, strengthened the dispersed structure of Kyoto's dye industry. According to the kimono dyer T. Kawada, an integrated system would make the total re-dyeing fee much higher than that in the non-integrated structure. He observed in a discussion forum that the washing fee for re-dyeing, when outsourced to a specialised artisan, was 50–60 yen, but if dyers started to integrate washing, it would cost 180 yen, after taking idle time into account.[40] The third condition was that coordinators were needed to attend to each piece, both for the highly segmented production side in Kyoto and for customers nationwide. As noted, the *shikkai* played this coordination role.

Establishment of national network by Shikkai

Re-dyeing enabled Kyoto production factories to be connected directly to consumers all over the country via the *shikkai*. Figure 2 illustrates this network. The re-dyeing process

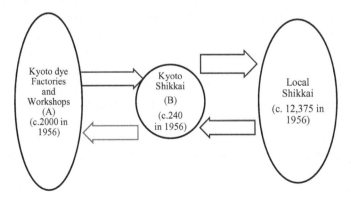

Figure 2. Shikkai's national MTO network. Source: Based on the figures by Izushi, 1968, p. 69 and Nakamura,1982, p. 349. Note: () show approximate numbers in 1956.

was as follows. First, Kyoto dye/paint/print factories (A) made sample rolls or, as was the case later, published sample books. The Kyoto *shikkai* (B) mediated the sale of these sample rolls and books to the local non-Kyoto *shikkai* (C) as well as other kimono retailers and distributors. Local *shikkai* (C), who were mostly in charge of cleaning and maintenance of kimono, showed these samples to customers and received re-dyeing orders. Local *shikkai* (C) would commission these re-dyeing orders to the Kyoto *shikkai* (B). Kyoto *shikkai* (B) coordinated the re-dyeing processes, with at least 6–7 specialised artisan workshops or factories, checking every stage in the process. When the re-dyed item was finished, Kyoto *shikkai* (B) would send the item to the local *shikkai* (C), who would deliver it directly to the consumer.

Only after the introduction of modernised chemical dyes from the mid-1870s onwards was this nationwide re-dyeing order network established. The possibility of re-dyeing was limited if the natural plant dye was used.[41] The number of Kyoto *shikkai* had grown significantly by the mid-1920s. Kyoto's dye industry was reorganized along two lines: dyers or *shikkai*.[42] Indeed, Takahashi noted in 1925 that Kyoto had 1,100 *shikkai* offices that had more than 3,000 employees; if family members are included, the number of employees exceeded 10,000.[43] Further, a newspaper article in 1927 noted that Kyoto police estimated as much as 10,000 *shikkai* operating in Kyoto, reflecting the increase in the door-to-door salesperson *shikkai*.[44] At the same time, the number of local *shikkai* grew. In 1926, there were 17,166 local *shikkai* dispersed across Japan, connecting customers at diverse locations with the Kyoto *shikkai*.[45] The extensive reach of Kyoto *shikkai*'s re-dyeing order network is highlighted in the complaints Kyoto police received concerning fraud and breach of contracts both inside and outside Japan, sometimes as far away as Shanghai and Dalian.[46] The increase in the local *shikkai* was also the result of modernisation and mechanisation, as small and mid-scale local dyers who could not afford the larger investment in facilities became local *shikkai*.

Re-dyed items were the backbone of the Kyoto dyed kimono industry that lasted for decades during economic booms, recessions, and wartime shortages. During the economic boom in 1914-1919, the *shikkai* guilds recorded that re-dyeing orders accounted for 60% of all orders.[47] When recession hit in 1920, followed by worldwide depression, kimono dealers faced intense competition amid lower demand.[48] The proportion of re-dyed items in the total market seems to have increased in these years, and, in particular, mechanised re-dyeing printing grew.[49] On the other hand, MTS kimono wholesalers suffered from fluctuations in kimono prices; for example, they had to sell low during a drop in prices in 1933, whereas the *shikkai* who could count on stable re-dyeing demand enjoyed peak business in the 1935–1939 period.[50] The Japan–China war from 1937 caused a serious shortage of white kimono fabrics. By then, re-dyeing comprised 90% of all orders. Moreover, strict production control was introduced in the same year.[51] Shortly afterwards, in 1940, production of luxurious items was banned, regardless of their being new or re-dyed.[52] Although Kyoto kimono industrialists succeeded in reversing the ban, almost all the *shikkai* had to stop operation or change jobs in 1942, when the entire industry was ordered to reorganise under the re-establishing of business enterprise ordinance, which made it mandatory to abolish small and medium-sized enterprises or to integrate them into larger enterprises.[53] After the war, many of these *shikkai* returned to their business.[54] Since the regulation of silk production continued until around 1949, re-dyeing orders continued to account for most of the business in the industry, comprising 60% of all orders, well into the 1950s.[55]

Re-dyeing of kimono in mid-1950s and mid-1960s

However, in the mid-1950s and mid-1960s, when the problem of the shortage of white fabrics was solved and dyed kimono production was skyrocketing, the Kyoto *shikkai* achieved impressive growth. In 1956, the total revenue of 170 *shikkai* offices (1,294 employees) belonging to the *shikkai* guild was 2 billion yen.[56] In 1965 their turnover with 247 *shikkai* offices (2189 employees) grew six-fold to 12 billion yen.[57] The Kyoto *shikkai* offices downsized after the war, with nearly 80% of firms employing less than 10 people, and 40% less than 5.[58] Nevertheless, the *shikkai* kept on facilitating the two networks of Kyoto dyers and the nation-wide clientele. On average, one Kyoto *shikkai* in 1956 was in contact with 14.5 dye preparation workshops, 106.6 dye factories, and 67.7 plain dye factories in Kyoto, while in 1965, the average numbers of facilities had changed to 17.3, 87.8, and 5.4, respectively.[59] On the other hand, in 1955, Kyoto *shikkai* received orders from 14,242 facilities (or, an average of 86.9 facilities per *shikkai*), of which 86.9% or 12,375 were local *shikkai* and the rest were kimono retailers and department stores.[60] The percentage of local shikkai only dropped by 5% in 1966.[61] The geographical distribution of the contracts was spread far and wide. In 1955, regions adjacent to Kyoto and within a 50–150 km radius, such as the Kinki and Chubu areas, accounted for only 12% and 8.8%, respectively, of the contracts. However, distant regions, such as Tokyo (15.9%; 460–500 km away), southern Kyushu (18%; 500–900 km away), and northern Hokkaido (12.3%; 1,400–1,600 km away), had higher proportions.[62]

Re-dyeing orders were crucial for maintaining this network. In 1967, the local *shikkai* in Tokyo maintained close bonds with Kyoto *shikkai* and re-dyeing orders were key to these relationships. There were four types of operations of the Tokyo local *shikkai*, who were dispersed in small shops over 23 Tokyo wards, as follows: (1) cleaning and mending; (2) re-dyeing orders; (3) new dye orders; and (4) sale of MTS pieces.[63] No local *shikkai* in Tokyo concentrated on re-dyeing although it was the leading source of their revenue, comprising more than one third on average (34%).[64] In addition, the larger their business, the more crucial re-dyeing became. By then, Tokyo dyers were the primary collaborators of the local *shikkai* in Tokyo. However, 70% of the local *shikkai* in Tokyo ordered re-dyeing and new dyeing from Kyoto.[65] Kyoto dominated the orders directed outside of Tokyo, with other places accounting for only 12%.

Re-dyeing was the primary operation for the Kyoto *shikkai* in both 1956 and 1965. With the rise of MTS production, Kyoto *shikkai* diversified their operations into (1) coordinating MTS dyes; (2) selling white kimono fabrics; (3) selling dyed MTS kimonos; or (4) selling woven MTS kimonos. Though these operations contributed much to their revenue growth, still in 1965, none of these activities became dominant.[66] Of the Kyoto *shikkai*, 93.5% conducted re-dyeing and for 78.2%, re-dyeing was a major activity, accounting for 50% of their business, as Tables 2 and 3 show.

The decrease of re-dyeing from the 1970s onwards

After the 1970s, re-dyeing orders fell rapidly, preceding the fall of MTO demand. The reasons for the rapid decline were complex, as total kimono production fell. One of the most influential factors was the re-luxurisation of the kimono. Since the 1970s, Japanese women started to wear more European-style garments for daily wear and casual wear. Kimonos began to be worn more as ceremonial or formal wear.[67] Under an unprecedented economic boom in

Table 2. Re-dye operations in Kyoto Shikkai business in 1956 and 1965.

Employees	Firms no. 1965	Re-dye%	New dye %	Re-dye only firm % 1965	Re-dye/total over 50% firm % 1965	Firms no. 1956	Re-dye%	New dye %
Above 30	10	63.0	37.0	0%	100.0%	5	83.1	16.9
20–29	5	72.8	27.2	0%	80.0%	4	75.3	24.7
10–19	31	62.2	37.8	3.2%	67.7%	26	80.6	19.4
5–9	77	66.8	33.2	0%	77.9%	67	76.0	24.0
1–4	107	67.3	32.7	3.8%	79.4%	68	70.6	29.4
Total	230	64.8%	35.2%	5	180	170	78.0	22.0

Source: For 1956: Muneto and Kuromatsu, 1959, p. 120 and p. 125. For 1966: Izushi, 1968, pp. 38–42; Izushi,1972, pp. 63–66.

Table 3. Kyoto Shikkai's revenue sources in 1965.

	MTO	MTS	Wholesale/retail		
	Re-dye	New dye	Blank	Dyed K	Woven K
No. Companies	241 230	37	122	70	35
Percentage	97.5% 93.1%	15.4%	50.6%	29.0%	14.5%
Over 50% of revenue no (no. of 100%)	185(81) 180(5)	13 (4)	3	13(2)	1
Percentage	76.8% 78.2%	5.4%	1.2%	5.4%	0.4%

Source: Izushi, 1968, pp. 38–42; Izushi, 1972, pp. 63–66.

Japan, the unit price of the kimono soared. The re-luxurisation did not lead to an increase in re-dyeing orders. Between 1956 and 1965, more expensive hand painting and stencil dyeing began to gain prominence and accounted for nearly 60% of orders for Kyoto *shikkai* in 1965, at the expense of plain or mechanised dyeing, whose proportions dropped signifi-cantly compared to those in 1956, as Table 4 shows.[68] This change in the product mix partly explained the slight decrease in re-dyeing orders, which had a far higher proportion than plain or mechanised dyeing. As the kimono was more used for formal wear, there was little demand for downgraded re-dyed kimonos, operated as semi-formal wear. Moreover, in the 1970s, synthetics were taking over for cheaper kimonos. Re-dyeing of synthetics was pos-sible, if done by resin processing, but doing so did not meet the cost and quality standards. Furthermore, white silk kimono fabrics were no longer manufactured in anticipation of mul-tiple re-dyeing, and thus, it became increasingly difficult to re-dye kimono silk fabrics in general.

As re-dyeing orders were the backbone of the national network, the MTO production was harmed by the decrease in re-dyeing orders. A smaller market with higher unit price seems to have provided favourable conditions for MTO production to flourish. However, for Kyoto's MTO mechanism, as described in the previous sections, these conditions were unfavourable. The luxurisation of the kimono increased the cost for making sample rolls or publishing sample catalogues.[69] In the national network of the *shikkai*, the samples had to be distributed to many.[70] For Kyoto's numerous but tiny dyeing workshops, the cost was prohibitive. Kyoto dye factories should have regrouped or adopted the franchising system to share the cost, but the specialised structure under *shikkai* coordination limited this outcome.[71] Therefore, it was a natural choice for the Kyoto factories to switch to MTS production, under which there was no need to make samples. Kyoto dyeing factories started incorporating MTS pro-duction faster than the *Shikkai*. In 1966, two-thirds of the factories were involved in MTS

Table 4. Product categories among Shikkai orders 1956 and 1965.

	Hand	Stencil	Mechanized	Plain	Black	Others
1955 Shikkai	5.2%	44.7%	19.5%	18.3%	10.4%	1.9%
1965 Shikkai	5.9%	51.7%	17.3%	11.3%	10.9%	2.9%

Source: Muneto and Kuromatsu, 1959, p. 124. Izushi, 1967b, p. 41.

production. In a questionnaire from the same year, the majority of the factories expressed pessimistic forecasts for future re-dyeing demand.[72]

Given this situation, the most active members of Kyoto *shikkai* reformed themselves, and began calling themselves *sensho*, which can be translated as 'a master of dyeing'. They organised annual collective exhibition tours and collaborated with department stores to take MTO orders after 1971.[73] However, this did not help maintain the original network of the Kyoto and local *shikkai*, as *sensho* were reliant on wholesalers and department stores in expanding their endeavours. Their once strong links with the local *shikkai* began to fade. More expensive kimonos require larger spending for maintenance, and this demand was just sufficient to enable the decreasing number of local *shikkai* to survive by repositioning themselves as specialised cleaners for formal kimono wear. In summary, the network that expanded during popularisation could not adapt to the demands of luxurisation.

Conclusion

Of the three strategies of post-consumer textile waste management, refashioning, the make-over of used clothes, is gaining attention because it conserves resources, and thereby adds value. However, refashioning is generally evaluated as an emerging business, rather than an established one; further it is seen as a niche market.[74] This article showed a highly successful case of mass-scale refashioning business operation that was systematically integrated with the clothing industry. From the 1920s to the 1960s, at least a quarter, and on average, more than half of the dyed kimono production in Kyoto, was re-dyed makeover. This study showed that the re-dyed kimono was the engine for mass consumption, and was the primary contributor in making dyed kimono production possible throughout the phases of demand expansion, recession, recovery, and unprecedented boom.

Supply shortage of white fabrics was not the only reason for the industry to become proactive in incorporating refashioning into their business. Re-dyeing created a stable source of revenue for MTO production. Further, re-dye operations contributed significantly to Kyoto achieving its central place in kimono production. Piece-wise, custom-order kimono production, supported by re-dyeing demand, enhanced Kyoto's strong reputation for quality and technique. Kyoto earned praise for its quality and techniques in both high-end and low-end products by showcasing its dye techniques and skills in providing various choices during the re-dyeing process. Refashioning helped Kyoto in branding its kimono throughout Japan during the popularisation phase.

This article analysed the nationwide network of dye-coordinators called the *shikkai*, who enabled the expansion of the MTO system for refashioning and facilitated the piece-by-piece re-dyeing operations via numerous specialised dye factories and artisans in Kyoto. The article confirms the validity of analysing the formation of a facilitative body— in this case, the *shikkai*—to support the analysis frameworks of previous literature on waste management. From the methodological perspective, the article took a total industry approach, which implies that it connected the waste management operation with the production, distribution, and consumption. Further, we believe our study on re-dye contributes to the present literature on the fashion industry by highlighting refashioning enabled mass scale MTO production of clothes. Our result verified the choice of MTO and MTS as important factors in determining the scale of post-consumer textile waste management.

In comparison to the present-day refashion business, our case could be more efficient and cut costs at various phases of its operations: collection phase, sorting and grading phase, disassembly phase, redesign phase, and distribution and selling phase. Our findings further suggest that refashioned items in our case were formal to semi-formal wear that would downgrade by frequent re-dye. The owner knowingly bought the item as a re-dyeable luxury item. Our case suggests that the refashioning business was a highly knowledge-intensive operation, which required a suitable allocation of product-related knowledge. In present-day refashioning, the designer is solely responsible for the knowledge and skills. In our case, product-related knowledge was more equally allocated between consumers, mediating coordinating *shikkai*, and the MTO manufacturers. Our study suggests that the further task required to be done for making refashioning a flourishing enterprise is designing a knowledge allocation mechanism within the industry that urges sharing of the product-related knowledge among the operators involved, including the active involvement of the consumer.

However, we must be careful in equating, the refashioning operations of the study with those of present-day businesses. Previous literature on waste management and business history demonstrated that recycling was a historically conceptualized and constructed operation. It was precisely the failure of re-dyeing operations to last beyond the 1970s that supports the findings of previous literature on waste management; that is, from the early 1960s onwards, there was a paradigm shift in how waste management business should be structured. Stokes et al. noted that the change was ushered in by the 'reconceptualization of long-standing practice of "salvage" as "recycling".'[75] While salvage is a straightforward business of collecting household waste that has a stable demand in the market, recycling is distinguished from the former by its consideration of non-economic factors, such as concern for environmental well-being. From this perspective, the refashioning in our case could be placed as the last mass-scale, straightforward operation of 'salvage' rather than the complicated and technology-intensive operation of 'recycling'. From the perspective of textile waste management, our case exemplifies the kimono industry's failure to shift from the mass-scale salvage segment to a recycling one. Nevertheless, our case suggests therefore that the historical processes of post-war post-consumer textile waste management of fashion industries and the waste management business can be analysed together. Such analysis will help to bridge the gap between the operations used from the 1930s to the 1960s and the present-day ones, as well as clarify the reasons why present-day textile waste management strategies (recycling, reusing and refashioning) are structured in a certain way. Further investigation of the facts highlighted in our case, for example the aspect of the choice of fibres, will provide hints to resolve these issues.

Notes

1.   Blackburn, *Sustainable Apparel.*
2.   Stokes et al., *Waste Business*; Jones, *Green Entrepreneurship.*
3.   Dssanayake and Sinha, "Sustainable Waste", 80.

4.   Ibid, 85-87.
5.   Strasser, *History of Trash*, 28; Stöber, "Europe Repair Trade," 147.
6.   Oldenziel and Hard, *Europe Consumers*; Gerasimova and Chuikina, "Repair Society."
7.   Oldenziel and Hard, *Europe Consumers*; Gerasimova and Chuikina, "Repair Society;": Twigger Holroyd, "Dress Leisure."
8.   Tranberg Hansen, *Salaula*.
9.   Norris, "Indian Saris;" Norris, "Cloth Economies."
10. Izushi, *Yuzen Dyeing*, 68.
11. Muneto and Kuromatsu, *Modernization Yuzen*, 124. Calculation and estimations are based on this work.
12. Under MTO, production is triggered by a sales order. Under MTS, suppliers estimate the sales-sand produce. In the clothing industry, the former is custom-made and the latter is ready-to-wear.In the field of operational research, hybrid MTO and MTS production systems have been much discussed since Williams, *Special Products*.
13. The origin of the dye coordinators could be traced to as early as the ninth century. For further historical development of the *shikkai*, see Takahashi, *Secret Kyoto*, 10 and Iwaki and Takatera, *Origin Shikkai*, 40.
14. For published articles and studies, see Izushi, *Kyoto Yuzen*; Izushi *Yuzen Dyeing*;Izushi *Kyoto Dye*; Nakamura, "*Japanese Textile*;" and Nakamura, *Dyed Kimono*. See note 8 for the survey of investigation reports.
15. Iwaki, *Shikkai Postwar* and Iwaki and Takatera, *Origin Shikkai*.
16. Yamamoto, "Labour Division."
17. Franck, "Kimono Fashion," 33-34; Tamura, *Socioeconomic History*, 133-175. Franck'sexcellent study, which traced the changing consumption pattern of clothing between the 1880s and 1990s, refers to the kimono's long term usage and its 'revamping' by new collars and sleeve cutting, but re-dyeing was not mentioned. Tamura's book provides chapters on the innovations introduced in chemical dyes or changing consumption patterns, but re-dyeing was not referred.
18. The details are described in note 8.
19. Takahashi, *Secret Kyoto*; Murakami, *Modern Yuzen*. Moreover, the paper also based itsanalysis on guild publications, newspaper articles, and Kyoto Chamber of Commerce's investigation report in Kyoto gofuku *shikkai, Anniversary Pamphlet*; Kyōto orimono oroshishō kyōkai, *Kyoto Textile*; Osaka asahi shinbunkyoku, "*Shikkai Complaints*."
20. Each investigation yielded multiple reports and studies. The 1956 investigation is covered in Kyotoshi keizaikyoku, *Kyoto Kimono*; Izushi, *Kyoto Yuzen*; and Muneto and Kuromatsu. It is mentioned in Izushi, *Kyoto Dye*. The 1965 investigation led to Izushi, MTO Yuzen; Izushi, *Kyoto Shikkai*; Izushi, *Yuzen Dyeing*; it is also briefly mentioned in Izushi, *Kyoto Dye*. The results of the 1972 and 1982 investigations are in Doshisha University Institute, *Japanese Textile Studies*; Izushi and Omura, Kyoto Dyeing; Nakamura, "Japanese Textile." In addition, Tanaka, "Kyoto Yuzen Decline" provides an overview of production since the 1970s.
21. Kyotoshi keizaikyoku, *Kyoto Yuzen*.
22. Tsushōsangyōshō senikyoku seniseihinka, *Investigation report*.
23. Kyotoshi keizaikyoku, *Tokyo Shikkai*.
24. Kyōzome oroshi shōgyōkumiai, *Shikkai Merchandizing*.
25. The width of dyed kimono fabric changed to 37cm after 1965.
26. Popularisation in this article is defined as the phenomena in Japan from the 1880s to the 1960s, wherein one woman owned multiple types of kimono. Franck, "Kimono Fashion," and Tamura, *Socioeconomic History*, associated the phenomena more with the emergence of fashion. For Yūzen or other luxurious kimono, whose use was limited to the elites, popularisation means that they began to be produced in larger quantities and became incorporated as formal wear for middle class women. The structural changes that the Kyoto Yūzen industry went through since early modern era can be listed as follows:

     (1) Establishment of Kyoto dyed kimono as luxury item for the elite nationwide (1670-1800)
     (2) Popularisation phase, with the introduction of synthetic dyes, mechanisation, and new fibres (spun silk/cotton/wool) (1890s-1930s)

(3)   Wartime halt in production (1939-1945)
(4)   Post-war recovery, re-acceleration of popularisation and mass production (1950s-1970s)
(5)   Demand shrinkage and re-luxuriation after 1972

27. Doshisha University Institute, *Japanese Textile Studies*, 240-247; Muneto and Kuromatsu, *Modernization Yuzen*, 77-78; Kyotoshi keizaikyokyoku, *Kyoto Shōkōjōhō*, 46).
28. Izushi, *Yuzen Dyeing*, 68.
29. Nakamura, "Japanese Textile," 311-335
30. Ibid., 364-392.
31. Tsushōsangyōshō senikyoku seniseihinka, *Investigation Report*, 19.
32. Nakamura, "Japanese Textile," 357.
33. Omura, *After Care*, 30-33.
34. Franck, "Kimono Fashion," 3; Tamura, *Socioeconomic History*, 16.
35. Kyoto Prefectural University *Kyoto Memories*.
36. They were used as gifts and dowry items. Interview with Mr. G. Hayashi, who was active as a *shikkai* from the 1960s inwards, on 16th January, 2018.
37. Kyotoshi keizaikyokyoku, *Kyoto Yuzen*, 50. Mr. G. Hayashi, mentioned in the previous note, confirmed the cost.
38. Kyotoshi keizaikyoku, *Investigation Report*, 55. The plain colour dye fee is an estimation.
39. Kyoto Prefectural University, *Kyoto Memories*.
40. Kyotoshi keizaikyoku, *Kyoto Yuzen*, 50.
41. Ibid., 55. Chemical coal tar dye was imported from 1870 onwards, and from 1871, the government research lab *Seimikyoku* in Kyoto supervised improvements in its application. Chemical dye was applied for Yūzen dye as early as 1874, first to wool and muslin, and then to silk crepe. Mixing chemical dye with the starch (*Utsushizome*) invented around 1879 enabled Yūzen to develop a simultaneous resist and dye processes for silk, radically shortening the production phase, and enabling mass production, besides allowing the inclusion of various colour nuances: Kyoto orimono oroshishō kyōkai, *Kyoto Textile*, 44-45.
42. Takahashi, *Secret Kyoto*, 101
43. Ibid., 108.
44. Osaka asahi shinbun kyoku, "Shikkai Complaints," 247.
45. Iwaki and Takatera, *Origin Shikkai*, 43. They counted the numbers from *Nihon yōzome gofuku senshoku gyōsha meikan* (Lexicon of Kyoto dye products seller and dyers), published in 1926.
46. Osaka asahi shinbun kyoku, "Shikkai Complaints," 248. They supervised 627 cases during 1923–25. In response, the *shikkai* guild associations stressed that they were contractors, operating under a fixed fee. Takahashi, *Secret Kyoto* also confirms that the Horikawa police branch in Kyoto received 90 complaints in a month. Takahashi, *Secret Kyoto*, 109-110.
47. Kyōzome oroshi shōgyōkumiai, *Shikkai Merchandizing*, 30.
48. Ibid., 21.
49. Izushi, *Yuzen Dyeing*, 68.
50. Kyōzome oroshi shōgyōkumiai, *Shikkai Merchandizing*, 30.
51. Ibid., 25
52. Kyoto orimono oroshishō kyōkai, *Kyoto Textile*, 53-56.
53. Muneto and Kuromatsu, 39-40; Kyoto orimono oroshishō kyōkai, *Kyoto Textile*, 57-70.
54. Izushi, *Yuzen Dyeing*, 74-75
55. For deregulation of silk, see Kyoto orimono oroshishō kyōkai, *Kyoto Textile*, 74-77. For re-dye rate, see Nakamura, "Japanese Textile," 357; Iwaki, *Shikkai Postwar*, 639.
56. Muneto and Kuromatsu,123.
57. Izushi, *Kyoto Dye*, 66; Izushi, *Kyoto Yuzen*, 38.
58. Ibid., 120. According to Izushi, *Kyoto Shikkai*, 35, in 1966, the percentage of firms employing less than 10 and less than 5 was 77.6% and 48.6%, respectively.
59. The drop in the number of plain dye factories was remarkable, but the exact reason for the drop is unknown. For 1956, see Muneto and Kuromatsu, 120. For 1965, see Izushi, *Yuzen Dyeing*, 46.
60. Muneto and Kuromatsu, 127.
61. Izushi, *Kyoto Shikkai*, 43.

62.   Muneto and Kuromatsu, 128.
63.   Kyotoshi keizaikyoku, *Investigation Report*, 6 and 10-12.
64.   Ibid., 7.
65.   Ibid., 22-25
66.   Izushi, *Kyoto Dye*, 64)
67.   Franck, "Kimono Fashion," 169-170.
68.   Izushi, *MTO Yuzen*, 41.
69.   Izushi, *Yuzen Dyeing*, 24-27; Nakamura, *Dyed Kimono*, 155-159
70.   Izushi, *Kyoto Dye*, 47
71.   Izushi, *Studies Kyoto*, 71. Indeed, 54.6% of Kyoto *shikkai* in 1965 joined some group. However, lack of flexibility in sharing individual networks is repeatedly pointed out; see Yamamoto, "Labour Division," 35-40.
72.   Izushi, *Kyoto Shikkai*, 50-51
73.   Kyoto kōgei, *Sōritsu 45*, 1-15.
74.   Dssanayake and Sinha, "Sustainable Waste", 80.
75.   Stokes, *Waste Business*, 301.

Acknowledgements

This research was supported by the JSPS Grants in Aid (15H03233 and 15KK0059). I am grateful to Professor Keiko Suzuki, Dr Aya Ueda, Professor Mihoko Aoki and Dr. Masako Yamamoto and their colleagues from Art Research Centre, Ritsumeikan University, Professor Rie Mori, and those in a related project who provided insight and expertise that greatly assisted the research. I am also immensely grateful to Masako Kitaura of Senshū Sano Gofuku Kitaura, who connected me to the valuable artisanal skills and innovative endeavours in the field. My heartfelt gratitude to Mr. T.Hayashi at Shikkai Hayashi; Mr. T. Yoshida at the Kyoto Kimono Clinic; and Mr. Y.Ezoe, Mr. T.Mori at Chisō and Ms. Kato at the Institute of Chiso Arts and Culture (http://www.icac.or.jp) for sharing their expertise. I would like to express my sincere gratitude to Professor Haneda Masashi at the University of Tokyo, who manages two research platforms that explore new approaches to Global History (http://coretocore.ioc.u-tokyo.ac.jp), for giving me generous and valuable opportunities to explore the field of second-hand clothing circulation in global perspective. I also thank my colleagues and advisors of the research project Linking Cloth-Clothing Globally (http://www.lccg.tokyo) for their overall support. Part of the initial paper was presented at the panel 'Fashion and Technology: Consumers, Democritization of Luxury and New Technologies', organized by Professor Emanuela Scarpellini of the University of Milan. I express my sincere gratitude to her, Professor Naoko Inoue at Josai University and the other participants at the panel for the early discussions. In addition, I would like to express my sincere gratitude to Professor John Styles at the University of Hertfordshire and Professor Pierre Yves Donzé at the University of Osaka for their valuable comments in the later stages of my research; any errors remaining are my own. Finally, I would like to thank the anonymous reviewers and the editors Jennifer Le Zotte and Karen Tranberg Hansen for their comments and support.

Disclosure statement

No potential conflict of interest was reported by the author.

References

Blackburn, R.S. *Sustainable Apparel: Production, Processing and Recycling*. Woodhead Publishing Series in Textiles 1. Cambridge: Woodhead Publishing, 2015.

Dissanayake, G., and P. Sinha. "Sustainable Waste Management Strategies in the Fashion Industry Sector." *The International Journal of Environmental Sustainability* 8, no. 1 (2012): 77–88.

Doshisha University Institute for Humanities and Science (Ed.) (1982). *Wasō orimonogyō no kenkyū [Studies on Japanese-style Textile Industry]*. Kyoto: Minerva Publishing.

Franck, P. *The Japanese Consumer: An Alternative Economic History of Modern Japan*. London: Cambridge University Press, 2009.

Franck, P. "Kimono Fashion: The Consumer and the Growth of the Textile Industry in Pre-War Japan." In *The Historical Consumer: Consumption and Everyday Life in Japan 1850–2000*, edited by P. Franck, and J. Hunter, 151–175. New York: Palgrave Macmillan, 2015.

Gerasimova E., and S. Chuikina. "The Repair Society." *Russian Studies in History* 48, no. 1 (2009): 58–74.

Iwaki M. "Sengo *Shikkai* to Sono Yakuwari [*Shikkai* in Postwar Days and their Roles]." *Nihon Kansei Kōgakkai Ronbunshi* 9, no. 4 (2010): 637–643.

Iwaki M., and M. Takatera. "*Shikkai* no naritachi to sono hensen [Origin and History of *Shikkai*]." *Nihon Kansei Kōgakkai Ronbunshi* 11, no. 1 (2012): 39–45.

Izushi, K. "Dentō Sangyō ni Okeru Kōzō Henka: Kyoto atsurae yūzengyō wo chūshin to shite [On the Structural Change in Order-made Yūzen Industry in Kyoto]." *Dōshisha shōgaku [Studies on Commerce]* 9, no. 6 (1958): 666–687.

Izushi, K. "Atsurae uūzen no genkyō to dōkō. Kyōyūzengyō jittai chōsa kekka [The Present State of Affairs and Trends in MTO Yūzen production: The Results of the Investigation]." *Kyoto Shōkōjōhō*, No.75, Kyotoshi Keizaikyoku, 1967a.

Izushi, K. "Yōzome oroshishō no genkyō to mondaiten: Yōzome oroshishōgyō jittai chōsa no kekka wo chūshin toshite [Present State of Affairs and Problems of Kyoto Shikkai: Centering on the results of Shikkai investigation report]." in *Kyoto Shōkōjōhō*, 76, Kyotoshi Keizaikyoku, 1967b.

Izushi, K. "Kyoto atsurae yūzengyō no kōzō. Sono dentōsangyō toshite no seikaku wo chūshin toshite [The structure of Order-made Yuzen Dyeing Industry in Kyoto]." *Dōshisha Shōgaku [Studies on Commerce]* 19(4) (1968): 51–86, Kyoto: Dōshisha shōgakkai.

Izushi, K. *Kyoto senshokugyō no kenkyū [Studies on Kyoto Dye and Weaving Industry]*. Kyoto: Minerva Publishing, 1972.

Izushi, K., and S. Omura. "Kyoto senshokugyō jittai chōsa hōkokusho [Present state report of Kyoto dyeing and weaving industry]." *Kyoto Shōkōjōhō*, 79, Kyotoshi Keizaikyoku, 1979.

Jones, G. *Profit and Sustainability. A History of Green Entrepreneurship*. Oxford: Oxford University Press, 2017.

Kyoto gofuku *shikkai* dogyō kumiai. *Kyoto gofuku shikkai dōgyōkumiai sōritsu jusshūnenkinenshi [10th Anniversary Pamphlet of Kyoto Gofuku Shikkai Dogyō kumiai]*. Kyoto: Kyoto gofuku *shikkai* dōgyō kumiai, 1928.

Kyoto kōgei senshō kyōdō kumiai. *Sōritsu 45 shūnen kinenshi [45th Anniversary Book]*. Kyoto: Kōgei senshō kyōdō kumiai, 2006.

Kyoto orimono oroshishō kyōkai. *Kyoto orimono shijō no gaiyō [Overview of the Kyoto textile market]*. Kyoto: Kyoto orimono oroshishō kyōkai, 1957.

Kyoto Prefecutral University. Kyō no kurashi kenkyūkai, Kioku no nakano kyō no *kurashi chōsa kenkyū* [Investigations and Research on Kyoto life in the *memories*], Kyoto: Annual Report for Grants in Aid, 2003.

Kyoto shōkō kaigijo. *Kyō yūzen ni kansuru chōsa [Investigation on Kyoto Yūzen industry]*. Kyoto: Kyoto shōkō kaigijo, 1940.

Kyotoshi keizaikyoku. "Kyō yūzen gyōkai no arikata wo kataru [Discussion on the state of Kyoto Yūzen Industry]." *Kyoto Shōkōjōhō* 29 (1957):45–55, Kyoto: Kyotoshi keizaikyoku.

Kyotoshi keizaikyoku. Kyōyūzen no seisan to ryūtsū [Production and distribution of Kyoto Yūzen Kimono]. Kyoto Shōkōjōhō, Special Edition, Kyoto: Kyotoshi keizaikyoku, 1958.

Kyotoshi keizaikyoku. *Tokyo tonai ni okeru shikkaigyō jittaichōsahōkokusyo [Investigation report on shikkai in Tokyo region]*. Kyoto: Kyotoshi keizaikyoku, 1967.

Kyōzome Oroshi Shōgyōkumiai. *Yōzome oroshi no ayumi [Steps of Kyoto Shikkai Merchandizing Association]*. Kyoto: Kyōzome oroshi shōgyōkumiai, 1974.

Munetō, K. and I. Kuromatsu, eds. *Dentōsangyō no kindaika [Modernization of Traditional Industries–The Structure of Yūzen Industry Kyoto]*. Tokyo: Yuhikaku, 1959.

Murakami, A. and Yūzen kyōkai 1927. *Kindai yūzenshi* [History of Modern Yūzen] Reprint Kyoto: Geijutsudo, 2012.

Nakamura, K. "'Wasō *Senshoku* kakō kōgyō no sanchi kōzō bunseki' [Analysis on the production regions of kimono dye application industry]." In *Wasō orimonogyō no kenkyū [Studies on Japanese-style Textile Industry]*, edited by Dōshisha University Institute for Humanities and Science, 306–393. Kyoto: Minerva Publishing, 1982.

Nakamura, K. "Somegofuku no jukyūkikō to kōzō henka (1) [Dyed Kimono's Supply and Demand System and Structural Changes]." *Dōshisha Shōgaku [Studies on commerce]* 39, no. 6 (1988):147–177.

Norris, L. "Recycling and Reincarnation: The Journeys of Indian Saris." *Mobilities* 3, no. 3 (2008): 415–436

Norris, L. "Urban Prototypes. Growing Local Circular Cloth Economies." Business History, published online: Oct 30, 2017, https://doi.org/10.1080/00076791.2017.1389902

Oldenziel, R., and M. Hard. *Consumers, Tinkerers, Rebels: The People who Shaped Europe*. London: Palgrave Macmillan, 2013.

Omura, S. *Shimatsu to zeitaku no aida [Between After Care and Luxury]*. Tokyo: Koseishuppansha, 1993.

Osaka asahi shinbun kyoku 1927. "Kujō hyakushutsu no kyō Shikkaiya [Kyoto *Shikkai* with Hundreds of Complaints]." In Osaka asahi shinbun kyoku, *Shōbai ura omote tsuzuki [Vol. 2 of Business Front and Back]*. Reprint, Tokyo: Iwanami Shoten, 2014.

Stöber, G. "Premodern Sustainability? The Secondhand and Repair Trade in Urban Europe." In *Cycling and Recycling. Histories of Sustainable Practices*, edited by R. Oldenziel, and H. Trischler, 147–167. New York and Oxford: Oxford University Press, 2016.

Stokes, R.G., Köster, R., and S. C. Sambrook. *Business of Waste: Great Britain and Germany, 1945 to the Present*. New York: Cambridge University Press, 2013.

Strasser, S. *Waste and Want: A Social History of Trash*. New York: Metropolitan Books, 1999.

Takahashi S. *Kyōzome no hiketsu [The Secret of Kyoto Dyeing]* 1925. Reprint Kyoto: Kyoto Shoin, 1974.

Tamura H. *Fasshon no shakai keizai shi [A Socioeconomic History of Fashion]*. Tokyo: Nihon keizai hyōronsha, 2004.

Tanaka, N. "Kyoto Kohaba yūzengyō no suitaikeikō bunseki to shōraitenbō [Analysis on the decline of Kyoto Kohaba Yūzen Industry and Future Prospective]." *Ryukoku Business Review* 13 (2012): 35–53.

Tranberg Hansen., K. *Salaula: The World of Secondhand Clothing in Zambia*. Chicago: University of Chicago Press, 2000.

Tsushōsangyōshō senizakkakyoku seniseihinka (MITI, Bureau of Textile products). *Senshokuseirigyō Jittaichosa Hōkokusho* [Investigation Report of Current State of Dye Industries]. Kindaika kihonkeikaku sakuteishiryō [Records for Basic Plan of Modernization] No. 6, Tokyo: Tsushōsangyōshō senizakkakyoku seniseihinka, 1966.

Twigger Holroyd, A. "Perceptions and Practices of Dress-related Leisure: Shopping, Sorting, Making and Mending." *Annals of Leisure Research* 19, no. 3 (2016): 275–293.

Williams, T. M. "Special products and uncertainty in production/inventory systems." *European Journal of Operational Research* 15, no. 1 (1984): 46–54.

Yamamoto M. "*Dentōsangyō ni okeru bungyōsei no kōzai*" ["The Merits and Demerits of Labour Division in Traditional Industries Seen through the Ritsumeikan University Yuzen Kimono Project"]. *Journal of the Japan Society of Design* 68 (2016): 35–48.

The work of shopping: Resellers and the informal economy at the goodwill bins

Jennifer Ayres

ABSTRACT

In this article, I examine the material and everyday practices of a community of thrift-shoppers at the Goodwill Bins. Their practices reveal that shopping in these cutthroat environments is anything but leisurely. By attending to how these spaces are utilised as resources for independent ventures in the informal economy, I show how the occupation of reselling blurs the lines between consumption and production, and shopping and work. I argue that the thrift store can be viewed as a microcosm of the broader shifts occurring in the economy and the latest capitalist reorganisation of work into non-standard and precarious forms.

Introduction

Unbeknown to many, thrift stores hum with the activity of creative shoppers and micro-entrepreneurs collecting electronics to repair, repurposing and harvesting raw materials for art projects, collecting metal objects to sell for scrap, and reselling things like books, 'distressed' furniture, vintage clothing and tools at flea markets, yard sales, boutiques and online. These are just a few of the economic resources thrift stores unofficially offer, not including the array of official social services non-profit organisations provide.

Thrift stores are a rapidly growing segment of the retail sector that many consider 'recession proof': when the economy tanks people come running. The National Association of Resale Professionals (NARTS), an industry trade group for used goods resale and consignment stores, says, 'Resale attracts a new demographic of both suppliers and customers during difficult economic times.'[1] On the 2016 Forbes list of the 100 largest charities the Salvation Army ranks #4 and Goodwill Industries ranks #10.[2] Goodwill is one of the largest non-profit thrift store chains, with more than 2,900 retail thrift stores across the United States and Canada,[3] and reported earnings of $5.6 billion in revenues in 2015[4]– almost a 30 per cent increase from $3.7 billion in revenues in 2009. CEOs of regional districts make six-figure salaries; the salary of the CEO of the Southern California district is more than $500,000 per year,[5] but that figure rises to $1.1 million when total compensation is calculated.[6] Goodwill also reports that it diverted more than 3 billion pounds of clothing and household goods from landfills in 2015.[7] Considering these figures makes it clear that the thrift store is worthy of study for its impact on the economy, beyond its unique contributions to consumer and material culture.

Goodwill banks on the culture of overconsumption that gives away goods because they are simply not desirable anymore, rather than cultures of scarcity where goods are given away only when depleted of value and use. For items deemed unsalable, i.e. trash, Goodwill outsources the labour of picking and sorting to its customers through its special liquidation Outlet stores (known colloquially as the 'Bins'). In exchange for the opportunity to scavenge Goodwill's trash, the customers (who I call 'Regulars') pay for their finds by the weight, at $1.29 per pound, and Goodwill eliminates most of the costs and inefficiencies of labour associated with retail (jobs like pricing, sorting, displaying, customer service, etc.).

Thrift stores like the Bins are dynamic and heterogeneous spaces owing to the changing inventory of used objects for sale and the diversity of patrons. These patrons engage in a variety of income-generating strategies through secondary markets in the informal economy. Thrift stores like the Bins are also spaces in which local immigrant and ethnic entrepreneur communities and networks converge, and where disparate service workers and self-employed workers congregate. The thrift store figures prominently in my analysis as an autonomous semi-public space that is often appropriated as a work site. I focus on the distinction between *shopping* and *working* at thrift stores in order to complicate the received wisdom about the nature of production, consumption and shopping. Indeed, it is through this examination of precarious work and thrift stores that the dichotomy between production and consumption breaks down and illuminates a much richer material world and social order in its absence. Examining how work and leisure operates in these environments interrupts narratives that condemn and conflate shopping with consumption – especially if it involves women shopping for clothes. So, this research also offers a feminist intervention, that shopping for clothes to resell and consume is no less valid than procuring groceries or provisioning necessities or any other political economic activity.

Literature review

The secondhand economy is one where people buy secondhand items for various reasons, such as: limited budget, concerns for the environment, the diverse array of styles to choose from and exclusivity (the fact that no one else will have the same object). The ability to perform and display distinction while saving money (what Gregson and Crewe term 'the value imperative' driving both new and secondhand consumption) is a key pleasure and rationale of thrifting.[8] There can be a politics to thrifting that can take the form of reuse, sustainability, anti-consumption and anti-fashion. And it is important to acknowledge the pleasures of thrifting: the occasional treasure find and the deployment of a range of senses to aid in the hunt for interesting shapes, patterns, textures or designs that catch the eye – all without necessarily requiring purchase. The thrift store offers to many a social outing, as a free hands-on museum of bad taste and obsolesced fashion. The thrift store is also a place of possibility where one can find necessities and engage differently with retail surroundings. Found secondhand objects invite us to imagine and create narratives about their pervious uses, wearers and social lives.[9]

Whether it is 'antiques', 'vintage', 'secondhand' or just plain 'used', all of these terms reflect a category of post-consumer goods that are recovered from discards and transformed into treasure. In order to be re-valorised as rare antiques, for example, objects must move temporally and spatially into the category of trash in order to be rescued from obscurity and be transformed into a value-added category.[10]

Secondhand clothes are characterised by the ambiguity, flux and impermanence of their value.[11] Botticello focuses on the symbolic dimensions of value creation in the rebranding of secondhand clothes by middlemen, like traders and shop and stall owners. As clothing moves spatially from ragmill to market stall the transformation in its value is almost entirely symbolic and contextual, reminding us about the subjective nature of value.[12] In an earlier essay, Botticello explores how clothes sorting requires a particular kind of tacit knowledge of how people come to know what is valuable.[13] She identifies workers as key agents in recognising value and the tricks they develop to determine the value of an object. For instance, while workers wear dust masks, they do not wear gloves because gloves interfere with their ability to feel if a material is silk or cotton, and if it is wet or dry. Another worker takes a suspected wool garment and runs it along her neck to test if the fibres are scratchy and thus confirm if it is wool.[14] This illuminates that determining the value of used clothing often requires a corporeal, tactile, and embodied engagement (beyond quick and detached visual assessment). Botticello's attention to worker practices is important for my consideration of how thrifters in the Bins also come to develop their own work attire and uniforms for the task of picking.

Transformation requires essential shifts in categories of trash to treasure and a 'sleight of hand' to assist in the change of context that allows value creation.[15] Norris draws on Thompson's 'rubbish theory' to argue that this unseen process transforming post-consumer waste back into commodities is crucial to the value and status claims reused commodities make.[16] Norris states that it takes a special eye and specialised labour to recognise, produce and extract value from castoff clothing. Hawley also attends to the tacit knowledge it takes to find rare valuables in a heap of miscellany by offering key conceptual frameworks.[17]

The literature on thrift stores, thrift store fashion, vintage, and secondhand clothing circulations in the United States and United Kingdom is the most relevant strand of literature for this project (Hoff,[18] McRobbie,[19] Tinkcom, Fuqua, and Villarejo,[20] Mendvev,[21] Goldsmith,[22] Cline,[23] Steward,[24] LeZotte[25]). Gregson and Crewe's research findings dovetail nicely with scholarship on the interplay between the local and global in international clothing markets.[26] Attending to the geography and cross-cultural hybridity of the US–Mexico Borderlands, Hill looks at the habits of everyday trading and municipal salvage operations,[27] while Gauthier explores the transnational lives of 'ant traders' or *fayuqueros* who bring consumer goods across the border to resell while evading customs.[28] Parker and Weber also study the geography of selling secondhand goods in Chicago,[29] offering a nice contrast to Gregson and Crewe's UK based studies.[30] LeZotte offers one of the most compelling and comprehensive accounts in the literature on this subject with a historical analysis of Goodwill thrift stores.[31]

The circulation of secondhand clothing transcends national borders and is a global phenomenon (Hansen,[32] Milgram,[33] Clark,[34] Fontaine,[35] Rivoli,[36] Cline[37]). Thanks to Hansen's body of work, we know that the secondhand clothing trade is a valued institution in many areas of Africa as part of a large and established informal economy that crisscrosses all over the continent.[38] Because of decades of research in the midst of globalisation, Hansen is able to offer a particularly compelling analysis of Zambian consumption and modernity that challenges typical narratives of the local and global.[39] A key dilemma she investigates is whether the import of secondhand clothing is helping or hindering the Zambian nation while it is undergoing economic liberalisation. Hansen shows that *saluala* (secondhand clothes) becomes a straw man for larger anxieties about globalisation and inequitable North–South trade relationships. The use of cheap castoffs in personal style and wardrobes is not an easy example of Western domination either. She explains:

> Save for the origin of saluala garments, there is nothing particularly 'Western' about how people in Zambia deal with them. Saluala clothing practices and their incorporation of nonlocal cultural inspirations are not adequately explained as a result of hegemonic domination by the West. The process is interactive… and it draws importantly on local cultural notions of how to dress[40]

Ultimately Hansen's work illuminates how re-commodified castoffs are repurposed for thoroughly rooted and local experiments in style, and how this surplus flow of cheap clothes allows entrepreneurial ventures in secondary markets in the informal economy.[41]

If we study the way thrift stores are utilised as prime grounds for sourcing raw materials to transform and resell for small independent ventures, we can see that the informal economy plays a significant role in how people across the socio-economic stratum creatively stretch their limited incomes. Thus, the informal economy literature is essential to make sense of the activity I describe in the Goodwill Bins. Pulling from this literature allows the discussion to move away from a focus on the individual, style, identity and narratives, and towards a broader social and cultural analysis of the effects and practices of reselling secondhand goods.

While there is an established body of scholarship on economic development and the informal economy in the Global South,[42] some scholars have critiqued how this canon implicitly stigmatises the informal economy by neglecting to examine its prevalence in the global North and all capitalist societies.[43] The informal economic activity of garbage picking and scavenging is prevalent around the world. Examples range from Columbia,[44] China,[45] South Africa,[46] and the lives of *catadores* (cardboard recyclers) throughout Mexico,[47] and Brazil.[48]

Thankfully more studies of the domestic informal economy are emerging. Studies on the informal economy in the United States are often foundational texts across the humanities, covering topics like: elaborate systems of reciprocity while on Welfare;[49] Christmas-tree book resellers in Greenwich Village;[50] Latino day-laborers in California;[51] West African street traders in Harlem;[52] illicit hustles in Chicago projects;[53] making a living off dumpster diving in an affluent Dallas suburb;[54] Silicon Valley's high-tech vs. service and informal economy divide;[55] work ethic among homeless pro-recyclers of San Francisco;[56] and Ikea's encroaching gentrification of Red Hook's food-cart vendors.[57]

This literature also highlights important factors for choosing self-employment in the informal economy – factors like being in control of one's work and work schedule. Yet this scholarship also illuminates that many people who create livelihoods on the margins do so owing to their inability to access formal labour markets. Nevertheless, the factors of autonomy and flexibility that come with informal ventures should not be underestimated. Indeed, the informal economy allows marginalised people to organise along lines of work and kin and exert claims to space not otherwise possible in the formal economy. This is part of the reason why we have seen an explosion in entrepreneurial ventures post-Recession: the labour market has contracted and ejected people from formerly stable positions, professions and careers. There has a been a corresponding surge in under-the-table informal economic activity as people take on extra gigs and side hustles to make ends meet while also pursuing riskier forms of work where the potential for personal freedom and success are higher. When unemployment, underemployment and stagnant wages dominate, it should come as no surprise that people decide to change their careers and work for themselves – choosing autonomy and flexibility over dead-end and soul-crushing jobs.

Study Design

This research is based on three months of participant observation at one particular Goodwill Outlet in Northern California in 2010. Participant observation in this site consisted of shopping, aimless browsing and socialising in the store for six or more hours a day, often split in two shifts, six days a week. The store structure, dynamics and culture formed the bulk of my fieldnotes. I recorded how many times a day bins were rotated and at what times; what busy and slow days looked like; how many customers in the store constituted 'busy'; what languages were spoken; who collected what and if there were observable age, gender and ethnic patterns as to who worked with particular materials. Since I sew clothes and do photography as hobbies, there was always more than enough material to look at and objects to investigate in the store. I took photographs in order to better remember the scene, atmosphere and particular objects. Through positioning myself as a semi-permanent fixture of the store I gained rapport with other Regulars and conducted semi-structured phone interviews.

Case study: The Goodwill Bins

Goodwill Outlets are also known as Goodwill 'As-is' stores, Bargain Barns, Bargain Bins, and colloquially referred to as the 'Bins'. For the most part, Goodwill Outlets are attached to a centralised Goodwill Industries warehouse that receives, processes, sorts and redistributes donated goods back to Goodwill thrift stores throughout a region. In some regions the Outlet is part of a post-retail division or part of salvage operations. Everything in the store is 'last-chance'; it either did not sell at a regular thrift store or was deemed unfit for sale and all the goods are heaped in large blue bins and sold by weight at $1.39 per pound. The wheeled bins are rotated in – "fresh" bins – and out – 'old' bins – about four times a day. The contents of the 'old' bins are dumped into a compactor or bale machine for further disposal (Figure 1); 'fresh' bins are swarmed by patrons and rapidly tilled for goods (Figures 2 and 3). Since the bins are rotated frequently the contents of the store are changed entirely more than once a day. This is why people visit the store multiple times a day for new goods or they just stay at the store the whole day (Figure 4).

The people aggressively digging through the bins constituted a community of die-hard patrons, the Regulars, who routinely hung out at the store, as if it were their full-time job, 10 am to 5 pm Monday to Friday. This set the tone for a brisk pace of business between patrons who bartered goods and fought for treasure to collect and resell. Their practices revealed that shopping in these particular bustling and cutthroat environments was anything but leisurely. Because this store sold things by the pound, and did not have to individually display or manage items, it could sell loose scraps of paper, bedpans, 'brand new' Christmas tree tinsel from the 1960s still in the box, household electronics, mirrors, china, picture frames, miscellaneous wires and stained carpet all mixed up in the same bin. Clothes were not conveniently colour-coded or hung up on racks, housewares were not winningly displayed on shelves, and no antiques gathered dust in glass cases because this site was not meant for

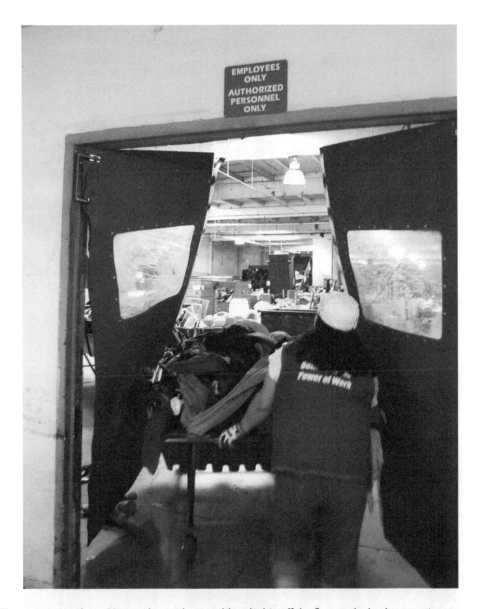

Figure 1. In Northern CA, a worker pushes an old, stale, bin off the floor to the back processing area.

leisurely shopping; it was a site to clear out Goodwill's excess garbage, a site to work in, to buy wholesale for other endeavours, and to find treasure (Figure 5).

The rotating bins of goods mimics the rotating cast of characters in Bins stores (Figure 6). Like the open-air bazaar, the Bins foster a heterogeneous environment that unintentionally provides one of the most ethnically and racially integrated spaces in the urban landscape (Figures 7, 8, 9). A vibrant range of informal micro-entrepreneurial activity occurs in these spaces: white middle-class women buy interior decorating props to stage houses for sale; Russian families collect blankets, bedding and vintage clothing for sale at monthly swap meets or upscale San Francisco vintage stores; Japanese dealers and hipster youths search out vintage clothes to resell on eBay or in their own vintage shops; men of various ethnicities

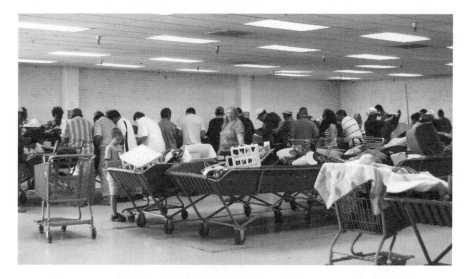

Figure 2. A new bin change in CA and ensuing frenzy.

Figure 3. In NY, shoppers are made to wait behind a line taped to the floor while new bins are wheeled out onto the floor. After a tedious wait jockeying for the best position in line, the whistle blows, releasing them to make a mad dash towards the new bins.

and nationalities gather metal wares to strip down and sell to scrapyards; Latinas collect work wear and Nike athletic shoes; Latinos repair and refurbish household electronics; white male book resellers use barcode scanners to research book prices on Amazon; West African men accumulate carts full of blue jeans; Ghanaian men buy trade English paperbacks to sell back home; and all kinds of people buy goods that might fetch more money later at a garage sale or flea market booth. While this characterisation is provisional, it is important to offer it

Figure 4. Shoppers or workers? Regulars in NJ wait on the sidelines with their carts for the next bin change when fresh merchandise will replace stale bins. An empty box of cat litter can be seen from the closest bin begging the question whether the contents of the store are trash or treasure.

in order to counter the assumptions that 'there is nothing good' (i.e., of value) at thrift stores, or that only a specific class, gender, or ethnicity of people deal with used goods (Figure 10). Regulars have many different motivations, besides saving money, for shopping and working at the Goodwill Outlet.

Whereas price in retail thrift stores will bar people from accessing certain goods, in the Goodwill Outlet the patron has access to almost everything. No purifying work has been done by Goodwill to cleanse its inventory. The goods are only provisionally separated into four main categories: books, glassware, wares and textiles. Customers do the work of selection themselves, and goods are much cheaper because of this. While a T shirt is $4 in most Goodwill retail thrift stores, in Goodwill Outlets it will be under $1 based on its light weight. By selling what is not usually offered up for sale at conventional thrift stores, Goodwill Outlets can be used as a reuse and salvage depot where one can find 300 empty cd jewel cases, vintage dresses reeking of mothballs and without their buttons, a full-size human skeleton Halloween decoration, tea pots missing their lids, and five pounds of Lego pieces scattered throughout the entire store. All it takes is a person with a creative imagination, knowledge of specialised markets and the patience to find and accumulate select items for repurposing, resale, and revaluation (it might also help to be slightly obsessive-compulsive to ensure methodical collection of every piece of a set and every piece of puzzle, button, bone and Lego that may have been dispersed throughout the bins). And with the recent contraction of the labour market, this store model offers low-barrier experimentation with self-employ-ment. Yet it also requires a person who can see value in trash while suspending symbolic

Figure 5. A young girl watches as professional book resellers, all men, sort through the book bins in Northern CA.

systems of cleanliness that pathologises garbage. Patrons understand dirt as a necessary hazard of the store and as a trade-off for access to rare goods (Figures 11, 12, 13).

The Regulars who depend on the Bins for their livelihoods collectively transform these sites into spaces of community (Figures 14, 15). Regulars work in close quarters with other patrons and employees, and this closeness facilitates the building of bridges, alliances, business partnerships and intense rivalries between both Regulars and employees. The continuous flow of used goods is critical to establishing a steady following of recyclers and resellers. In fact, anywhere Goodwill Outlets are located, there are bustling coteries that spend their days and nights loitering in the store waiting for a fresh bin of wares, books or clothes to be rolled out (Figures 16, 17).

Figure 6. A regular patron at a Bins in NV. He got tired of people starring at his one 'good' eye, so he wears these sunglasses. The Bins are great for people-watching because of idiosyncratic personal styles like this.

Filthy hands and dirty work

The smell, grit, grime, noise, odours, dust, dirt and commotion from random objects and cutthroat patrons all combine to make the Bins an overwhelming affront to most senses and standards of decency. Some Outlets do not have air conditioning, water fountains, reliable bathrooms or enough shopping carts, so the discomfort of not being able to wash your

Figure 7. Two elderly retirees catch up with each other over their shopping carts in Northern CA.

hands, stow your findings or wipe the sweat off your brow keeps casual shoppers away. The many different polluting, and even caustic, elements found in the Bins does the work of filtering out people who are afraid to get their hands dirty or do not have the patience or time to thoroughly dig for treasure (Figure 18).

Online reviews of Goodwill Outlets sensationalise not only the dirt, but also the filthy people who seem to be permanent store fixtures. Internet reviewers around the US log onto Yelp.com to capture and share the dirt and uniqueness of the Goodwill Outlet in their part of the country. The filth associated with Goodwill Outlets stems from a combination of the inferior used, stained, damaged or smelly goods; the lingering odours, smells, noises, and unaesthetically appealing store; and the dirty, unkempt shoppers who look and smell strange. It is both the stock of informal resellers posted up in Goodwill Outlets and the mixture of salvageable goods with trash for sale that create 'seedy' and 'sketchy' reputations for these lawless sites. Journalist Wescoat Sanders explains,

> 'Like junkies, the pickers at The Bins are hooked more on lifestyle than the drug itself. They may find a valuable object on any given day, or even several valuable objects, but when those objects are sold, the search begins anew.'[58]

On the Internet, Yelp and Google reviewers emphasise the threat of bodily dirt in sweat and stenches that linger to construct the Goodwill Outlet as contaminating on multiple levels. In 2010, one Yelp.com review of a Goodwill Outlet in Seattle stated, 'If the smell of those lovely "fragrant" items in the bins doesn't make you gag, the pervasive body odor of at least one person in the store probably will'.

The symbolic thrill of others whom the Yelp reviewers want to come close to, but not touch, and the power of dirt to illuminate transgressions in the social order are ideas indebted to the classic work of Douglas who argued, 'As we know it, dirt is essentially disorder.'[59] She identifies cleanliness as a cultural production, a construct particular to cultures at specific

Figure 8. Latinas sorting though clothes and waiting for new bins of clothing to come out in Northern CA.

historical moments, and dispels beliefs that hygiene and cleanliness are universal, objective, ahistorical or inherent traits. Douglas' famous phrase, 'Dirt is matter out of place' identifies transgressive substances as those that violate the social systems of order.[60] The cultural

Figure 9. Men sort through textiles and inspect a bin full of pants and jeans in Northern CA.

conflation of dirt with disorder is apt for viewing the Goodwill Outlets' perceived disreputability and chaotic atmosphere. Douglas illuminates the spatial dimensions of categories that prescribe active vigilance and maintenance to ensure dirt stays in the garden and doesn't creep inside the home. She says, 'Dirt is a relative idea. Shoes are not dirty in themselves, but it is dirty to place them on the dining table.'[61] What happens when this social order is upended, like in the jumble of miscellaneous used goods in the Bins? What do people do after they accidentally touch or brush against something defiling, and why?

The startling realisation that clothes in the Outlet are unwashed can make people recoil in disgust. A common occurrence in the Bins is undesirable contact with used underwear while going through the bins of textiles, precipitating a visceral reaction from psychic contamination. While some people might not care about accidental contact with polluted used goods, other people may be so offended by the thought of contact with used underwear that they stop shopping and leave the store. I have witnessed people enter the store and hurry for the door when realising the work and physical engagement with used goods

Figure 10. A vintage dealer takes a call while going through a new bin of textiles.

required of them. Detachment is necessary at the Bins to keep the self intact from symbol-ically threatening substances.

It is not just the smells, physical stains, soils or flaws of a garment that make it worn and polluted but also *who* is perceived or imagined to have worn it before – at the heart of why

Figure 11. Signage warning about unattended shopping carts and an unattended shopping cart with a 1970s vintage Barbie dream home.

people do not want to reuse things is the unfounded but readily cited association of used clothes with health hazards from the inferior hygiene practices of strangers, the poor and racialised others.[62] As Hoff shows, used hand-me-downs from relatives are perceived as

Figure 12. Scrappy Christmas traditions at the Northern CA bins usually involve several warning signs in English and Spanish not to touch the display and that the presents under the tree are, sadly, for display only.

acceptable because those bodily presences are known.[63] Used clothes from the thrift store, however, could have had any body in them.[64] To some people, used things are just inherently dirty, and no amount of washing or sustainability discourses will change their ingrained fears. This is the reason many people refuse to even go to a thrift store; 'For some the associations of secondhand clothing with the unknown other, possibly dead, bodies is sufficient to deter them from even entering.'[65]

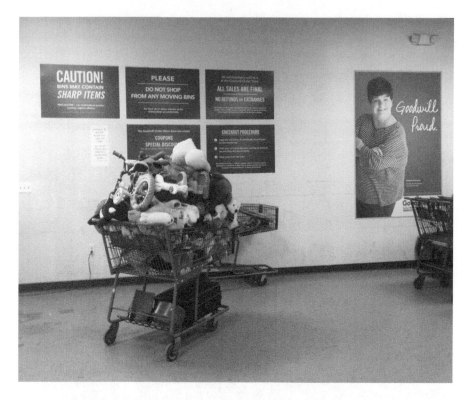

Figure 13. A typical scene at the Bins. Someone's cart is packed full of the day's pickings with store posters displayed prominently in the background warning customers about the nature of the store.

This tolerance for dirt is not merely reflective of a permissive disposition or 'open mind', however; it is essentially a job requirement of Regulars. There are limits to abstract notions of purity and symbolic notions of cleanliness: At some level no one wants to come into contact with a dirty diaper. Hawkins argues that we need to focus on the material:

> 'Psychoanalysis doesn't help make sense of the shifting place of waste in everyday life and material culture; how our ordinary encounters with it are implicated in the making of a self and an object world. It reduces waste to a phobia, understanding it only as a threat to self-certainty.'[66]

So, it is more than the abstract stigma of dirt that constitutes Goodwill Outlets as 'gross' or dangerous. For example, when 20 people are rapidly digging through the same jumble of wares, the weight of heavy objects can suddenly shift and crush or slice hands.

To 'shop' the Outlet entails a substantial amount of careful work in order to go through the bins. Since the nature of 'shopping' at the Bins means 'getting dirty' and requires sweating, competition, wearing special gloves or a makeshift uniform, it is easier to make the case that shopping in this site more closely resembles work (sometimes hazardous). This work also requires a certain physical engagement that necessitates occupying retail space differently: defensively guarding your cart, plunging your hands into an unknown mass of objects, manually heaving piles of clothing around in order to sort through them, weaving through congested aisles, and enduring the lapse of any semblance of a 'personal bubble' in order to compete against the elbows and arms that go flying to grab goods first. Outlet patrons are adept at navigating hazardous conditions and tolerating the filth of the store in exchange

Figure 14. An African-American man playfully poses for a picture strumming a guitar he has just found in Northern CA.

for access to a range of unsorted goods that may be trash or might turn out to be treasure. Thus, Outlets require an alternative engagement with dirt that shifts definitions of used goods from trash to a resource that can be reclaimed, recirculated and revalued.

A major reason that Regulars overlook the negative and hazards of the Bins is because Goodwill Outlets supply the raw resources for reselling ventures and these ventures offer autonomy. In his ethnography of a Michigan landfill Reno finds that scavengers also deploy alternative understandings of trash. He says,

> For scavengers, discarded wastes are neither simple utilities nor necessarily polluting, but complex and potentially enriching materials. To say that scavenging waste is about possibility rather than necessity, about what people make of waste rather than what they must do with it, is not to deny the very real constraint and indignities often associated with the practice. Rather, it is to recognize the agency and creativity of scavengers[67]

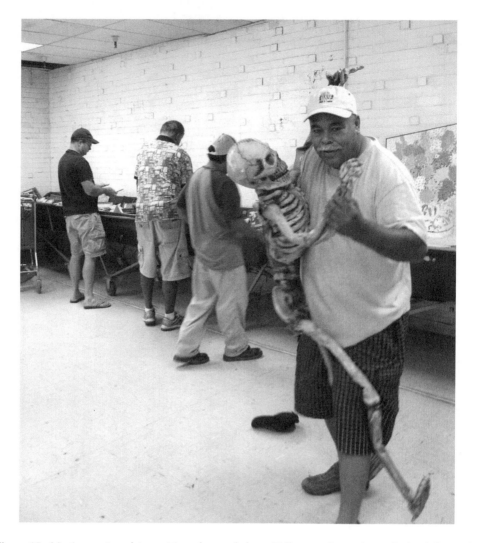

Figure 15. A Latino contemplates getting a heavy skeleton Halloween decoration and takes it for a spin first, in Northern CA.

Through paying attention to material practices of the seemingly trivial behaviours and informal dress codes of Regulars in the Bins we can see how these practices negotiate both the symbolic boundaries of cleanliness and material realities of personal safety. Long-term patrons of Goodwill Outlets devise many different strategies to deal with the dirt and chaos. A league of patrons suited-up in makeshift uniforms of Crocs, dust masks and gloves, is a peculiar element unique to Goodwill Outlets. The protective gear worn by patrons alerts newcomers that these spaces have a very different symbolic and socio-cultural order than traditional thrift stores or retail settings. These practices are not specific to one community or region; across the country, and without any formal instruction, Regulars adopt these same practices. These measures may seem absurd to newcomers, but the dangerous conditions of some Goodwill Outlets make these precautions necessary. A dedicated pair of heavy-duty gloves for work in the Goodwill Outlet demonstrates the ways Regulars tolerate possible

Figure 16. In AZ, an African-American eBay reseller of plus size lingerie and swimwear partners up with a Latina to search for goods together- when she finds blue jeans she throws them her way in exchange to all the lingerie and swimwear her friend comes across. The daunting rows of bins and physical stamina it takes to manually comb through all of bins makes forming arrangements like this ideal.

harm in exchange for access to cheap used goods. The elements of this uniform establish individuals as part of the community of everyday patrons and help make Regulars visible as a serious labour force compared with casual shoppers. These makeshift strategies at dealing with the dirt also perform symbolic functions of marking time in the day and the space of the Outlet as a work site where a uniform is needed. A uniform specifically for work in the Outlet can make the informal entrepreneurial work feel more legitimate through defining time off and on the clock. The uniform allows patrons to frame their time and role at the Goodwill Outlet differently: exposure to hazards just comes with the job and must be

Figure 17. In CA, a shopper brings her cute dog inside to hang out in the shopping cart while she shops.

tolerated. Reno finds a symbolic dimension to the worker's uniforms that parallels the Bins. He says, 'Workers invest in ideological and material separations between "work" and "home." Different rituals of purification intercede between these realms, as many employees throw out their work gloves, wash their hands and arms, and change their uniforms and boots at the end of their shift.'[68]

Here is my own cumulative list of hazards encountered in the clothing bins of Goodwill Outlets across the country during multiple years of patronage and research: used blow-up sex dolls, broken glass, earwigs, dirty diapers, spiders, wet pieces of clothing, fleas, amateur pornographic polaroids, dead bugs, glass bongs, rodent faeces, knives and urine and faeces-stained goods. I got a rash from poison oak contaminated clothes, engaged in shouting matches over goods, received cuts from sharp objects, had goods stolen out of my cart, got hit in the hip with a moving bin, and had my credit card stolen by a cashier. Acquaintances in Portland, OR have reported getting scabies from the Bins as well. During a visit to an Outlet in California, a man walked past me with a bloody gloved hand: he pulled off his heavy-duty gardening glove to show me where a loose food-processing blade in the wares had sliced right through the glove into his thumb. One informant rattled off a list of the most horrific and amazing items he had found in the Bins: explosives, hypodermic needles, guns, drugs,

Figure 18. This Outlet in AZ was in a converted warehouse parking lot and would routinely flood in the monsoon seasons. Whatever has fallen on the wet floor is not picked up. In the background predominantly Latino men pick through electronics in a new bin.

porn, alcohol, 38 special ammunition and '9 mm brand new in the box,' 1918 Kodak Landcamera with matching case found separately, 18 k diamond ring, Jose Canseco auto-graphed baseball, four- and five-leaf clovers. He even reported being handed a briefcase by another man that contained a live scorpion.

Regulars protect their bodies by wearing dust masks and plastic gloves and guard their property by cloaking their shopping carts in blankets to hide their findings from potential thieves. When carts are scarce, even the carts themselves can be stolen; intentionally, or not, shopping carts with collected items are swiped and the merchandise is tossed into a nearby bin – essentially undoing someone's whole workday. Aisles get congested so shopping carts are often left in another aisle nearby. The lawlessness of idle and unattended carts taking up space in aisles is a source of constant tension between patrons and Goodwill employees.

Goodwill often does not alert patrons about where to sort and stow their shopping carts. These unidentified zones lead to strife and harassment over what parts of the store are off-limits for storing carts or sorting. Thus, patrons resort to covering their shopping cart with a blanket to hide the contents as well as mark the cart as belonging to a regular patron. A sea of shopping carts covered with blankets and parked along a wall is another distinctive element of Goodwill Outlet culture that demonstrates how patrons exert their own order on the chaos and improvise their own methods for managing risk (Figure 19).

Figure 19. A vintage dealer has parked his shopping cart full of the days findings, covered it in a blanket he has also found, and then placed a stuffed animal he christens 'Mimi' on top to watch over his possessions.

With all this dirt and these hazards, why are so many people Regulars? Many sighed to me in a sort of helpless resignation that there is simply 'no other place like it'. Since time is the only real investment needed to make it in this venture, the Bins offer a low-risk and addictive gamble. Even when bad things do happen (like cuts and injuries from objects and fights with other Regulars) the store is unrivalled in the unpredictable assortment of goods it offers. The gamble is what makes the store addicting as well – many feel they could never 'quit' the store or stay away from it for too long without worrying about the potential treasure they might miss out on. You may have your purse stolen or encounter something awful once in a while, but the bad is buffered by the chance of finding rare objects, the life-affirming moments of exchange with strangers, the random acts of kindness, and the public intimacy formed with Regulars and employees.

Discussion

This case provides thick description and gritty texture of the physically exhausting and symbolically polluting elements of digging at the Goodwill Outlet stores. The physical hazards and tolls of these sites and this kind of labour reveal that 'picking' in this environment most closely represents scavenging labour, and thus production, rather than the casual activity of shopping that we associate with consumption. Through attending to how these spaces are utilised as resources for independent ventures and work in the informal economy, I have shown how the line between shopping and labour is blurred and ambiguous in practice. The lack of an articulation between these lines matter profoundly for how we understand work, value work, create collective class identities and resist work's domination of our time. It is clear that previous distinctions between work and leisure in industrial capitalism hold little relevance or analytical insight for work and life under late capitalism.

The ambiguity between labour time and leisure time, and production and consumption matters because it reflects an ongoing problem: the reorganisation of work into freelance, creative, and flexible 'on-demand' forms that erases a set work day, defined workplace and a defined class of workers. Whereas twentieth-century labour power agitated and organised for an eight-hour work day and protections at their workplace, post-industrialism has introduced work that is temporally and spatially delinked: work is now hypermobile and always on. The larger stakes of this delinking is that work is cannibalising leisure time, creating precarity and leading to a culture of overwork – even the phrase 'work/life balance' has become a thing of the past.

Connections and conclusions

It is clear that there is a larger relationship between thrift stores, the informal economy and the reorganisation of work into precarious forms (contract, subcontract, freelance, temp and intern being a few of these forms). The concepts of polarisation and uneven development are essential to understanding what gives rise to the informal economy and how it plays out in local spaces like the thrift store. The informal economy and strategy of cobbling together transitory gigs is about survival but also about being competitive in an urban creative class setting of post-industrialism. In her work on globalisation and the city, Sassen develops the idea of polarisation to address how inequality stems from fundamental changes in capitalism and she explains how this inequality affects the organisation of work.[69] The shift in capitalism from manufacturing to services and information polarises the labour market into a small percentage of elite knowledge-intensive jobs and a large pool of low-wage service work. The way of life promised by Fordism, home ownership and a decent career with benefits and retirement has been eroded since capitalist restructuring in the late 1970s and 1980s moved 'good' unionised jobs like manufacturing offshore, imported immigrant service workers and introduced new forms of low-paid flexible work (part-time, freelance, subcontracted) and flexible workers (temps, interns, adjuncts). Sassen understands informality as a global expansion of subcontracting and exploitation in working conditions. Sassen's main point is that informality has arisen directly out of economic restructuring in New York City and is not some sort of short-lived mutation or fluke, 'The growth of the informal economy in New York City represents not a regression from or an anomaly in an otherwise advanced capitalist economy, but a fundamental aspect of the postindustrial city.'[70]

Thus, to this larger problem, we can look to the micro and analyse how people on the ground are adjusting and navigating to post-Recession work and life. People are adjusting to the demands of neoliberalism and their ejection from formal labour markets by improvising their own enterprises. These self-made enterprises grant thrift store informal workers something dead-end entry-level jobs in the formal economy cannot: control over their schedules, autonomy and dignity. While avoiding dirty diapers, picking through used clothes and digging through trash might not be conventionally understood as dignifying, it is the ability to make one's own life without a boss that is dignifying, humanising and worthy of respect. We may do well to turn to those in the informal economy, the ones without externally imposed work/leisure schedules, for advice and wisdom on how to structure our days and time beyond simply subsisting or surviving.

Without attention to the structural and the historical aspects of work and economy, the microeconomic ceases to matter, and there is no framework in which to analyse how thrift stores might offer something more than places for shopping and consumption. This is why in order to understand the broader economic conditions that the informal economy emerges from, we need to attend to their effects on space: we need to examine the related development of cities, urban life, and the 'new geography work.'[71] It is important to think about the potential use of the shared and cohabitated space of the Bins to organise, as a physical meeting ground that facilitates cross-class coalitions between employees (often treated as disposable in dead-end retail jobs) and the patrons of the store that are self-employed in the informal economy as resellers and refurbishers that have no protections and all risk.

If the image of unorganised and self-employed scavengers fighting for garbage in a warehouse conjures up other post-apocalyptic or dystopian imagery, the utopian counter should look to the Global South as the model for the future of organising scavengers. The inability to recognise common conditions of precarity between workers in different sectors like creative 'knowledge economy' workers, service workers, and informal economy workers points to a larger debate about the demise of unions and the possibility of cross-class coalitions under post-Fordism. Ross states;

> Though they occupy opposite ends of the labour market hierarchy, workers in low-end services, both formal and informal, and members of the "creative class," who are temping in high-end knowledge sectors, appear to share certain experiential conditions. These include the radical uncertainty of their futures, the temporary or intermittent nature of their work contracts, and their isolation from any protective framework or social insurance. These common conditions have prompted…the formation of a multi-class precariat[72]

Although Ross focuses on the potential alliance between labour and environmentalism, he articulates pertinent concerns for my focus on workers in the informal economy. Discussing workers in the US knowledge economy, Ross argues that,

> Organizers will have to approach precarity as an experiential norm for people, not as an unlucky, temporary circumstance that can be remedied simply by acquiring a union card. If the labor movement is to be a resurgent force on the new landscape of irregular work, then the most precarious may have to be accorded moral, and ultimately organizational leadership within cross-class coalitions[73]

These coalitions will need to acknowledge and respect the key differences between workers like nationality, citizenship status, race and sexuality that make some workers more vulnerable than others. Finally, another implication that might be drawn from this analysis is that in order for informal workers to recognise the value of other informal and/or service workers' labour, sufficient institutional and organisational resources must exist within and through which workers may recognise themselves and others.

Notes

1. NARTS. 'Resale Thrives in a Slow Economy'. July 8, 2015. https://www.narts.org/i4a/pages/index.cfm?pageid=329
2. https://www.forbes.com/sites/williampbarrett/2016/12/14/the-largest-u-s-charities-for-2016/#658f65244abb
3. https://www.goodwill.org/wp-content/uploads/2014/10/Goodwill-Industries-International-2013-Annual-Report.pdf
4. https://www.forbes.com/companies/goodwill-industries-international/
5. https://www.huffingtonpost.com/john-hrabe/the-worst-corporation-in-_b_1876905.html
6. https://watchdog.org/83209/policies-tax-dollars-enrich-goodwill-execs/
7. https://www.goodwill.org/wp-content/uploads/2015/07/2015-Annual-Report_lr.pdf
8. Gregson and Crewe show that secondhand consumption is not anti-consumption but bears a striking resemblance to first-hand consumption; 'Secondhand' frequently bears a marked similarity to the practices that shape designer purchasing and consumption in the first cycle: difference, taste and individuality' (2003): 11. Secondhand buyers commonly perform the well-researched work of savvy shoppers by knowing what a bargain is, and when something is a ripoff. Additionally, extracting a gem from a thrift store or flea market demonstrates the ultimate skill of smart shopping. Gregson and Crewe add: 'The sale is a manifestation of their learnt and embedded knowledge/s, not imposed by an external value regime.' (2003): 57.
9. See Appadurai, *The Social Life of Things*; Stallybrass, *Marx's Coat* and *Worn Wolrds*; Tinkcom, Fuqua, and Villaerjo, *On Thrifting*; Gregson and Crewe, *Secondhand Cultures*.
10. See Thompson, *Rubbish Theory*; Strasser, *Waste and Want*; Gregson and Crewe, *Secondhand Cultures*; Hawley, 'Digging for Diamonds'; Norris, *Recycling Indian Clothing*; Botticello, 'Between Classification…' and 'Fashioning Authentic Selves'; Brooks, *Clothing Poverty*.
11. Fontaine describes this process as a 'psychological economy'; 'This "psychological" economy compounds the difficulty of precisely defining the value of secondhand objects in circulation. In fact, they incorporate all sorts of value: a value linked to their utility, to their degree of rarity, a value linked to the price of the raw materials of which they are composed or to the cost of the labour involved in their production, and a changing value linked to the age of the object in relation to the fashion cycle' (2008): 11.
12. Botticello, 'Fashioning Authentic Selves, 2013.
13. Botticello, "Between Classification…' 2012.
14. Ibid., 173.
15. Norris traces the life of silk saris as they become too worn or unwearable. She finds secondhand saris command their own trade where they are deconstructed into industrial quantities that

are then reincorporated in commodities where the fragments live on as decorations, rather than body coverings. She says, 'The thread running through all these recent studies is that work is required to make objects suitable for further exchange, once they are no longer suited to their initial use. It is this work that creates new value for used clothing' (2010): 15. She further explains; 'For these products to be accepted a sleight of hand must transform the used garment into an antique…The politics and practicalities of hidden transformations are essential for the translation between regimes of value and the creation of new modalities' (2010): 174. Writing about value and the global trade of used clothes in India, Norris argues, 'This transformational creation of a second life for old garments itself constitutes an important trans-national flow of materials, an efficacious waste stream of fiber, cloth, color and pattern that bears endless potential to re-create value, yet one that remains largely within an unacknowledged global underworld associated with dirt and decay' (2010): 4.

16. See Thompson, *Rubbish Theory*, 1979. Oxford: Oxford University Press. Norris also says 'Clothing must become rubbish in order for such transformations to be successful; their conversion into new consumer goods with high value depends on their being largely conducted in secret, enabling them to move between regimes of value' (2010): 133.

17. Hawley, 'Digging for Diamonds', 2006.

18. *Thrift Score*, by Al Hoff, formerly a DIY zine by the same name, focuses on the author's thrifting adventures and argues that thrift stores offer a kind of archaeological dig that excavates the excesses of consumerism.

19. McRobbie's earliest influential work was on the counter-cultural heritage of London and identifies rag markets as both sources of entrepreneurial employment and street fashion from the ground up in the 1960s through the 1980s. Her attention to post-war subcultures and their relationship to distinctive visual and material culture is one of the only accounts that explains why certain cultural locations and identities were drawn to entrepreneurship and business in vintage. Little has changed from McRobbie's 1998 description of secondhand clothing to now: 'Secondhand style owes its existence to those features of consumerism which are characteristic of contemporary society. It depends, for example, on the creation of a surplus of goods whose use value is not expended when their first owners no longer want them. They are then revived, even in their senility, and enter into another cycle of consumption' (1998): 29. Because of the layers and levels of knowing distinction, McRobbie sees through claims that buying secondhand is anti-consumption and argues the ragmarket is where there is simultaneously 'an even more refined economy of taste at work' (1998): 29. Indeed, the market for vintage grew after McRobbie's publication and is now such a popular market we tend to take its rise to popularity for granted.

20. The authors assert that thrift stores are excellent places from which to think about political economy of material objects as each object in the thrift store provokes questions about its conditions of possibility. The collective line of questioning 'what is this? What is this for? What does it do? How was it made? Why was it bought and brought into this world in the first place?

21. Mendevev offers a detailed case study of a Savers thrift store in the Midwest where she found that the corporation operating the thrift store actively played up and exploited narratives about cultural capital by advertising its store as a 'retail melting pot' and through catering to an explicitly named 'urban hipster' demographic.

22. Goldsmith focuses on clothes that are donated to farmers markets in Union Square, NYC.

23. Cline, *Overdressed*, 2012.

24. Steward, 'What Does that Shirt Mean to You?' 2017. Steward also studies shoppers at the Bins in Portland, Oregon and found basically two types of Goodwill Outlet shopper in their narratives: one group she terms 'thrift seekers' as their thrifting is a competitive game; the other group she terms 'creativists' who thrift out of personal creativity they see as superior to other consumers.

25. LeZotte, *From Goodwill to Grunge*, 2017

26. As cultural geographers, Gregson and Crewe argue that symbolic location is needed to differentiate between new retail spaces and secondhand spaces, especially when there is overlap between the goods being sold (imitation sharpies, fake designer purses, liquidated backstock of consumer household items, etc.). The role of symbolic location in creating used

clothing markets is why, for them, 'geography matters, fundamentally to the constitution of secondhand worlds' (2003): 49.

27. Hill, 'El Dompe', 2009.

28. Gauthier, 'The Fayuca Hormiga', 2009.

29. Parker and Weber, 'Secondhand Spaces', 2013.

30. Gregson and Crewe, *Secondhand Cultures*, 2003.

31. LeZotte, *From Goodwill to Grunge*, 2017. She make the astute observation that secondary markets and salvage operations were typically the domain of recent immigrants, specifically Jewish immigrants, and that the formalisation of an itinerant trade into global non-profits (like Goodwill Industries International and the Salvation Army) worked to Christianise the business of rags (2017): 7. One of LeZotte's main contributions to this field of literature is through demonstrating the role secondhand exchange, as a profitable industry, has played in the development of infrastructure in nineteenth and twentieth century America, and the development of the twentieth century consumer.

32. See Hansen, *Salaula*, 2000a, and Hansen, 'Charity, Commerce, Consumption', 2008.

33. Milgram also found that bargain hunting for deals and secondhand clothes are not unique to America. Through her ethnographic research among 'ukay-ukay' traders in the Philippines, she found that young people especially enjoyed hunting and digging for treasure as a pleasurable shopping activity and routine (2005): 146. She also noticed that savvy shoppers wanted foreign clothes because clothing from the West was known to be stylish and durable. Like Hansen, Milgram also points out that this did not constitute cultural imperialism, however, because the quality of construction and wide variety of styles were actually far superior and cheaper compared with the local market options.

34. Clark's research also supports Milgram's findings about the popularity of secondhand clothing imports in Hong Kong in the late 1990s. For my purposes, Milgram's and Clark's research, respectively, illustrate that shopping for secondhand clothes is not just a pastime of hipsters (young privileged people), but especially appealing to youths all over the world who use clothing as a medium to express their identities and collective affiliations.

35. Fontaine, *Alternative Exchanges*, 2008.

36. Rivoli, *The Travels of a T-Shirt*, 2009.

37. Both Rivoli (*Travels of a T-Shirt*) and Cline (*Overdressed*) focus on contemporary secondhand clothing trades as a way to investigate the commodity chain and examine how the fashion industry has changed in the last 30 years. Rivoli does this in order to offer an informative journey into economics and world trade, while Cline does this in order to offer a narrative about ethical consumption.

38. See Tranberg, Karen Hansen, 'Charity, Commerce, Consumption: The International Secondhand Clothing Trade at the Turn of the Millennium – Focus on Zambia' in *Alternative Exchanges: Secondhand Circulations from the Sixteenth Century to the Present*, ed Laurence Fontaine. New York: Berghahn, 2008.

39. Hansen explains, 'As a local phenomena, salaula is part of a countrywide wholesale and retail scene with its own consumption politics and cultural economy of taste and style. And as a global phenomenon, the explosion of Zambia's salaula trade and its associated trading activities and consumption practices are the products of a little-known, almost entirely unregulated global commodity chain' (2000a): 249.

40. Hansen, *Salaula*, 251.

41. Hansen challenges the conventional assumption that developing nations are passive victims of globalisation by highlighting how the secondhand clothing trade in Zambia offers quality and abundance of fashion for cheap, thus allowing Zambians more ways to experiment with expressing their identities. Once we look at how clothes are reused to create idiosyncratic and contemporary fashions we can no longer accept the narrative that people are passive victims of globalisation, where the 'third world' is seen as the economic and historical dust bin of the linear progress of 'first world' consumption and culture.

    She lays out what this process of recommodification looks like: 'The transformations of the West's castoff clothing into new garments in Zambia, initiated in interactions at the point of wholesale, continues through the retail process. Unhinged from its origin, the decommissioned value of the West's discarded clothing is changed anew in the retail process. The process of redefinition hinges on the meaning of the term Salaula – selecting from a pile in a manner of rummaging. Processes that express this are evident, for example on "opening day," when a bale is cut open for resale, its contents are counted and individual items are assessed for quality and price. At this moment, when the clothes are ready to enter into another cycle of consumption, it is important to remember that they have not been meddled with. Both traders and customers prefer to open bales publicly, so that customers can select on the spot. A bale that is opened in the market in full view is considered to contain "new" garments. If it were opened privately at home, the trader might put aside choice items, causing customers to suspect that they are being presented with a second cut and not "new" clothing' (2008): 182. Hansen follows the transformation of secondhand clothes from discards into desirable garments and investigates a central link in the commodity chain: the role of tailors. She illuminates that tailors set up as an ancillary industry alongside Salaula markets and help translate the foreign used clothes into updated and stylish one-of-a-kind garments for the discriminating Zambian. She also says, 'In recent years the clothes displayed in the boutique section of Lusaka's salaula markets are hung up "fresh" from the bale, that is, with wrinkles and fold. Prewashed and ironed clothing in the opinion of traders and customers alike leaves the suspicion that the clothes are "thirdhand," meaning previously owned and worn by Zambians' (2008): 183.

42. See Hart, 'Informal Income Opportunities,' 1973; De Soto, *The Other Path*, 1989; Castells and Portes, 'World Underneath,'1989; and Portes and Haller, 'The Informal Economy,' 2005.
43. See Boruchoff, 'Latin Americans at Home Abroad,' 2008; Galemba, 'Informal and Illicit Entrepreneurs,' 2008; and Marcelli et al., *Informal Work in Developed Nations*, 2010.
44. Birkbeck, 'Self-Employed Proletarians in an Informal Factory,' 1978.
45. Yang, 'At the Bottom of the Heap,' 2015.
46. Samson, 'Accumulation by Dispossession and the Informal Economy,' 2015.
47. Medina, *The World's Scavengers*, 2007.
48. Millar, 'Making Trash into Treasure,' 2008.
49. Stack, *All our Kin*, 1974
50. Duneier, *Sidewalk*, 1999.
51. Valenzula, 'Day Labourers as Entrepreneurs?' 2001.
52. Stoller, *Money Has No Smell*, 2002.
53. Venkatesh, *Off the Books*, 2006.
54. Ferrell, *Empire of Scrounge*, 2006.
55. Zlolniski, *Janitors, Street Vendors, and Activists*, 2006.
56. Gowan, 'New Hobos or Neo-Romantic Fantasy?' 2008.
57. Zukin, *Naked City*, 2010.
58. Wescoat Sanders, 'Junks Last Chance,' 2004.
59. Douglas, *Purity and Danger* (1966): 12.
60. Ibid., 48.
61. Ibid.
62. See Gregson, Brooks, and Crewe, 'Narratives of Consumption and the Body,' (2000): 112.
63. Hoff, *Thrift Score*, 1999.
64. Gregson, Brooks, and Crewe, 'Narratives of Consumption and the Body,' (2000): 109.
65. Ibid., 107.
66. Hawkins, *The Ethics of Waste* (2006): 3–4.
67. Reno, 'Your Trash is Someone's Treasure,' (2009): 33.
68. Ibid. (2009): 40.
69. Sassen, 'The Informal Economy,' 1991.
70. Ibid. (1991): 94.
71. Ross, *Nice Work if You Can Get It* (2009): 11.
72. Ibid. (2009): 6.
73. Ibid. (2009): 9.

Disclosure statement

No potential conflict of interest was reported by the author.

References

Alexander, Catherine, and Joshua Reno. *Economies of Recycling: The Global Transformation of Materials, Values, and Social Relations*. New York: Zed, 2012.

Appadurai, Arjun, ed. *The Social Life of Things: Commodities in Cultural Perspective*. Cambridge UK: Cambridge University Press, 1988.

Balli, Cecilia. "Ropa Usada [Used Clothes]." In *Puro Border: Dispatches, Snapshots and Graffiti from La Frontera*, edited by Luis Humberto Crosthwaite, Bobby Byrd and John Bird. El Paso: Cinco Puntos Press, (2002): 183–190.

Birkbeck, Chris. "Self-Employed Proletarians in an Informal Factory: The Case of Cali's Garbage Dump." *World Development* 6, no. 9-10 (1978): 1173–1185.

Boruchoff, Judith A. "Latin Americans at Home Abroad." Review of Janitors, *Street Vendors, and Activists: The Lives of Mexican Immigrants in Silicon Valley*. *Latin American Research Review* 43, no.1 (2008): 225–234.

Botticello, Julie. "Between Classification, Objectification, and Perception: Processing Secondhand Clothing for Recycling and Reuse." *Textile: The Journal of Cloth and Culture* 10, no. 2 (2012): 164–183.

Botticello, Julie. "Fashioning Authentic Selves: Secondhand Clothing and the Materialization of Enduring Values." *Critical Studies in Fashion & Beauty* 5, no. 1 (2013): 111–124.

Brooks, Andrew. *Clothing Poverty: The Hidden World of Fast Fashion and Second-Hand Clothes*. London: Zed Books, 2015.

Castells, M., and A. Portes. "World underneath: The Origins, Dynamics and Effects of the Informal Economy." In *The Informal Economy: Studies in Advanced and Less Developed Countries*, edited by A. Portes, M. Castells and L. A. Benton, 11–37. Baltimore, MD: John Hopkins University Press, 1989.

Clark, Hazel. "Second Hand Fashion in Hong Kong." In *Old Clothes, New Looks: Second Hand Fashion*, edited by Palmer, Alexandra and Hazel Clark. New York: Berg, 2005: 155–170.

Cline, Elizabeth. *Overdressed: The Shockingly High Cost of Cheap Fashion*. New York: Penguin, 2012.

Davila, Arlene. *Culture Works: Space, Value, and Mobility across the Neoliberal Americas*. New York: New York University Press, 2012.

Dávila, Arlene. *El Mall*. Berkeley: University of California Press, 2016.

De Soto, Hernando. *The Other Path*. New York: Harper & Row, 1989.

Douglas, Mary. *Purity and Danger*. London: Routledge, 1966.

Duneier, Mitchell. *Sidewalk*. New York: Farrar, Straus and Giroux, 1999.

Entwistle, Joanne. *The Aesthetic Economy of Fashion: Markets and Value in Clothing and Modeling*. London: Berg, 2009.

Ferrell, Jeff. *Empire of Scrounge: Inside the Urban Underground of Dumpster Diving, Trash Picking, and Street Scavenging*. New York: New York University Press, 2006.

Fontaine, Laurence, ed. *Alternative Exchanges: Second-Hand Circulations from the Sixteenth Century to the Present*. New York: Berghan Books, 2008.

Galemba, Rebecca B. "Informal and Illicit Entrepreneurs: Fighting for a Place in the Neoliberal Economic Order." *Anthropology of Work Review* 29, no. 2 (2008): 19–25.

Gauthier, Melissa. *The Fayuca Hormiga of Used Clothing and the Fabric of the Mexico-U.S. Border*. PhD Thesis. Concordia University, 2009.

Goldsmith, David. "The Worn, the Torn, the Wearable: Textile Recycling in Union Square." *Nordic Textile Journal*. Vol 1. 2012: 16–29.

Gowan, Teresa. "New Hobos or Neo-Romantic Fantasy? Urban Ethnography beyond the Neoliberal Disconnect." *Qualitative Sociology* 32, no. 3 (2009): 231–257.

Graeber, David. *Toward an Anthropological Theory of Value*. New York: Palgrave, 2001.

Gregson, Nicky, and Louise Crewe. *Secondhand Cultures*. New York: Berg, 2003.

Gregson, Nicky, Kate Brooks, and Louise Crewe. "Narratives of Consumption and the Body in the Space of the Charity/Shop." In *Commercial Cultures: Economics, Practices, Spaces*, edited by Peter Jackson, Michelle Lowe, Daniel Miller and Frank Mort, 101–121. London: Berg, 2000.

Hansen, Karen Tranberg. *Salaula: The World of Secondhand Clothing and Zambia*. Chicago, IL: University of Chicago, 2000a.

Hansen, Karen Tranberg. "Other People's Clothes? The International Second-Hand Clothing Trade and Dress Practices in Zambia." *Fashion Theory* 4, no. 3 (2000b): 245–274.

Hansen, Karen Tranberg. "Charity, Commerce, Consumption: The International Secondhand Clothing Trade at the Turn of the Millennium – Focus on Zambia." In *Alternative Exchanges: Secondhand Circulations from the Sixteenth Century to the Present*, edited by Laurence Fontaine. New York: Berghahn Books, 2008: 221–234.

Hart, Keith. "Informal Income Opportunities and Urban Employment in Ghana." *The Journal of Modern African Studies* 11, no. 01 (1973): 61–89.

Hawkins, Gay. *The Ethics of Waste: How We Relate to Rubbish*. Lanham: Rowman and Littlefield, 2006.

Hawkins, Gay, and Stephen Muecke, eds. *Culture and Waste: The Creation and Destruction of Value*. Lanham: Rowman and Littlefield, 2003.

Hawley, Jana M. "Digging for Diamonds: A Conceptual Framework for Understanding Reclaimed Textile Waste Products." *Clothing and Textiles Research Journal* 24, no. 3 (2006): 262–275.

Hill, Sarah. "El Dompe, Los Yankees, and Las Segundas: Consumption's Other Side in El-Paso-Ciudad Juarez." In *Land of Necessity: Consumer Culture in the United States- Mexico Borderlands*, edited by Alexis McCrossen. Durham: Duke University Press, 2009: 298–319.

Hoff, Al. *Thrift Score*. New York: Harper Collins, 1999.

Hou, Jeffrey. "Night Market in Seattle: Community Eventscape and the Reconstruction of Public Space." In *Insurgent Public Space: Guerrilla Urbanism and the Remaking of Contemporary Cities*, Hou Jefffey, ed. New York: Routledge, 2010: 111–222.

Hrabe, Jon. "Goodwill's Charity Racket: CEOs Earn Top-Dollar, Workers Paid Less than Minimum Wage". *Huffington Post*. 2012. https://www.huffingtonpost.com/john-hrabe/the-worst-corporation-in-_b_1876905.html

Hrabe, Jon. "Goodwill Minimum Wage Loophole Will Shock You". *Huffington Post*. 2013. https://www.huffingtonpost.com/john-hrabe/goodwill-minimum-wage_b_3246824.html.

Hrabe, Jon. "Policies, Tax Dollars Enrich Goodwill Execs". 2013. https://watchdog.org/83209/policies-tax-dollars-enrich-goodwill-execs/

LeZotte, Jennifer. *From Goodwill to Grunge: A History of Secondhand Styles and Alternative Economies*. Chapel Hill: UNC Press, 2017.

Marcelli, Enrico. "The Diverse Nature of Informal Work in California." In *Informal Work in Developed Nations*, edited by Enrico Marcelli, Colin C Williams and Pascale Jossart, 168–176. New York: Routledge, 2010.

Marcelli, Enrico, Colin C. Williams, and Pascale Jossart, eds. *Informal Work in Developed Nations*. New York: Routledge, 2010.

McRobbie, Angela. *Be Creative: Making a Living in the New Culture Industries*. Cambridge: Polity, 2016.

McRobbie, Angela. "Second-Hand Dresses and the Role of the Rag Market." In *Zoot Suits and Second-Hand Dresses*, edited by Angela McRobbie. Boston, MA: Unwin Hyman, 1988: 23–49.

McRobbie, Angela. "A New Kind of Rag Trade?" In *The Consumer Society Reader*, edited by Juliet B. Schor and Douglas B. Holt. New York: The New Press, 2000: 433–445.

Medina, Marcel. *The World's Scavengers: Salvaging for Sustainable Consumption and Production*. Lanham: Altamira Press, 2007.

Medvedev, Katalin. "It's a Garage Sale at Savers Every Day: An Ethnography of the Savers Thrift Department Store in Minneapolis." In *Exchanging Clothes: Habits of Being II*, edited by Christina Giorcelli and Paula Rabinowitz. Minneapolis, MN: University of Minnesota Press, 2012: 230–253.

Milgram, Lynne B. "Second Hand Clothing in the Philippines." In *Old Clothes, New Looks: Second Hand Fashion*, edited by Palmer, Alexander and Clark, Hazel. New York: Berg, 2005: 135–154.

Millar, K. "Making Trash into Treasure: Struggles for Autonomy on a Brazilian Garbage Dump." *Anthropology of Work Review* XXIX(2), no. 2 (2008): 25–34.

NARTS National Association of Resale Professionals. Press release, "Resale Thrives in a Slow Economy." Accessed July 8, 2015. https://www.narts.org/i4a/pages/index.cfm?pageid=329

Neuwirth, Robert. *Stealth of Nations: The Global Rise of the Informal Economy*. New York: Pantheon Books, 2011.

Nightingale, Demetra Smith and Stephen A. Wandner. *Informal and Nonstandard Employment in the United States: Implications for Low-Income Working Families*. Washington DC: The Urban Institute, 2011.

Norris, Lucy. *Recycling Indian Clothing: Global Contexts of Reuse and Value*. Bloomington: Indiana University Press, 2010.

Palmer, Alexander, and Hazel Clark, eds. *Old Clothes, New Looks: Second Hand Fashion*. New York: Berg, 2005.

Parker, Brenda, and Rachel Weber. "Second-Hand Spaces: Restructuring Retail Geographies in an Era of E-Commerce." *Urban Geography* 34, no. 8 (2013): 1096–1118.

Portes, Alejandro, Manuel Castells, and Lauren A. Benton, eds. *The Informal Economy: Studies in Advanced and Less Developed Countries*. Baltimore, MD: John Hopkins University Press, 1989.

Portes, Alejandro, and William Haller. "The Informal Economy." In *The Handbook of Economic Sociology*, edited by Neil J. Smelser and Richard Swedberg, 403–425. Princeton: Princeton University Press, 2005.

Reno, Joshua. "Your Trash is Someone's Treasure: The Politics of Value at a Michigan Landfill." *Journal of Material Culture* 14, no. 1 (2009): 29–46.

Rivoli, Pietra. *The Travels of a T-Shirt in the Global Economy: An Economist Examines the Markets, Power, and the Politics of World Trade*. Hoboken: John Wiley and Sons, 2009.

Rojas, James. "Latino Urbanism in Los Angeles." In *Insurgent Public Space: Guerrilla Urbanism and the Remaking of Contemporary Cities*, ed Jefferey Hou. New York: Routledge, 2010: 36–44.

Ross, Andrew. *Nice Work If You Can Get It*. New York: New York University Press, 2009.

Samson, M. "Accumulation by Dispossession and the Informal Economy – Struggles over Knowledge, Being and Waste at a Soweto Garbage Dump." *Environment and Planning D: Society and Space* 33, no. 5 (2015): 813–830.

Sassen, Saskia. *Globalization and Its Discontents: Essays on the New Mobility of People and Money*. New York: The New Press, 1998.

Sassen, Saskia. "The Informal Economy." In *Dual City: Restructuring New York*, edited by John H. Mollenkopf and Manuel Castells, 79–101. New York: Russell Sage Foundation, 1991.

Smith, Robert. *Mexican Immigrant Women in New York City's Informal Economy*. New York: Columbia University-New York University Consortium, 1992.

Stack, Carol B. *All Our Kin: Strategies for Survival in a Black Community*. New York: Harper and Row, 1974.

Stallybrass, Peter. "Marx's Coat." In *Border Fetishisms: Material Objects in Unstable Spaces*, edited by Patricia Spyer, 183–207. London: Routledge, 1998.

Stallybrass, Peter. "Worn Worlds: Clothing, Mourning, and the Life of Things." In *Cultural Memory and the Construction of Identity*, edited by D. Ben-Amos and L. Weissberg, 35–50. Detroit, MI: Wayne State University Press, 1999.

Steward, Shelly. "What Does That Shirt Mean to You?: Thrift-Store Consumption as Cultural Capital." Working paper. Department of Sociology, University of California-Berkeley, 2017.

Stoller, Paul. *Money Has No Smell*. Chicago, IL: University of Chicago Press, 2002.

Strasser, Susan. *Waste and Want: A Social History of Trash*. New York: Henry Holt and Company, 1999.

Stuadt, Kathleen. *Free Trade: Informal Economies at the U.S. Mexico Border*. Philadelphia, PA: Temple University Press, 1998.

Thompson, Michael. *Rubbish Theory: The Creation and Destruction of Value*. New York: Oxford University Press, 1979.

Tinkcom, Matthew, Joy Van Fuqua, and Amy Villarejo. "On Thrifting." In *Hop on Pop: The Politics and Pleasures of Popular Culture*, edited by Henry Jenkins, Tara McPherson, and Jane Shattuc, eds. Durham: Duke University Press, 2002: 459–471.

Tu, Thuy Linh. *The Beautiful Generation: Asian Americans and the Cultural Economy of Fashion*. Durham: Duke University Press, 2011.

Valenzuela, Abel Jr. "Day Labourers as Entrepreneurs?" *Journal of Ethnic and Migration Studies* 27, no. 2 (2001): 335–352.

Venkatesh, Sudhir. *Off the Books: The Underground Economy of the Urban Poor*. Boston, MA: Harvard University Press, 2006.

Wescoat Sanders, Justin. "Junk's Last Chance." *The Portland Mercury* 29 July. 2004.

Yang, Lichao. "At the Bottom of the Heap: Socioeconomic Circumstances and Health Practices and Beliefs among Garbage Pickers in Peri-Urban China." *Critical Asian Studies* 48, no. 1 (2015): 1–9.

Zhang, Lin. "Fashioning the Feminine Self in 'Prosumer Capitalism': Women's Work and the Transnational Reselling of Western Luxury Online." *Journal of Consumer Culture* 10(1): (2015): 1–21.

Zlolniski, Christian. *Janitors, Street Vendors, and Activists: The Lives of Mexican Immigrants in Silicon Valley*. Los Angeles, CA: University of California Press, 2006.

Zukin, Sharon. *Point of Purchase: How Shopping Changed American Culture*. New York: Routledge, 2003.

Zukin, Sharon. *Naked City: The Death and Life of Authentic Urban Places*. New York: Oxford University Press, 2010.

Valuation in action: Ethnography of an American thrift store

Frederik Larsen

ABSTRACT

This article documents the workings of a contemporary second-hand thrift store in California. The ethnographic notes collected during six-months fieldwork and subsequent returns present accounts of the practices, values and people involved in turning the remainders of consumption into cultural commodities, and the interwoven relations between object and people. The process of transformation is best understood in a nexus between gift and market exchange as an act of categorisation. Revisiting Mary Douglas' statement on dirt as matter of classification, the article shows how value is momentarily fixed in the objects to allow them to re-enter second-hand economies, and how categorisation is an attempt to manage the reality of disorder.

When I first started working at the Community Thrift Store in San Francisco I was immediately sent to 'the back door'. 'This is where people drop off donations and we do the first round of sorting', Armun[1] told me when he showed me around. 'From here they are sent to the different departments'. The back door is located on the right side of the building opening onto a small street where vehicles can pull up and people can unload donations directly onto the dock. Inside there is an area for unloading and different crates and carts where the employees will drop the donation designated for the various departments. From here the donations enter a crucial stage in their 'social lives' of transformation, from being discards to becoming cultural commodities.[2] The journey is perilous and many of them never reach that goal, but are instead discarded once again. Those that do survive that journey are remarketed to become part of the growing second-hand economy.

At the back door the Community Thrift accepts responsibility for donations regardless of their condition. Whether or not the objects can be sold, at whatever price, the organisation now considers them their responsibility and deals with them in one way or another. This responsibility has several implications: most importantly, it means that everything that enters is thoroughly considered and every effort is made to make the object marketable. The organisation lives up to its name by being thrifty and making the most of donations. If the objects cannot be sold individually they are sold on in bulk to other second-hand organisations or recycled. Due to this sense of responsibility, the employees and the managers do what they can to utilise the donations, and this attitude is ingrained in the organisation's way of operating.

This article documents the workings of a contemporary second-hand thrift store in California. It offers descriptions of the actions, considerations and circumstances of performing valuations in the context of a thrift store. The ethnographic notes were collected during six months of fieldwork and subsequent returns, and present accounts of the practices, values and people involved in turning the remainders of consumption into cultural commodities. In the process stories are used to elucidate the interwoven relations between the things, the people and the community. The primary objective of this article is to give a detailed view of the everyday activities of a thrift store. As such it offers a view of contemporary practices to supplement historical accounts. Therefore the ethnographic details are only contextualised towards the end of the article to initiate an analytical understanding of valuation practices. Taking Mary Douglas' statement on dirt as a point of departure,[3] the article shows how values are temporarily fixed in the objects in order to allow them to re-enter the second-hand economies. The process of categorisation of the objects constitutes sense-making practices that allow cultural value to be attached to the objects. The process of transforming discards creates a nexus between gift and market exchange and the valuations manifest a number of values that collectively bring second-hand objects to market. These involve economic factors and knowledge of the market as well as social value for the community and emotional value attached to the process of donating. Identifying categorisation as pivotal in bringing second-hand objects to market, the article shows how valuation practices are constantly adapted to the realities of disorder and how things, no matter how rigorous the practice, continue to fall through the gaps.

The tavern guild community thrift store

The Tavern Guild Community Thrift Store organisation is based in San Francisco. It is a registered charity that divides its profits between more than 200 local charities. The organisation was founded in 1982 by a group of restaurateurs and bar owners in the gay community in response to the AIDS epidemic, as a way to raise money for victims of the disease. In the beginning the organisation only raised money for HIV and AIDS charities, but it has since expanded the types of charities to include animal sanctuaries, shelters, healthcare centres and many others.[4] The operation is run by 22 paid employees, managers and assistant mangers, and an executive director. The organisation is located in a large warehouse on Valencia Street in San Francisco where all its activities are housed. The store has a large pink façade facing Valencia Street, one of the most popular streets in the area, with new stores popping up all the time. The area has undergone a gentrification process since the late 1990s when the area first became popular with technology entrepreneurs. After the dotcom 'bubble' burst at the end of the millennium, the gentrification slowed off, but has resumed and intensified in recent years, leaving Community Thrift in a central and highly coveted retail location. The area is now inhabited by a mix of people from all ethnic groups and income levels, a diversity clearly reflected in the store's clientele.

The community thrift store is one of many charity run organisations utilising discarded household goods such as clothing, furniture, homewares electronics and other objects as a means of generating profit for charitable causes. As such it is located in a history of charity organisations utilising the surplus of consumer goods created by increasing industrial production. Modern thrift stores first emerged during the first decades of the twentieth century in the US.[5] The number of second-hand stores and the size of the trade then greatly increased in the 1970s with the emergence of a budding interest in protecting the environment. Especially since the mid-1990s, many western countries have seen a dramatic rise in interest in used objects.[6] The Community Thrift operates within this context and while thrift shops, as Le Zotte notes,[7] now cater to a wide audience, the Community Thrift is dedicated to serving its community. What that means specifically is explored in the following. The Community Thrift operates like many other charity organisations in the USA and in Europe by collecting and accepting material donations for resale, from which it generates all of its revenue. People donate their unwanted objects – clothes, furniture, kitchenware, art works, CDs, books, etc. – and the employees, some paid and some volunteers, sort, value and price the objects before they are remarketed. Charity organisations make up a large segment of second-hand economies especially in what could be described as the beginning of the value chain; the point where second-hand objects are 'produced' as objects for markets, out of what people donate. In recent years eBay and similar online platforms have facilitated direct sales between end-customers, but in the markets I have studied (US, Denmark and Thailand) charity organisations still report increasing sales.

The ethnographic fieldwork that forms the basis of this article was carried out in and around the organisation over a period of six month. I entered the Community Thrift as a volunteer and was trained in all the different stations along the trajectory from donation to sale. That the organisation was willing to offer me so much instruction made the approach very useful, and I describe this method as an apprenticeship. Learning how to perform valuations allowed me to get a much closer understanding of all the different aspects. Ingold has described this type of role in fieldwork as a 'skilled practitioner,'[8] highlighting the participatory and experiential aspects: 'the novice becomes skilled not through the acquisition of rules and representations, but at the point where he or she is able to dispense with them'.[9] The ethnographic account that follows describes the journey objects take from donation to resale with a focus on the practices and considerations that go into re-establishing them as valuable commodities.

The beginning of the journey

The first station in the journey from donation to resale is 'the back door'. Inside the door, which is more like a gate, the donations go through the primary stage of rough sorting. Next to the gate there is a sign informing donors of which items the organisation accepts and what it does not accept. Most of the time, two employees are stationed here to assist donors and perform the initial sorting. The donors are relatively involved in this process, since they hand over the donations directly to the employees. Most of the time this meeting is quite uneventful, but there are instances where these meetings become more engaged. The first day I worked at the back door I experienced some of the emotional aspects of handling used objects:

> This first donor drove up to the gate with his whole car filled with boxes. They all contained his late wife's clothes and shoes. She had recently passed away and he was getting rid of all her clothes. 'It's hard,' he said, a little emotionally, as he dropped the first box on the ramp. I helped him carry the boxes to the gate and they were all marked with a description of the content of the box: 17 pairs of new socks, trouser suits, dresses, etc. He had also printed out an inventory of all the objects and noted the prices of all the things. The total amount came to over $5,000. Karen handed him a receipt that he filled out with his name, date, the amount and, at the bottom of

the receipt, the name of the charity he wanted the money raised to go to. He wanted to donate the money to a women's shelter his wife had volunteered for from time to time.

Most of the encounters are less emotional, but many 'drop-offs' are prompted by emotional events in people's lives: moving house, clearing out relative's belongings and even weight loss.[10]

When the donations have been dropped off, some are rejected and some are discarded, but most are divided into boxes, bags and crates to be taken to the different departments of 'homeware', 'clothing', 'books', 'art and music', and 'electronics'. The first sorting does not entail any pricing, but it does involve an initial valuation in the form of decisions as to which objects need to be discarded immediately and which of the remainder should go where.

After the rough sorting stage, the objects are taken to the different departments for closer inspection and valuation. The departments have different ways of performing valuations, but there are similar concerns for all of them. The most important feature in the valuation is the condition of the object, since most objects have to be in good material condition to be remarketed. In rare cases, the brand or name of the artist behind an object can justify it being remarketed despite flaws, but formal indicators like designer names or label are mostly secondary to material condition. Desirability and demand is usually the next feature considered. Most objects will go out on display if they are not broken or flawed, a though if they are highly sought-after they may still be remarketed with minor flaws. Conversely, if there is a lot of the same type of objects then some may be discarded. In the following text I will describe in more detail how the objects are handled to exemplify the practices and considerations involved.

When a crate of electronic devices is brought from the back door into the electronics department, Ralph, one of the employees working in this department, cleans and tests each object. A crate can include anything from TVs to phones, memory cards, blenders, lamps, and amplifiers. CD players are plugged in and connected to speakers and PCs are connected to monitors and all content is erased. Coffee makers are only turned on: 'no coffee is actually being brewed!' Ralph tells me jokingly. He keeps odd plugs, bulbs, batteries and adaptors so that he can test any objects that come in without leads or cables. If the objects work they are priced, and if not they are either marked 'as is' and labelled as non-functioning, or are recycled. Customers who can fix them will buy the objects at a lower price, Ralph tells me. Odd cables, memory cards and other accessories are sold for approximately 50–75 c. He prices stuff based on his knowledge of what customers will buy, combined with a sense of 'What would I pay?', 'How new or old is this?' and 'What do we usually charge?'. Ralph will mostly price stuff at 'something-plus-25-cents', or 'something-plus-75-cents'. Prices like $8 are rare, he says, and so is $5.50. He is completely aware that this is a psychological matter, but still keeps to the 'principle'. In the clothing department the objects, in this case clothes, also undergo a thorough inspection before they are priced and remarketed. First the employees at the back door accept the clothes, then attach charity numbers and put the clothing in crates. These crates are then moved to the clothing area where they are sorted into usable items and recyclable items (or consigned to the $1 bin). The initial inspection ensures there are no holes in the clothes and that they are clean. The usable items are stacked and the stacks are separated with a piece of tape indicating the different charity the clothes were donated to. Tags are then attached with the charity code on them and the clothes are divided into men's and women's. They are then moved again into subsections according to clothing types: jackets, trousers, tops, etc. From there they are priced individually and placed on hangers and brought to the shop floor.

The first time I worked in the clothing department, Karen showed me how to price designer jeans. She looked at the brand, and from her knowledge of what people want she priced them accordingly. The average price is between 16–23 dollars if there is nothing wrong with the jeans. If they are a more popular brand or style they will go higher; if there is a small stain or they show too many signs of wear, they will go for a lower price. Clothing priced above $17 is put in a special section and chained to the rack to prevent theft. The $1 bin, meanwhile, is where all the stuff is placed that is too good to recycle but too worn or stained to go in the ordinary section. After Karen had instructed me I started performing pricing in the clothing department myself. The first time I did this I valued women's and men's jackets. The jackets had already been sorted and tagged with the charity code. I performed the final run-through, assigned a price and put them on hangers. They are placed on a rack that only contains items ready to go out into the store. In order to assign a price I examined the state of each jacket and determined whether it was a 'high end' brand. If it was not I referred to a list Karen had given me specifying the price-range of different types of clothing. The list is divided into categories of styles and brands. Women's t-shirts are priced between $2.50 and $3, though a vintage or brand T-shirt, for example, can go for up to five dollars. Outdoor jackets are more expensive, as are items from brands like J Crew, GAP, and Jones of New York. While I was working on the jackets, Meeta came over to see how I was doing. I had found a few vintage pieces among the items I was valuing that should go in a separate section, as well as a few things with stains or tears. Meeta, who is the manager in the clothing department, explained to me that one of the advantages of having different people doing the sorting and pricing is that different people see different things.

The ordinary and the unique

Although much of the work involves routine tasks for the employees, every day something new comes in that needs special attention and requires the employees to spend time conferring with colleagues or looking the object up online. These special items can be very different. On one occasion, an old – almost antique – pewter thermos was donated. It was brought in inside a box with a lot of other objects and was immediately identified as something that had to be looked up. A few days later, when the 'look-up' box was full, Karen went through it and looked up the thermos online. I did a similar search and found it on eBay priced at almost $100. Karen decided to set the price at 32 dollars and 50 cents, which reflects the particular status of the object, but still a significantly lower price than it might fetch online. This corresponds with the overall pricing strategy of the Community Thrift. The aim is to price objects so that they bring in as much money as possible for the charities, but also that they should be accessible. Accessibility is considered in relation to regular customers who may not be able to afford expensive items, but also to cater for professional buyers. Professional buyers make up a relatively large portion of the customer base and they generate a lot of revenue, as well as taking quite a number of items out of the store and thereby making room for new objects. The price should be low enough for professional buyers to want to purchase the items and be able to sell them on with a profit.

Valuation in action

The journey through the organisation represents a symbolic and social transformation for the objects, but a large number of physical movements are involved in order to bring about this transformation. From the back door to the different departments and the sales floor, objects are constantly moved around. The series of movements can be seen as a process of refinement with ever-higher levels of attention being given to details at every station. The stations are fixed while the objects flow through them. Employees move them from station to station, often prompted by a lack of space as more objects flow in. After their valuation in different departments, the objects are put in boxes or on racks once they have been tagged, ready to go onto the sales floor.

Even ordinary items like mugs, T-shirts and paperbacks need individual inspection and consideration to ensure their condition is up to standard. With most objects the condition has to be perfect. At the same time, because the organisation has a strong commitment to generating as much profit for the charities as possible, the inspection and consideration of each object is taken very seriously. Everything that is donated is valued. One day when I was working at the back door with Scott pricing objects, I came across some office supplies that were left at the bottom of a box: some pins, a roll of tape, some post-its, pens, etc. I asked Scott if he ever priced stuff at less than fifty cents, because I had just priced a number of items slightly bigger and more attractive than these at fifty cents. He told me they did not and said I should 'bundle them together'. Bundling means finding a way to ensure the items stay together, either by securing them with tape or using one of the various sized bags they keep for the same reason. I made bundles of ten pens and an eraser for two dollars, or three post-it blocks, or three packets of staples + five pens. I then taped up the bags, priced them and put them in 'office supplies' in the homeware section of the store. As an expression of the thrifty approach adopted in the Community Thrift, investing some time ensures the leftover objects become marketable. Over the six months I worked in the warehouse I heard again and again the statement that 'we just want the stuff to sell'. No one prices objects in the expectation that the items will hang around until the right buyer (maybe) turns up: the objects must 'move'. This is an underlying principle, just like the principle that the organisation will try to raise as much money as possible from the donations they receive.

In all departments the objects are tagged with different coloured tags to make it easier to identify how long the object has been on display in the store. This information is used when employees 'pull' objects from the store after they have failed to sell within a certain amount of time. The objects are then either reduced in price, which requires a new tag, or discarded, in which case they end up in boxes or bags and are placed at the back entrance. These bags and boxes are then collected by companies that either resell or recycle them in various ways.

Having worked my way through the back area, I was allowed to work at the sales counter as well. Helping customers with the items at the counter allowed me to observe another aspect of handling used goods that is also time-consuming. When someone asks to see a camera for example, you take the cameras out and place them on the counter. Most of the time the customer wants to see several cameras in order to be able to decide and compare. This is a lengthy operation mostly because the customers cannot test the cameras so they have to examine them closely to check for flaws. Some of the digital cameras come with chargers, but this also takes time due to the need to plug them in, replace the battery and turn on the camera. The same goes for phones. In that case, customers can check if the phones turn on properly, but not if they can actually make calls. A lot of the customers buying electronics are return customers who know the drill. One of the regular customers is a professional buyer who comes in often and looks up the online value of the cameras on his phone. He hangs out in a corner, typing in style numbers and brands on his phone, looking to see if he can make a profit on any of the items.

By working at the counter I was able to observe the last stage of the journey of the objects as they leave the Store. Most of them go out without any interference, but some, especially the more expensive items, are reduced in price if they are to be sold to a returning customer or if a customer buys more things at once. One day, for example, Armun gave a 25% reduction on a clock he sold to a customer who was also buying two speakers. Armun told me he gave the reduction because the customer was going to buy the speakers and because the clock had been sitting in the store for three weeks. In some cases the objects only leave the store temporarily. Some of them return because people no longer have any use for them and decide to re-donate, while others return because some of the customers shop in the store as a form of hobby. These customers spend a long time browsing for things they want. They buy objects, sometimes every day, and then re-donate them. Sometimes the stuff comes back with the price tag on it showing that it was bought very recently.

Zooming in on valuations

Training and working in the different departments gave me an embodied understanding of what valuations entail and how formal indicators and tacit subjective knowledge, as well as sensations, emotions and energy levels, all play a part in the process. Most of my observations were grounded in these experiences, but I also used additional tools and methods like Interviews and casual conversations to clarify how my experiences related to those of other more experienced sorters. To supplement my knowledge, I conducted sessions of joint interviews during the sorting of individual objects as they were donated. The following is an excerpt from my notes from one such session:

> Zack, Scott and I sat down in the homeware department and looked at the box in front of us. The first object Scott took out of the box was an metal teapot in Arabic style. It had a plastic ring round the top of the lid, which Scott removed to make it look more attractive. He said it didn't really affect the price whether this ring was on or off, but he removed it anyway. Zack agreed on the price and Scott put a pink price tag on the teapot indicating the monthly colour code and stamped with the price and a charity code, in this case 176, which indicates that the object has been donated to raise money to Safehouse, a local charity dedicated to providing housing to homeless women who have been involved in sex-work.

> The second object was a handmade wooden candleholder. It was made of real wood, which Zack noted was important, and it had a 'mid-century modern' look to it, although it was not marked. Scott and Zack both considered it special and so the final price was set at $4.25.

> Next were four martini glasses which Scott and Zack considered to be quite nice but nothing exceptional. They were priced at $2.25.

> Immediately after, Scott pulled out another set of martini glasses. They were longer than the first four and generated some debate back and forth, since Zack thought they should be priced the same as the first four glasses while Scott insisted that they should be priced higher because they were longer and more attractive. In the end Scott won the argument and they were priced at three dollars each.

We went through a number of other objects, amongst which was a set of French glass plates. According to Scott they were valuable, but since they were scratched he did not want to put a high price on them. Zack, on the other hand, would not have them put in the store at all and discarded them immediately because of their condition.

What these sessions helped me identify was the individual involvement and judgements in the valuations. Although the underlying principles clearly inform the fundamentals of valuations, ultimately it is a personal call that decides the price and whether the objects will continue the journey.

Last stage of commoditisation

Objects that have been discarded during the valuation or after being 'called' in the store are collected in bags and boxes and put in a corner in the back area, to be picked up by other companies that either recycle them or sort them again to see if there is anything of value. The donated clothes that go to recycling are those that have turned out to be too dirty or in too poor condition. There are also items that have been in the store for a long time but have not sold. These clothes are all put in plastic bags and are picked up several times a week, by a recycling company. I observed the pickups of most of the different types of objects, from pottery to clothing and books. In the book department Drew explained how the decision is made to get rid of books that have been in the store for too long: 'I try not to get rid of stuff that might sell, but you have to throw some things away'. Like all the others working at the Community Thrift, Drew is highly aware of the organisation's principle that they want to make as much money for the charities as possible, so that getting rid of stuff that might sell is a difficult decision. Since the company that picks up the books pays by bulk and not by individual value, there is no need to throw out valuable books. The process of creating or capturing the value of the donated objects relies on a combination of organisational principles and ad hoc judgements. As the objects leave the thrift store, either as recycled material or by being sold they enter a larger second-hand economy that constitutes the context of valuation practices.

Categories of value: Understanding the practices of valuation

At the intersection of consumption and production, second-hand exchanges touch on a number of fields. Studies have documented charity and thrift shops,[11] second-hand markets in different parts of the world,[12] the global flows of used commodities,[13] and the impact of second-hand trade on cultures all over the world.[14] Only a few studies have addressed the collecting and sorting that takes place in organisations[15] and charity organisations.[16] The studies mentioned here take different approaches to the subject, but most are joined by the attention to the movement of objects and the importance of contextualising second-hand objects to understand their value. One of the ways this is done is through the use of cultural categories.

Matter out of place

Following Mary Douglas,[17] making sense of second-hand objects can be seen mainly as a matter of categorization. Her statement that 'dirt is matter out of place' offers a structural approach and suggests that categories produce dirt. Framed by this approach Botticello argues, when describing the sorting process in second-hand industries, that, by turning the process around and categorising dirt or discards, the sorting process creates order and the potential for value.[18] Before the sorting begins, the piles of donations are unrecognizable as commodities and carry very little value. What goes on in the Community Thrift can thus be described as a transformation through categorisation.

Sorting, or categorisation, creates a structure, a trajectory, through the organisation. This structure is relatively stationary since the different employees inhabit different stations throughout the organisation. The mobility is in the objects. The trajectories that the objects follow highlight the instability in the lives of things. And in the Community Thrift there are several possible trajectories. By establishing trajectories the organization attempts to manage the continuous flow of donations. The particular interference the structure imposes on the flow are the actions that transform the discards into commodities. As Kopytoff describes, writing biographies of things can help make sense of the instances where things change states.[19] The present account offers an augmented view of this event in 'the life of things' where the objects change from one state to another. What happens inside the Community Thrift is an event with several possible outcomes, to which I will subsequently return.

Practicing valuations

The structure I have described rests solely on the systems of routinised actions that the employees and managers perform. In fact, practicing valuation is in itself what creates value, both by making sense of the objects and by investing time and energy in them. These actions organize objects and social relations and are themselves organised. Practices are always unique and at the same time a repetition of previous recognizable practices. A defining feature of practices as described by Reckwitz, is the interconnectedness of activities, knowledge and objects and those connections are evident in valuation processes.[20] Repetition is crucial to valuation as to other practices. As 'a routinized type of behaviour which consists of several elements, interconnected to one other: forms of bodily activities, forms of mental activities, things and their use, a background knowledge in the form of understanding, know-how, states of emotion and motivational knowledge,'[21] practices are at once individual and collective. As a single action or even a set of actions, a valuation is not rooted in a wider structure of meaning. Through the interconnectedness of the organisation, the individual and the social context, valuations are stabilised and are central to the process of turning discards into commodities.

Rubbish in disorder

I have used the term discards about the objects as they arrive. They could also be understood as rubbish. Thompson,[22] when defining his seminal approach to the study of economic value in second-hand markets describes rubbish as a 'region of flexibility',[23] which allows for different outcomes. According to Thompson, consumer objects have transient value that at some point turn them into rubbish. But by entering the rubbish state they also have the possibility to gain durable value as antiques or collectibles. In Thompson's view, transfers occur between transient, rubbish and durable states in that order. Objects do not move from durable to transient or from rubbish to transient. The Community Thrift mainly handles objects that Thompson would define as transient, namely household goods. The employees and volunteers enforce a structure that aims to categorise the rubbish and turn it into valuable objects. Therefore the durable state in this analysis includes objects that have been reinstated as commodities, whether durable or transient. In the Community Thrift the categories are less defined and some objects are donated as transient and continue as transient even after the valuations. Also, durable objects such as artworks and antiques are donated because of their value even though they go through a rubbish state. Thompson describes the process of moving objects from one state to another as a transfer. He focuses on structural processes, but as the transfers in the Community Thrift involve a number of practices and actions I expand the term and describe them as a transformation instead. The objects move as part of an active engagement and the categorisations make the objects recognizable as commodities. In that sense, the term transformation better indicates the activities and the change that is involved.

The ambiguity in the process has led me to describe the donations as discards instead of rubbish. I use the term discards because it can refer to objects that are considered rubbish as well as objects that are considered valuable but have been discarded by their previous owner anyway. Either way, the donations arrive because they have been discarded and are physically and categorically in disorder. The disorder, or being out of place in Douglas' terms, is a potentially powerful state and preserving or allowing some degree of disorder is valuable. However, the primary action which the donations activate is categorisation through structure and a move out of the rubbish state.

Performative disorder

No matter how well the objects are categorised, some of them challenge the structures that the employees tirelessly seek to enforce. At any given time, a box containing cups, paperclips, three pens, a pair of jeans and five books may be donated, activating the process in which the employees begin organising the different objects. Almost every donation raises new questions and requires slight adaptations to the system. The individuality of the objects means that each category of the systematisation needs to be broad. At the same time, knowing exactly where things go and why is important in order to perform a valuation and pricing of the object that balances the different dimensions described above. While the individuality of each object is crucial to their transformation into valuable commodities, at the same time it hinders a seamless flow from discard to commodity. I have described the transformation as a movement from disorder – matter out of place – into commodities through meaningful structures and categories. On one level, therefore, a semiotic, structuralist level, the objects are transformed into valuable commodities; while on another level the individual nature of the objects resists this structure and changes the categories. Don Slater points out that ambiguity is not a property of objects but of classification and practices, and goes on to outline a number of ways in which ambiguity affects objects in markets and in consumption.[24] Along the lines of Douglas's argument, Slater describes the potentiality of ambiguity as both a risk and an opportunity. Being uncategorizable is a potential taboo, but also a possibility for change. In the sorting of second-hand objects, uncategorizable objects are certainly potent and their position can result in a higher value. It may also mean that the object is discarded or disappears in the store because it does not sit comfortably among other similar objects.

Adjusting categories is one of the clearest expressions of the performative nature of the valuation structure. At any moment in time, the Community Thrift operates with a specific number of more or less defined categories that appear stable to the employees and the customers. Over time, however, these categories change: new categories are invented and old ones are abandoned to fit the demands of the customers or the objects. Some of them are formal categories that are written down and enforced throughout the sorting process. Karen told me how children's wear had been a category for a period of time, but had later been abandoned, to the point where the Community Thrift no longer accepts children's clothes. This category was removed due to the amount of work it took to keep that section of the store clear. According to Karen, customers shopping for children's clothes would often take all the clothes off the hangers and just leave them on the floor. An executive decision was thus made to stop offering them altogether. Other categories are removed or established more unnoticeably based on the donations that come in. Sometimes there are a lot of similar items, or a lot of things that can be grouped together. During the time I worked in the Community Thrift, crystal glassware was one particular section that appeared and disappeared regularly. At other times there were a lot of ceramic items. So the different sections grow or diminish or even disappear over time to make place for something else. The temporary categories are an efficient means of creating order even of more specialised objects.

As Botticello notes, donations produce categories that reclassify objects.[25] Creating categories is a way of creating meaning and becomes a way of establishing relations between employees (who now know where to put things) and customers (who now know where to find them). In the Community Thrift it is clearly visible how the systematisation and categorisation of the objects along the trajectory through the process is crucial for the value creation. Each category relates the objects to other similar or comparable objects and to other external contexts. It also became clear to me how categorisation is disrupted by the contingency of objects and their materiality. The fact that nobody knows what or how much will be donated also disturbs the categories. And the uncertainty of what the donations will include means that there has to be a certain amount of openness. However, for the individual doing the job of putting things out on the shelves, the sections are very helpful since they help you go through the cases quickly. In the book department, for example, there were many sub-sections, and as I got familiar with the different sections I felt a certain sense of satisfaction every time I was able to find the right spot for a book. After having done this for a while, I was able to find the right place for almost everything. The objects and the contingency in the donations and their material qualities affect the categorisation, as do individual performances of practices.

Problematic categorisations

The problem with categories is not only a matter of ambiguity in the sorting process. The way the sections of the different departments are organized can also be problematic. One day when I was putting out new books I was approached by a man who found the 'ethnic studies' section of the book department problematic. He had been hovering for a while and finally came up to me very politely and told me that he objected to the way all non-white authors were grouped into this section. He also found it problematic that James, the volunteer who usually puts out the new books who is African American, in his view, was being forced to adhere to a racist or western-centric system of categorisation. Another similar issue became clear to me when a woman asked for books in Spanish and I had to direct her to the 'foreign language section'. In a neighbourhood where most people speak Spanish, it is hardly a foreign language. Also books with a gay theme were always put in the gay-interest section and not in fiction. Considering the Community Thrift's strong commitment to promoting racial, gender and sexual diversity and equality, it is hard to imagine that there is a deliberate strategy to suppress or misrepresent minorities. The reason, in the specific case of the Spanish books for example, is in part the fact that few of the donors, especially the donors of books, are Spanish-speakers. For that reason a section of books in Spanish would be very small and that is probably why the books end up in the foreign language section. Another, bigger, issue is that it is much easier to assign objects to broad categories when you have to get the stuff out quickly. Finding the right place to put an object creates a sense of satisfaction, and as the person doing the job you become immune to the content of the category. The differ-ence between the categories is what matters in the practice, not the qualitative content. That does not mean that the categories are fixed or are conceived similarly by everyone. When either customers or employees contest the categorisation or their implications their situated and sometimes problematic, meanings are revealed. Categories are performative. Establishing problematic categories that act against explicit values in the organisation, such as equality, demonstrates how practices are individual and collective at the same time. The interconnectedness of activities, formal and tacit knowledge in the practices that establish categories can result in contradictory outcomes.

Thrift in the thrift store

The experience of working in the Community Thrift and being taught how to perform val-uations showed how the dominant value that guides practices throughout the organisation is thrift. At every station along the trajectory, as well as in the larger structures of the organ-isation, being thrifty – i.e. using resources in a considered way and not being wasteful – is expressed through actions and words. From taking responsibility for the donations at the beginning of the trajectory to bundling office supplies or pricing bedding that accidentally enters the flow, the employees make the most of whatever they receive. Thrift is often at odds with pure economic rationality, since the investment of time involved in making objects valuable does not always transform into higher economic output. Being thrifty certainly means making the most of the donations, but not only in terms of economic gain. Making the best use of the donations includes bundling objects, reducing prices, looking things up, testing, cleaning and sorting. Thrift as a value in the organisation can perhaps be understood as what Graeber describes as an 'infravalue'.[26] Being thrifty is not an end in itself but a means to obtain other values. By being thrifty, the Community Thrift is able to create economic, social and emotional value. Thrift has mainly been treated as a feature of consumption and the household;[27] It is closely associated with saving and even, as Podkalicka and Potts point out, with 'conspicuous conservation'.[28] As Miller describes it, thrift is an attempt to stop resources flowing out of the household. In the context of the thrift store, however, thrift is mainly a way of moving things along.

Return to rubbish theory, gifts and commodities

Thompson's rubbish theory highlights the presence of objects that are no longer wanted or valued by their current owner and how value decay and material decay do not go hand in hand.[29] The objects linger long after they are no longer valuable to anyone. Second-hand markets exist because of this fact; but the specific knowledge of these practices makes it clear that as soon as the object enters a larger social relation, the possible value of the object become a subject of negotiation. It is clear that one of the purposes of the Community Thrift is to determine whether an object is in one of the states along the trajectory from discard to commodity; but in the thrift store objects can pass from rubbish to transient again – at least if discards are the same as rubbish. If ridding oneself of unwanted objects is to consider them rubbish then the donations that the Community Thrift accept are, for the most part, rubbish. But only a fraction of these enter a durable state after they have been discarded. Most of the objects re-enter the precarious position, where their value is diminished over time due to wear and desirability. Many objects gain value from this process even if they do not become durable, but the value they gain is not constant. A Pyrex bowl in a thrift store is in most cases more valuable than it was to the person who discarded it. But it will only retain that value as long as demand is high. Fluctuations in prices in second-hand markets are very common. Many traders I have talked to attest to this. Objects that seemed to be a solid investment ten years ago can suddenly fall out of favour with customers and their prices drop radically.

Thompson is concerned with the economic aspect of second-hand markets. But in the thrift store other types of value are also in play. A concern for the community and offering affordable household goods is a form of social value central to the Community Thrift. The emotional aspect of donating to a charity a loved one would have liked to help is valuable to the donors and increasingly an environmental concern is becoming important to the organisation. In this article I will not present a lengthy analysis of how these values interact with each other, but briefly suggest that the practices of valuation in the thrift store display properties of both market and gift exchanges.

Writing biographies of things, as Kopytoff suggests, offers a temporal understanding of the changing nature of objects in a social sphere. He describes how objects change category over time as a result of biographical events such as buying, giving, selling, etc. It is one of these events, or sets of events, that is the focus of this article: the remarketing of used objects. These events, the result of a number of practices that include donating, sorting and valuation, transform objects from a relatively invaluable bulk of discards into singular-ized commodities. Gifting and commoditisation are equally important, and as such the value of these objects is affected by both. Kopytoff suggests that an object can be an heirloom and a commodity simultaneously to different people in accordance with different value systems.[30] In the process of remarketing used objects the objects have to potentially be both to the same person, i.e. the person sorting them. As Graeber, Miller and others note, the dichotomy between gift and commodity as completely separate states is too simple.[31] In the Community Thrift the objects arrive as gifts in one sense, as they are donated to charity, but they are also potential commodities. Otherwise the Community Thrift would not accept them. They are also potential rubbish, since nobody knows if the Community Thrift can make use of the donations. If the objects were treated only as potential commod-ities, more things would be looked up and sold online, the prices would be higher, and many of the cheaper objects would be discarded. In fact, as Armun described to me, the Community Thrift would most likely cease to exist in this case, since they would generate more money from the sale of the warehouse than they would from many years of operating. In other words, commodification of the entire operation could, potentially make more economic sense. An entirely economic analysis would likely find several instances of inefficiency in the operation, but looking at the elements of a gift exchange these practices make sense as part of the aim of the Community Thrift. As Cliff expressed it: 'we could do the eBay thing to make more money, but that kinda defies the purpose of a thrift store'. Gift exchange is not only carried out by donors, it pervades the whole organisation: from sorters 'giving' their time to bundle non-valuable objects to pricing structures that are sensitive to the economic circumstances of some of their customers, to the employees allowing patrons to nap or hang out in the furniture department, and to the overall aim of the organisation to generate money to the various charities they partner with. The gift givers, that is the donors, are also caught up in this duality: they are not necessarily driven by altruism alone, since, for example, they can get a tax refund from making the donation. In some cases, donating unwanted items may even provide absolution from indulging in overconsumption. But focusing on the practices involved and how employees and donors invest actions and concern in them makes it possible to consider both economic market-driven structures and social and emotional influences as well. Considering only the social aspects of the exchange of donations also creates a simplified image of the reality of second-hand markets. Graeber offers an inclusive concept of value that can grasp both market and gift relations, by suggesting that value, in the broader sociological sense as well as economic, is constituted by the actions, thought and energy invested in an object.[32] In the context of the thrift store the actions invested in something, be it in the value of an object or an organisation, is a potentiality in that relation until it is capitalised. Capitalising or making something exchangeable in the form of an abstracted medium of equivalence releases that potential and renders the relation stale. But in the Community Thrift the capitalisation of (some of the) value generates social value in other areas. It is clear that thrift is the dominant value in the Community Thrift and making the most of the donations transcends all aspects of valuation practices. Seen as an expression of thrift, the negotiations between economic and social and emotional values create coherent patterns of value.

The remainders and dirt

The process of turning donations into cultural commodities relies on knowledge, experience, actions and principles. Categorisation constitutes the primary form valuing the objects with the activity itself creating value by investing time and energy in the object. As a form of conclusion, however, I want to point attention to what is left behind: throughout the process from donation and sorting through pricing and selling, waste is constantly being generated. Although the whole process is one of re-establishing discards as valuable commodities through rigorous practices of categorisation, something is always left behind. Things are broken or get dirty or are just not saleable. Looking at the 'uneven remainders' a central concept in the emerging field of discard studies,[33] illustrates how valuations in the second-hand trade create a system that orders (read: dominates) objects into systems of meaning. However, it is also a system that relies on these remainders and on the individual employees' ability to creatively recontextualise them. Although some discard literature has a tendency to romanticise waste, the attention to structures and organising as a form of domination is important to keep in mind. The spectre of the cultural taboo of impurity that Douglas describes still lingers. By retaining a sensibility to the disorder, ambiguity and dirt that is part of this process, discarded objects form a commentary on organisational attempts to marginalise waste both materially and symbolically. The account of the practices of valuation that I have presented above testifies to the adaptability and creativity of the employees in making the most of the donations, no matter how small or unmanageable they are. Disorder is an important element of valuations that also provides the opportunity for value. It is also an illustration of an adaptable organisational system that, no matter how well it categorizes, creates remainders. Thrift as an infravalue, even a form of 'tactic' in de Certeau's terminology,[34] is a situated response to reality of the flow of objects that allows the organisation and especially the individual employees to navigate the larger structure and balance different kinds of values.

Notes

1. Armun is the director of the Community Thrift; All names have been altered throughout.
2. Appadurai, Social Life of Things.
3. Douglas, Purity and Danger.
4. A full roster of the different charities can be found here: http://www.communitythriftsf.org/charities/
5. Le Zotte, Not Charity, 170).
6. Crewe & Gregson, Alternative Retail Spaces.
7. Le Zotte From Goodwill to Grunge.
8. Ingold, The Perception of the Environment.
9. (Ingold, Ibid: 415).
10. One donor I spoke to had recently lost a lot of weight. He was donating a large amount of expensive and colourful shirts, and he expressed a combination of joy over the weight loss and sadness that he could not wear the shirts anymore.
11. Horne & Maddrell, Charity Shops and Le Zotte, Not Charity,.
12. Hansen, Salaula.
13. Crang et al. Rethinking governance and Gregson et al. Following things.
14. (Gregson et al. Second-Hand Cultures; Gregson & Crewe Performance and possession; Norris Recycling Indian Clothes and Rivoli The Travels of a T-shirt.
15. (Botticello, Between Classification.
16. (Abimbola The International Trade; Horne & Maddrell Charity Shops.
17. Douglas, Purity and Danger.
18. Botticello, Between Classification.
19. Kopytoff, Cultural biography of things.
20. Reckwitz Towards a Theory.
21. (Reckwitz, ibid: 249–50).
22. Thompson, Rubbish Theory.
23. Thompson in Parsons, Thompson's Rubbish Theory: 390).
24. Don Slater Ambiguous goods.
25. Botticello Between Classification.
26. Graeber It is value: 233).
27. Miller, A Theory of Shopping.
28. Campbell in Podkalicka & Potts, Towards a general theory.
29. Thompson, Rubbish Theory: 8–9).
30. Kopytoff, Cultural biography of things.
31. Graeber Towards an Anthropological Theory and Miller Alienable Gifts.

32. (Greaeber *Towards an Anthropological Theory*: 45).
33. (Schaffer, *Discard Studies Compendium*.
34. de Certeau, *Practice of Everyday Life*.

Acknowledgements

I would like to thank the employees, volunteers and Managers at the Community Thrift Store for their immense help with this research. I would also like to thank the editors and reviewers for their helpful comments and suggestions.

Disclosure statement

No potential conflict of interest was reported by the author.

Bibliography

Abimbola, O. "The International Trade in Second-Hand Clothing: Managing Information Asymmetry between West African and British Traders." *Textile* 10, no. 2 (2012): 184–199.

Appadurai, A. "Introduction: Commodities and the Politics of Value." In *The Social Life of Things*, edited by A. Appadurai, 3–63. Cambridge: Cambridge University Press, 1986.

Botticello, J. "Between Classification, Objectification, and Perception: Processing Secondhand Clothing for Recycling and Reuse." *Textile* 10, no. 2 (2012): 164–183.

de Certeau, M. *The Practice of Everyday Life*. Berkeley and Los Angeles: University of California Press, 1984.

Crang, M., A. Hughes, N. Gregson, L. Norris, and F. Ahamed. "Rethinking Governance and Value in Commodity Chains through Global Recycling Networks." *Transactions of the Institute of British Geographers* 38, no. 1 (2012): 12–24.

Crewe, L., N. Gregson, and K. Brooks. "Alternative Retail Spaces." In *Alternative Economic Spaces*, edited by Andrew Leyshon, Roger Lee & Colin C. Williams. 74–106. London: Sage Publications Ltd., 2003.

Denegri-Knott, J., and E. Parsons. "Disordering Things." *Journal of Consumer Behaviour* 13 (2014): 89–98.

Douglas, M. *Purity and Danger –An Analysis of the Concepts of Pollution and Taboo*. London: Ark, (1966) 1985.

Graeber, D. *Toward an Anthropological Theory of Value*. New York: Palgrave, 2001.

Graeber, D. "It is Value That Brings Universes into Being." *HAU: Journal of Ethnographic Theory* 3, no. 2 (2013): 219–243.

Gregson, N., and L. Crewe. "Performance and Possession: Rethinking the Act of Purchase in the Space of the Car Boot Sale." *Journal of Material Culture* 2 (1998): 241–263.

Gregson, N., and L. Crewe. *Second-Hand Culture*. Oxford & New York: Berg, 2003.

Gregson, N., M. Crang, F. Ahamed, N. Akhtar, and R. Ferdous. "Following Things of Rubbish Value: End-of-Life Ships, 'Chock-Chocky' Furniture and the Bangladeshi Middle Class Consumer." *Geoforum* 41 (2010): 846–854.

Hansen, Tranberg K. *Salaula: The World of Second Hand Clothing and Zambia*. Chicago: University of Chicago Press, 2000.

Horne, S., and A. Maddrell. *Charity Shops, Retailing, Consumption and Society*. London and New York: Routledge, 2002.

Ingold, T. *The Perception of the Environment: Essays on Livelihood, Dwelling and Skill*. London & New York: Routledge, 2000.

Kopytoff, I. "The Cultural Biography of Things: Commoditization as Process." In *The Social Life of Things*, edited by A. Appadurai, 64–92. Cambridge: Cambridge University Press, 1986.

Le Zotte, J. "Not Charity, but a Chance': Philanthropic Capitalism and the Rise of American Thrift Stores." *The New England Quarterly* 86, no. 2 (2013): 169–195.

Le Zotte, J. *From Goodwill to Grunge: A History of Secondhand Styles and Alternative Economies*. Chapel Hill, NC: The University of Northern Carolina Press, 2017.

Miller, D. *A Theory of Shopping*. Ithaca NY: Cornell University Press, 1998.

Miller, D. "Alienable Gifts and Inalienable Commodities." In *The Empire of Things: Regimes of Value and Material Culture*, edited by F. Myers, 91–115. Santa Fe: School of American Research Press, 2001.

Moeran, B. *Notes for a Theory of Value*. Working Paper. Frederiksberg: Creative Encounters Research Programme, 2009.

Norris, L. *Recycling Indian Clothing –Global Contexts of Reuse and Value*. Bloomington: Indiana University Press, 2010.

Parsons, E. "Thompson's Rubbish Theory: Exploring the *Practices* of Value Creation." *European Advances in Consumer Research* 8 (2008): 390–393.

Podkalicka, A., and J. Potts. "Towards a General Theory of Thrift." *International Journal of Cultural Studies* 17, no. 3 (2014): 227–241.

Reckwitz, A. "Toward a Theory of Social Practices: A Development in Culturalist Theorizing." *European Journal of Social Theory* 5, no. 2 (2002): 243–263.

Rivoli, P. *The Travels of a T-Shirt in the Global Economy: An Economist Examines the Markets, Power and Politics of World Trade*. Hoboken, N.J.: John Wiley & Sons, 2014.

Shaffer, G. Camp. *Discard Studies Compendium*. January, 2017. http://discardstudies.com/discard-studies-compendium/.

Slater, D. "Ambiguous Goods and Nebulous Things." *Journal of Consumer Behaviour* 13 (2014): 89–87.

Stark, D. *The Sense of Dissonance: Accounts of worth in Economic Life*. Princeton & Oxford: Princeton University Press, 2011.

Thompsons, M. *Rubbish Theory*. Oxford: Oxford University Press, 1979.

History as business: Changing dynamics of retailing in Gothenburg's second-hand market

Staffan Appelgren 🆔

ABSTRACT

This article traces developments in the second-hand market over the last 15 years in Gothenburg, Sweden. Outlining how the second-hand market is characterised by rapid shifts in ownership, location and type of business, it explores how retailers perceive and negotiate these shifting forces. With an analytical focus on people and things in motion, it aims to increase our understanding of the factors and forces involved in such movement and transience. The article shows how retailers develop an adaptive apparatus for navigating the second-hand market and that market growth translates into motion and flux rather than stability.

Introduction

We, who run Rosens Antikvariat today (Lovisa and Lars) succeeded Jonas and Marita. They called their bookshop Liljans Antikvariat. Liljans Antikvariat has ceased to be a physical bookshop, but continues to trade in second-hand books online. Jonas and Marita in their turn succeeded the bookshop from Ulf, who ran Vasastadens Antikvariat. Ulf managed second-hand bookstores for many years in Gothenburg, and today runs one in Borås city called Aderno Antikvariat. Before Ulf moved into Aschebergsgatan 21, the bookshop was called Röde Orm for eight years during the 1990s. Today, Antikvariat Röde Orm, run by Stein, is located in the Haga district.[1]

Message on website, Rosen's antiquarian bookshop, Gothenburg

This bookshop has now closed. Thank you all for your visits during the years we have had the pleasure to run this wonderful little second-hand bookstore.[2]

Subsequent message on the same website

The quotations above, written a year apart, illuminate the rapid and intricate shifts in ownership, location and type of business that are common in second-hand markets. Like the things that circulate through this market, the infrastructure facilitating these flows – physical shops, businesses and shopkeepers – is characterised by motion and flux.[3] When I began fieldwork on second-hand markets in Gothenburg, Sweden, in 2014, I experienced this flux immediately. The volatile nature of the second-hand market – shops coming and going, owners changing, businesses relocating – was apparent when I started to search for information on the Internet, and then walk through the city to cross-check it. I quickly discovered that what I assembled on the Internet did not match the situation in the streets. Already in the first district, I saw a second-hand bookstore with a notice announcing that it had shut down the week before. Cursing my luck, I took notes and carried on. A few hundred metres down the street, a popular vintage clothes store had a sign on the door saying that it would soon be turned into an Internet shop. I began to worry whether I would have time to conduct my research before all the shops went out of business and the whole project come to nothing.

Simultaneously, public interest in second-hand, vintage and retro seemed higher than ever before. In Sweden, as in many countries, buying second-hand, once associated with poverty and low status, became the latest in fashion, with lifestyle magazines, Internet blogs and television programmes communicating its benefits and attractions.[4] Indeed, acquiring goods in ways that differ from the dominant modern form of purchasing newly produced commodities has become mainstream in many parts of Swedish society. By this I mean that alternative forms of acquisition – buying, receiving, sharing, swapping and simply finding (even in your own closet) pre-used and unwanted stuff – have entered into a dialectical relationship with the dominant model of acquiring goods, producing a situation in which reuse has lost much of its critical edge while conventional consumption has gained a sustainability dimension. Buying and using second-hand stuff is now a common everyday phenomenon, not a hip alternative championed by trendsetters and celebrities, nor a radical act of anti-materialism, nor associated with the stigma of poverty as has been discussed in other cases.[5] Lately, even Swedish state authorities have been affected by the passion for pre-loved things, leading to a debate about the tax exemption enjoyed by charities and promoting reuse as part of moral citizenship.[6]

Considering how mainstream history as business has become, perhaps one cannot talk about a second-hand 'scene' in Gothenburg anymore.[7] The established second-hand shops, charities, flea markets, car boot sales, yard sales, online auctions, social media communities, swapping apps, housing associations' reuse rooms, swapping events, etc., are now supplemented by major conventional retailers carrying their own line of second-hand commodities.[8] However, while this growth and diversification happens throughout Sweden, Gothenburg is particularly fertile ground for these phenomena. A major European port and hub for Northern European trade and commerce for well over two centuries, Gothenburg has seen a continuous inflow and outflow of migrants, commodities and ideas, and the circulation of people and things has been a cornerstone in the city's socioeconomic development. This is still reflected in the city's economy and industry and encapsulated in the city's slogan: 'Sustainable City – Open to the World'.[9] Shipping, shipbuilding, commerce, finance, textile, fisheries and manufacturing have all been important industries, and while some have not survived global competition (most significantly shipbuilding), most have overcome years of crisis through transformation and restructuring, and now contribute to Gothenburg's hybrid economy where industry, trade and commerce constitute the backbone alongside cultural and creative industries. Today the city, with a population of half a million, is home to a lively alternative arts scene, hosting significant music and film festivals, local fashion labels and a vibrant bar and café culture. The rise in popularity of retro and vintage sits well with its creative arts culture and 'sustainable ethos', seen for example in the annual mega flea market. It also sits well with how the city has become increasingly segregated with expanding income gaps and growing poverty.[10]

With the spread of second-hand consumption, and the increase in its popularity and state interest in its potential, why did my observations of second-hand shops in Gothenburg seem to indicate a sector in trouble? Once I began conducting interviews with shop-owners, I became aware that my initial impressions were an effect of my own expectations. My assumptions had been informed by a 'sedentarist' perspective in which fixity and stability constitute established points of departure for analysis, and where mobility and flux are considered irregularities and anomalies. This perspective, which has dominated social analysis, has led to the omission or downplaying of processual and emergent aspects of social life. In the context of the second-hand market, such a perspective risks overlooking the forces behind this dynamism and how they can be understood as inherent to this particular market. Conventional retailing's linearity has privileged this type of assumption, but the circularity of second-hand retailing provides an opportunity to rethink how the flows of commodities restructure the retail infrastructure. By shifting the perspective to seeing movement and transformation of people and things as analytical fundamentals, I began to re-evaluate the character of this market, seeing change as an aspect of conducting business with pre-owned and used material culture.

By tracing developments in the second-hand market over the last 15 years in the city of Gothenburg, I aim to increase our understanding of the factors and forces involved in such movement and transience, and how shop-owners negotiate them. I compare data available in a 2003 overview of Gothenburg's second-hand market to a 2014 survey conducted by our research team and material collected through recent fieldwork and interviews with market actors.[11] I use quantitative data about the development of shops, actors and business concepts over time to measure the changes that have occurred over the years and establish a framework for interpreting the personal narratives and understandings of some of the actors involved.[12]

While the quotations above pertain to second-hand book businesses, here I focus on how the market for used objects for interior design and home decoration, such as furniture, lamps, chinaware, utensils, trinkets, gadgets, toys, etc., has evolved. The bewildering and rapidly changing labels of second-hand goods and actors are part of the market's transient nature. Some categories of used items, such as classic antiques, artworks, cars, watches, coins, books and vinyl records, have their own specific histories and trajectories, and will not be of central concern here. I focus on trade with everyday objects for the home and the body to relate the market's unfolding to developments in the wider society, specifically the doctrine of circular economy that has become a cornerstone in the Swedish government's sustainable consumption strategy. According to this, reuse and recycling play crucial roles in turning waste into resources, combatting the environmentally destructive consequences of further diffusion of materials in waste management and helping achieve a more efficient use of limited economic resources.[13]

Scholarly engagement with second-hand, retro and reuse has tended to focus on consumers and the exchange itself rather than on traders.[14] When traders have been studied, they tend to belong to the categories of charities and sellers on flea markets, garage sales and car-boot sales.[15] Research specifically on second-hand retailers and their businesses, in contrast, tends to be concerned with circulations between the Global North and the Global South.[16] In what follows, my aim is neither to establish actual causal factors for the mobility of the second-hand market in Gothenburg, nor to assess the reliability or accuracy of shop-owners' perceptions of such factors. Rather, I convey a sense of how key actors on this market spoke about, made sense of and handled the fluctuations and changes that they experienced, to further our understanding of the shifting nature of this field.

The ebb and flow of shops

In 2003, arts and culture journalist and author Björn Höglund published an overview of second-hand shops in Gothenburg. This is not an academic analysis, but a comprehensive guide directed at readers interested in touring the city's second-hand scene.[17] The guide lists second-hand shops in seven categories (second-hand and antiques, antiquarian book-shops, stamps and coins, flea markets, second-hand clothing, second-hand records and charities), and contains brief information and a short evaluation of each shop, as well as maps of a several districts where second-hand trade was particularly dense. As such, it makes a useful comparison to the current second-hand scene.

When I compare second-hand stores in Gothenburg in 2003 with the current situation, the second-hand market looks highly transient. Of the 121 shops listed in the guide, only 50 are still in operation; three out of five shops have closed in less than 15 years. Second-hand and antiques shops fared the worst, with two out of every three shops having disap-peared. This category contains the second-hand shops trading in furnishings and interiors products that are my focus. Interestingly, the other category containing shops with a similar business focus, charities, shows an entirely different trend. Nearly all of the 15 shops in the guide are still in operation, some after having been reorganised or merged. This suggests that smaller, privately owned and commercially operated second-hand stores (the first cat-egory) are more vulnerable to market shifts and trends and broader social developments than charities. The latter are generally backed by larger non-profit organisations, and so have the capacity and resources to persevere through periods of decline and transform themselves in the face of new demands. My interviews with representatives of charities confirm that even if the pressure has increased on charities to deliver good economic results, many have been successful in making their operations more efficient, expansive and business-like. Thanks to the exemption from taxes on second-hand goods that charities enjoy (unlike for-profit second-hand businesses), and staff who are often recruited as part of publicly subsi-dised labour market programmes[18] (thus keeping labour costs down), charities are economically stable operations on a competitive commercial market. Indeed, major charities like the Salvation Army's Myrorna and Emmaus Björkå have formed a lobby organisation to strengthen the position of second-hand charities on the market.[19]

When our research team set out to investigate the circulation of objects on Gothenburg's second-hand market, we mapped the field to get a grasp of the number of second-hand shops and their business profiles. The categories of shops trading in used and old things vary over time, and concepts, such as second-hand, retro, vintage and reuse, shift in content and popularity.[20] However, by and large, the 2003 guide and the 2014 survey overlap in content. Of the 88 establishments listed in our 2014 survey, 78 are still in operation today (two and a half years later) and 10 shops have closed. All the discontinued shops fall into the category of shops dealing in furnishings and interiors objects, meaning that 10 out of 55 shops have shut. In other words, nearly every fifth shop has been discontinued in two and a half years' time. This shows that in the short time span of two and a half years there is considerable change, and suggests that the wider timespan of 15 years very likely includes an even higher number of actual shops appearing and disappearing, including some which show up in neither the 2003 guide nor the 2014 survey, since they only existed for a short period within this time span.

Looking at the numbers from the perspective of new businesses, rather than closed shops, a similar pattern emerges. Comparing the 2014 survey with the 2003 guide, there are 42 shops that are not mentioned in the earlier source. While a few might have been overlooked in the first survey, most are new shops emerging in the 11 years that have passed. Seven of these shops have already closed, meaning that the 35 remaining shops are the ones that now constitute a vital part of the second-hand scene in Gothenburg. Comparing 2014 with early 2017, we find that no less than 17 new second-hand shops have opened, suggesting an increase in the pace of new shops opening.

In short, the period between 2003 and 2014 the number of shops were relatively constant, whereas the last few years have seen more new shops (17) than closed ones (10). A cautious interpretation suggests that there is an increase in the number of shops during the last few years, and that previously the number of shops was relatively constant. Above all, it is clear that the market has been volatile, with shops, owners and businesses coming and going.

'It all goes in waves'

The number of discontinued businesses and the frequency of new shops appearing can be read as indications of market decline and growth respectively. Shop-owners often shared this contradictory view of the market. Many agreed that we were currently witnessing a general interest in second-hand on a scale not seen before, with wider and more intense circulations of used stuff. This 'love affair' is mentioned already in the 2003 guide, where the author notes that public interest is 'greater than ever' and shops are 'opening constantly'.[21] Still, converting this popularity and success of the market into stable and expanding business operations was challenging for my informants. 'It all goes in waves,' sighed one of the shop-owners when pondering the market he tried to navigate.

Shifting the analytical focus to mobility is not intended to diminish the challenges shop-owners face, but to cast a different light on the situation, illuminating factors and forces contributing to this transience and highlighting the practices people employed to navigate a changing environment. More than being a problem for retailers to work out, mobility is an everyday reality that they work with and through. What were their experiences of this transience over time? How did they understand the mutability of the market? How did they negotiate a field that continuously transforms due to both internal and external forces?

Changing profits and margins

'Once I came across this leather sofa and sold it for 20 times the price. Such things you just don't find anymore.' Anders was the owner of a second-hand shop in an urban area that once had many second-hand shops, most of which had closed down. He was sorting through his stockpile of second-hand stuff that he had purchased to sell in his shop. Buying was a continuous activity, he told me, with certain peak periods during the year for sourcing trips to ensure there would always be 'cool things' to sell in the shop. These things would wait in storage if there was no room for them in the shop, if there were multiples of the same item or if they needed a bit of care. Sometimes unsold stuff would return to storage. It was a space for handling market fluctuations and uncertainties by building up stock, but had over the years become a reservoir of unsold items, triggering costs rather than yielding profits. For the shop-owner, the storage had become a burden that needed to be taken care of. For the anthropologist it was an archaeological treasure of second-hand objects assembled over 15 years. As we sorted, examined and carried away stuff, Anders generously shared the histories and memories behind the objects, their design-historical value and how they had fared in the second-hand market over the years.

The storage was an assemblage of missed opportunities for making profit, and our task was to re-evaluate the items and find channels for their further circulation. Their faded attraction triggered narratives about their successful peers that were sold in their prime, such as the leather sofa. Anders told me that previously it had been easier to turn a small investment and a little effort into a large gain. This golden age of second-hand retailing had no clear delimitation in time, but Anders thought it was before second-hand, flea markets and retro became a national craze and 'everyone became an expert on second-hand'.

The theme that business used to be easier and more lucrative recurred in many conversations and interviews with shop-owners. Many reminisced that before, the gap between purchasing price and selling price, the net profit, was wide, largely controlled by expert retailers. They spoke about how coveted and marketable things had been easy to find, and, being able to distinguish the valuable from the ordinary, they could pick out the cherries and turn them into a handsome profit. One shop-owner recalled how he used to bid for things at the local auction house with little competition from others, since auctions were usually held during the mornings, when most people were at work. He would then carry the stuff a few hundred metres to his shop and sell it by afternoon with a good return.

According to the shop-owners, things changed in late 1990s and early 2000s. With the rapid increase in popularity of second-hand goods and the emergence of widely accessible information on the Internet, shop-owners saw the price gap diminish considerably. The problem, they stated, was not that there was a shortage of beautiful and desired old things. On the contrary, increased demand for and circulation of second-hand items have led to their preservation, rather than disappearance. Margareta, who runs a tidy and popular second-hand shop in the inner city, commented that 'there is wonderful stuff out there, and easy to get, but it is expensive, sometimes crazily expensive'. Retailers felt that, today, everyone was out there looking for economic value in old things. 'People want to know the value of their belongings,' said one shop-owner, concluding that people had started to see their possessions as commodities with commodity potential and repeated 'commodity phases' in their life trajectory.[22]

For retailers, diminishing net profit meant pressure to make their sourcing more efficient and their sales more effective. It also necessitated routinely explaining why they could not pay the prices people expected when buying stock. Sometimes people understand, sometimes they don't, said one shop-owner and continued: 'Anyway, I tell them to sell it on Tradera (an online auction site).' When customers had what she saw as unrealistic expectations, she felt it was better to suggest that they sell it themselves rather than trying to reach an agreement. If the item was in mint condition, my informants thought the threshold for when it was worth the trouble to buy it from someone walking through the door was a 50% margin, meaning the sellers of the stock would be paid half the estimated revenue. If sold quickly, this would cover tax, costs and yield a small profit.

The declining value of expertise was not the only reason for the experience of diminishing profits. Margareta, who specialised in Scandinavian design from the 1950s to the 1970s, suggested that a crucial difference today was that 'original' items from these decades, now peaking in the second-hand market, were rapidly disappearing. In other words, although actual objects from this era proliferated, they were rarely available directly from the people who bought them new, the 'original consumer'. In her experience, the vast majority of things for sale from these decades had already entered into the second-hand circuits, and most of their profit margin had been exploited. This suggests that, analytically, one should not only distinguish between the linear consumption of first-cycle goods, and the circular consumption of second-hand things, but also single out first-cycle objects within the second cycle, and the 'original consumer' from subsequent consumers. [23] 'Virgin' second-hand goods have a greater chance to enter the second-hand market underpriced, thereby affording opportunities for a greater profit margin when discovered.

Surfing the ebb and flow of trends

The second-hand market shares one crucial transient feature with first-cycle retailing in a market economy: demand. Trends in the second-hand market come and go, despite the fact that novelty and fashion have been said to stand in contrast to the value of patina as the standard and currency of social status.[24] What stood out in the experiences of the retailers I interviewed was a sense that the pace of trends has intensified, requiring retailers to be more sensitive to the shifts of popular taste. 'You have to be right here and right now with your stuff. It's crazy really,' said Peter, who managed a second-hand shop noticeable for its well-organised premises. Sometimes one would misjudge a trend. Anders, for example, ended up with a handful of unsold Italian bathroom cabinets, gathered after demand had already peaked, and people had moved on to something else. He picked up one of them and explained that they were made in the 1960s and popular in Sweden at the time. Some years ago, they suddenly re-emerged on the market as popular second-hand goods, and sold quickly. 'They used to be around SEK 700, but now you can only get like SEK 350, if you are lucky.'

Trends and demand were negotiated differently by my informants. Some were pragmatic and tried to build a reputation for having the latest stuff available. Others would refrain from taking in items to meet temporary demands, instead keeping their own business focus, and also for reasons of reputation. As one shop-owner exclaimed when I asked him what he would not take into the shop: 'Lisa Larson figurines! They just don't fit into the shop's profile.' Clearly, he thought these popular cute ceramic figurines from the mid-1950s onwards would undermine his carefully curated shop and be bad for his business, even if he knew he could make some money from them in the short run.[25] Others cleverly reconciled diverging business interests by being strict with what was sold in the shop, and using other channels, such as online auctions, for selling 'inappropriate' objects they knew would bring in money.

Working with and through trends, and developing strategies for handling this unpredictable terrain, was seen as a manifestation of a shift in authority. Information and knowledge used to be the perquisite of the retailer on the second-hand market, much in line with Clifford Geertz's classic study of the bazaar economy. Geertz argues that since information is not openly accessible in the bazaar, buyers need to form close relationships with specific merchants.[26] This observation fits with how my informants spoke about retailing prior to the changes around the millennium shift. Then, expert knowledge used to be accessible to shop-owners through books, evening courses and subscriptions to high-profile designer, craft or art magazines. For shop-owners on the second-hand market today, however, this kind of information is free and readily available to anyone, and new authorities have appeared, setting the agenda and initiating trends. Many pointed to popular niche magazines, TV shows, and blogs and other social media platforms as highly influential in what became trendy.[27] Another category of trendsetters was interior designers, styling homes for sale on the real-estate market. Retailers gave examples of trends that had emerged through these channels, both singular types of items, such as the craze for deer heads a few years earlier, as well as broader classes of objects, such as the popularity of having a group of different Windsor-style chairs around the eating table.

Thus, while knowledge and authority were understood as once having been external to the market, vested in design and art history experts and marked by a stability, it was now experienced as diffuse, with a number of trendsetting voices who had more or less formal education but the social and aesthetic power to influence audiences.[28] Moreover, a clear difference in types of usable knowledge had emerged. Knowledge in design history had increasingly been accompanied, or even supplanted, by knowledge of what was currently in vogue. Here, we see a reversal of Geertz's hierarchical relationship between patron and client. Listening to customers had become an important means of acquiring crucial information about the market and staying in tune with the trends.

Sourcing: 'The eternal hunt'

Information about market desires was only one side of the trade, however. The other uncertainty that needed attention, consideration and work was sourcing. 'It's a damned job, really. It's an eternal hunt,' as one retailer put it. Margareta, who had a close friend running a shop in mainstream retailing, sighed enviously: 'It's new clothes that they just, like, order, and that's a bit unfair, right?' Unlike ticking boxes in an order form, sourcing was understood to be as shifting and unpredictable as the trends.

To cope with the vagaries of sourcing, retailers established different strategies. One was secrecy, having one's own favourite haunts, and making purchasing trips to distant rural areas and small towns, or even abroad. Another was forming networks and alliances, both vertically and horizontally. All retailers had developed some form of sourcing network, sometimes including repair. Most sophisticated was probably Annika and Sten's network around The Thrift Shop. They had been in business for nearly eight years and their shop was popular and well stocked with 1950s and 1960s objects, with ceiling lamps as a speciality. Despite having entered the business after the 'golden age', their business appeared to have expanded with the current vogue of second-hand. Their shop was a nexus of suppliers and sales channels. Their main task was to sort and direct the flows of things.

Three major channels constituted their base for the continuous inflow of marketable things. The first was a clearance company that would buy up large quantities of used items such as the estate of a deceased person and provide The Thrift Shop with 'a pile' of what the clearance company thought would be of interest. A second was two wholesalers, who would offer objects that they knew were on The Thrift Shop's list of wanted things. Where and how the wholesalers got their things was a mystery they would not disclose, but the shop-owners guessed it was through flea markets, auctions and private persons in a wide catchment area in the countryside. Lastly, private persons would contact the shop with pictures of items they wanted to sell. This ranged from individual objects to a whole house full of things, in which case the shop-owners would contact the clearance company. What The Thrift Shop did not do, but some of the other shop-owners regularly did, was to source in the field themselves. Sourcing was something they had done intensively when they entered the market: indeed, finding 'cool' and exciting items was the very reason they got involved in the first place. With time and the expansion of the shop, however, sourcing had become too time-consuming and was best delegated to specialists. Annika and Sten took on the role of managing and directing flows of things in and out of their business operation.

The flow of second-hand stuff out of The Thrift Shop, and their diverse channels, were as regulated as the inflow. Assessing and sorting were crucial to directing flows and creating revenues. Simply keeping things out was as important as assembling stock, since unwanted items were time-consuming and incurred costs. This, Annika and Sten explained, meant turning offers down and disappointing people with unrealistic hopes. Next was unwanted things that had made it over the threshold of the shop, mainly through the items that they received from the clearance company, but also objects that had been unsold in the store for too long. In rare cases things would be disposed of, but a preferred option, especially for newer second-hand items, i.e. used things that as yet had little historical value, was to donate them to charity. A third option, and the only one creating revenues, was to send them to a countryside auction, where customers had different expectations from those in the city. This option was further refined by sending various types of items to different destinations, depending on local demand. These strategies were aimed at items not meeting the stop's standard or profile. For objects deemed to be rare or have high value, there were basically two options. First, the shop-owners had started another second-hand company that specialised in more upmarket second-hand and antiques. They could easily transfer such objects to this shop, sporting a different profile and aimed at a different clientele. A second option was to hand an item over to a renowned auction-house to make sure the best possible price was attained.

While these hierarchical networks seemed functional and smooth, networking horizontally with owners of similar shops in the city was more sensitive. In the case of Annika and Sten, this dimension of networking was less developed and important. They felt that even if other shops claimed to offer the same type of goods, they in fact rarely did. Annika maintained that a customer on the hunt for a particular item who was directed to another shop would still return in the future. Other shopkeepers also said that they did not see the benefit of networking with other shops in the same trade. Peter, who ran a vintage clothing store, saw this as an important difference between second-hand apparel and furnishings. In his experience, shops trading in second-hand and vintage clothes would collaborate, even to the point of publishing a map of similar shops, whereas shop-owners trading in furnishings had a more cautious approach. Many confirmed this indirectly. Except for a few trusted friends in the business, reserve characterised the relationships between shops. Not wanting to disclose sourcing strategies, fear of jealousy and an undefined suspiciousness were mentioned as reasons for keeping a certain distance from each other on the market.

The role of external factors

Most aspects of market transience brought up in interviews referred to developments within the market's unfolding. However, two other factors that shop-owners identified as significant had more an external character. These were the expansion of the Internet and escalating real estate prices.

The Internet was the most significant change over the last 15 years that shop-owners mentioned. Both challenges and opportunities followed in its wake, with actors having different capacities to navigate in the new landscape. Auction houses went online to enlarge their market, private persons intensified trade through online auction sites, knowledge became readily available and new trendsetters emerged through blogs and social media. However, intensified connectivity and speed also meant an increase in public interest in second-hand things, leading to an intensification in exchange of things as well as tips, stories and pictures about the latest finds. With more than 20 years in the business, Bengt, who ran a shop specialising in military collectibles and antiques, had seen all these changes, and experienced how a tight network of second-hand shops along one of the city's wealthiest streets had faded away. 'We used to be nine shops here, along this street,' he said, pointing along the sloping street. 'Now it's only me.' Older shop-owners had struggled to keep up with new technologies.

Another reason for the demise of shops in this once prominent second-hand district was something that many touched upon when discussing how the market had evolved over time. A favourable rent arrangement, with only one price increase in 10 years, was a key reason Bengt had survived. Not everyone had been that lucky. An elderly couple who had run a second-hand shop further down the street had suddenly seen their rent doubled, then doubled again a few years later. Bengt was of the opinion that some real estate owners used this method to squeeze out the shop tenants. 'But we are not all Seven-Elevens or trendy chain cafés,' he sighed, hinting at his lack of leverage against such setbacks.

Conclusion

Second-hand retailing differs from conventional retailing in that there is no direct manufacturer or wholesaler to order new products from when stock is low or size is sold out. Yet, trends and fashions are as erratic and demand as unpredictable as on most first-cycle markets. The second-hand shops covered in this article experience considerable uncertainty and movement in supply and demand. They find themselves in a flexible and transient market, continuously striving to secure marketable goods to match the standards and expectations common in conventional retailing.[29]

Over the last 15 years Sweden's market for second-hand goods has gone from a socially and economically marginal phenomenon, to a trendy alternative to mass-consumption, to a consumption-reinforcing popular past time, to an optimistic expression of hope for the circular economy's capacity to solve major environmental and economic challenges of our time through reuse, upcycling and sharing. Still, second-hand retailing meant uncertainty and hardship for many shop-owners in Gothenburg. 'It's shockingly bad business in this trade, right ... in a trade that is very trendy', 'You have to marry rich, or have a wealthy partner', 'People come to us, and think what we do is fantastic ... but I can't pay any bills from that, really' are comments I collected when we discussed the general business climate. Some talked about an unfair market, where they as store-based commercial retailers felt squeezed between charities, on the one side, and private online-traders, on the other. Charities and online traders were understood to operate under more economically advantageous circumstances, the former through government subsidisation and the latter through government inattention. Others spoke in visionary terms about a trade rooted in popular ideas about the circular economy as extending the lifespan of things and reducing waste. Reuse businesses and repair shops should, they argued, be targeted for government interventions such as start-up support programmes and tax easements. Furthermore, by fostering local consumption and revitalising the local economy, the trade was also socially sustainable. This viewpoint accords with the government's new strategy for sustainable consumption, but concrete policies to substantiate this new political will had yet to appear.

Understanding second-cycle retailing demands an analytical perspective that accounts for the dynamism inherent in the circulation of second-hand things. First-cycle retailing as a waystation on the linear trajectory of the conventional production/consumption system (the 'take, make and dispose model'[30]) makes the orchestrated coordination of production, marketing and sales feasible and desirable, preferably on the principles of 'lean production' and 'just-in-time'.[31] Stable access to resources, materials and products along the commodity chain ensures retailers' capacity to meet market demands and can measure how well-oiled and efficient the production machine is. Not so in second-cycle retailing. While first-cycle manufacturers and retailers have been (at least, until recently[32]) unconcerned with the after-life of the commodities they have produced, distributed and sold, thinking of them as the responsibility of public waste management operations, this is exactly the point where second-cycle actors source for commodity potential. While the former makes from scratch, the latter forages among what exists.[33] 'Leanness' and 'timing' are needed to produce things for consumers, but also in order to produce consumers for things. Retailers' role as matchmakers between people and things makes second-cycle business unpredictable and complex, and dependent on knowledge and information. Navigating the transient terrain of reuse, recycling and repair demands strategies and routines that closely follow the shifts of the market. Capacity and infrastructure for sourcing, information retrieval, sorting and assessing, storage, repair and multiple outlets were all part of an adaptive apparatus for navigating as a second-hand retailer. Even so, the rapid shifts in physical shops, business operations and shopkeepers in Gothenburg over a 15-year period suggests that the dynamism of this market extends even further. The popularity of second-hand shopping and sustainable consumption contributes to an infrastructure of shops, business operations and actors where growth translates into motion and flux rather than stability. The inflow of used things further destabilises the infrastructure as retailers search for proper outlets for their continuous circulation. A mobility perspective is useful for understanding the challenges and opportunities that these actors face, how they make sense of this shifting reality that is at once both promising and unfavourable, and why shops vanish while the market expands.

In the 2003 guide to second-hand shops in Gothenburg, the author lists a number of familiar motives for shopping second-hand, such as nostalgia, sustainability and bargaining, concluding that it is to 'shop with one's heart'.[34] For the shop-owners I knew, who navigate a shifting terrain on a fluctuating income despite the market's expansion, and await the desired reforms, the reason for keep trying to make business of history seemed to be to 'sell with one's heart'.

Notes

1. http://rosensantikvariat.se/2013/03/gamla-agare/. Accessed January 11, 2017.
2. http://rosensantikvariat.se. Accessed January 11, 2017.

3.   See Larkin, 'The Politics and Poetics' for a discussion on the role of infrastructure and Tsing, 'The Global Situation' for a dynamic view of 'channel making'.

4.   Appelgren and Bohlin, 'Growing in Motion'; Fredriksson, 'Second-Hand Values'; Knowles, 'Locating Vintage.'

5.   See for example Balthazar, 'Made in Britain'; Gregson and Crewe, *Secondhand Cultures*; Pipyrou, 'Cutting *Bella Figura*.'

6.   See Göteborgs Posten, 'Momskrav' and Ministry of Finance Sweden, 'Strategy.'

7.   Straw, 'Some Things' discusses the concept of scene.

8.   The major e-commerce company Ellos is one example of this: https://www.ellos.se/page/vintage-collection. Accessed Januari 27, 2018.

9.   The city of Gothenburg's international website: http://international.goteborg.se. Accessed January 27, 2018.

10. Malmberg, Andersson and Östh, "Segregation"; Scarpa, "Looking Beyond."

11. This study is part of the research project 'Re:heritage. Circulation and Marketisation of Things with History', funded by the Swedish Research Council 2014–2017.

12. Methods of the 2003 and 2014 surveys will be presented in detail below. The recent fieldwork was carried out intermittently during 2015–2016, involved semi-structured interviews and conversations with 17 shop-owners in Gothenburg, as well as participant observation in two shops. The latter included participating in everyday on-site routines, excursions related to sourcing and sorting activities in storage locations. This study follows the ethical guidelines for social sciences developed by the Swedish Research Council, including informing informants on the research project and their rights in participating and withdrawing, seeking voluntary participation and consent, as well as maintaining confidentiality and anonymity: http://www.codex.vr.se/texts/HSFR.pdf.

13. Gregson et al., 'Interrogating'; Ministry of Finance Sweden, 'Strategy.'

14. Botsman and Rogers, *What's Mine*; Appelgren and Bohlin, 'Circulating Stuff'; Jenss, *Fashioning Memory*; Gregson and Crewe, *Secondhand Cultures*; Alexander and Reno, *Economies of Recycling*; Czarniawska and Löfgren, *Managing Overflow*.

15. Gregson and Crewe, *Secondhand Cultures*; Horne and Maddrell, *Charity Shops*; Larsen, 'Objects'; Sherry Jr., 'A Sociocultural Analysis'; Hansson and Brembeck, 'Market Hydraulics'; McColl, 'It's Vintage'; Nickel, 'Thrift Shop'; Watt and Dubbeld, 'Enchanting'; Herrmann, 'Gift or Commodity.'; Herrmann, 'New Lives'; Herrmann, 'Valuing Affect'; Herrmann, 'Negotiating Culture'; Herrmann, 'Garage-Sales'; Brembeck and Sörum, 'Assembling Nostalgia.'

16. Hansen, *Salaula*; Norris *Recycling Indian*; Brooks, 'Riches from Rags'; Milgram, 'Reconfiguring Margins.' For research on retailers in the Global North see Baker, 'Retailing Retro'; Crewe, Gregson and Brooks, 'The Discursivities' and Handberg, 'Montreal Modern.'

17. Höglund, *Gamla grejer.*

18. Charities in the second-hand market are often enrolled in active labour market policies directed at long-term unemployed persons and thus provide labour market training opportunities financed by government funding. This arrangement often has the duals goal of involving the unemployed in productive labour and promoting sustainable consumption.

19. Ideell Secondhand, see further http://www.ideellsecondhand.se

20. See Gregson and Crewe, *Second-Hand Cultures*; Franklin, 'Consuming Design'; Cassidy and Bennett, 'The Rise of Vintage'; Baker, *Retro Styles*; and Fischer, 'Vintage' for more on these categories.

21. Höglund, *Gamla grejer*, 7–8.

22. Cf. Denegri-Knott and Molesworth, '"I"ll sell this'; Fredriksson, 'E-handelns virtuella.' See Appadurai, 'Introduction', 13–17 for a discussion of the commodity phase.

23. See Gregson and Crewe, *Second-Hand Cultures*, 2–13 for a discussion on first and second cycle consumption.

24. McCracken, *Culture and Consumption*.

25. Lisa Larson is a Swedish ceramicist and designer.

26. Geertz, 'The Bazaar Economy.'

27. See, for example, Fredriksson, who explores the role of bloggers, 'Shabby Chic.'

28. Cf Baker, 'Retailing Retro' and Appelgren and Bohlin 'Second-hand as "Living".'
29. Crewe, Gregson and Brooks, 'The Discursitivities of Difference', 63–64.
30. See for example https://www.ellenmacarthurfoundation.org/circular-economy
31. Enkawa and Schvaneveldt, 'Just-in-Time'.
32. For the world's largest furniture retailer, IKEA, closing the loops of material flows is now an explicit corporate goal according to their latest sustainability report. However, this mainly translates into aiming to recycle materials, rather than facilitating the reuse of things. IKEA Group, "Sustainability Report."
33. See Appelgren and Bohlin, "Growing in Motion" for a discussion about making new objects and growing second-hand things.
34. Höglund, *Gamla grejer*.

Acknowledgments

I would like to thank Anna Bohlin and Maris Gillette for reading drafts and giving helpful comments, and the editors and anonymous reviewers for constructive criticism and suggestions.

Disclosure statement

No potential conflict of interest was reported by the author.

Funding

This work was supported by the Swedish Research Council under [grant number 421-203-1923], the research project 'Re:heritage. Circulation and Marketisation of Things with History'.

ORCID

Staffan Appelgren (iD) http://orcid.org/0000-0001-8945-6757

References

Alexander, Catherine, and Joshua Reno, eds. *Economies of Recycling: The Global Transformations of Materials, Values and Social Relations*. London: Zed Books, 2012.
Appadurai, Arjun. "Introduction: Commodities and the Politics of Value." In *The Social Life of Things: Commodities in Cultural Perspective*, edited by Arjun Appadurai, 3–63. Cambridge: Cambridge University Press, 1986.
Appelgren, Staffan, and Anna Bohlin. "Circulating Stuff through Second-hand, Vintage and Retro Markets." *Special issue Culture Unbound: Journal of Current Cultural Research* 7, no. 1 (2015): 1–168.
Appelgren, Staffan, and Anna Bohlin. "Growing in Motion: The Circulation of Used Things on Second-hand Markets." *Culture Unbound: Journal of Current Cultural Research* 7, no. 1 (2015): 143–168.

Appelgren, Staffan, and Anna Bohlin. "Second-hand as 'Living' Heritage: Intangible Dimensions of Things with History." In *Routledge Companion to Intangible Cultural Heritage*, edited by Peter Davis and Michelle L Stefano, 240–250. London: Routledge, 2017.

Baker, Sarah Elsie. "Retailing Retro: Class, Cultural Capital and the Material Practices of the (Re)valuation of Style." *European Journal of Cultural Studies* 15, no. 5 (2012): 621–641.

Baker, Sarah Elsie. *Retro Style*. London & New York: Bloomsbury, 2013.

Balthazar, Ana Carolina. "Made in Britain: Brexit, Teacups, and the Materiality of the Nation." *American Ethnologist* 44, no. 2 (2017): 220–224.

Botsman, Rachel, and Roo Rogers. *What's Mine is Yours: The Rise of Collaborative Consumption*. New York, NY: HarperCollins, 2010.

Brembeck, Helene, and Niklas Sörum. "Assembling Nostalgia: Devices for Affective Captation of the Re:heritage Market." *International Journal of Heritage Studies* 23, no. 6 (2017): 556–574.

Brooks, Andrew. "Riches from Rags or Persistent Poverty? The Working Lives of Secondhand Clothing Vendors in Maputo, Mozambique." *Textile: The Journal of Cloth and Culture* 10, no. 2 (2012): 222–237.

Cassidy, Tracy Diane, and Hannah Rose Bennett. "The Rise of Vintage Fashion and the Vintage Consumer." *Fashion Practice* 4, no. 2 (2012): 239–261.

Crewe, Louise, Nicky Gregson, and Kate Brooks. "The Discursivities of Difference: Retro Retailers and the Ambiguities of 'The Alternative.'" *Journal of Consumer Culture* 3, no. 1 (2003): 61–82.

Czarniawska, Barbara, and Orvar Löfgren, eds. *Managing Overflow in Affluent Societies*. New York and Abingdon: Routledge, 2012.

Denegri-Knott, Janice, and Mike Molesworth. "'I'll sell this and I'll buy the that': EBay and the Management of Possessions as Stock." *Journal of Consumer Behaviour* 8, no. 6 (2009): 305–315.

Enkawa, Takao, and Shane J. Schvaneveldt. "Just-in-Time, Lean Production, and Complementary Paradigms." In *Handbook of Industrial Engineering: Technology and Operations Management*, edited by Gavriel Salvendy, 545–561. New York: Wiley

Fischer, Nancy L. "Vintage, the First 40 Years: The Emergence and Persistence of Vintage Style in the United States." *Culture Unbound: Journal of Current Cultural Research* 7, no. 1 (2015): 45–66.

Franklin, Adrian. "Consuming Design: Consuming Retro." In *The Changing Consumer*, edited by Steven Miles, Alison Anderson and Kevin Meethan, 90–103. New York: Routledge, 2002.

Fredriksson, Cecilia. "E-handelns virtuella etnografi: Om förtroende och tillit på Tradera." *Nätverket* 17 (2010): 33–59.

Fredriksson, Cecilia. "Shabby Chic och slitenhetens estetik." *Nätverket* 18 (2013): 36–42.

Fredriksson, Cecilia. "Second-Hand Values and the Making of a Green Fashion Eco-Market." In *Making Sense of Consumption*, edited by Lena Hansson, Ulrika Holmberg and Helene Brembeck, 197–212. Göteborg: Centre for Consumer Science, Gothenburg University, 2013.

Geertz, Clifford. "The Bazaar Economy: Information and Search in Peasant Marketing." *American Economic Review* 68, no. 2 (1978): 28–32.

Göteborgs Posten. "Momskrav mot second-hand står fast." http://www.gp.se/nyheter/ekonomi/momskrav-mot-second-hand-står-fast-1.79657

Gregson, Nicky, and Louise Crewe. *Second-Hand Cultures*. Oxford: Berg, 2003.

Gregson, Nicky, Mike Crang, Sara Fuller, and Helen Holmes. "Interrogating the Circular Economy: The Moral Economy of Resource Recovery in the EU." *Economy and Society* 44, no. 2 (2015): 218–243.

Handberg, Kristian. "Montreal Modern: Retro Culture and the Modern Past in Montreal." *Culture Unbound: Journal of Current Cultural Research* 7, no. 1 (2015): 67–89.

Hansen, Karen Tranberg. *Salaula: The World of Secondhand Clothing and Zambia*. Chicago: University of Chicago Press, 2000.

Hansson, Niklas, and Helene Brembeck. "Market Hydraulics and Subjectivities in the 'Wild': Circulation of the Flea Market." *Culture Unbound: Journal of Current Cultural Research* 7, no. 1 (2015): 91–121.

Herrmann, Gretchen M. "Gift or Commodity: What Changes Hands in the U.S. Garage Sale?" *American Ethnologist* 24, no. 4 (1997): 910–930.

Herrmann, Gretchen M. "Negotiating Culture: Conflict and Consensus in U.S. Garage-Sale Bargaining." *Ethnology* 42, no. 3 (2003): 237–252.

Herrmann, Gretchen M. "Garage Sales Make Good Neighbors: Building Community through Neighborhood Sales." *Human Organization* 65, no. 2 (2006): 181–191.

Herrmann, Gretchen M. "New Lives from Used Goods: Garage Sales as Rites of Passage." *Ethnology* 50, no. 3 (2011): 189–207.

Herrmann, Gretchen M. "Valuing Affect: The Centrality of Emotion, Memory, and Identity in Garage Sale Exchange." *Anthropology of Consciousness* 26, no. 2 (2015): 170–181.

Höglund, Björn. *Gamla grejer i Göteborg – en guide till antikt och second hand*. Göteborg: Tre Böcker Förlag AB, 2003.

Horne, Suzanne, and Avril Maddrell. *Charity Shops*. London: Routledge, 2002.

IKEA Group. "Sustainability Report FY16." http://www.ikea.com/ms/en_US/img/ad_content/IKEA_Group_Sustainability_Report_FY16.pdf

Jenss, Heike. *Fashioning Memory: Vintage Style and Youth Culture*. London: Bloomsbury Academic, 2015.

Knowles, Kim. "Locating Vintage." *Necsus. European Journal of Media Studies* 4, no. 2 (2015): 73–84.

Larkin, Brian. "The Politics and Poetics of Infrastructure." *Annual Review of Anthropology* 42, no. 1 (2013): 327–343.

Larsen, Frederik. *Objects and Social Actions – on Second-hand Valuation Practices*. PhD diss. Copenhagen Business School, 2015.

Malmberg, Bo, Eva Andersson, and John Östh. "Segregation and Urban Unrest in Sweden." *Urban Geography* 34, no. 7 (2013): 1031–1046.

McColl, Julie, Catherine Canning, Louise McBride, Karina Nobbs, and Linda Shearer. "It's Vintage Darling! An exploration of vintage fashion retailing." *The Journal of The Textile Institute* 104, no. 2 (2013): 140–150.

McCracken, Grant. *Culture and Consumption: New Approaches to the Symbolic Character of Consumer Goods and Activities*. Bloomington: Indiana University Press, 1988.

Milgram, B. Lynne. "Reconfiguring Margins: Secondhand Clothing and Street Vending in the Philippines." *Textile: The Journal of Cloth and Culture* 10 no. 2 (2012): 200–221.

Ministry of Finance Sweden. *Strategy for Sustainable Consumption*. Fi2016:7, 2016.

Nickel, Patricia Mooney. "Thrift Shop Philanthropy: Charity, Value, and Ascetic Rehabilitation." *Cultural Politics* 12, no. 2 (2016): 173–189.

Norris, Lucy. *Recycling Indian Clothing: Global Contexts of Reuse and Value*. Bloomington: Indiana University Press, 2010.

Pipyrou, Stavroula. "Cutting bella figura : Irony, Crisis, And Second hand Clothes in South Italy." *American Ethnologist* 41, no. 3 (2014): 532–546.

Scarpa, Simone. "Looking Beyond The Neighbourhood: Income Inequality And Residential Segregation In Swedish Metropolitan Areas, 1991–2010." *Urban Geography* 37, no. 7 (2016): 963–984.

Sherry, Jr., Jr., John F. "A Sociocultural Analysis of a Midwestern American Flea Market." *Journal of Consumer Research* 17, no. 1 (1990): 13–30.

Straw, Will. "Some Things a Scene Might Be: Postface." *Cultural Studies* 29, no. 3 (2014): 476–485.

Tsing, Anna. "The Global Situation." *Cultural Anthropology* 15, no. 3 (2000): 327–360.

Watt, Kathryn, and Bernard Dubbeld. "Enchanting The Worn-Out: The Craft of Selling Second-Hand Things at Milnerton Market, Cape Town." *Social Dynamics* 42, no. 1 (2016): 143–160.

Second-hand vehicle markets in West Africa: A source of regional disintegration, trade informality and welfare losses

Abel Ezeoha, Chinwe Okoyeuzu, Emmanuel Onah and Chibuike Uche

ABSTRACT

This article critiques the second-hand vehicle markets in the West African region, focusing on the triad trading arrangements among Nigeria, Benin, Togo, and Niger. These countries are connected by a number of underlying conflicting interests in the second-hand vehicles trade. Benin and Togo are incentivised by the revenues derived from re-export trade and port operations. Niger provides a proxy market for the illegal re-export of these vehicles to Nigeria, with the latter suffering huge welfare losses as a major consuming nation. We conclude that by offering conflicting benefits to the West African countries, the second-hand vehicle market provides disincentives against true regional integration.

1. Introduction

Trading in second-hand vehicles is arguably one of the most popular and complex intraregional cross-border businesses on the West African Coast. The popularity is such that two West African countries (Nigeria and Benin) rank among the top markets for used vehicles exported from Europe and America.[1]

Benin Republic alone reportedly harbours the largest market for such vehicles in Africa.[2] The economic benefits of the intraregional cross-border trading in second-hand vehicles are reported in terms of employment generation and increases in public revenue via import duties. On the other hand, the challenges and complexities of this form of trade have also been overwhelming – resulting in issues such as environmental concerns, regional disintegration, trade informality, illegality, and welfare losses.

The interplay of costs and benefits of the second-hand vehicle markets in West Africa can be attributed to the structural formation of the sub-regional bloc itself. In essence, the establishment of the Economic Community of West African States (ECOWAS) in 1975 marked the beginning of an economic and social integration process in that region of Sub-Saharan Africa. One of the primary goals of ECOWAS is 'to promote cooperation and development in all fields of economic activity' through the 'elimination of customs duties and other charges of equivalent effect in respect of the import and export of goods among member states, abolition of quantitative and administrative restrictions on trade among member countries, [and] abolition of obstacles to the free movement of persons, services, and capital between member states'.[3] Achieving this laudable integration goal requires that each of the Community's 15 member countries meet the demand and supply conditions for integration. The demand conditions require that market actors must perceive integration as being equitably in their best interests; while the supply side involves 'the conditions under which political leaders are willing and able to accommodate demands for regional institutions at each step of the integration process'.[4] These conditions are challenged in several African countries, particularly in West Africa where such attempts have been qualified as 'an integration of incomplete states' because the affected states 'cannot fully lay a claim to complete nationhood and suffer from internal insecurities'.[5]

The resulting effect of the dysfunctional regional structure is that little progress has been recorded in real terms in the pursuit of ECOWAS' long-term goal of attaining fully integrated economic and monetary union. Movement of people, for instance, is free in principle, but in practice it is besieged with challenges such as hostility from native populations, insecurity of life and property, and incessant harassment and extortion by border security agents.[6] Although the West African Economic and Monetary Union (WAEMU) has recorded significant progress in terms of attaining a common currency and free-trade zone since its establishment in 2000, the progress of its sister body, the West African Monetary Zone (WAMZ) remains virtually the opposite. The two sub-regional blocs remain sharply divided along colonial lines – the Francophone and the Anglophone ECOWAS member countries.[7]

In practice, many of the movements of people and goods that take place in the region are informal, generating global controversies on issues such as human trafficking and the trading of illicit goods and services. Even before colonialism took hold in the region, there was a near absence of 'state interest' in the ways that people within the region related. According to Azam, this meant that cross-border trade was based much more on common ethnic roots than on any formal integration effort.[8] The official designation of the border between Nigeria and Benin, for instance, merely resulted in the Shade Yoruba tribe being divided into two – one part belonging to French Dahomey and the other to Anglophone Nigeria.[9] Due to strong ethnic ties, border towns and migrants prefer to relate economically on informal terms rather than by using formal rules. Attempts to enforce national border policies, in line with the evidence established by Golub Stephen and Mark Pitt, intensify the degree of informality and encourage large price differences that provide an immediate impetus to trade diversion and smuggling.[10] In turn, informality breeds bilateral conflicts, illegality, and results in a higher degree of welfare losses in the constituent countries.[11] Meager's observations on the West African border trade show how informality erases the incentive to cooperate among countries in Africa by weakening the fiscal capacity and monetary control, undermining domestic productive capacity, and undermining the legitimacy and probity of the states.[12]

The second-hand vehicle markets in the West African region therefore present a good case for how informality can breed disintegration, illegality and welfare losses. The market, which, by the early 1980s, was limited to a restricted trade within Nigeria has an interesting history. The items of second-hand trade were originally called *Belgium*, because most of them were then sourced from Belgium by West African migrants in Europe. In 1986, the name changed to Tokunbo cars, derived from a Yoruba personal name Adetokunbo (which literally means 'a crown [ade] returns [bo] from overseas [ti] okun), given to 'a child conceived or born away from home, generally [for Nigerians] in Europe'.[13] The Tokunbo name is tagged to the fact that second-hand vehicle imports from Europe and America were mostly by the Nigerian diaspora, who used that as a source of repatriating wealth.

Arguably, more than any other country in the region, Nigeria suffers huge welfare losses as a result of the booming cross-border trade in second-hand goods. The country's large population, high incidence of poverty, endemic official corruption, and existence of porous borders, all join to make it highly vulnerable to negative externalities associated with the importation of used vehicles into West Africa. In the words of Fadahunsi and Rosa, 'the Nigerian cross-border trade is particularly interesting, as it takes place in an environment of long-standing illegality and corruption'.[14] While Benin and Togo (the major re-exporting countries) benefit immensely in terms of increased employment and government revenue, Nigeria suffers huge losses arising from a decline in customs' revenue, environmental risks, frustration of domestic industrial development plans, and increasing waves of illicit trade.

By focusing on the cross-border consequences of the second-hand vehicle trade in the West African region, our study provides a meaningful contribution to the literature on the international trade in second-hand goods. Over 35 years into its existence, the regional body (ECOWAS) is yet to attain a reasonable level of trade and economic integration. This is evident from the 2016 Africa Regional Integration Index, which placed it second to last among the eight officially recognised Regional Economic Communities (RECs) in Africa. We attempt to contextualise the skewed welfare losses/gains, illegality, and informality resulting from the cross-border second-hand goods trade and posit that they are among the key factors militating against the regional integration efforts by member countries. We also argue that the second-hand vehicle trade discourages bilateral cooperation and intensifies trade wars among West African neighbours. In effect, no optimal policy options appear to be on the ground, either at country level or at sub-regional level, to deal with the threats and challenges associated with the expanding influence of the second-hand vehicle trade in the West African region. We show how the welfare effects of the intraregional second-hand vehicle market in West Africa are asymmetrically distributed, not just between buyers and sellers, but also between countries. Following this approach, we structure the rest of the article as follows: Section 2 summarises issues relating to port politics and development in West Africa; section 3 critiques the trade policy and port governance issues in the second-hand vehicle markets in the region; section 4 illustrates how the market for second-hand vehicle induces informality and illegality in cross-border trade; section 5 examines the welfare losses associated with second-hand vehicle trade; and section 6 concludes the article.

2. Ports Politics and Development in West Africa

Seaport systems and operations play a dominant role in intraregional trade relations in the West African region. This is because most of the constituent countries are not industrialised and, as such, rely on imports from outside the region to meet domestic needs. Countries with deep-sea resources are always seen to have more competitive advantages than their inland counterparts, mostly because such resources offer opportunities for increased transhipment welfare benefits. Post-independence port policies are therefore ostensibly designed to capture a larger share of regional transhipment activities. This trend surfaced in the 1980s, when many of the countries started repositioning their ports systems around the benefits of transhipments. The most ambitious project, according to Iheduru, was

Senegal's Port Autonomie Dakar (PAD), which was built in 1988 to serve as a sub-regional load centre, including feeder services to Mali, Mauritania, Guinea-Conakry and Guinea-Bissau.[15] Other concurrent seaport expansion programmes in the region within the same period include that of Ivory Coast (in 1987) and Ghana (in 1988 and 1990). A report on the ambitious move of the Ivorian government typifies the intense competition that existed over transhipment businesses. According to the report,

> Cote d'Ivoire's rush to install new gantry cranes in Abidjan in 1987, against professional advice, typified its desire to garner as much of the sub-region's transshipment trade as possible. According to an Ivorian official, those cranes were installed simply "'because Lagos [Nigeria] had one'".[16]

Nigeria and Benin are equally involved in the competition for transhipment businesses in the region. The influence of Nigeria is informed by the country's size and history. Before the start of seaport expansion programmes in other West African countries, Nigeria was already known as a major hub for transhipments in the region – both in commodities and in slave trades. For instance, in its pre-independence periods, surf ports were established at Quidah and Cotonou, in the then Kingdom of Dahomey (now Benin Republic) as the 'slave coast', in order that European traders could compete with the nearest rival, Lagos.[17] This act marked the first major attempt by the government of Dahomey to counter the influence of the Nigerian port system on regional trade flows. Between 1945 and 1956, Dahomey – and Niger-bound imports were diverted through Lagos' ports due to long delays in the loading and discharging of ships at Quidah and Cotonou (which sometimes stretched to 556 idle days).[18] But the costly nature of the Lagos-Porto Novo route eventually forced the French colonial government to expand the Cotonou port and improve the rail-road route from Cotonou inland to the Niger Republic[19]. This move was part of a strategy to divert a substantial proportion of the latter's imports through Lagos. The expansion did not, however, resolve the issue of congestion, especially as trade volumes continued to increase along with economic modernity in neighbouring countries. This explains why, after independence in 1959, the Beninese government deemed it a viable policy option to rely on the engagement of private port operators to cope with increasing trade flows.

Because of their strategic role and influence in transhipment businesses in the region, both Nigeria and Benin have tended to compete along different lines, based on their respective port policies and reforms. In contrast to the situation in Benin, where private sector operators were part of the post-independence history of sea port development, in Nigeria, until the mid 2000s, the port system was monopolised by the Nigerian Ports Authority (NPA). This monopoly was further reinforced by Decree No. 38 of 1999, which reinvigorated the power of the NPA to control all public and private tasks in the water transport sub-sector.[20] This means that, comparatively, the port systems in Benin and in other West African countries have historically had a more flexible outlook than in Nigeria. The dry port policy adopted by the Nigerian government in March 2006 (as a public–private partnership arrangement[21]), was a strategic reaction to the keen competition between Benin Republic and Nigeria for the maritime needs of Niger Republic and probably Chad Republic. This is reinforced by the fact that of the six designated dry ports, only Kaduna (an industrial state at the heart of Nigeria's north central region) was operational at the end of 2015. The effectiveness of this policy was however limited by the matched concessionary policy adopted by Benin, following the Beninese government's award of a 25-year concession to the French company

Groupement Bollore, in November 2008, 'to build and operate the South Wharf Container Terminal'.[22]

As highlighted above, competition in seaport reforms and operations in West Africa is not restricted to Nigeria and Benin. For instance, a plan to build a shared port at the common frontier of Togo and Benin Republic failed because of the differing economic interests of the two Francophone neighbours. This was despite the French government's commitment to fully finance the project. Whereas the major incentive behind port development in Lomé, Togo was to achieve independence from Ghana in the provision of port services, Benin Republic was interested in liberating itself from the dominance of Lagos ports in the handling of its shipments and those of her Francophone neighbours, Niger Republic.[23] The divergent interests in bilateral relations among countries in West Africa essentially constitute a key part of the narrative on how intraregional commodity trading can be a basis for regional disintegration, trade informality and welfare losses. As enunciated by Okello Oculi, 'informal cross-border trade is claimed to have been fuelled, since the 1970s across West Africa, by small and weak economies of Benin, Togo and the Gambia which adopted the strategy of low-tariff policies to attract foreign imports from outside Africa for transit to richer neighbouring economies of Mauritania, Senegal and Mali (for Gambia); Nigeria and Burkina Faso and Niger (by Togo and Benin)'.[24]

3. Policy and Port Governance Issues in the Second-hand Vehicle Trade

The second-hand vehicle market in West Africa generally operates based on a sovereign triad structure. At one point of this triad is Nigeria, with its protectionist port operation and import policies, which is explained by the fact that the country constitutes the final destination for a greater proportion of second-hand vehicle imports into West Africa. The national interest from this perspective is to control and, if possible, prevent the shipment of defective and old vehicles into the country; this calls for a series of high-import tariffs and the imposition of non-tariff protections. At another point is Benin and Togo, whose fiscal operations are tied to revenue from re-export trade and port operations. In pursuit of this common interest, the governments of these countries deliberately put in place liberal trade policies, considered to be among the freest in the Sub-Saharan African region. Their respective trade policies allow for the importation of goods of all kinds into the countries and the subsequent re-export of such goods to neighbouring West African countries.[25] Evidence suggests, for instance, that of the total imports of used cars into Cotonou Port in Benin, about '90 percent are destined for Nigeria, with 5 percent for Niger and 5 percent for the domestic market'[26]; and that out of every set of four vehicles for the Nigerian market, three are discharged in Cotonou.[27]

For second-hand vehicles imported through Benin and Togo, no formal arrangements are in place to guarantee their quality and condition, mostly because these imported vehicles never leave the ports and find their way onto the streets and cities of Benin and Togo. An aspect of the Beninese trade policy, for example, prohibits the sale of Nigerian-bound imported goods within the Benin territory, and the importer of such goods are given 'only three days to get his cargo across the border'.[28] In effect, the re-exporting and port operational role of both Benin and Togo earns them the sobriquet 'Warehouse States' – a term originally used to refer to the role of Benin in West African trade relations.[29]

At the last point of the triangular West African second-hand vehicle trade arrangement is Niger. Benin and Niger are members of the WAEMU customs union,[30] which means that the countries are economically more integrated in terms of free movement of persons, goods, services and capital. Benin is endowed with deep-sea resources, which makes it a strategic location for serving the export and import trading needs of its landlocked neighbours, such as Burkina Faso and Niger. Niger, in contrast, is a landlocked country with no sovereign access to seaports. Port shipment to Niger is therefore through Benin, with minimal (or, in some cases, zero) import duty charges, based on the WAEMU free-trade and common currency arrangements. Interestingly, both countries share common land borders with Nigeria. Technically, this geographical proximity facilitates Niger as an alternative channel for moving goods from Benin to Nigeria. Consequently, Niger is recorded as having provided a proxy market for second-hand vehicles destined for Nigeria since 2003. The widely acclaimed view is that, in practice, to avoid duties, vehicles designated as transit to third countries 'are some-times placed under the transit regime to Niger, and then unofficially diverted to Nigeria'.[31] This strategy allows the importers and the Beninese authority to conceal the identities of the original destination and to circumvent the Nigerian government's ban on second-hand vehicle importation via land routes.

Lack of transparency in the second-hand vehicle imports created an opportunity for money laundering and trading in illicit commodities.[32] The case of money laundering was, for example, implicated in an investigation report by the United States Drug Enforcement Administration (DEA). The report indicted 'two Lebanese exchange houses, Kassem Rmeiti & Co. For Exchange (Rmeiti Exchange) and Halawi Exchange Co. (Halawi Exchange), as conduits through which hundreds of millions of dollars are moved in cash into the U.S to buy cars which are then shipped to Cotonou where most 'Tokunbo' cars on Nigerian roads are brought into the country'.[33]

As expected, increased seaport politics among the West African countries complicated port management systems, resulting in indiscriminate importation and dumping of sec-ond-hand goods, congestions, and repression of domestic industries' productive capacity.[34] The first major port congestion crisis, considered as one of the worst in the world,[35] occurred in Nigeria between 1975 and 1977, and was matched by the government's attempt to expand and modernise the country's port facilities. The second such port congestion crisis took place in the mid 1980s and an attempt to resolve it focused mostly on the use of fiscal policy based on the expansion of the country's import 'prohibition list'. In particular, the Nigerian govern-ment attempted to resolve the problem of port congestion by imposing stringent import restriction policies that resulted in a ban on certain commodities or, in some cases, the imposition of exorbitant tariff structures. Against the principles of economic integration, unconventional trade wars grew among West African countries, with national trade policies overriding regional interests.

A major tool for the trade wars is fiscal policy. In Benin, in 1985, an erstwhile 'fiscal policy on state monopoly on imports was abolished and replaced by a license system'; and in 1987, 'the licensing requirements were further abolished'.[36] In 1993, the Beninese government stretched its trade liberalisation policies by abolishing all other restrictions,[37] with the primary target of boosting export revenue via increased flow of trade. From then on, the government has maintained a system of fiscal policy and port governance measures that are not only deliberately targeted at wooing Nigerian importers, but have equally resulted in making the Port of Cotonou one of 'the best ports in the region in terms of the speed at which cargo is unloaded'.[38] According to Benjamin, Golub, and Mbaye, in both Benin and Gambia 'since the early 1970s, the authorities have sought to maintain trade taxes below those of neighbouring countries in a deliberate attempt to re-export to their larger neighbours'.[39] Togo and Benin also compete in terms of fees and speed of service discharge. Describing this tariff-linked competition, it is contends that whereas 'Benin sacrificed some of its transit trade in order to collect a larger amount of revenue', 'Togo collects very little revenue on transit and re-exports, in order to boost competitiveness'.[40]

The pursuit of divergent policies was also a common characteristic of the Nigeria-Benin bilateral trade relations.[41] From Nigeria's perspective, the argument for the second-hand goods market, which include anti-dumping and protection of infant industries, finds strong merits in the economic externalities theory. Equally, on the side of Benin (and Togo), increased trade flows of second-hand vehicles is promoted as a strategy for increasing public revenue for national development. For Nigeria, there are more incentives to control the importing of used cars than there is for Benin, Gambia, and Togo. Nigeria has an infant auto industry that consistently begs for protection and promotion. An example is the National Automobile Policy which was introduced in 2014 as a strategy for localising automobile manufacturing in the country. Neither Togo, nor Benin has such an automobile industry policy framework. As an end-user of imported second-hand vehicles also, Nigeria is more exposed to the environmental and health risks associated with such products than any of the neighbouring countries, which, in most cases, operate as transit ports.

4. Welfare Effects of the Second-hand Vehicle Trade

The second-hand vehicle market generates both welfare gains and losses. On the positive side, in Africa, such markets satisfy the need for low-priced, high-quality goods. It equally generates other forms of positive externalities, especially in terms of employment, entrepreneurial engagement, and opportunities for increased public revenue. Problems arise because the welfare benefits of the second-hand goods trade are, in most cases, unevenly distributed among trading partners. At the national level, the benefits are skewed in favour of the dealers, who presumably have information advantages over the sellers, and the welfare losses are skewed against the buyers, who traditionally lack information. At the regional level, the welfare benefits favour the transhipment or re-export countries, whereas the losses are focused on the buying countries. In this section, we show how the uneven distribution of the benefits and losses arising from the second-hand vehicle trade stifles trade formalities and regional integration. In doing this, we discuss the welfare effects of second-hand trade in terms of trade illegality and informality, the consequences on regional economic integration, and the welfare losses to different stakeholders.

4.1. Illegality and informality in second-hand vehicle markets

The rhetoric in the extant literature emphasises that: second-hand markets for vehicles provide incentives for smuggling, crimes, trade diversion and money laundering;[42] and that the markets stunt regional industrial growth by crowding out and dis-incentivising the growth of domestic manufacturing firms. This is because, at the regional level, the economic costs of the second-hand markets spread from just the consequences on microeconomic agents (buyers and sellers) to macroeconomic burdens on the government and society at large.

In Nigeria, a ban on the importation of cars by land routes from neighbouring countries has been in force since 2004. Movements of imported second-hand cars from Benin, Togo and other West African countries into Nigeria are officially adjudged illegal from the point of view of the Nigerian authorities. In a BBC African Business Report, a World Bank senior economist in Benin said that 'the Beninese legally import the vehicles from Europe, but then export them illegally to Nigeria'.[43] From the Nigerian perspective, the massive markets for second-hand vehicles between Nigeria and its West African neighbours are mostly illegal because the trade is banned by law, and informal because there is no official documentation process to support or facilitate the trade. In contrast, the Beninese and Togolese governments have no significant restrictive policies in place to control the flow of second-hand vehicles and other consumer goods – a stance that makes the market legal from the perspective of Benin and Togo.

Ironically, the process of illegally diverting Benin-bound imported vehicles to Nigeria is formalised. This is evident in the existence of

> a well-established set of procedures for obtaining documents from customs authorising the diversion of cars to Nigeria, where the fees and taxes for obtaining the authorisations amount to about CFAF400,000 per car. This includes a fee for a customs escort to accompany the car to the Nigerian border,[44]

This was acknowledged by one of the dealers, who was quoted as saying that: 'As a way of encouraging us to continue to patronise them, the Benin government offers rebate to Nigerian importers'; and 'apart from paying what is generally viewed as a healthy tariff system, the Nigerian importer in Benin is further granted 15 percent tariff less what is paid by his Beninoise counterpart'.[45] Consequently, buyers of such cars ultimately save 'up to 30% buying cars in Benin, rather than buying it directly in Nigeria'.[46]

Erosion of confidence in the Nigerian port governance system, due to corruption and arbitrary service charges, is also implicated as a major cause of trade diversion.[47] It has, for instance, been argued that 'like a ripple, high port charges led to customer apathy which in turn led to cargo diversion wherein millions of metric tonnes of Nigeria-bound freight were diverted to neighbouring ports of Cotonou, Lome, Tema, Accra, and the rest.'[48] The barriers imposed by the Nigerian government provide a huge incentive for Beninese and Nigerian smugglers to persistently 'conduct informal trade across the borders on products ranging from agricultural commodities to used cars'.[49]

4.2. Consequences on regional economic integration

The complexities in the regional market for second-hand vehicles in West Africa are aggravated by the near absence of effective institutional counteracting mechanisms for fair trade. Consequently, trading in second-hand vehicles is shrouded in illegitimacy and deliberate attempts to circumvent official trade rules and tariffs.[50] The existing counteracting mechanisms are either weak or costly and their signalling power is inadequate in terms of enhancing the competitiveness of good products.[51] In other regions, economic integration has proved to be an effective tool for discouraging trade informality and reducing the costs of formal importation and exportation with enhanced compliance to existing regulations.[52] However, in the West Africa sub-region, attempts to use such frameworks to promote smooth regional trade are often faced with compliance problems. Due to lack of cooperation, an individual country's policy efforts trigger opposing counteractions from neighbouring countries.

Table 1. Quantitative Restrictions on Second-hand vehicle Import (based on allowable age-limit of cars into Nigeria).

Year	Allowable Age Limit
1994–2002	8 years
2002–2004	5 years
2004–2008	8 years
2008–2009	10 years
2010–2013	15 years
2014–2015	10 years
2016	15 years

As shown in Table 1 above, against the desired policy goal, the more the Nigerian government eases its quantity restrictions on the age limits of vehicles permitted to be imported into the country, the more viable the alternative Beninese and Togolese cross-border trading routes become. This is also considering the fact that prices are naturally negatively correlated with the age of commodities.

Regardless of the trade policy of Nigeria, the Cotonou second-hand vehicle and consumer product markets are officially structured and governed around the overwhelming demand for second-hand products in Nigeria. This is especially in light of the fact that up to three quarters of consumer goods officially imported through the port of Cotonou are re-exported to the Nigerian market.[53] Benjamin, Golub, and Mbaye specifically report that the high demand by Nigerians has fuelled second-hand vehicles markets as 'Benin's most significant re-export since about 2000'; and that the trend also resulted in steep increases in imports of vehicles from 50,000 in 1996 to an 'all time high of 300,000 in 2007'.[54] A 2014 BBC report also alleged that as many as 25,000 vehicles are re-exported into Nigeria from Benin on a monthly basis.[55]

As part of the formalisation process of the second-hand vehicle re-export business, and in circumvention of the Nigerian government's trade restriction rules, Benin also takes advantage of the strategic location of Niger. It does so by ensuring that used car imports officially destined for Niger are diverted to Nigeria. In support of this claim, Benjamin, Golub, and Mbaye provide evidence that shows that "of 230,000 cars declared for shipment to Niger in 2001, only 15,000 ended up there"; "'almost all the rest wound up in Nigeria'".[56]

Apart from the competitive and strategic trade policies of Benin and Togo, the port governance system also contributes to illegalising and de-formalising the import of second-hand vehicles into Nigeria. In contrast to what pertains in Benin, a great deal of mis-governance takes place at the Nigerian end of the trade. In effect, 'the unofficial re-export trade operates in a thinly disguised collusion with high government officials in Nigeria'.[57] Where collusion is difficult, smuggled vehicles are escorted or self-driven by security agents across border posts, which makes interception very difficult and eases evasion from immigration. This is again a reaction to the high level of inefficiency in the port governance system.[58] Unlike the case in Nigerian seaports, where official agents and unofficial touts compete in the second-hand vehicle market space, at the Beninese and Togolese end of the market, customs is the only uniformed agency an importer has to contend with, and there is absolute order in the entire port clearing system.[59] The Beninese-Togolese-Nigerian second-hand vehicle trade relation is thus a good demonstration of how divergences in trade policies can frustrate regional economic cooperation among neighbouring countries.

4.3. Welfare Losses from Second-hand Vehicle Trade

At the regional level, the economic costs of the second-hand markets have wider consequences. There are the burdens of increased environmental externalities, the cost of regulating informality and illegality, and, above all, problems associated with trade creation and
trade diversion.[60] In the words of Chu and Delgado:

> the illegal importation of used vehicles falls outside formal economic activities, which in turn are
> not taxed, negatively affecting government revenue inflows. Additionally, informality removes
> the incentive for businesses to improve their customer service and productivity. Thus, growth
> potential is reduced; fewer jobs are created, driving more people into the informal sector, further
> limiting growth in a self-reinforcing cycle.[61]

Trade creation and diversion constitute by far the most significant manifestation of the
regional market for used vehicles. In this case, trade creation arises when cheap imports
from neighbouring countries increase to replace inefficiently produced, high-cost domestic
products.[62] On its own, trade diversion implies shifting the source of imports from lower-cost
sources outside the regional bloc to a higher-cost source within it.[63] Because of the quality
uncertainty associated with the second-hand vehicle trade, especially in poor developing
regions, the positive welfare effects of trade creation and diversion are rarely recorded at
the macroeconomic or regional level. Asante attributes this to the fact that existing external
trade is usually large, relative to their domestic production and the fact that intragroup trade
is a minor component of their total trade.[64]

Specifically, the welfare losses from the market for second-hand vehicles can be analysed
from the perspective of individual and deadweight losses. The individual losses accrue to
buyers and dealers as specific economic agents in the market, while the deadweight losses
relate to the consequences of informality and illegality (in terms of public revenue losses,
retardation of domestic industries, and unemployment), as well as the negative externalities.
Agbo summarised these losses to include the influx of 'all sorts of abandoned, discarded,
wrecked, ruined, or worn out vehicles or end-of-life vehicles', revenue loss to the government,
increased border crimes, and deflation in the capacity of the country's infant domestic automobile industry.[65]

4.3.1. Welfare losses to the government

As mentioned above, top of the list of welfare losses accruing to government and society at
large include: the huge costs of fighting border crimes and maintaining border security;
negative economic externalities relating to environmental damage caused by the importation of defective vehicles; and loss of public revenue due to trade diversion. On the fiscal
side, evidence reveals that Nigeria lost a stunning N136 billion (over US$900 million) in 2013
as a result of the diversion of cargo to other ports in the sub-region.[66] The World Bank also
reported that over $400 million, representing about 25 percent of the 2010 total annual
revenue collected by the Nigerian Customs Service, is lost through smuggling activities
across the land frontier borders.[67] Mostly in the case of Nigeria, corruption by port officials
renders any form of fiscal policy objective unrealizable and provides incentives for the sustenance and protection of illegal re-exports.

Growth in the regional market for second-hand vehicles and consumer goods has also
transformed a number of countries in the West African sub-region into a haven for smuggling
businesses. 'So extensive is current smuggling that it has transformed border crossings into

booming towns and markets'.[68] The enormous extent of smuggling activities is also well-doc-
umented historically. It is reported, for instance, that 'in 1981, the value of smuggled goods
between Nigeria and Benin was an estimated 12 billion francs CFA ($US58 million)', and that,
seeking to evade import controls, Nigerian businessmen used Benin's Port of Cotonou as
their major conduit for illegal overseas imports.[69] Accounting for this is the existence of
complex border-linked trade routes between Nigeria and its neighbours.[70] This makes unofficial re-exports easy to move, either by road or water, with the existence of numerous and
ever-changing tracks along the long borders with Nigeria.

The growing intensity of the smuggling business in Nigeria creates incentives for other
crimes such as human trafficking, piracy, money laundering, and a transformation of the
buying countries into a dumping ground for all sorts of defective and environmentally hazardous goods.[71] Nigeria, for example, is credited with being 'the main source of piracy in the
region, accounting for 29 piracy incidents, including two hijackings, 11 ships boarded, 13
vessels fired upon and three attempted attacks'.[72] The cost of fighting smuggling-related
border crimes imposes a large-scale financial burden on the government. Lack of cooperation
in border security management among neighbouring countries also weakens efforts at
integration.

No doubt, the welfare losses incurred by Nigeria in the regional second-hand goods
market constitute major welfare gains to Benin and Togo. The market for used cars in Benin
is phenomenal, accounting for 43 percent of trade flows, about 45 percent of Cotonou's port
revenues,[73] as well as nearly 75 percent of the GDP.[74] However, the transit policy in the country
is believed to be a source of revenue leakage to the government, leading to a situation where
used cars (and other goods) marked for transit to landlocked countries, in order to suspend
tax payments, are diverted and smuggled to Nigeria.[75] Togo's economy is traditionally centred
on the activities at the Port of Lomé, with re-export trade at the port accounting for more
than 25 percent of total exports.[76] Benin has a relative advantage over Togo. First, Benin is
the closest CFA country to Lagos, and as such maintains an 'important role for trade between
Nigeria and many of the countries of the region'.[77] Whereas there is a direct border link
between Benin and Nigeria, this is not the case with Togo and Gambia, who do not share a
direct geographical border with Nigeria. Trade flows are carried out through Togo by longer
land routes, which invariably increase the cost of shipping over and above costs incurred in
Benin.

While there are some welfare gains for Togo and Benin, the neighbours are constantly
locked in trade wars, using tariffs as a key strategic tool and working completely against the
tenets of WAEMU. Moreover, mass cross-border migration and trafficking also makes conflicts
contagious – as in the case of the Boko Haram insurgency, the impacts of which were as
severe in some neighbouring countries as they were in Nigeria.

4.3.2. Welfare losses to consumers in the market
The welfare effects of the second-hand vehicle market to consumers can equally be positive
or negative. The positive effects include the ease of accessibility and affordability that such
markets provide. It has been posited, for instance, that the utility preferences of consumers
in developing countries are enhanced in the global market for used vehicles because of the
limited supply of new vehicles, price differentials and differing depreciation rates across
countries.[78] It is arguable that without the existence of this market, very few persons in poor
regions like West Africa could own a vehicle. On the other hand, welfare losses to consumers

of second-hand vehicles come in the form of the higher likelihood of buying defective cars at exorbitant prices, as well as the associated costs and risks of using such cars. As earlier identified, the market for second-hand vehicles in the West African sub-region is traditionally characterised by a large information deficit and price-quality disparities against buyers. Due to quality uncertainty, most of the time end-users who buy such vehicles lack the capacity to actually determine their worth and so often pay more than they should. The loss in con-sumer surplus increases in step with the number of intermediaries, more so because each intermediary rationally struggles to maximise its own utility surplus.

Consistent with the analytical framework used by Abimbola for second-hand clothing, in practice, the buyers know nothing about the quality of the vehicles in the source countries in Europe and in America, and are ignorant of the damage that may have occurred as the vehicles exchange hands from the Beninese importers to the Beninese re-exporters and finally to the Nigerian dealers.[79] In the case of Nigeria, where most of the cross-border sec-ond-hand vehicle trade is informal and illegal,[80] due to legal restrictions by the Nigerian government, there is an absence of effective formal counteracting mechanisms for protect-ing consumers (such as formal rules, insurance, and warranties). Buyers are also reportedly incentivised to transact informally to minimise costs and avoid paying double import duties, to the transshipment country and the home country. In the presence of illegality, the dealers along cross-border routes invest little in building their reputations. Rather, they wilfully exacerbate quality uncertainty and undermine transparency in the trading process.

As Golub argued, the consumer welfare losses associated with the second-hand vehicle trade in West Africa are felt more in the buying countries (such as Nigeria and Niger) than in the re-exporting countries (like Benin, Togo and Gambia).[81] This is because, in the absence of effective harmonisation in regional trade policies and rules, the re-exporting countries have little incentive to expend resources on guaranteeing the quality control and standards of used vehicles in transit to neighbouring countries.

4.3.3. Welfare losses to producers and dealers in the market

The welfare effects of the second-hand vehicle trade are also skewed against producers and dealers in importing and re-exporting countries. On the positive side, evidence shows how the market has induced entrepreneurial growth in the region. In essence, the blurring of legality and illegality in the market provides a wider profit margin for the traders – making it possible for them to 'target any goods irrespective of their legal status if potential profit margins are high'.[82] The immense job losses in the regional markets, occasioned by the recent economic recession in Nigeria, underscores the importance of the market for generating entrepreneurial growth in the West African sub-region. A recent report illustrates how 'mechanics, drivers, electricians, and painters have all lost their jobs' due to the absence of Nigerian buyers in the Beninese and Togolese markets.[83]

The most significant welfare loss accruing from the second-hand vehicle market is the crowding-out effect. A report in the Nigerian newspaper *BusinessDay* exemplified this crowd-ing-out effect by highlighting that the dependency on imported new and used cars has brought about a situation where, in recent years, 'the pioneer car assembly plants have fallen into disrepair'.[84] The producers' welfare losses, in the case of West Africa, are worsened by the fact that the economic policies in place to protect the industry are either poorly designed or inefficiently implemented.[85]

5. Conclusion

Nigeria has the largest demand for second-hand vehicles in Sub-Saharan Africa. Ironically, the Nigerian government imposes the stiffest tariffs and non-tariff measures against the importation of such commodities. There is currently a restrictive ceiling of fifteen years age limit for vehicles permitted into the country, and vehicles that are within this bracket attract an import tariff of 35 percent, the highest in the region. The prevailing harsh business environment in the country invariably makes the survival of domestic vehicle assembling plants near impossible and newly assembled vehicles out of the reach of most citizens. Additionally, port congestion and administrative bottlenecks make Nigerian seaports unviable due to the delays in the clearing of legally imported goods. The structural defects in the Nigerian trading policies and port operational system are the main reason for the booming second-hand vehicle markets in the sea-rich neighbouring West African countries of Benin and Togo. To take maximum advantage of the situation in Nigeria, these countries operate some of the freest and most liberal trade policies in Africa. There are few or no restrictions and no formal arrangements in place to guarantee the quality and conditions of the second-hand vehicles imported into these countries, mostly because the imported vehicles never leave the ports and reach the streets and cities of Benin and Togo.

Historically, the second-hand markets have been a source of social integration and tend to serve the specific goal of satisfying the need for low-priced, high-quality goods. A major problem identified in this article is the uneven distribution of the resulting benefits and losses. Whereas the interests of Benin and Togo are commonly tied to the associated revenue potentials from re-export trade and port operations, Nigeria suffers huge welfare losses relating to public revenue losses, environmental risks, frustration of domestic industrial development, and increased waves of illicit trades. Differing benefits and losses result in differences in trade and monetary policies. Due to the associated welfare losses, Nigeria's trade policy is highly restrictive on second-hand vehicles. In contrast, the huge welfare benefits accruing to Benin and Togo provide them the incentive to operate liberal trade policies. The differences in policy thrusts provide significant incentives for informality in the market, whereby such vehicles are traded legally in Benin and Togo, but illegally in Nigeria. Benin uses its common border with Niger as a proxy market to circumvent the Nigerian government's high tariff and non-tariff restrictions on the importation of second-hand vehicles.

By offering conflicting benefits to the West African countries, the second-hand vehicle markets provide a major disincentive against true regional economic integration; and an attempt to achieve effective regional integration among ECOWAS member countries would require a true harmonisation of all aspects of trade policies on influential commodities such as second-hand vehicles. Such regional efforts should centre primarily on harmonising country-specific policies and trade rules relating to age limits of vehicles, health and quality specifications, transshipment and re-export policies, and the applicable national tariff structures. Currently, the ECOWAS liberalisation policy and common external tariffs (CET) system have no explicit pronouncements on controlling the growing influence of the ubiquitous second-hand vehicle trade. The common import tariffs adopted by the member countries to curb smuggling and enhance intraregional trade flows are yet to be fully implemented. When the tariffs come into force, member countries can enforce them only when the gains and losses from sub-regional trade are relatively evenly distributed.

Notes

1. UNECE. 'Used Vehicles: Global Overview' *UN Environment Background Paper*, 2017 https://www.unece.org/fileadmin/DAM/trans/doc/2017/itc/UNEP-ITC_Background_Paper-Used_Vehicle_Global_Overview.pdf; Also see Coffin, David, Jeff Horowitz, Danielle Nesmith, and Mitchell Semanik. '"Examining Barriers to Trade in Used Vehicles."'
2. Ribstein, Sophie and Jason Boswell. 2014. 'Benin's Second-hand Car Trade', *BBC African Business Report*, September 5, 2014. http://www.bbc.co.uk/news/business-29061377
3. Anyanwu, *Monetary Economics: Theory, policy, and Institutions,* p. 389.
4. Matthews, *Regional integration and food security in developing countries.*
5. Qobo, Mzukisi. "The challenges of regional integration in Africa: In the context of globalisation and the prospects for a United States of Africa", p. 16.
6. Adepoju, Aderanti. "Migration in West Africa", 37–41.
7. Uche, "The politics of monetary sector cooperation among the Economic Community of West African States members."
8. Azam, *Trade, Exchange Rate, and Growth in Sub-Saharan Africa.*
9. Blum, "Cross-border flows between Nigeria and Benin: what are the challenges for (human) security?".
10. Golub, Stephen. "Informal cross-border trade and smuggling in Africa", 179.-200; Pitt. "Smuggling and price disparity." 447–458.
11. Golub, Stephen. "Informal cross-border trade and smuggling in Africa"; Fadahunsi and Rosa, "Entrepreneurship and illegality: insights from the Nigerian cross-border trade", 397–429.
12. Meager, Kate. 'A back door to globalisation? Structural adjustment, globalisation and transborder trade in West Africa', 57–75.
13. Guyer, Jane I. *Marginal gains: monetary transactions in Atlantic Africa,* p. 87.
14. Fadahunsi and Rosa. "Entrepreneurship and illegality: insights from the Nigerian cross-border trade", 397–429.
15. Iheduru, *The political economy of international shipping in developing countries,* p. 154.
16. Cited in Iheduru, p. 155.
17. For evidence of this, see 0821415719_intro.pdf.
18. White, "New ports in Dahomey and Togo", p. 161.
19. Ibid., p. 162.
20. Federal Government of Nigeria, 'Draft National Transport Policy'. 2010.
21. Online source: Oxford Business Group, 2016.
22. White, "New ports in Dahomey and Togo".
23. For details, see Ibid.
24. Oculi, "Cooperation and Integration in African: The Case of Informal Cross Border Trade", p. 3.
25. Beuving, "Nigerien second-hand car traders in Cotonou: A sociocultural analysis of economic decision-making", 353–373.
26. Benjamin, Golub, and Mbaye, "Informality, trade policies and smuggling in West Africa", 381–394.
27. This latter view is indeed an open secret widely expressed in the local media. See for instance *Leadership* [Nigeria] newspaper of 5 September 2016, 'Customs Loses N600bn to Diverted Vehicle Imports'; and *New Telegraph* [Nigeria] newspaper of 12 October 2016, 'Benin republic Controls 63% of Nigeria's Vehicle Imports'.
28. *Daily Trust* [Nigeria] newspaper, 'Nigeria's Chaos, Benin Republic Gains', 19 February, 2012.
29. LARES. Le commerce frontalier entre le Bénin et le Nigeria. Rapport de synthèse. CFD : février 1995, 60 p.
30. Other members of West African Monetary and Economic Union (WAEMU) are Burkina Faso, Cote d'Ivoire, Guinea Bissau, Mali, Senegal, and Togo.
31. Benjamin, Golub, and Mbaye, "Informality, trade policies and smuggling in West Africa", p. 390.
32. Beuving, "Nigerien second-hand car traders in Cotonou: A sociocultural analysis of economic decision-making".

33. Freeman, Michael, and Moyara Ruehsen. "Terrorism Financing Methods: An Overview/ Perspectives on Terrorism".
34. Dossou, Sinzogan; and Mensah, 'Economic Growth in Benin: Lost Opportunities', 87–118.
35. Akinwale and Aremo. "Concession as a catalyst for crisis management in Nigerian Ports." 117–126.
36. Sacerdoti, Emillio. 'Benin: recent economic developments', 96–102.
37. Ibid.
38. See a USITC cable titled Study on Benin: Effects of Infrastructure Conditions on Export Competitiveness, Wikileaks, October 3, 2008. The Port of Cotonou acts has a free port status, which implies that trade is permitted before custom declaration.
39. Benjamin, Golub, and Mbaye, "Informality, trade policies and smuggling in West Africa."
40. Golub, "Informal cross-border trade and smuggling in Africa", p. 198.
41. Sacerdoti, Emillio. 'Benin: recent economic developments'.
42. Blum, "Cross-border flows between Nigeria and Benin: what are the challenges for (human) security?".
43. Ribstein, S. and Boswell, J. 'Benin's second-hand car trade' Africa Business Report, 5 September 2014.
44. Benjamin, Mbaye, and Diop. *The informal sector in Francophone Africa: firm size, productivity, and institutions*, p. 203.
45. *Daily Trust* "Nigeria"s Chaos, Benin Republic's Gains', Shehu Abubakar, Cotonou Feb 19 2012.
46. BBC News (2014), 'Benin's second-hand car trade', African Business Report, September 5.
47. Marjit, Sugata, Sudeep Ghosh, and Amit Biswas. 'Informality, corruption and trade reform', 777–789.
48. Nigerian Ports: The Perils Of Demurrage, by Chigozie Chikere http://247ureports.com/nigerian-ports-the-perils-of-demurrage-by-chigozie-chikere/
49. United States International Trade Commission. 'Export Opportunities and Barriers in African Growth and Opportunity Act Eligible Countries', Inv. 332–464, DIANE Publishing, 2005, 5–7.
50. Cantens, Thomas, Robert Ireland, and Gaël Raballand. "Introduction: borders, informality, international trade and customs." 365–380.
51. See for instance Bond, 'A direct test of the' Lemons' model: The market for used pickup trucks." 836–840.
52. Lesser and Moisé-Leeman. 'Informal cross-border trade and trade facilitation reform in Sub-Saharan Africa', p. 6.
53. Soule, Obi, and Club. *Prospects for Trade between Nigeria and its Neighbours.*
54. Benjamin, Golub, and Mbaye, "Informality, trade policies and smuggling in West Africa." p. 203.
55. Ribstein, Sophie and Jason Boswell, 'Benin's second-hand car trade' BBC Africa Business Report, 5 September 2014.
56. Benjamin, Golub, and Mbaye, "Informality, trade policies and smuggling in West Africa.", p. 227.
57. Ibid.
58. *Daily Trust* "Nigeria"s Chaos, Benin Republic's Gains', Shehu Abubakar, Feb 19 2012.
59. Ibid. "Sunday Trust was on the entourage of the Senate Committee on Transport investigative committee to Benin Republic recently".
60. Golub, Stephen. "Informal cross-border trade and smuggling in Africa".
61. Chu and Delgado. "Used vehicle imports impact on new vehicle sales: The Mexican Case", p. 351.
62. Andic, Fuat, Suphan Andic, and Douglas Dosser. *A theory of economic integration for developing countries: illustrated by Caribbean countries.*
63. Robson, Peter. *Integration, development and equity: economic integration in West Africa*, p. 6.
64. Asante, Samuel KB. *Regionalism and Africa's development: expectations, reality and challenges.*
65. Agbo, COA. "Recycle materials potential of imported used vehicles in Nigeria." 118–128.
66. Administrator, "How TEMA May Emerge West African Hub Port', *The Journal of Freight and Energy*, July 31, 2014. http://www.journalngonline.com/2014/07/31/how-tema-may-emerge-west-african-hub-port/
67. *Daily Trust*, 'Nigeria's Chaos, Benin Republic's Gains', Shehu Abubakar, February 19 2012.

68. Sandbrook and Barker. *The politics of Africa's economic stagnation,* p.141; For more evidence on this claim, see Golub (2012)
69. Sandbrook and Barker. *The politics of Africa's economic stagnation.*
70. Azam, *Trade, Exchange Rate, and Growth in Sub-Saharan Africa.*
71. Folami and Naylor. "Police and cross-border crime in an era of globalisation: The case of the Benin–Nigeria border", 859–879.
72. Administrator (2014), How TEMA May Emerge West African Hub Port, *The Journal of Freight and Energy*, July 31, http://www.journalngonline.com/2014/07/31/how-tema-may-emerge-west-african-hub-port/
73. Benjamin, Golub, and Mbaye, "Informality, trade policies and smuggling in West Africa."
74. Blum, "Cross-border flows between Nigeria and Benin: what are the challenges for (human) security?".
75. Goretti, Manuela, and Hans Weisfeld. *Trade in the WAEMU: Developments and Reform Opportunities.*
76. WTO, 'Trade Policy Reviews: First Press release,' Secretariat and Government Summaries, January, 1999.
77. Azam, *Trade, Exchange Rate, and Growth in Sub-Saharan Africa.*
78. Coffin, Horowitz, Nesmith, and Semanik. "Examining Barriers to Trade in Used Vehicles."
79. Abimbola, Olumide. "The international trade in secondhand clothing: managing information asymmetry between West African and British traders." 184–199.
80. Fadahunsi and Rosa, "Entrepreneurship and illegality: insights from the Nigerian cross-border trade", 397–429.
81. Golub, Stephen. "Informal cross-border trade and smuggling in Africa".
82. Fadahunsi and Rosa, "Entrepreneurship and illegality: insights from the Nigerian cross-border trade", p. 397.
83. Allegresse, Sasse and Paul, Carsten. 2017. 'Nigeria recession deals blow to smuggling hub' *Benin Reuters World News*, March 30. https://www.reuters.com/article/us-nigeria-benin-smuggling/nigeria-recession-deals-blow-to-smuggling-hub-benin-idUSKBN17125X
84. Ekere, Ndy. 2016. 'Options for developing the Nigerian automotive industry', *BusinessDay Day*, December 19. http://www.businessdayonline.com/options-developing-nigerian-automotive-industry/
85. Chu and Delgado. "Used vehicle imports impact on new vehicle sales: The Mexican Case", 347–364.

Disclosure statement

No potential conflict of interest was reported by the authors.

Bibliography

Abimbola, O. "The International Trade in Secondhand Clothing: Managing Information Asymmetry between West African and British Traders." *Textile* 10, no. 2 (2012): 184–199. doi:10.2752/17518351 2X13315695424310.

Adepoju, A. "Migration in West Africa." *Development* 46, no. 3 (2003): 37–41. doi:10.1177/ 10116370030463006.

Agbo, C. O. A. "Recycle Materials Potential of Imported Used Vehicles in Nigeria." *Nigerian Journal of Technology* 30, no. 3 (2011): 118–128.

Akinwale, A. A., and M. O. Aremo. "Concession as a Catalyst for Crisis Management in Nigerian Ports." *The African Symposium: Journal of African Educational Research Network* 10, no. 2 (2010): 117–126.

Andic, F., S. Andic, and D. Dosser. *A Theory of Economic Integration for Developing Countries: Illustrated by Caribbean Countries*. London: Routledge, 2010.

Anyanwu, J. C. *Monetary Economics: Theory, Policy, and Institutions*. Hybrid Publishers, 1993.

Asante, S. K. B. *Regionalism and Africa's Development: Expectations, Reality and Challenges*. Springer, 2016.

Azam, J. *Trade, Exchange Rate, and Growth in Sub-Saharan Africa*. Cambridge University Press, 2007.

Benjamin, N. S. Golub, and A. A. Mbaye. "Informality, Trade Policies and Smuggling in West Africa." *Journal of Borderlands Studies* 30, no. 3 (2015): 381–394. doi:10.1080/08865655.2015.1068203.

Benjamin, N., A. A. Mbaye, and I. T. Diop. *The Informal Sector in Francophone Africa*. World Bank Publications, 2012.

Beuving, J. J. "Nigerien Second-Hand Car Traders in Cotonou: A Sociocultural Analysis of Economic Decision-Making." *African Affairs* 105, no. 420 (2006): 353–373. doi:10.1093/afraf/adi106.

Blum, C. *Cross-Border Flows between Nigeria and Benin: What Are the Challenges for (Human) Security?* Abuja: Friendrich-Ebert Stiftung Regional Office, 2014.

Bond, E. W. "A Direct Test of the Lemons' Model: The Market for Used Pickup Trucks." *The American Economic Review* 72, no. 4 (1982): 836–840.

Cantens, T., R. Ireland, and G. Raballand. "Introduction: Borders, Informality, International Trade and Customs." *Journal of Borderlands Studies* 30, no. 3 (2015): 365–380. doi:10.1080/08865655.2015.10 68207.

Chu, T., and A. Delgado. "Used Vehicle Imports Impact on New Vehicle Sales: The Mexican Case." *Análisis Económico* 24, no. 55 (2009): 347–364.

Coffin, D., J. Horowitz, D. Nesmith, and M. Semanik. "Examining Barriers to Trade in Used Vehicles." Staff Research Papers | USITC No. 044, 2016.

Dossou, A. S., J. Sinzogan, and S. Mensah. "Economic Growth in Benin: Lost Opportunities." In *The Political Economy of Economic Growth in Africa, 1960–2000*, edited by B Ndulu, 87–118. Cambridge: Cambridge University Press, 2008.

Fadahunsi, A., and P. Rosa. "Entrepreneurship and Illegality: Insights from the Nigerian Cross-Border Trade." *Journal of Business Venturing* 17, no. 5 (2002): 397–429. doi:10.1016/S0883-9026(01)00073-8.

Folami, O. M., and R. J. Naylor. "Police and Cross-Border Crime in an Era of Globalisation: The Case of the Benin-Nigeria Border." *Security Journal* 30, no. 3 (2017): 859–879. doi:10.1057/sj.2015.17.

Freeman, M., and M. Ruehsen. "Terrorism Financing Methods: An Overview." *Perspectives on Terrorism* 7, no. 4 (2013). http://www.terrorismanalysts.com/pt/index.php/pot/article/view/279/html.

Golub, S. S. "Entrepot Trade and Smuggling in West Africa: Benin, Togo and Nigeria." *The World Economy* 35, no. 9 (2012): 1139–1161. doi:10.1111/j.1467-9701.2012.01469.x.

Golub, S. "Informal Cross-Border Trade and Smuggling in Africa." In *Handbook on Trade and Development*, edited by Morrissey, Oliver, Ricardo A. López, and Kishor Sharma, 179–200. Cheltenham: Edward Elgar Publishing, 2015.

Goretti, M., and H. Weisfeld. *Trade in the WAEMU: Developments and Reform Opportunities*. No. 8-68. International Monetary Fund, 2008.

Guyer, J. I. *Marginal Gains: Monetary Transactions in Atlantic Africa*. 1997 vols. University of Chicago Press, 2004.

Iheduru, O. C. *The Political Economy of International Shipping in Developing Countries*. University of Delaware Press, 1996.

Lesser, C., and E. Moisé-Leeman. *Informal Cross-Border Trade and Trade Facilitation Reform in Sub-Saharan Africa*. OECD Trade Policy Papers, No. 86, Organization for Economic Cooperation and Development. 2009.

Marjit, S., S. Ghosh, and A. Biswas. "Informality, Corruption and Trade Reform." *European Journal of Political Economy* 23, no. 3 (2007): 777–789. doi:10.1016/j.ejpoleco.2006.06.001.

Matthews, A. *Regional Integration and Food Security in Developing Countries*. 45 vols. Food & Agriculture Organization, 2003.

Meager, K. "A Back Door to Globalization? Structural Adjustment, Globalization and Transborder Trade in West Africa." *Review of African Political Economy* 30, no. 95 (2003): 57–75. doi:10.1080/03056240308374.

Oculi, O. "Cooperation and Integration in African: The Case of Informal Cross Border Trade." *Africa Vision* 525 (2005): 3.

Pitt, M. M. "Smuggling and Price Disparity." *Journal of International Economics* 11, no. 4 (1981): 447–458. doi:10.1016/0022-1996(81)90026-X.

Qobo, M. "The Challenges of Regional Integration in Africa: In the Context of Globalisation and the Prospects for a United States of Africa." *Institute for Security Studies Papers* 2007, no. 145 (2007): 16.

Raballand, G., and E. Mjekiqi. "Nigeria's Trade Policy Facilitates Unofficial Trade but Not Manufacturing." In *Putting Nigeria to Work*, edited by Volker Treichel, 203–228. World Bank Publications, 2010.

Robson, P. *Integration, Development and Equity: Economic Integration in West Africa*. 52 vols. Routledge, 2010.

Sacerdoti, E. *Benin: Recent Economic Developments*. IMF Staff Country Reports, Issues 96–102, International Monetary Fund. 1996.

Sandbrook, R., and J. Barker. *The Politics of Africa's Economic Stagnation*. Cambridge University Press, 1985.

Soule, B. G., C. I. Obi, and S. Club. *Prospects for Trade between Nigeria and Its Neighbours*. Organization for Economic Cooperation and Development (OECD), 2001.

White, H. P. "New Ports in Dahomey and Togo." *Geography* 46, no. 2 (1961): 160–163.

Uche, C. U. *The Politics of Monetary Sector Cooperation among the Economic Community of West African States Members*. World Bank Working Paper, 2001. doi:10.1596/1813-9450-2647.

Urban prototypes: Growing local circular cloth economies

Lucy Norris 🆔

ABSTRACT
Circular economy (CE) models are driving the next restructuring of global textile production and secondary markets, but their socio-political configurations are largely untested. New textile recycling technologies have the potential to redirect material resource flows, disrupt global secondary markets and reconfigure the waste hierarchy. Mainstream CE modelling tends to include people simply as product users in a system of material flows governed by large brands. However, anthropological research into collaborations of small-scale urban designer-producers show how they are using CE principles to prototype new regional cloth economies that aim to reproduce the types of societies they wish to live in.

Introduction: Concepts of the circular economy

This article takes a critical view on different conceptions of the circular economy (CE) and its potential to enable new ways of living sustainably. Here the focus is on the fashion and clothing sector, in particular current and future configurations of the second-hand clothing (SHC) and textile recycling economies. The field of textiles and fashion is one of the most pertinent arenas in which to explore emerging strategies of sustainability and the circular economy, since textiles and clothing have always been intimately entangled with human social, cultural and political forms.[1] A recent documentary film estimates that up to one in six people on the planet are now involved in textiles and fashion, and claims that it is the world's second most polluting industry after oil.[2] This growth has been driven since the 1980s by the increasing manufacture and over-consumption of 'fast fashion', enabled by improved integration of supply chains and the shorter lead-times that characterise 'quick response' production, providing a high turnover of cheap clothing in high street stores, and resulting in the related increase in unwanted garments further down the line.[3] Fundamental concerns about the industry's negative environmental impacts and poor labour conditions in both production and disposal practices, and its highly visible role in underpinning continued global economic inequality, are increasingly voiced.[4]

The holistic concept of a circular economy is promoted as a solution to the 'sustainability and thrive-ability for both business and planet' – it is systemic by design, close-looped, restorative, waste-free, based on effectiveness and runs on renewable energy.[5]

CE supporters portray it as an exciting and whole new way of transforming the economy into a regenerative system that will, as a baseline, exist within planetary limits. This attractive proposition is a social construct which grew out of the sediment layered by many different concepts that have been in existence for some time now.[6]

The report from the International Reference Centre for the Life Cycle of Products, Processes and Services (CIRAIG) identifies 10 concepts that have provided the conceptual building blocks for CE thinking over the past few decades, namely sustainable development, ecological transition, green economy, functional economy, life-cycle thinking, cradle-to-cradle thinking, shared value, industrial ecology, extended producer responsibility and eco-design.

The CE's most active proponent is the Ellen McArthur Foundation (EMF), which was founded to accelerate the global transition to a CE, and in 2014 established *Project Mainstream*, a partnership with the World Economic Forum and McKinsey & Co.[7] They have published a raft of reports on innovative systems thinking, circulating material streams, intelligent assets, scaling up strategies and regional opportunities within India and the EU.[8] The best-known diagrammatic iteration of the concept also derives from the EMF,[9] which shows an industrial system split into biological and technical material cycles, with materials flowing through different feedback loops as the products are, in the technical cycle for example, used, shared, maintained, reused, refurbished and effectively recycled.

The move towards a CE requires substantial infrastructural changes in design thinking, materials science and new technologies, industrial production, user engagement, maintenance and reuse markets and waste management. The push towards implementing the CE is growing, following global concerns about resource security,[10] climate change and population growth. The EU has issued an action plan, 'Closing the Loop',[11] making this a key policy of what is currently the world's largest trading region. CE policies and/or laws are also in place in China, Japan, South Korea, France, Scotland, Canada and the Nordic countries.

The changes that are called for are largely in the areas of industrial production, innovative technologies, and financial and business systems. The EMF and its growing number of global CE100 business partners are strongly attached to the underlying premise that economic growth must be maintained and can be decoupled from resource depletion through designing effective (rather than efficient) systems and harnessing natural capital,[12] rather than championing alternatives to growth such as 'steady state economics',[13] or achieving 'prosperity without growth'.[14] In the US it is also the business case for reducing dependency on scarce external resources and maximising profits which is driving interest in CE principles, rather than environmental arguments.[15]

As the human geographer Hobson observes, these initiatives have tended not to address the socio-political implications of moving towards a CE, have obscured other transformative pathways and practices, and have not considered what forms and processes of governance would facilitate an effective and equitable CE.[16] She asks further,

> what are the implications of a CE for quotidian spaces and practices, as the patterns and rhythms of everyday socio-materiality are potentially reconfigured? ... [D]oes [the CE] productively merge disparate discourses and actors to garner much-needed action around the manifold issues of sustainability?'[17]

Hobson asks how geographers' approaches to materiality, emergence and everyday activism can engage with CE topics, and investigate the possibilities for citizen engagement and reconfigured material practices around the CE.

Critical thinking that can be brought to bear on mainstream CE models, which assume the power of global capital and regulation to effectively govern a circular system, includes work on the agency of materials whose affordances may prove problematic for attempts to govern their life-cycles, and work on the aims of different socio-political groups who engage with it. Gregson and Crang point out that waste has been primarily identified by the social sciences in terms of the categories and politics of waste management, and defined by waste treatments (disposal technologies or resource recovery strategies) and their connection to policy.[18] Much research on waste is therefore anchored in the idea of humans acting upon the world, in keeping with Latour's critique of the modern dualistic division of the world into the natural and the social.[19] In contrast, an approach to waste that sees it as being 'historically mutable, geographically contingent, and both expressive of social values and sustaining to them' draws on Douglas' work on the symbolic nature of the categorisation of certain matters as waste.[20,21] This leads Gregson and Crang to ask 'how different matters matter differently?'[22] They reference Gille's work on the changing social construction of waste in socialist and post-socialist Hungary,[23] and point out the way in which various forms of matter have different affordances and become governed differently under different regimes.

Much CE modelling focuses on material flows stripped of their sociality; people are configured simply as consumers or users that must be encouraged to keep materials circulating through a series of loops, taking little account of the fundamental ontological significance of the relationships between people, materials and things in shaping our world, or of the changing nature of property rights that these entail. In an exhibition celebrating the uncontrollable nature of matter and its unforeseen metabolisms, the accompanying text posits an uncomfortable truth behind the CE:

> It refers to a logic in which goods are seen as containers for materials that are only temporarily consolidated and will be reclaimed as assets as soon as a product cycle ends. ... Liquid consumption will replace ownership and intermittent access will replace belonging under the pressure of the constant movement demanded by capitalism – a trend that is already foreshadowed by the current 'sharing economy'. Goods are rented, loaned and leased rather than owned by the user; goods become services as their assets, the materials that they contain, need to stay 'in the hands' of the companies producing them. Accordingly, much of the work of managing materials within circular economic models will be comprised of surveilling the status of these distributed resources through networked technologies – a situation that raises questions about privacy, data management and growing energy consumption.[24]

There is a wealth of entanglements between people, materials and things that emerge from desires to reshape our societies and build very different circular economies in the future. These alternative social and political visions of sustainable living in socially embedded economies include people and practices operating in the interface between the market and non-market economies. Examples include the designers, artists and activists exploring the application of concepts such as open source to the CE.

Its proponents believe that only by being transparent, sharing knowledge about materials, design principles and technologies, can the complex problems posed by transitioning to a CE be solved within the time frames required for action. This knowledge also includes open standards, transparent supply chains, decentralised and distributed collaboration, so that designers and makers can build solutions together. Social activists in Berlin's new Circular Lab are fighting to change the terms on which material and technical reconfigurations are taking place, and use open source principles to foster collaboration and take advantage of the 'abundance of natural capital' they are attracting.[25] They work to increase the circulation of things, question how much transparency is needed within a system in order to transition to full circularity, to grow social participation, and start by placing people in the centre, creating a form of what Hart terms 'human economies'.[26]

Fashion and clothing design is one area where independent designers struggle to gain access to technical information about materials and processes in order to judge their appropriate capacities. The ingredients and properties of materials that achieve certification from the Cradle-to-Cradle Products Innovation Institute, for example, are locked behind a wall of intellectual property rights (IPR) that makes it impossible for such research to be shared. Designers who are permitted to use some of these materials in their projects may find it hard to develop them afterwards, due to the confidentiality agreements in place. And without access to information about the material properties, it becomes impossible to develop the kind of alternative, locally based, socially embedded systems envisaged. As independent CE designer and German Sustainability prize-winner Ina Budde commented, 'the idea is that the CE movement should focus on user flows and not material flows. We need to focus on the product's worthwhile-ness, its look and feel – [circular] fashion understands this, that value grows through use'.[27]

Fashion hacktivists such as Otto von Busch also work with open source principles;[28] he encourages us all to share fashion as an open technology of the self, and as a form of civic engagement and community capacity-building. Berlin-based fashion designer and software coder Cecilia Palmer established the upcycling label Pamoyo in 2007 as an open source business that shares patterns with makers under a Creative Commons licence. 'The pattern is only an idea, a concept, it only becomes a product when someone actually makes it'.[29] She also runs Fashion Reloaded, participatory swap, make and restyle events that use open source tactics to encourage DIY/DIT (Do It Yourself / Do it Together) skills and 'change the fashion game' from the bottom up. Drawing on the philosophy of the maker movement, she says 'if you can't open it, you don't own it! … [T]his is very easy to do with fashion ... everyone *can* take a pair of scissors to a garment, but not everyone does'.

The next section in this article outlines the latest and projected developments in textile recycling technologies, second-hand clothing markets and CE thinking within the mainstream, large-scale textile and fashion sectors, and suggests that these may affect the future structuring and relative value of these markets by potentially privileging recycling over reuse. By way of contrast, the third section looks at emerging micro-economies of cloth, using a case study from Bristol (UK). This shows how independent young designers and small businesses are working to create meaningful lives and building collaborative production and service models within local economies. These help them to prototype the kinds of CE infrastructures they require to be active participants in reproducing the types of societies and human-centred economies they wish to grow and inhabit.

Textile recycling and the CE

The circular economy is rapidly gaining interest amongst the fashion and textile sector globally as a potential systems solution to the challenges of resource vulnerability, traceable and sustainable supply chains, the recovery of materials from users, and the effective recycling of pre- and post-consumer textile waste.

In April 2015, textile up-cycler Cyndi Rhoades, CEO of Worn Again, publicly announced that her company was joining forces with H&M and the Kering group (owner of global luxury and sports brands) to speed up development of an innovative chemical recycling technology.[30] The recycling of textiles into regenerated fibres, yarns and non-wovens has relied upon mechanical technologies that have changed little since their development 200 years ago and have resulted in a range of very low-quality products.[31]

The current global estimates of used clothing pathways are stark.[32] In 2015, about 50 million tons of used clothing was sent to landfill or otherwise disposed of, and it is estimated that only 20% of used clothing is collected globally (though this varies widely, with approximately 40% in the UK, 14% in the USA). Of that 20%, 55% is sent to reuse markets, 40% is down-cycled and 5% is waste. There is just a tiny amount of recycling textiles back into textiles.[33] Rhoades declared that she has no interest in disrupting current reuse markets, which she endorsed as environmentally friendly (although this global trade *is* controversial in terms of the social and economic inequality that underpins it).[34] Rather she wants to increase the overall amount of material collected, and develop the technology to maintain the value of those textiles that are then recycled.

The principles of cradle-to-cradle thinking underpin the modelling of the CE in textiles.[35] Materials need to be separated into either biodegradable or technical cycles, and products containing inseparable mixtures of the two are 'monstrous hybrids'.[36] About 35% of all new textiles worldwide are poly-cotton, and these comprise 75% of the total amount of textiles sent for recycling, currently about 55 million tons. Worn Again's proclaimed breakthroughs in the chemical recycling of old clothing are, first, the ability to separate synthetic polyester from cellulosic cotton in mixed-fibre fabrics through a process of dissolution, allowing each to be extracted and reprocessed into new yarn. Polyester can be returned to the granular state and reintroduced into the production cycle.

The second breakthrough concerns the recycling of natural cellulosic fibres, such as cotton and bamboo textile waste. A solution of cellulose can be extruded to create a man-made cellulosic fibre, similar to viscose and lyocell. Through effective recycling, Worn Again aims to create the equivalent of virgin fibres in terms of quality, price and environmental standards. According to Rhoades, the technology will enable a linear supply chain to become circular loops, with consumers urged to become active participants by providing the raw materials back to businesses. The circular business case is (a) consistent supply of materials (there are already enough used textile materials in existence to remake a year's supply of new), (b) reduced dependency on external factors such as the weather, oil prices etc., and (c) brands will be able to set very high, but achievable, sustainable goals.

Other consortia are developing related technologies, business models and design strategies to start 'closing the loop'. Aalto University has partnered with the University of Helsinki to develop IONCELL-F, a sustainable manmade cellulosic fibre that can be made from wood, waste paper and cardboard, and waste cotton textiles. Technical research is investigating the possibility of preserving colour during the recycling, to reduce the need for re-dyeing.[37] They are partners in the EU Horizon 2020 consortium project Trash2Cash, as is SOEX, Europe's largest commercial textile recycler and owner of subsidiary i:Co, the company that works with H&M and other high street brands to collect used clothing in stores across Europe.

One step earlier in the cycle, the Holy Grail for revolutionising the used textiles economy is the mechanised sorting of used textiles by material to provide the feedstock for this more effective recycling. Fibersort is the fibre-recognition technology being developed by another consortia since 2015, comprising Wieland Textiles, Valvan Baling Systems, Metrohm Applikon, Worn Again, Faritex, Salvation Army ReShare and Circle Economy.[38] In order to process the approximately 500 kilotons (kt) of textile waste collected in the UK, Netherlands, Germany, Belgium and France alone, the Valvan machine will need to be able to process large volumes of material quickly to make it commercially viable, while recognising the various material component parts of complex garments.

The successful development and implementation of a coordinated, capital-intensive reshaping of the technological landscape of textile resource recovery appears to be several years off. However it suggests that there will be profound changes in global SHC and textile recycling markets, as well as an impact on design and primary production. Once such circular systems start to emerge at scale, a key question will be to what extent major brands or consortia operate closed-loop or open systems. In the former, businesses aim to recuperate materials from their own products via leasing models, dedicated take-back schemes and investment in proprietary technology, while in the latter, circular systems are envisaged as operating as a series of open networked platforms coordinating the exchange of resources. The Circle Market, run by Amsterdam-based Circle Economy, is piloting the latter, testing an online European marketplace for post-industrial, pre- and post-consumer recyclable textiles.[39] Yet building economic relationships between expensive technologies such as Fibersort and systems such as the Circle Market could result in far more complex models of the interface between open source CE and IPR regimes.

There is the potential for economic tension between sorting used clothing for reuse markets, and sorting for mixed chemical recycling, resulting in a possible privileging of reuse over recycling. The reverse logic of hand sorting heterogeneous garments for reuse markets (largely in developing countries) depends upon highly networked brokers who can obtain stock cheaply and subsidise lower quality goods by reliable mid-market exports and identifying the 'diamonds' that accrue a good profit from the right buyers.[40] This balance may change if textile recyclers invest in expensive sorting equipment to cope with large volumes of increasingly poor quality fast fashion destined for recycling – as feedstock for recycling technologies, it may provide a more reliable return. Another factor is likely to be the increasing number of bans and restrictions,[41] and proposed bans,[42] on SHC in developing country markets, and the relative precariousness of those import hubs dependent upon serving neighbouring black markets.

In recognition of the potential of circular systems to fully and effectively recover the materials from fast-flowing products and allow for a positive reframing of 'fast fashion', design researchers at the University of the Arts, London (UAL), as part of Sweden's *Mistra Future Fashion II* programme,[43] are working on the principle that the speeds of materials must be matched to user needs,[44] rather than simply demonising 'fast fashion' and assuming slow is better. Slow fashion is a movement that supports developing deeper emotional ties to clothing, from buying better quality, sustainably produced garments, to maintaining and repairing clothing well and handing it on responsibly afterwards.[45] All of these are fundamental building blocks of CE thinking and enhance both the longevity of clothing and the social relationships woven into them but do not in themselves ensure the circulation of resources.

A complementary strategy, sustainable 'super-fast fashion', would open up a space for 'short-life' garments made out of renewable resources to be quickly used then recycled, while 'long-life' clothing could be circulated through multiple lives before being reclaimed. Prototypes of the first have included biodegradable *A.S.A.P. (Paper Cloth)*[46] and the latter through *Fast ReFashion* which enables users to refashion durable garments at home.[47] UAL's designers are beginning to work with textile technologists to design new materials for the variable speeds of the CE, and with Swedish retailer Fillipa K to develop their in-house leasing and take-back models.

But as the economics of production and reproduction of textiles changes, numerous questions arise regarding the temporal, spatial, political and economic character of these new circular economies. Will these systems be locally or regionally based, or organised in global nodes to take advantage of economies of scale and existing textile competencies? Will their locations follow sources of cheap labour and/or a lack of regulation?[48,49] Will these models be dominated by closed-loops where material resources and IPR are protected by global capital, or will materials, services and products circulate via networked open platforms? What will it mean for the cycles of reuse, maintenance and repair that are an integral part of CE thinking – will these services also be kept in-house by multinational brands, or will a wealth of independent service models develop alongside them? Who will manage the materials and goods that fail to recirculate?

Crucially, the question remains as to what importance social justice and economic equality will be given in emerging CE models and their relationship to concepts of global sustainability. As Raworth argues in *Doughnut Economics*, a safe operating space for humanity to thrive in must not exceed the environmental ceiling of limited resources, the planetary boundaries, but must also be founded on a set of social boundaries that prevent human deprivation.[50]

Urban cloth economies

One area in which to explore some of these questions is urban micro-economies, looking at the successes and failures in growing local CEs and their connectivity to both small-scale communities and global business networks. The city is becoming a key site for researching the effective flow of resources; 'regenerative cities' or 'circular cities' are emerging as places with integrated systems, flexibility, cooperative behaviour, localisation, recycling and renewable resources.[51] These concerns resonate with an anthropological interest in infrastructure, broadly described as

> technologically-mediated, dynamic forms that continuously produce and transform socio-technical relations. That is, infrastructures are extended material assemblages that generate effects and structure social relations, either through engineered (i.e. planned and purposefully crafted) or non-engineered (i.e. unplanned and emergent) activities. Seen thus, infrastructures are doubly relational due to their simultaneous internal multiplicity and their connective capacities outwards.[52]

The following is a description of a micro-cloth economy in Bristol. The city was not historically a traditional 'textile town', and lacks the embedded infrastructure required for the large-scale production of cloth or clothing. Nor did it have the associated industries that are found in textile towns for recycling by-products and manufacturing waste. Rather it has attracted a small group of designer-makers and local businesses that are interested in seeing what types of collaborations they can build with the resources they have to hand, and how to fill in the gaps they uncover.

The Bristol Textile Quarter[53]

The south-western city of Bristol in the UK promotes itself as a creative hub of green industries, social entrepreneurs and ethical businesses. With a population of less than half a million, it established its own local currency, the Bristol Pound, in 2012, and was awarded the title of 'European Green Capital' in 2015. It is home to the Soil Association (the organic certification body), the UK's branch of Tridos (the Dutch ethical bank) and Sustrans (which promotes a national cycle network). It is also registered as a Sustainable Food City, developing 'responsible and resilient local and regional food systems'.[54]

In 2014, a small group of independent women in their late 20s and early 30s met at a sustainable fashion conference; they were running their own fashion and textile businesses and were looking for local work space. When part of an old Victorian warehouse became available in the Barton Trading Estate, they moved in together. The 'Bristol Textile Quarter' (BTQ) was established as a collaborative workspace, founded and run by Emma Jane Hague. Having spent five years in an Andean village running a vertically integrated textile project for women producing high-fashion items from local wool, Hague was inspired by both the Textile Arts Centre in Brooklyn, whose mission is to 'unify and empower the local textile community, and advocate for the handmade',[55] and Made in New York, which supports local manufacturing in the city in partnership with the Pratt Institute.[56]

BTQ's mission is to 'build a more resilient textile economy in Bristol and the South West', and its website challenges:

> if Bristol can think and care so much about how it feeds itself, then why aren't we thinking and caring about how we clothe ourselves too? The vision for Bristol Textile Quarter is to offer both an online platform and a physical space in which the local textile community can start to connect, collaborate and explore what a more resilient local textile economy might look like.[57]

The BTQ occupies most of the lower floor, and membership in early 2016 included costume designer Linda Higginson,[58] contemporary and vintage upholsterer *A Peculiar Grace*, sustainable clothing label *Tamay & Me* (producing hand-embroidered indigo jackets in Vietnam), Emma Hague's own *Working Wool* initiative and the up-cycled fashion label *Antiform*, founded by Lizzie Harrison. The space offers facilities such as handlooms and knitting machines for hire on a daily or weekly basis, as well as organising events to facilitate collaboration between local makers, designers, fibre producers, students and educators.

Some of the enterprises based at Barton Road are drawing on the rich regional heritage of wool manufacturing in the South West of England. The *Working Wool* initiative was established by Hague together with *Fernhill Farm*, a holistic eco-farm in the local Mendip Hills which produces *Fernhill Fleece*, to develop an 'immersive learning experience' to raise awareness of wool as a natural, sustainable fibre; the project is now run through the BTQ. The BTQ has also established a South West England affiliate of *Fibershed*, the California-based grassroots movement that supports the development of transparent, regional and regenerative fibre systems, and has been prototyping the production of regionally grown and woven community-supported cloth. This 'soil-to-soil clothing' is part of a movement 'to bridge the gaps between values, technology, the circular economy and people' through a focus on local stories to make these connections visible, putting human values at the forefront of innovation and supporting equitable economies.[59]

The upper floor of the building houses the studio of award-winning designers *Dash + Miller Ltd*, specialising in the development and production of bespoke hand-woven textiles for the international fashion and interior industries. In 2015, *Dash + Miller* and the BTQ established *The Bristol Weaving Mill Ltd* at one end of the ground floor, involving one young woman, Leila, spending nine months single-handedly rebuilding and re-engineering a salvaged textile loom. Promoted as an artisanal micro-mill based in the heart of Bristol, the equipment has been especially rebuilt to be as flexible as possible, to produce minimum orders of 5–10 m of fabric using a wide range of fibres and weaving techniques including jacquard and dobby, with a 'no-boundaries approach to design and production'.[60] The mill specialises in producing sustainable, locally sourced woollen cloth and fancy tweed for interiors, as well as a variety of high-quality experimental fabrics for women's wear and catwalk fashion, and is producing the first commercial cloth in Bristol for 90 years.

Bristol Cloth

In 2015, a collaborative effort between the Bristol Weaving Mill, Fernhill Farm, the BTQ and Bristol-based natural dyers *Botanical Inks* resulted in a competition to design a Bristol Cloth. Working with a palette of white, pale grey, dark grey and deep mustard, dyed using waste onion skins from local organic restaurants, the cloth would be produced from Fernhill Farm's 100% Shetland wool in a dobby weave. The design brief asked,

What does Bristol's social fabric look like?
What kind of cloth does Bristol need?
How would you weave Bristol?
What woven designs were traditionally born out of the South West?

Finalists from the South West had their designs on public show as part of the Bristol Green Capital Lab's events, and the Bristol Cloth partners chose the winner together with a public vote. The successful finalist was Falmouth-based textile designer Wendy Kotenko, with a locally inspired basket-weave design.

BTQ's aim is to make textile and fashion supply chains as local, sustainable and transparent as possible, characteristics of the Slow Fashion movement. Bringing together potential collaborators under one roof, and prototyping Bristol Cloth production, enables designers to find out where the gaps are in processing relatively small quantities locally, and seek out sustainable solutions. Finding spinning facilities in the region that could provide a cost-effective service for the small volumes required (about 30–40 kg of fleece at a time), while also being able to ensure no cross-contamination with fibres from elsewhere, was challenging; the raw fibre has to be sent to Yorkshire. If required to be finished, the woven wool cloth is sent North again for the final processing, although it is also perfectly functional (and beautiful) in its 'unfinished' state.

This design and production network has also opened up other opportunities that could incorporate second-hand clothing into a broader aim of founding a regional circular economy, involving designers, users and recyclers. The micro-mill has experimented with using reclaimed yarn for one of its fabrics, and there is potential to use recycled yarns in the future, perhaps eventually derived from local sources of used clothing, as explored in the next section.

Antiform

The label Antiform is a core member of the BTQ, with its founder Lizzie Harrison bringing a different perspective and experience to the collaboration. Until her move to Bristol in 2014, Harrison had co-founded and run a number of clothing and fashion projects in Leeds from 2008 to 2014, challenging ways of thinking about new and used clothing in the broader fashion landscape and community development.[61] She describes her aim at the time as being 'to develop a community-based closed-loop project model for textiles recycling'. Her practice-based research, carried out through the project *ReMade in Leeds*, entailed her choosing to work within a single postcode in a diverse residential neighbourhood in Leeds by setting up a small garment factory in a normal street. Meeting the challenge of how to keep unwanted clothing in circulation locally involved finding new ways to sort, redirect and redistribute it. This included encouraging people to turn out their wardrobes and bring forgotten items to the project, setting up a clothes exchange programme, a repair and alteration service, a sewing café offering upskilling classes, fashion hacking events encouraging people to redesign their own clothing, and establishing a social enterprise next door for unemployed local women that upcycled unwanted clothing into new designs for the associated fashion label *Antiform*. For Harrison, it was all about 'using local skills and under-valued material resources to create local fashion'.[62]

Harrison's research found that for most of the local community, the act of engaging with fashion was synonymous with going high street shopping and buying something new, while second-hand clothing was sold in very different social settings and hence perceived very differently. A photographic study she conducted with co-founder Jade Whitson-Smith mapped out the local fashion landscape, highlighting the aesthetic differences between the central retail areas of Leeds, characterised by well-lit glass-fronted shops on the high street, and the provision of repair and alteration services, tucked away in run-down premises in residential areas.[63] Blurring these differences and establishing community engagement with used, worn and worn-out clothing as fulfilling fashion practice became one of Harrison's central aims.

Much of ReMade in Leeds' work was iterative, trialling ideas in as many settings as possible, finding out what worked on the ground and whether the projects or products had viable markets and made a meaningful difference to local populations. Clothes swaps, 'Swishing parties' and online apps are now transforming the circulation and redistribution of unwanted garments around the world, whether the model falls under the umbrella of the 'sharing economy', or through various degrees of monetised exchange facilitated by profit-making platforms. Leeds Community Clothes Exchange is one of the projects Harrison originally founded in her studio in 2007. Inspired by the concept of increasing local resilience through the Transition Town Movement,[64] it is now being successfully run by local volunteers. Today it takes place in the local Community Centre, with 1500 members swapping 2500 garments every month. Visitors can bring up to 20 garments with them, provided that they are clean and in good condition. In return they get a token for each one, which they can use to simply swap for something else. Any unused tokens are logged in a database for the next visit, or donated to support vulnerable people in the local women's refuge or centre for refugees who need clothing – they can then come along anonymously and pick out what they want.[65] Homemade cakes and vegetarian Indian food are on offer, and the chance to catch up with friends during the afternoon are some of the biggest attractions.[66] Swappers who have brought along clothing often meet the other swappers who are acquiring them. Harrison reports that people show a real sense of pride when someone else decides they like a garment enough to take it home with them. It is the conviviality of the occasion and the acknowledgement of each other's taste and judgement that gives it added value for participants.

When ReMade in Leeds' repair and alteration service was established, it created a boutique atmosphere. Customers would book an appointment, try on their garment in the fitting room and discuss the repairs or alterations they wanted. When they returned, they would again try on the garment, and, if satisfied, it would be wrapped in tissue and put into a bag. The boutique environment also included a café, music and an atmosphere where people were encouraged to feel as though they were going out with a group of girlfriends on a Saturday afternoon and were expressing their identity through fashion.

Rather than putting herself forward as the designer who needs to take control of the whole system to effect positive change, Harrison sees herself as much as a facilitator and collaborator, who works with whomever and whatever she finds on the ground to reframe the way in which maintaining and circulating used clothing is perceived as an enjoyable part of the fashion experience, without making people feel that these are worthy practices. Understanding why some approaches fail on the ground has also been an invaluable experience, for example over-ambitious expectations regarding capacities to make the repair of badly designed, cheaply made fast fashion viable. For Harrison, these projects

> personify the idea of acting locally and offer inclusive and accessible platforms for local communities to participate in fashion events, run fashion services and create new kinds of fashion product. The activities in themselves address sustainability through their very nature … but they also contribute to larger ideas … around building resilience and creating diversity.[67]

Harrison is still exploring how to develop appropriate services and spaces to enjoy fashion and the process of re-fashioning, to make these valid fashion experiences for the mainstream consumer. It is this shift, rather than the new recycling technologies that promise to 'tidy up the mess of over-consumption behind the scenes', which she believes lies at the heart of the successful development of a circular textile economy.

Growing a circular textile economy in Bristol

These activities take what designer-maker Amy Twigger-Holroyd recently described as the 'domestic circular economy';[68] they develop the concepts of community-building and circularity at the level of a city-wide cloth economy, building practice-based knowledge about what actually happens to clothing from the initial acts of consumption and clothing's eventual disposal as a base from which to devise appropriate sustainable strategies. As the scope of activity widens, non-market and marginal initiatives increasingly engage with mainstream market-based producers, retailers and recyclers, reinforcing the argument that CE solutions will not be developed in isolation and demand collaboration across economic spheres. It should also be noted that while so many of the 'movers and shakers' of new CE thinking in this article are women, this appears to be so across all sectors, from those leading capital-intensive technological research and innovative high street retailers through to independent designers, academics and environmental activists. Gender is highly visible in this sector but it is not obvious how it is being configured in the work to create new economies, and research into the structures of power in the political cultures in which these women are operating would generate useful insights into the challenges that women face and how this impacts upon the roles they develop.[69]

Since relocating to the Bristol Textile Quarter, Harrison has been involved in the development of the Bristol Cloth through design advice, but is already thinking about how to incorporate recycling grades of used local textiles into a fabric run. Of course the textiles and clothing bought and used by local people are not locally produced but are part of highly distributed global assemblages, yet once discarded into the current system they constitute a local material resource for which more sustainable pathways are needed.

Just a quarter of a mile away is the South West of England's largest commercial textile recycling facility, Bristol Textile Recyclers (BTR), employing 70 people, 40 of whom work on the sorting lines. Established in 1972, in early 2016 the family firm was struggling to find commercially viable end markets for the increasing proportion of low-quality clothing; six of their competitors had closed down during the preceding year. BTR bought 20 tons a day (the equivalent of three adult male African elephants, as our host Aimee visualised it) but were only able to make a profit on 50% of it, the rest being too poor-quality. They buy most of their stock from charity shops and school collections, so their suppliers had already picked out the best-quality items; yet the top-quality 'cream' grades had previously comprised 15% of their stock, before falling to about 1%. As a result, they were only making a profit on the 0.5% which stayed in the UK as reusable garments, another 0.5% which was sold to Eastern Europe (their buyers accepted only new clothing, preferably with tags), and just half of the 88% that was sold to Africa and Pakistan. A further 8% were recycled as wipers, while the last 4% they had to pay to be recycled by a third party as energy from waste.

Of their export sales, that to Africa was summer clothing: these markets are vulnerable to changing fashions and currency exchange fluctuations, meaning that the high reputation and size appropriateness of used clothing from the UK had to be balanced against possibly cheaper material from the USA. These markets are also vulnerable to the imposition of future bans and restrictions (see above), or conversely the lifting of bans upon which smuggling currently depends.[70] Much of the winter clothing sent to Pakistan may well end up being recycled for fibre; some is bundled into mixed shipments of shoes and bric-a-brac. Yet there were specific goods for which the firm did not have a market, for example fleece dressing gowns, which were compacted and given to refuges, clothing collections for the Jungle Camp in Calais, or sent to animal shelters for use as bedding. To comply with the EU Waste Framework Directive to recycle 50% of household waste by 2020 and reduce the amount going to landfill, it will become economically impossible for UK recyclers to pay to 'waste' these materials. In an industry known for secrecy, BTR is unusually open about its business challenges, and puts a lot of effort into working with local schools and charities to raise awareness of the problems with recycling low-quality clothing and the potential value of good-quality used textiles. Supporting the principles of slow fashion and reuse, the company works with local up-cyclers designing from waste, and welcomes the public to its premises to buy vintage clothing and to see for themselves the volumes of low-quality clothing that are generated locally.

In the meantime, BTR is placing great hope in the ability of new sorting technologies such as Fibersort to become viable as investments, and advances in fibre-to-fibre regeneration to create new recycling markets for its low-quality stock. However, the proximity of BTR to BTQ and regular networking via regional textile recycling forums opens up the possibility that some of this locally collected material could be incorporated as recycled material into cloth woven in Bristol. This could increase the resilience of the local textile economy by adding diversity of resources to the current mix and demonstrating the potential for closing the loop locally.

The quantities involved are designed to be very small at the outset, and this would not pose a viable circular solution to the problems of mass consumption of fast fashion in our linear system. Yet as a prototype, its most significant value could be in making the connections between these global and local circulations of cloth and clothing visible through a narrative that acts as a new conceptual metaphor. There is a lack of transparency surrounding clothing's production, retail and disposal in the global textile industry's existing linear model, and a lack of knowledge about the materials, technologies and global power relations that underpin it. The prototype as a material representation encourages a reframing of the way in which fashion and textiles might be perceived to be embedded in the local economy and connected to individual behaviours. Furthermore, the evolution and implementation of local *circular* systems are complex ideas, and their technical and material embodiments can be used as communication tools to improve the next iteration.

George Lakoff's early linguistic work on metaphor showed how it shapes perception;[71] and more recently he asserted that framing is a moral exercise that shapes the character of a political movement.[72] His work has been adopted by advocates of sustainable third sector development,[73] and now also by the CE movement, with the aim of constructing new moral frameworks for sustainable behaviour.[74] Frame analysis was first developed by Goffman,[75] and has also been applied to the role of material culture in constructing the contexts of human action in ritual and everyday life, and shaping our expected behaviours accordingly.[76]

Material culture theorists recognise that objects also exert agency through their material biographies and forms. For Appadurai, objects condense experience – they are icons of other ways of living, they carry their histories within them and exert a demand on us. 'While they are often regarded as tools of fixity, they are in fact testaments of circulation'.[77] The Bristol Cloth is a complex woven textile constructed from multiple material and social resources, imbued with the spirit of connecting people, creating local urban environments and fostering circularity. It also has potential agency as an artwork: anthropologist Alfred Gell's theory of art suggests that through abduction we infer human intentionality through the agency of artefacts, which become the distributed mind of their creators through their circulation, in turn affecting those with whom they come into contact.[78] As Küchler contends, this analysis is vital for 'recovering the way images serve as the thread of thought, entangling expectations with experience in ways that root agency not in action, but in imagination'.[79]

Conclusion

It is suggested that the large-scale technical innovations in the pipeline, driven by consortia whose members are all major stakeholders in the CE, are going to be able to endlessly circulate materials through technologies that will separate out polluted materials and purify them before returning them to the status of 'virgin fibres' ready to be consumed once more. Such technologies ought to empower us to conceive of ourselves as responsible consumers supporting the rituals of separation and sacrifice in order to support the common good, mediated by global business that organises the continued circulation of materials and products behind the scenes, selling us the rights to use certain materials in certain forms for a period of time. In the purest, glossiest representations of this utopian vision, secondary economies could eventually cease to exist, with users simply leasing brand new products until they are ready to be recycled within closed-loops and replaced. In this transcendental economy geared towards planetary salvation, now it is not just the domestic household user that redeems themselves through proper moral behaviour, but industry and big business that can grant themselves absolution.

Drawing on Marx's theory of commodity fetishism,[80] Graeber observes that 'the factory floor and incinerator are just as properly kept out of sight as the hospital ward and crematorium'.[81] This encourages us to think that objects, like human beings, are 'discrete, free-standing, self-identical entities', rather than 'ongoing processes, patterns of change, fundamentally entangled in the world around them', and it is this that enables us to apply clear property rights to them.[82] Mainstream models of circular economies operating at the global level introduced at the beginning of this article, of which a circular fashion economy is a leading example, tend to ignore the constitutive role of exchange in building social relations, focusing simply on the effective circulation of materials and products, and conceiving of people as 'users' in a service economy.[83]

This article has briefly referred to alternative forms of sociality and property relations engendered through the shared and redistributive economies,[84] the open source movement as a political project that can be applied to varied forms of production and exchange, and acts of repair and maintenance as political interventions. But it also aims to show how CE experimentation at the local community level in Bristol has provided a social and political space in which these approaches, in market and non-market iterations, can come together. Building a local infrastructure of designer-makers and users to grow local capacity makes visible the work of making and remaking things and the messiness of decay and disposal practices, and helps uncover which practices lead to success or failure. It also exposes the types of property relations embedded within clothing during various iterations, the complexity of the value systems through which it circulates as fashion, fabric or fibre, and how it is through the negotiating of exchange from one sphere to another that both economic and social value is created.

As Steven Jackson writes about 'Broken World Thinking', we live in a world characterised as 'on one hand, a fractal world, a centrifugal world, an always-almost-falling-apart world. On the other, a world in constant process of fixing and reinvention, reconfiguring and reassembling into new combinations and new possibilities.'[85] This article argues that attention to emergent circular urban cloth economies opens up a complex new site for studying the meanings of cloth in small-scale alternative groups embedded within large-scale capitalist economies, and to understand how the material properties of cloth, its metaphorical role in connecting and tying, and its use to consolidate social relations and mobilise political power, continue to be powerful tools for remaking social worlds.[86]

Notes

1. As a broad spectrum of anthropologists, political economists and textile historians describe; see for example Weiner and Schneider, *Cloth and Human Experience*; Küchler and Miller, *Clothing as Material Culture*; Lemire, *Fashion's Favourite*; Mukerji, *From Graven Images*.
2. Morgan, *The True Cost*.
3. see Rivoli, *The Travels of a T-Shirt*; Norris, "Introduction: Trade and Transformations."
4. Siegle, *To Die For*; Brooks, *Clothing Poverty*; Hoskins, *Stitched Up*; Greenpeace International, *Toxic Threads*; Norris, "The Limits of Ethicality."
5. CIRAIG, "Circular Economy."
6. Ibid., 5.
7. "Project MainStream Helping Scale."
8. "Circular Economy Reports & Publications."
9. "Circular Economy System Diagram."
10. EEF, "Materials for Manufacturing"; McKinsey & Co., "Resource Revolution"; McKinsey & Co., "Manufacturing the Future."
11. European Commission, "Closing the Loop."
12. Ellen MacArthur Foundation, "Towards the Circular Economy 1."
13. Daly, *Towards a Steady-State Economy*.
14. Jackson, *Prosperity Without Growth*.
15. US Chamber of Commerce Foundation Corporate Citizenship Centre, "Trash to Treasure."
16. Hobson, "Closing the Loop or Squaring the Circle?," 89.

17. Ibid., 90.
18. Gregson and Crang, "Materiality and Waste."
19. Latour, *We Have Never Been Modern*.
20. Gregson and Crang, "Materiality and Waste," 1027.
21. Douglas, *Purity and Danger*.
22. Gregson and Crang, "Materiality and Waste," 1027.
23. Gille, *From the Cult of Waste*.
24. Buehler, "Inflected Objects #2 Circulation."
25. "OSCEdays."
26. Hart, Laville, and Cattani, *The Human Economy*.
27. Budde, interview, June 2016.
28. Von Busch, 'Fashion-Able."
29. Fuad-Luke, Hirscher, and Moebus, "Open Fashion & Code," 189.
30. "Worn Again Joins Forces."
31. Oakdene Hollins Ltd, SATC Ltd, and NIRI Ltd, "Clothing Recycling Report"; Morley, Bartlett, and McGill, "Maximising the Reuse and Recycling"; Norris, "Shoddy Rags and Relief Blankets."
32. All figures provided in Rhoades, "Keynote: Materials."
33. A few well-known closed-loop solutions have been developed over the past few years, which currently rely on returning garments to dedicated recycling factories in single locations. For example, Patagonia's Common Threads programme enables their fleeces to be recycled by the Japanese company Teijin into polyester filament. Mud jeans, based in Amsterdam, is pioneering the idea of circulating denim, running a leasing scheme for jeans, which can then turned into sweaters through mechanical yarn reclamation in a factory in Spain. Dutch aWEARness has created a circular supply chain for its own workwear made from 100% recyclable polyester, Returnity®, which recycles clothing in a factory in Tunisia.
34. The structural impact of the international free-market trade in second-hand clothing on local developing economies has been widely debated, in particular to what extent it conflicts with the aims and scope of international development policies. See Brooks, "Stretching Global Production Networks"; Norris, "The Limits of Ethicality"; Norris, "Introduction: Trade and Transformations"; Hansen, "Controversies." The appropriation of second-hand styles as cultural resource are comprehensively discussed in Hansen, *Salaula*.
35. Braungart and McDonough, *Cradle to Cradle*.
36. Ibid.
37. Niinimäki et al., "Colours in a Circular Economy."
38. "Could FIBERSORT Change the Textiles".
39. "Circle Market: Fuelling the Recovery."
40. Hawley, "Digging for Diamonds"; Crang et al., "Rethinking Governance"; Norris, "Introduction: Trade and Transformations"; Brooks, "Riches from Rags or Persistent Poverty?"; Abimbola, "Managing Information Asymmetry"; Botticello, "Between Classification, Objectification and Perception"; Milgram, "Activating Frontier Livelihoods."
41. International Trade Administration, "Worn (Used) Clothing."
42. see for example Brooks, "East Africa's Ban."
43. "Mistra Future Fashion."
44. Earley and Goldsworthy, "Designing for Fast and Slow."
45. Fletcher, *Craft of Use*.
46. Politowicz and Goldsworthy, "A.S.A.P. (Paper Cloth)."
47. Earley, "Fast Refashion – Textile Toolbox."
48. Gregson et al., "Doing the 'Dirty Work'."
49. Crang et al., "Rethinking Governance."
50. Raworth, *Doughnut Economics*.
51. "Circular Cities Network."
52. Harvey, Jensen, and Morita, *Infrastructures and Social Complexity*.
53. The data for this section were largely gathered during a field visit to Bristol in February 2016 and ongoing conversations with Harrison, followed up with interviews with Harrison and Hague during winter 2016/17

54. "Bristol Food Policy Council."
55. "Textile Arts Centre."
56. "Made in NYC."
57. "Bristol Textile Quarter."
58. Higginson has documented her challenge to make all of her own clothing in a year at http://mademywardrobe.com/blog/ (accessed June 14, 2017).
59. Silvestri, "Keynote."
60. "The Bristol Weaving Mill."
61. Harrison, "Fashion and Community."
62. Ibid., 247.
63. Whitson-Smith and Harrison, "Mending Fashion."
64. Hopkins, *The Transition Handbook*.
65. This equitable anonymity is in contrast to other initiatives that focus on asymmetrical exchange when giving a charitable gift, for example the London-based charity Hubbub's scheme whereby mothers package up their babies' outgrown clothing and give them to less well-off mothers at organised meet-ups.
66. Zee, "Swap till You Drop."
67. Harrison, "Fashion and Community," 249.
68. Twigger Holroyd, "Shifting Perceptions: The Re-knit Revolution."
69. The multiple strategies women adopt in order to make a living in Berlin's independent creative fashion economy is discussed in McRobbie, *Be Creative*, Chapter 5.
70. Norris, "The Limits of Ethicality."
71. Lakoff and Johnson, *Metaphors We Live By*.
72. Lakoff, *The All New*.
73. Crompton, "Common Cause."
74. Lakoff gave a keynote at the online Disruption Innovation Festival 2016: https://www.thinkdif.co/headliners (accessed January 15, 2017).
75. Goffman, *Frame Analysis*.
76. Miller, "Materiality: An Introduction."
77. Appadurai, "The Migration of Objects."
78. Gell, *Art and Agency*.
79. Küchler, "Threads of Thought," 26.
80. Marx, *Capital*, Chapter 1.
81. Graeber, "Afterword: The Apocalypse of Objects," 283.
82. Ibid., 280.
83. Norris, "Clothing in Circulation."
84. Botsman and Rogers, *What's Mine Is Yours*.
85. Jackson, "Rethinking Repair," 222.
86. Weiner and Schneider, *Cloth and Human Experience*, 2–3.

Acknowledgements

A heartfelt thanks to all of those designers, makers and recyclers who took time out of busy schedules to show me around their businesses, reflect upon their experiences and share their visions for the future of the fashion industry. I am grateful to Susanne Kuechler at the Department of Anthropology, UCL for an honorary research fellowship that provided valuable access to library resources, and to Rebecca Earley at Textiles Environment Design, for inviting me to become a Visiting Fellow at the University of the Arts London. I would also like to thank the three anonymous reviewers for their helpful comments, and the editors Jennifer Le Zotte and Karen Tranberg Hansen for their overall support.

Disclosure statement

No potential conflict of interest was reported by the author.

ORCID

Lucy Norris ⓘ http://orcid.org/0000-0002-2567-3426

References

Abimbola, Olumide. "The International Trade in Second-Hand Clothing: Managing Information Asymmetry between West African and British Traders." *Textile: The Journal of Cloth and Culture* 10, no. 2 (2012): 184–199.

Appadurai, Arjun. "The Migration of Objects: Circulations against Representation in Ethnological Collections." Presented at the Dictionary of Now: Thing, Ethnologisches Museum, Dahlem, Berlin, 10 October 2016.

Botsman, Rachel, and Roo Rogers. *What's Mine Is Yours: How Collaborative Consumption Is Changing the Way We Live*. London: HarperCollins UK, 2011.

Botticello, Julie. "Between Classification, Objectification and Perception: Processing Secondhand Clothing for Recycling and Reuse." *Textile: The Journal of Cloth and Culture* 10, no. 2 (2012): 166–183.

Braungart, W., and M. McDonough. *Cradle to Cradle: Rethinking the Way We Make Things*. USA: North Point Press, 2002.

Bristol Food Policy Council. Accessed January 17, 2017. http://sustainablefoodcities.org/findacity/cityinformation/userid/36

Bristol Textile Quarter. "Bristol Textile Quarter." Accessed January 17, 2017. http://bristoltextilequarter.co.uk/about/

Brooks, Andrew. *Clothing Poverty: The Hidden World of Fast Fashion and Second-Hand Clothes*. London: Zed Books, 2015.

Brooks, Andrew. "East Africa's Ban on Second-Hand Clothes Won't Save Its Own Industry." *The Guardian*, 4 May 2016, sec. Guardian Sustainable Business. https://www.theguardian.com/sustainable-business/2016/may/04/east-africa-kenya-ban-second-hand-clothing-imports-west.

Brooks, Andrew. "Riches from Rags or Persistent Poverty? Trading Second-Hand Clothes in a Mozambican Market." *Textile: The Journal of Cloth and Culture* 10, no. 2 (2012): 222–237.

Brooks, Andrew. "Stretching Global Production Networks: The International Second-Hand Clothing Trade." *Geoforum* 44 (2012): 10–22.

Buehler, Melanie. "Inflected Objects #2 Circulation - Otherwise, Unhinged." Exhibition text. Future Gallery, Schöneberger Ufer 59, Berlin, 29 June 2016.

Busch, Otto von. "Fashion-Able: Hacktivism and Engaged Fashion Design." PhD diss., University of Gothenburg, 2008.

CIRAIG. *Circular Economy: A Critical Literature Review of Concepts*. Montreal: International Reference Centre for the Life Cycle of Products, Processes and Services, 2015. http://www.ciraig.org/pdf/CIRAIG_Circular_Economy_Literature_Review_Oct2015.pdf.

"Circle Market: Fuelling the Recovery, Reuse and Resale of Textiles – Circle Economy." Accessed January 17, 2017. http://www.circle-economy.com/case/circlemarket/

"Circular Cities Network." Accessed January 17, 2017. https://www.ellenmacarthurfoundation.org/programmes/government/circular-cities-network

"Circular Economy Reports & Publications From The Ellen MacArthur Foundation." Accessed January 17, 2017. https://www.ellenmacarthurfoundation.org/publications

"Circular Economy System Diagram - Ellen MacArthur Foundation." Accessed January 17, 2017. https://www.ellenmacarthurfoundation.org/circular-economy/interactive-diagram

"Could Fibersort Change the Textiles Recycling Landscape? – Circle Economy." Accessed January 17, 2017. http://www.circle-economy.com/the-fibersort-pilot-empowering-enabling-textile-to-textile-recycling/

Crang, M., Alex Hughes, Nicky Gregson, Lucy Norris, and F. Ahamed. "Rethinking Governance and Value in Commodity Chains through Global Recycling Networks." *Transactions of the Institute of British Geographers (NS)* 38, no. 1 (2013): 12–24.

Crompton, Tom. *Common Cause: The Case for Working with Our Cultural Values*. London: World Wildlife Fund UK, 2010. http://assets.wwf.org.uk/downloads/common_cause_report.pdf.

Daly, Herman E. *Toward a Steady-State Economy*. San Francisco: W.H. Freeman, 1973.

Douglas, Mary. *Purity and Danger: An Analysis of the Concepts of Pollution and Taboo*. London: Routledge & Kegan Paul, 1966.

Earley, Rebecca. 2013. "Fast Refashion – Textile Toolbox." http://www.textiletoolbox.com/exhibits/detail/fast-refashion/.

Earley, Rebecca, and Kate Goldsworthy. *Designing for Fast and Slow Circular Fashion Systems: Exploring Strategies for Multiple and Extended Product Cycles*. Nottingham Trent University, 2015. https://www.academia.edu/13232768/Designing_for_Fast_and_Slow_Circular_Fashion_Systems_Exploring_Strategies_for_Multiple_and_Extended_Product_Cycles.

EEF. *Materials for Manufacturing: Safeguarding Supply*. London: EEF The Manufacturer's Organisation, 2014. http://www.eef.org.uk/publications/reports/Materials-for-Manufacturing-safeguarding-supply.htm.

Ellen MacArthur Foundation. *Towards the Circular Economy 1: Economic and Business Rationale for an Accelerated Transition*. London: Ellen MacArthur Foundation, 2012.

European Commission. "Closing the Loop: An EU Action Plan for the Circular Economy." Communication from the Commission to the European Parliament, the Council, the European Economic and Social Committee and the Committee of the Regions, European Commission, 2015.

Fletcher, Kate. *Craft of Use: Post-Growth Fashion*. London: Routledge, 2016.

Fuad-Luke, Alistair, Anja-Lisa Hirscher, and Katharina Moebus, eds. "Open Fashion & Code: Interview with Cecilia Palmer." In *Agents of Alternatives: Re-Designing out Realities*, 182–189. Berlin: Agents of Alternatives (AoA), 2015. https://issuu.com/agentsofalternatives/docs/aoa_online_free_pdf.

Gell, Alfred. *Art and Agency: An Anthropological Theory*. Oxford: Clarendon Press, 1998.

Gille, Zusanne. *From the Cult of Waste to the Trash Heap of History: The Politics of Waste in Socialist and Post Sociaist Hungary*. Bloomington, IN: Indiana University Press, 2007.

Goffman, Erving. *Frame Analysis*. London: Harper & Row, 1974.

Graeber, David. "Afterword: The Apocalypse of Objects - Degradation, Redemption and Transcendence in the World of Consumer Goods." In *Economies of Recycling. The Global Transformation of Materials, Values and Social Relations*, edited by Catherine Alexander and Josh Reno. London: Zed Books, 2012: 277–290.

Greenpeace International. *Toxic Threads: The Big Fashion Stitch-Up*. Amsterdam: Greenpeace, 2012.

Gregson, Nicky, and Mike Crang. "Materiality and Waste: Inorganic Vitality in a Networked World." *Environment and Planning A* 42, no. 5 (2010): 1026–1032.

Gregson, Nicky, Mike Crang, Julie Botticello, Melania Calestani, and Anna Krzywoszynska. "Doing the 'Dirty Work' of the Green Economy: Resource Recovery and Migrant Labour in the EU." *European and Regional Studies* 10 (2014) 541–555: doi:10.1177/0969776414554489.

Hansen, Karen Tranberg. "Controversies About the International Secondhand Clothing Trade." *Anthropology Today* 20, no. 4 (2004): 3–9.

Hansen, Karen Tranberg. *Salaula: The World of Secondhand Clothing and Zambia*. Chicago: University of Chicago Press, 2000.

Harrison, Lizzie. "Fashion and Community." In *Routledge Handbook of Sustainability and Fashion*, edited by Kate Fletcher and Mathilda Tham. 243–252. Abingdon: Routledge, 2015.

Hart, Keith, Jean-Louis Laville, and Antonio David Cattani, eds. *The Human Economy*. London: Polity, 2010.

Harvey, Penelope, Casper Bruun Jensen, and Atsuro Morita, eds. *Infrastructures and Social Complexity: A Companion*, London: Routledge, 2017.

Hawley, Jana M. "Digging for Diamonds: A Conceptual Framework for Understanding Reclaimed Textile Products." *Clothing and Textiles Research Journal* 24, no. 3 (2006): 262–275.

Hobson, Kersty. "Closing the Loop or Squaring the Circle? Locating Generative Spaces for the Circular Economy." *Progress in Human Geography* 40, no. 1 (2016): 88–104. doi:10.1177/0309132514566342.

Hopkins, Rob. *The Transition Handbook. From Oil Dependency to Local Resilience*. Cambridge: Green Books, 2008.

Hoskins, Tansy. *Stitched Up: The Anti-Capitalist Book of Fashion*. London: Pluto Press, 2014.

International Trade Administration. "Worn (Used) Clothing." Accessed January 13, 2017. http://web.ita.doc.gov/tacgi/eamain.nsf/ff5dd4f75c7795ea8525762500657ba8/801e189cbcde7ed985257e7600439aea?OpenDocument

Jackson, Steven J. "Rethinking Repair." In *Media Technologies: Essays on Communication, Materiality and Society*, edited by Gillespie Tarleton, Pablo J. Boczkowski, and Kirsten A. Foot. Cambridge, MA: MIT Press Scholarship Online, 2014.

Jackson, Tim. *Prosperity Without Growth: Economics for a Finite Planet*. London: Routledge, 2011.

Küchler, Susanne. "Threads of Thought: Reflections on Art and Agency." In *Distributed Objects: Meaning and Mattering after Alfred Gell*, edited by Liana Chua and Mark Elliott. London: Berghahn Books, 2013: 25–38.

Küchler, Susanne, and Daniel Miller. *Clothing as Material Culture*. Oxford: Berg, 2005.

Lakoff, George. *The All New Don't Think of an Elephant! Know Your Values and Frame the Debate*. 2nd revised ed. White River Junction, VT: Chelsea Green Publishing, 2014.

Lakoff, George, and Mark Johnson. *Metaphors We Live By*. Chicago, IL: University of Chicago Press, 1980.

Latour, Bruno. *We Have Never Been Modern*. London: Prentice Hall, 1993.

Lemire, Beverly. *Fashion's Favourite: The Cotton Trade and the Consumer in Britain, 1600–1800*. Pasold Research Fund. Oxford: Oxford University Press, 1991.

"Made in NYC." Accessed January 17, 2017. http://madeinnyc.org/our-mission/

Marx, Karl. *Capital*. Translated by Samuel Moore and Edward Aveling. Vol. 1. (3 vols). 1995. Available at www.marxists.org/archive/marx/works/1867-c1/

McKinsey & Co. *Manufacturing the Future: The Next Era of Global Growth and Innovation*. McKinsey & Company, 2012. http://www.mckinsey.com/insights/manufacturing/the_future_of_manufacturing.

McKinsey & Co. *Resource Revolution: Meeting the World's Energy, Material, Food and Water Needs*. Translated by McKinsey Sustainability and Resource Productivity Practice. McKinsey Global Institute, 2011. http://www.mckinsey.com/insights/energy_resources_materials/resource_revolution.

McRobbie, Angela. *Be Creative: Making a Living in the New Culture Industries*. London: Polity Press, 2016.

Milgram, B. Lynne. "Activating Frontier Livelihoods: Women and the Transnational Secondhand Clothing Trade between Hong Kong and the Philippines." *Urban Anthropology & Studies of Cultural Systems and World Economic Development* 37, no. 1 (2008): 5–47.

Miller, Daniel. "Materiality: An Introduction." In *Materiality*, edited by Daniel Miller. Durham, NC: Duke University Press, 2005: 1–50.

Mistra Future Fashion. "Mistra Future Fashion." Accessed January 17, 2017. http://mistrafuturefashion.com/

Morgan, Andrew. *The True Cost*. Documentary, 2015. https://truecostmovie.com/.

Morley, N., C. Bartlett, and I. McGill. *Maximising the Reuse and Recycling of UK Clothing and Textiles: A Report to the Department for Environment, Food and Rural Affairs*. Aylesbury: Oakdene Hollins Ltd, 2009.

Mukerji, Chandra. *From Graven Images: Patterns of Modern Materialism*. New York: Colombia University Press, 1983.

Niinimäki, Kirsi, Eugenia Smirnova, Elina Ilen, Herbert Sixta, and Michael Hummel. "Colours in a Circular Economy." Presented at the Circular Transitions conference, Chelsea College of Art, UAL, 23 November 2016.

Norris, Lucy. "Clothing in Circulation." In *World Factory: The Game*, edited by Zoë Svendson and Simon Daw. London: Nick Hern Books, forthcoming 2017.

Norris, Lucy. "Introduction: Trade and Transformations of Second-Hand Clothing." *Textile: The Journal of Cloth and Culture* 10, no. 2 (2012): 128–143.

Norris, Lucy. "Shoddy Rags and Relief Blankets: Perceptions of Textile Recycling in North India." In *Economies of Recycling: The Global Transformation of Materials, Values and Social Relations*, edited by Catherine Alexander and Josh Reno, 35–58. London: Zed Books, 2012.

Norris, Lucy. "The Limits of Ethicality in International Markets: Imported Second-Hand Clothing in India." *Geoforum* 67 (2015): 183–193. doi:10.1016/j.geoforum.2015.06.003.

Oakdene Hollins Ltd, SATC Ltd., and NIRI Ltd. "Recycling of Low Grade Clothing Waste." 30 September 2006.

OSCEdays. *CRCLR Network*. Accessed January 17, 2017. http://crclr.org/oscedays/

Politowicz, Kay, and Kate Goldsworthy. 2014. "A.S.A.P. (Paper Cloth) - Textile Toolbox." http://www.textiletoolbox.com/exhibits/detail/sp-paper-cloth/.

"Project MainStream Helping Scale The Circular Economy." Accessed January 17, 2017. https://www.ellenmacarthurfoundation.org/programmes/business/project-mainstream

Raworth, Kate. *Doughnut Economics: Seven Ways to Think Like a 21st-Century Economist*. White River Junction, Vermont: Random House Business, 2017.

Rhoades, Cyndi. "Keynote: Materials." Presented at the Circular Transitions conference, Chelsea College of Art, UAL, 23 November 2016.

Rivoli, Pietra. *The Travels of a T-Shirt in the Global Economy: An Economist Examines the Markets, Power, and Politics of World Trade*. Hoboken: John Wiley, 2005.

Siegle, Lucy. *To Die For: Is Fashion Wearing Out the World?*. London: Fourth Estate, 2011.

Silvestri, Nikki. "Keynote." Presented at the Disruption Innovation Festival Launch, Royal Society of Arts, London, 11 July 2016.

Textile Arts Centre. Accessed January 17, 2017. http://textileartscenter.com/blog/

The Bristol Weaving Mill. "The Bristol Weaving Mill." Accessed January 17, 2017. http://www.bristolweavingmill.co.uk/about

Twigger Holroyd, Amy. "Shifting Perceptions: The Reknit Revolution." Presented at the Circular Transitions conference, Chelsea College of Arts, UAL, 23 November 2016.

U.S. Chamber of Commerce Foundation Corporate Citizenship Centre. *Trash to Treasure: Changing Waste Streams to Profit Streams*. Washington, DC: U.S. Chamber of Commerce Foundation Corporate Citizenship Centre. Accessed February 18, 2016. http://www.csrwire.com/press_releases/38721-U-S-Chamber-Foundation-Issues-New-Report-on-the-Business-Value-of-Circular-Economy

Weiner, Annette B., and Jane Schneider. *Cloth and Human Experience. Smithsonian Series in Ethnographic Enquiry*. Smithsonian Institute, Washington, DC: Werner-Gren Foundation for Anthropological Research, 1989.

Whitson-Smith, Jade, and Lizzie Harrison. "Mending Fashion: How Can We Engage the Wider Community of Fashion Consumers?" Conference presented at the Mendrs Symposium, Lake District, UK, July 2012. http://eprints.hud.ac.uk/20007/.

"Worn Again Joins Forces with H&M, Kering to Create Circular Resource Model for Textiles | Sustainable Brands." *Sustainablebrands.Com*. Accessed January 17, 2017. http://www.sustainablebrands.com/news_and_views/startups/sustainable_brands/worn_again_joins_forces_hm_kering_create_circular_resourc

Zee, Bibi van der. "Swap till You Drop: Why a Clothing Exchange Beats London Fashion Week." *The Guardian, 15 September 2014, sec. Life and style*. https://www.theguardian.com/lifeandstyle/2014/sep/15/swap-till-you-drop-clothing-exchange-beats-london-fashion-week.

Index

Note: Page numbers in *italics* indicate figures, those in **bold** refer to tables. Endnotes are indicated by the page number followed by 'n' and the endnote number e.g., 20n1 refers to endnote 1 on page 20.

For Product Safety Concerns and Information please contact our
EU representative GPSR@taylorandfrancis.com Taylor & Francis
Verlag GmbH, Kaufingerstraße 24, 80331 München, Germany